Do Not Stifle the Spirit

Do Not Stifle the Spirit

CONVERSATIONS WITH
JACQUES DUPUIS

Gerard O'Connell

ORBIS BOOKS
Maryknoll, New York 10545

ORBIS BOOKS
Maryknoll, New York 10545

Fathers and Brothers
MARYKNOLL™
TOGETHER IN GOD'S MISSION OF MERCY

Founded in 1970, Orbis Books endeavors to publish works that enlighten the mind, nourish the spirit, and challenge the conscience. The publishing arm of the Maryknoll Fathers and Brothers, Orbis seeks to explore the global dimensions of the Christian faith and mission, to invite dialogue with diverse cultures and religious traditions, and to serve the cause of reconciliation and peace. The books published reflect the views of their authors and do not represent the official position of the Maryknoll Society. To learn more about Maryknoll and Orbis Books, please visit our website at www.maryknollsociety.org.

Library of Congress Cataloging in Publication Data

Names: Dupuis, Jacques, 1923-2004, interviewee. | O'Connell, Gerard, interviewer.
Title: Do not stifle the spirit : Conversations with Jacques Dupuis.
Description: Maryknoll : Orbis Books, 2017. | Includes bibliographical references and index.
Identifiers: LCCN 2016053269 (print) | LCCN 2017017851 (ebook) | ISBN 9781608336876 (e-book) | ISBN 9781626982222 (pbk.)
Subjects: LCSH: Dupuis, Jacques, 1923-2004—Interviews. | Religions—Relations. | Religious pluralism. | Christianity and other religions. | Catholic Church—Doctrines—History.
Classification: LCC BX4705.D9234 (ebook) | LCC BX4705.D9234 A5 2017 (print) | DDC 261.2—dc23
LC record available at https://lccn.loc.gov/2016053269

For my beloved
Elisabetta, Edwin,
Juan Pablo, and Carolina

Contents

Preface

Classic authors like Cicero and St. Aelred of Rievaulx have written glowingly of the blessings that true friends bring. Over and over again, I saw how Jacques Dupuis, S.J., was blessed by the friendship of William ("Bill") Burrows, managing editor emeritus of Orbis Books, and Gerard ("Gerry") O'Connell, now Rome correspondent for *America* magazine. Both stood by him magnificently in the last years of life, as did other friends like Archbishop Henry D'Souza (archbishop emeritus of Calcutta) and John Wilkins (editor of the London *Tablet*).

Gerry persuaded Dupuis to respond to long and detailed interviews about his early life (in Belgium), his thirty-six years in India, and his final two decades at the Pontifical Gregorian University in Rome (1984-2004), which culminated in the severe stress and suffering caused by the Congregation for the Doctrine of the Faith (from October 1998 through to his death in December 2004). Those memoirs form the first part of this book. Dupuis had originally intended that Part II of this book should include three of his unpublished articles and some appendices. Since his death, however, all but one of those articles and the appendices have been published elsewhere as the editorial note explains. Consequently, this second part only contains the one hitherto-unpublished article in which he offers "a provisional balance sheet" of the five-year debate that followed the publication of his book *Toward a Christian Theology of Religious Pluralism*[1] and outlines the principal points on which he thought it necessary to clarify his position or introduce nuances.

A long chapter in *On the Left Bank of the Tiber*, my memoir about my own years at the Gregorian University (1974-2006),[2] tells the story of the CDF's investigation of Dupuis's *Toward a Christian Theology of Religious Pluralism*, their accusations, and the way their procedures left him deeply wounded. The secrecy and anonymity that marked those procedures would have met with censure even from the ancient Romans. In the Acts of the Apostles, Porcius Festus, the procurator of Judaea appointed by the Emperor Nero in AD 60, remarked apropos of the case against St. Paul: "It

---

1. Maryknoll, NY: Orbis Books, 1997.
2. Ballarat: Connor Court; Leominster: Gracewing, 2013, 213-51.

is not the custom of the Romans to hand over anyone before the accused had met the accusers face to face and had been given an opportunity to make a defense against the charges" (Acts 25:16). Would that Dupuis, right from the start, had been able to meet his accusers face to face and defend himself personally against their charges!

Let me add a few remarks to the story as Dupuis has told it in *Do Not Stifle the Spirit*. I read carefully the final, unpublished manuscript that he wrote for Médiaspaul Publishers (Montreal); it did not add anything noteworthy to what he had already published. His last published book,[3] however, added some significant modifications and additions to what he had already written in *Toward a Christian Theology of Religious Pluralism*. I spelled out those developments in an article, "Christ and the Religions."[4]

After the CDF's proceedings against Dupuis became known, friends like Jon Sobrino, S.J., Claude Geffré, O.P., and others made a point of going out of their way to visit him at the Gregorian. Dupuis had, however, never before met Jean Vanier, who had founded L'Arche, a world-wide series of communities for the intellectually disabled, and who would be the Templeton laureate in 2015. Guessing how wounded Dupuis felt, Jean phoned me ahead of a visit he was making to a L'Arche community in Rome and came to meet Dupuis over lunch in the Gregorian.

At some point in those painful, final years, Dupuis stopped coming to lunch with the community. But he was regularly there at the evening meal, often joined by Jesuit supporters like Herbert Alphonso, Philipp Schmitz, and Norman Tanner. On the evening of December 26, 2004, he stood up from table and started to fall. My left hand shot out instinctively and caught him in time.

The following evening I went out to eat with an Italian couple whose marriage was breaking up but for whom I could not do anything. Back at the Gregorian, Dupuis stood up in the refectory, fell, and hit his head on the hard corner of a wooden table. The superior drove him to a hospital, but they could do nothing. He died the following day, apparently of a cerebral hemorrhage. There was no autopsy, but when I went to view the corpse in the hospital's morgue, I could see a large hematoma on one of his temples where he had struck his head.

After the funeral Mass held in the community chapel at the Gregorian, I went out to lead the prayers when we buried Dupuis in the mausoleum

---

3. *Christianity and the Religions: From Confrontation to Dialogue*, trans. Phillip Berryman (Maryknoll, NY: Orbis Books, 2002).

4. *Gregorianum* 84 (2003): 347-62. I wrote this article after a first article commissioned for the *Gregorianum* was rejected. That first article, "Jacques Dupuis's Contribution to Interreligious Dialogue," was, however, published in *Theological Studies* 64 (2003): 388-97.

for Jesuits who die in Rome. A young Indian priest burned some incense and sang a hymn in Malayalam, the language of Kerala (southern India), before the metal coffin was placed in its niche. "Dupuis would have preferred a hymn in Bengali," the young priest said to me before the ceremony. "Don't worry," I assured him, "none of the others who are here can tell the difference."

In the years that followed the death of Dupuis, I set myself to investigate in depth and at length what the Scriptures teach about the salvation of God's "other peoples." The result was *Salvation for All: God's Other Peoples*,[5] a book dedicated to the memory of Dupuis, "a theologian of immense learning who always held that followers of other religions are persons to be encountered and not cases to be reduced to mere statements about them." I wrote his obituary for a 2010 supplement to the *New Catholic Encyclopedia*, discussed the way various writers had interpreted him in two articles,[6] and vigorously defended Bill Burrows's *Jacques Dupuis Faces the Inquisition* in a letter to the London *Tablet* (July 6, 2013). In *The Second Vatican Council on Other Religions*, I spent a chapter on the way Dupuis received and developed the teaching of Vatican II.[7]

Currently a stalemate seems to have descended on discussions in the theology of religions. In *A Christology of Religions* (forthcoming from Orbis Books), I seek to break this stalemate by introducing significant themes that have so far been simply ignored or largely ignored: the theology of the cross; the universal impact of Christ's high priestly ministry; the efficacy of love-inspired prayer for "the others," and the nature of the real faith available for those who follow "other" religions. I am only sorry not to enjoy the company of Dupuis, as he would have delighted in discussing these themes.

We should thank Gerry O'Connell, faithful friend of Dupuis, for preserving and now publishing what makes up the rich and varied chapters of *Do Not Stifle the Spirit*. Beyond shedding new light on a painful episode in the history of someone pursued by the CDF, this book will help people to appreciate the theology of Dupuis himself and the issues at stake when Christians think about those who follow other religious faiths. More than ever, our world needs the soundly based Christian thinking of Dupuis and his generous openness to "the others."

Gerald O'Collins, S.J., AC
Jesuit Theological College
Parkville, Australia

---

5. Oxford: Oxford University Press, 2008.
6. "Jacques Dupuis: The Ongoing Debate," *Theological Studies* 74 (2013): 632-54; "Was Jacques Dupuis a Neo-Rahnerian?" *Asian Horizons* 7 (2013): 568-81.
7. Oxford: Oxford University Press, 2013, 181-96.

Introduction

This interview book is the last testament of Fr. Jacques Dupuis, the renowned pioneering Belgian-born Jesuit theologian who died thirteen years ago in Rome. I consider it a work of historical importance and believe it could reopen, or at least contribute significantly to the reopening of, a theological debate on a subject of contemporary importance where there is still much to be understood.

In this brief introduction I shall explain both the genesis and the history of this book. Because Fr. Dupuis died on December 28, 2004, readers will no doubt want to know why it has taken so long to have it published. The question demands an answer; it will be given here.

I had my first extended conversation with Fr. Dupuis in October 1998, weeks after the Vatican's Congregation for the Doctrine of the Faith (CDF), then led by Cardinal Joseph Ratzinger, informed his Jesuit superiors that it had opened an investigation into his groundbreaking work *Toward a Christian Theology of Religious Pluralism* (Maryknoll, NY: Orbis Books, 1997). The book, now translated into several languages, discusses the relationship between Christianity and the other world religions, and explores what place these have in God's plan for the salvation of humanity.

Dupuis had been a consultor of the Pontifical Council for Interreligious Dialogue (1984-95) and a highly esteemed professor at the Pontifical Gregorian University (henceforth "the Gregorian") where his lectures attracted capacity audiences. He came to the Gregorian in 1984 to teach full time after spending thirty-six years in India where he had taught Christology, which he later described as "the one passion of my life." In India, he also served as one of the main theological advisers to the Catholic Bishops' Conference and produced, first in collaboration with Fr. Josef Neuner and later alone, the monumental and greatly appreciated work, *The Christian Faith in the Doctrinal Documents of the Catholic Church.*

When the CDF opened its investigation, I was the Rome correspondent for both the *Tablet*, an international Catholic weekly based in London, and for the Union of Catholic Asian News (UCAN), the main Catholic news agency in Asia. Both were keenly interested in his case, as was I. From then onward and up to three days before his death, I remained in regular contact with Fr. Dupuis. I visited him frequently at the Gregorian. We had dinner together many times, usually in the community's refectory. We conversed for hours on end, face to face or by phone. I witnessed how greatly he suffered in those last years of his life not only during the period of the investigation into his book (September 1998-February 2001), but also in the years following its conclusion and up to the eve of his death, when he felt he was under constant surveillance by the CDF and those connected with it.

In those years too I saw his profound, unshakable faith in Jesus Christ and his incredulity when the Congregation's officials, acting in the name of the church, accused him of doctrinal error, even heresy. He never knew who his accusers were, nor was he given an opportunity to speak with any of the Congregation's officials until the investigation had effectively reached its conclusion on September 4, 2000, as his fellow Jesuit, legal defender, and great friend, Fr. Gerald ("Gerry") O'Collins, recounts both in the preface to this book and in his fascinating autobiographical work, *On the Left Bank of the Tiber*.

I am a journalist specializing in Vatican affairs, not a theologian. Before becoming involved in the Dupuis case, I had read about the difficulties and sufferings other theologians before him had experienced at the hands of the CDF, or its predecessor—the Holy Office—because of their writings or lectures. The list is long, and includes such renowned scholars as Henri de Lubac, S.J., Yves Congar, O.P., and Edward Schillebeeckx, O.P.

From various conversations with church historians and theologians in Rome, I concluded that the Dupuis case was but the latest in this long series. I felt that quite apart from the theological issues involved in the search for truth, the way it was handled raised disturbing questions in terms of due process from a human rights perspective. It also raised some fundamental questions relating to justice and charity.

This whole question had been raised with cogency before the Dupuis case by the renowned Jesuit canon lawyer Ladislas Orsy, in an article first published in German in *Stimmen der Zeit* in June 1998 and reprinted in English in *Doctrine and Life* in August 1998 under the title "Are Church Investigation Procedures Really Just?" It took on particular relevance in the light of this new CDF investigation.

I monitored the Dupuis case closely, insofar as that was possible; and soon after it ended with the publication of the Notification by the CDF on February 26, 2001, which said his work contained "ambiguities" but no longer mentioned doctrinal errors or heresy, I approached Dupuis and asked if he would do an interview book with me covering his entire life, starting in Belgium, moving through his thirty-six years in India and ending in Rome. I explained that I wished to focus in particular on the CDF investigation into his pioneering *Toward a Theology of Religious Pluralism* and its aftermath. He was reluctant at first to engage in any such project, given all that he had been through, but eventually agreed after I persuaded him that it would give him an opportunity to put on public record his side of the story and to explain in the clearest way possible what actually happened as well as the theological issues at stake. I also suggested that this might help bring about a change in the way in which such processes are conducted in the future.

We began our "conversation," as he liked to call it, in 2002, and had finished the original project—Chapters 1 and 2 of this book—by June 29, 2003. At the end of that year, however, he confided his growing distress and dismay at the fact that even though he had been substantially cleared by the CDF's investigation, he had come to realize that he still remained suspect in its eyes. He felt under constant surveillance whenever he gave lectures in Italy or other countries. Moreover, he suffered too when he found it near impossible to get clearance from his superiors to publish articles that he had written; their reason, he said, was that they wished to protect him from getting into further trouble with the CDF, and indeed were under its instructions to contain his writings and public lectures.

Given this new situation, I convinced him to reopen and continue our conversation throughout 2004. This resulted in Chapter 3 of this book, "The Aftermath of a Trial."

I met Fr. Dupuis for the last time at six o'clock on Christmas Eve, 2004, at the Gregorian. We had agreed to this meeting by phone as I had finishing typing up the final draft of the text and wanted him to check it. I brought him the entire manuscript together with a bottle of good red wine to bring cheer to his Christmas.

As usual, he came down to the reception area to greet me and accompany me to his room. There was a great silence in the house that evening, as most of the professors had left to spend the festive season with their families or friends, but Dupuis had decided to remain. We chatted as we walked along the battleship-gray-painted corridors to his warm study/bedroom, which contained many books, an icon of Christ, objects from India, where he had spent thirty-six years, and much else.

Once inside, I gave him the draft manuscript, which he received with considerable joy. It included the complete text of the interviews I had conducted with him, either face to face or by email, over the previous three years, plus a collection of articles that he wanted to attach to this. He had already read most of the manuscript and only needed to review the new chapter. In actual fact, he corrected and approved the final text the very next day: Christmas day. The following morning, December 26, he asked a young Romanian student, whom he was befriending both spiritually and financially, to make photocopies of the entire work, for him and for me.

Two days later, on December 27, at the end of dinner that evening in the refectory of the Gregorian, as he stood up to leave, he fell and hit his head against a wooden table. He was rushed to the hospital where he died the next day, apparently from a brain hemorrhage.

I attended the requiem Mass celebrated in the community chapel of the Gregorian on December 30. It was celebrated by the superior of the community, who represented the Jesuit Father General, Peter-Hans Kolvenbach, who had long befriended Dupuis but sadly could not attend because he had an audience with Cardinal Ratzinger that same morning. Archbishop Michael Fitzgerald, then president of the Pontifical Council for Interreligious Dialogue, was one of the concelebrants. He was the only Vatican official at the Mass, but his presence was significant and a tribute to the man who had made a rich contribution to the PCID during his ten years as a consultor.

I was deeply moved before the Mass when I saw the young Romanian student mentioned earlier place a red rose on Dupuis's coffin. He had lost a good friend; the Catholic Church had lost a pioneering theologian who had contributed significantly not only to the church in India, but also to the universal church and the wider Christian community in the dialogue with the world's other great religions.

This interview book is his final contribution to that important relationship. It has a particular history, first regarding the genesis and the contents of this book and, secondly, relating to the reason why it has taken so long to publish it.

The book was my idea, but Dupuis chose the title: *Do Not Stifle the Spirit*. He also insisted on attaching three articles and three appendixes to the interview book, which offer a much fuller and deeper elaboration of points that he made in our conversations. Two of them, however, have already been published in other places (as the editorial note explains later in this book), and so are not included here. The third, "The Theology of Religious Pluralism Revisited: A Provisional Balance Sheet," is found in Chapter 4, since it is the only one that has not yet been published. In it, he highlights the main points on which he felt it necessary to clarify or to nuance his positions in the light of the discussion on his two books.

Since this book was finished on Christmas day 2004, why then has it taken thirteen years for it to appear in print?

To respond to that question, it is necessary to go back to the end of 2003, when we concluded the original project (Chapters 1 and 2). Father

Dupuis then wrote a letter to me in which he addressed the question of the book's publication. He stated clearly that he did not want this to happen while John Paul II was pope and while Cardinal Ratzinger was prefect of the CDF. Clearly, he did not want to risk having new problems with the CDF as a result of this book. He never even considered the possibility that Cardinal Ratzinger could succeed John Paul II as pope, since it was widely known that Ratzinger wanted to retire. Furthermore, since he knew the market well, he said he would look for a publisher once John Paul II and Cardinal Ratzinger were no longer in office. He confided then that Orbis should be given the first option, since it had published his earlier works.

In actual fact, Fr. Dupuis died more than a year before John Paul II, but then Cardinal Ratzinger was elected pope in April 2005 and governed the church as Benedict XVI until his resignation on February 28, 2013. Respecting Dupuis's expressed wish, I felt I could not publish this book in those years, and so the manuscript sat on a bookshelf in my study.

On March 13, 2013, the cardinal archbishop of Buenos Aires, Jorge Mario Bergoglio, was elected pope and took the name Francis. He was the first Jesuit to become pope. He brought a breath of fresh air and openness to the Catholic Church, together with a climate of greater freedom in many areas, including in the academic world and in the church's dialogue with the other Christian churches and the main religions of the world, as was evident in his talk to the bishops of Asia during his visit to South Korea, August 2014. Given this new climate in the church, I felt the time had come to seek a publisher for *Do Not Stifle the Spirit*. I mentioned this to Fr. Adolfo Nicolas, then head of the Jesuits, and asked if he wished to read the manuscript before publication, since in it Dupuis refers to many members of the Society of Jesus as well as the Gregorian University. He responded without hesitation, "I will read it when it is published!"

Then, in late January 2016, Fr. James Martin, the well-known American Jesuit, was in Rome and came for dinner. I showed him the manuscript and after rapidly glancing through it put me in contact with Jim Keane, an editor at Orbis Books. The rest is history.

During a visit to the Lebanon, May 2016, I briefly met Fr. Peter-Hans Kolvenbach at St. Joseph's Jesuit community, Beirut. He had been superior general of the Society of Jesus from 1983 to 2008, and strongly supported Dupuis. I told him that this interview book would soon be published, and when I mentioned that in it Fr. Dupuis expressed high praise and gratitude for the invaluable support he had given him, especially in those last difficult years, Fr. Kolvenbach looked at me and said, "I am honored!"

I feel sure that Fr. Dupuis is rejoicing in heaven at the publication by Orbis Books of his last testament. I too am happy that this work on which we labored for a long time now sees the light of day. I thank, in particular, Fr. Gerry O'Collins, for his invaluable advice and assistance in this whole endeavor.

I wish to conclude this introduction by quoting an extract from Fr. Dupuis's response to me when, on June 29, 2003, I asked him: "If at the end of time, Christ were to ask you to give an account of the work you have done, what would you say to him?" I do so because I believe his answer reveals better than anything else in this book the profound spirituality of this pioneering Jesuit theologian who dedicated his entire life to Jesus Christ and to his church. This is what he said:

> I cannot imagine myself giving to the Lord, on the other side of this life, an account of the work I have done. Nor do I think such an account on my part would be necessary. The Lord will know my work, even better than I know it myself. I can only hope that his evaluation of it will be more positive than that of some censors and, alas, of the church's central doctrinal authority.
>
> On my part, I would only wish to thank God for the gift of human life and for the call to share in his own divine life in his Son Jesus; I would also thank him for the full life which, for no merit of mine, he granted to me, his unworthy servant, for the many opportunities he offered me to learn to serve and love him.
>
> I trust that the Lord who reads the secrets of the hearts will know that my intention in writing what I have written and saying what I said has only been to express to the best of my ability my deep faith in him and my total dedication to him.
>
> Rather than being inclined to do the talking when we meet, I hope then to hear from the Lord, in spite of my failings and shortcomings, a word of comfort and encouragement. I pray that he may invite me to enter into his glory, forever to sing his praise. May I hear him say to me: "Well done, good and faithful servant; you have been faithful over a little, I will set you over much; enter into the joy of your Master" (Matt 25:21).

Amen.

Gerard O'Connell
Rome, Italy

Part I

A Bird's Eye View

— 1 —

The Antecedents

Gerard O'Connell: *Father Dupuis, Let me begin by thanking you for having accepted to hold these conversations. I am sure they will help a vast public to become familiar with your person and your work. I would like to begin by asking you some questions on your early life. Perhaps you could start by telling me about your parents, your family, the place where you were born in Belgium and where you spent the early years of your life, and went to school, and about the cultural milieu in which you grew up.*

Jacques Dupuis: I was born on December 5, 1923, in Huppaye, in the province of Brabant, Belgium. I come from a well-to-do family with a long tradition of liberal professions. My father, Fernand, was an engineer who became chief manager of an important factory of heavy metallurgy. My mother, Lucie, came from a tradition of notary professionals. In his professional work my father was very demanding of himself and of others; he was a perfectionist who did not tolerate mediocrity. But he was at the same time very human in his dealings with his more than one thousand subordinates, and an example to them of professional honesty and conscientiousness. He was extremely just in dealing with all and, notwithstanding the high demands he made, managed to endear himself to all under his direction.

My mother was nothing short of a saint. Her meekness, attention to others, and boundless generosity made her an ideal mother. I always thought that my parents complemented each other wonderfully well. Indeed, together they managed to build a most closely united family. We were four children, I myself being the third with a brother, Michel, and a sister, Monique, before me, and a brother, Andre, after me. The first three of us followed each other very closely in age and were educated together; the younger brother followed me by seven years. This closeness in age among the three of us built lasting bonds which endure even today, though I have been deprived of my only sister by her death in 1997, a loss I feel keenly even today.

Though born in Huppaye, I spent the whole of my youth in Charleroi, in the province of Hainaut, which was in those days one of the biggest industrial centers of Belgium, called "the black country" because of the many coal mines and factories, with their mountain-like heaps of coal refuse and blast furnaces forming the horizon. This is where my father exercised his profession. This is also where in 1929, at the age of five, I joined the Jesuit Collège du Sacré Coeur, where I would spend altogether twelve years of schooling, six in primary school and six in the humanities, or secondary school. All I know I have learned from the Jesuits. I am happy to report that I got an exquisite education at the Jesuit college, the likes of which would have been difficult to find elsewhere, even among Jesuit colleges. Especially the six years of Greco-Latin humanities were a thrill. Deep friendships were established between the students of the same class year, and between them and their teachers. There reigned among us a climate of emulation for academic excellence, for which the education I received at home (with the high demands my father made on his sons) served me well. We also enjoyed a high level of cultural formation in the arts, including music and the graphic arts. What most of all enhanced the formation received was the continual contact with the Fathers in the classroom, since five of the six years in the humanities had a Jesuit priest as "titular" teacher. And I must say that the men with whom we dealt for six years on a daily basis in the humanities were quite remarkable. Later, I often thought that perhaps the main reason why vocations have drastically fallen in recent decades is the fact that the students no longer enjoy, for lack of personnel, this deep and continued contact with the Fathers. This, I am afraid, works as a vicious circle, reducing the number of vocations and in turn the opportunities for similar contacts.

The ideal education which we were receiving was abruptly interrupted when, on May 7, 1940, during my second-to-last year of school, called "Poésie," Belgium was invaded by the German army. I volunteered at the age of sixteen for the army, but was refused [because I was] too young. As director of a big factory which was also producing war material, my father received orders to blow up the machines producing material which should not fall into the hands of the enemy, and to quit the country. This is how my whole family together left for France. We first landed in Normandy on the seashore in a place called Rivabella, more a holiday resort than a place of exile; but the Germans moved fast in their invasion of France and soon would have joined us. So, after two weeks we moved farther south and this time landed in Vandee, in a small, rather backward place called Aiguillon-sur-Mer, facing the Ile de Ré. This, I might well say, was my first experience of a Third World environment, even if the expression was unknown then. The floors were made of mud, and the fuel of cow dung; I would see this again much later in Indian villages. The setting in which we found ourselves was more one of camping than a home; but hardships have the advantage of deepening ties which are already profound, and we experienced utmost solidarity among ourselves. My father was anxious that I should not [spend] all this time of exile without pursuing my school studies. So I joined a French lycée situated not too far from the place, and I attended the second last year of schooling in preparation for the French "Bacho." The atmosphere was not too friendly toward Belgium, which was accused by some of having betrayed the allies by capitulating to Germany. I defended myself energetically, and am proud to report that in academic performance I could easily compete with the French students in the class. What happened next was that the Germans occupied even the forsaken place where we had landed, and there was no point in staying there any longer. German occupation at home would be better than in a foreign land. We thus made our way home in August 1940 to face the hardships of the German occupation, which would last till the liberation of Belgium by the American army in 1944.

Back home I resumed my studies in the college with the Fathers and those in the group of my companions who had remained in Belgium or had happily returned. The last year of schooling, called "Rhétorique," was especially rich and fruitful, as much from the academic point of view as from that of human relations. Hard years were to follow, which however do form character and prepare [one] to face the realities of life. Again, I wish to mention—for education at home is even more fundamental than that in school—how much I received throughout those years from my parents and family. To my father I am especially grateful for the sense of excellence which he conveyed to his children by the example of his own life and work, as well as by the high expectations he placed on us. To him I owe the ambition for perfection which I myself have tried to cultivate, and which served me well when I joined the Society of Jesus to follow St. Ignatius's ideal of seeking always greater service and the greater glory of God. Natural virtues learned in youth can be transformed through God's grace into supernatural gifts. To my mother I am even more indebted for her deep personal love and affection, her concern for my welfare, and the hopes she entertained secretly for my future.

G.O'C.: *Were you very religious as a young boy? When did you first think of becoming a priest? What did your parents say when you told them this? Why did you join the Jesuits?*

J.D.: I was full of life as a young boy, and very active as I grew up, much inclined to sport, including playing tennis, swimming every day, and cycling long distances. I was by no means a quiet or introspective temperament, but on the contrary was enterprising and always on the move. I was therefore not especially pious or "religious"; not more, I should say, than would be expected from a boy in my condition. Yet I was from quite a young age a daily mass server and communicant. Our home was just a five minutes' walk from the Jesuit college I attended and from the church attached to it. I and my mother were in church for daily mass at 7 A.M. My mother would attend the mass which I was serving for one of the Fathers. We would go back home together after mass and then, after breakfast, I left for school. The distance from home to the college was so short that I could still leave home when the bells rang for classes and be on time, provided I walked a little fast.

I mentioned above the close contact that existed in our college between the Fathers and the students—contact in the classroom, where we received a choice education, especially during the last years, and on the most important matters for life, such as the course of religion; but also contact outside the classroom, where we engaged in sporting or cultural activities with the Fathers in the precincts of the college. Many hours of physical and cultural activity were thus spent in a most friendly and virile atmosphere.

To the question of when and how I first thought of the possibility of becoming a priest, my answer is that there was no one special moment when I had a special grace of illumination. It came by itself by osmosis, as it were, through the intellectual and spiritual influence which the Fathers exercised upon me, though never with the slightest sort of pressure. The kind of life they lived, deeply committed as they were to service through education and deeply sincere in their religious commitment, impressed me deeply and, without my being completely aware, gradually became for me an example to follow and an ideal to realize in my own life.

I was not the only one to be thus impressed. From the class of thirty students to which I belonged, there came no less than nine vocations to the priestly ministry, six to the Society of Jesus, two to the diocesan clergy and one to the Benedictine order. Personally, I thus developed at once a priestly and a Jesuit vocation in the most natural fashion. It should be clear that in the circumstances I did not separate a priestly and a religious vocation; both came together and were practically inseparable. To this influence received from my teachers, I must add, with a feeling of deep gratitude, that without my knowing this at the time, ever since she had had children, my dear mother prayed that one of her sons might become a priest. This perhaps explains the feeling I always had of being the object of her special affection. Probably she had a presentiment that I would be the one. Years later, when in winter 1944 she was in a Louvain clinic for a cancer operation, I went to visit her before the operation took place, the outcome of which was uncertain. On that occasion she told me with great emotion that my vocation had been the greatest joy and grace of her life, for which she had prayed to God for many years. Eventually she was to die on May 7, 1945, from cancer at the age of forty-seven, on the very day when all the bells in town were ringing [to celebrate] the end of the war. She had offered her life that all of us might survive the hardships of the war. I have no doubt that I largely owe my vocation to my mother, to her example and her prayers.

I finished school in July 1941 and entered the novitiate in September. When I told my parents and family about my decision to join the Jesuits, their first reaction consisted in asking me to let the war finish before leaving home. Conditions during the Nazi occupation were indeed very hard, and it seemed better to postpone my decision to such time when, with the end of the war, there would be no danger to life and conditions would have improved. My answer was that there was no knowing how long the war would last and that I thought I should not postpone my decision. This seemed to make sense to my parents. For the rest, however, their reactions were varied. My mother saw in my vocation the realization of her deepest aspirations, though of course the separation would be especially painful; but she knew how to accept sacrifices and she would make this one for my sake. My father found it more difficult to understand and to accept. He had nourished high expectations for my future, as well as for that of my elder brother, in quite another direction, in the professional line. However, he never tried in any way to dissuade me or to interfere with what I thought to be my vocation, even if the call was not always easy to explain rationally. He insisted with me that, should I at any time regret my decision and discover that I had made a mistake, I should not hesitate to return home where I would always be welcomed back. Through God's grace this did not happen and my family have remained most attached to me ever since.

G.O'C.: *Where did you do your novitiate and your first training in the Society? Could you give a brief account of these first years of Jesuit training? Why and when did you choose to go to India?*

J.D.: There would be a lot to say about those seven years of early Jesuit training before I left for India at the end of 1948. The first years were under the German occupation, and even the years that followed bore the scars of all the hardships endured by the country and its people. We faced those hardships as young Jesuits in a deep spirit of solidarity. To give an idea of the hardships in which those years were spent, I may mention that the period was made up of three parts: two years of novitiate, two years of classical studies for the attainment of a licentiate in Letters, and three years of philosophy. I should therefore have known only three different residences during the period; instead I was in seven. I entered the novitiate in Arlon, in the Luxemburg province of Belgium. Less than six months after my joining, the German headquarters requisitioned our house, and we were given twenty-four hours to vacate. Even the library of the house had to be emptied and eventually found refuge in the loft of the church attached to the house, which was very spacious. We had to move to our country villa in a tiny place called Clairfontaine, very close to the Luxemburg border. The country was very beautiful, but the accommodation was sheer camping. Nevertheless, we carried on our formation, by deepening our spiritual life and life of prayer and studying the *[Formula of the] Institute of the Society of Jesus*, as well as material work and various experiments to test the strength of our vocation. However, when winter came (which in those parts can be very severe), it was impossible to continue camping in a villa without any kind of heating. We then moved even closer to the Luxemburg border, to a small place called Guirsch, and were put up in a small convent of nuns. There were only three old nuns, totaling among themselves some two hundred and fifty years. Already in this period I experienced the fact that physical hardships and difficult circumstances of life help form character, and I thank God for the solid formation I received during my very first years as a Jesuit.

The second period was called the Juniorate. It consisted of two years of academic studies in classics, Latin, Greek, and of course French literature, principally, at the Facultés Notre Dame de la Paix in Namur. Here too we had two different places of residence. We had been in our College of Wepion on the river Meuse, close to Namur, for a few months when the same story repeated itself. The occupying army (we were now in 1944) forced us to vacate the house within a short time and turned it into headquarters for officers of the German army. This time we went to our own farm in the countryside, in a tiny village called Suarie, where material conditions and the camping setup were considerably harder than they had been at Clairfontaine. We were now living and sleeping on the ground in stables which had been occupied by cattle. We white-washed the stables in a hurry to turn them into living, studying, and sleeping quarters. This time we had no chairs or tables; bundles of straw served the purpose. Even the altar on which mass was said every morning was made of bundles of straw. Despite those conditions, however, we carried on our studies and prepared formal yearly examinations, in which we all were successful. There was also work to be done in the fields and in the farm—not to mention watching the fields against robbers during the night—so that we might have something to eat and live by. But here more than anywhere else or at any other time during my long life in the Society, I experienced such a deep community spirit, made up of mutual concern, each one forgetting himself to think primarily of the others. This would not have been possible but for the guidance of a great Jesuit who was our rector—his name was Clement Plaquet—who managed to create among us an extraordinary spirit of brotherly charity, mutual help, and collaboration. To the precarious material conditions in which we were living were added the dangers to life from bombing raids; we also risked arrest and reprisals from the Nazi occupants. In those days life was lived from day to day, without any guarantee of being alive the next day. And it was in this setup that I lived what would remain the most tragic years of my life.

G.O'C.: *You mention the constant danger to life during the war. Could you spell out what you mean? What experiences did you have that put you in real danger?*

J.D.: Some memories of those years are especially vivid in my mind. One such memory is the bombing of Namur in 1944. The railway bridge over the river Meuse was an important strategic point used by the Germans to withdraw their troops. The American army wanted to blast the bridge. On a bright sunny day big American planes flew over the city and from a very high altitude dropped as many as ten or more bombs. From Suarie where we were camping, some five kilometers from the city, we could see the bombs shining in the sun when they fell from the planes in a horizontal position and gradually taking a vertical position as they came down. The whistling sound which they made while falling was deafening. There followed an enormous blast, when all the bombs hit the heart of the city. More than four thousand civilians were killed, while the bridge stood untouched. The next day, two small planes from the British Royal Air Force (RAF) dived over the bridge, dropped a few small bombs and broke the bridge without harming any victims. Meanwhile, relief work was being organized in the city. The municipal authority appealed for volunteers to help rescue the victims and unearth the dead. Our entire community of young Jesuits was engaged for weeks in relief work, pulling the wounded and dead bodies out of the ruins. The work was interrupted regularly because of repeated air-raid alarms; we had to go into underground shelters to save our lives.

Another tragic memory belongs to the time when Belgium was liberated by the American army. The American soldiers had reached Namur with their tanks and were patrolling everywhere in search of German soldiers trying to escape toward the forest, where they had a rallying point. The municipal authorities had requested our superiors to send a team of young Jesuits across the Meuse by boat, to bury dead German soldiers who were lying dead in the fields. It was full summer, and the temperature was exceptionally high for a Belgian season, with the result that the corpses of those poor Germans were fast deteriorating. It was urgent to bury them on the spot, unidentified. As we were busy doing this macabre job, other German soldiers were walking behind a fence with their guns pointing at us, hoping to escape to their rallying point in the forest. The Americans wanted to fire at them across the river but refrained from doing so because we were standing in between, doing our miserable job. They sent a little girl to tell us to return immediately to the other side of the river, so that they might shoot at the German soldiers hiding behind the fence, hoping to escape. We had hardly crossed the river again when the Americans began firing again and we could see the men falling on the other side.

Even apart from such tragic happenings, daily life was lived in thorough insecurity. The Germans came repeatedly and unexpectedly in search of persons. They would make us all line up with guns pointing at us, while they searched our living quarters for marks of activities connected with the "resistance." In the case of compromising evidence, the presumed guilty would be immediately taken away to some concentration camp. The Germans also searched for young people from Luxemburg, whom they would enroll by force in the German army. As we had in our community some scholastics from Luxemburg, we had to keep them hidden in a shelter in our own forest, where they remained permanently and where we brought them food three times a day.

G.O'C.: *Did any of your immediate family suffer and die in the war?*

J.D.: I have mentioned that my mother prayed and offered her own life— she died on the day of the ceasefire on May 7, 1945—that we might all escape and come out alive after the war. And so it happened, as far as my father and my brothers and sister were concerned. My father lived through the German occupation under continuous threat, because of his situation as chief manager of a big factory which before the war had been producing war material. He was constantly harassed by the Germans to produce such material for them. He constantly pleaded the impossibility of getting the factory to function in the present circumstances. In spite of constant harassment he survived, after having lived for years under terrible stress. As soon as the Americans came to liberate Belgium from the German occupation, the factory went into operation again and produced the armaments requested by the American army, for which my father received after the war an award from the American army.

An uncle of mine, Robert Lemaitre, the brother of my mother, was the one close member of the family to pay with his life for his patriotic activity. He had been a volunteer during the First World War and had fought in the trenches. After the war he had received many medals from the Belgian army for his exemplary behavior as a soldier during the war. He became a notary in Châtelineau, close to Charleroi. He had a very large house in which he had a hiding place built to shelter British pilots and officers of the Royal Air Force whose planes had been shot down by the Germans. He was denounced for anti-German activities. His house was thoroughly searched by the Germans, who found nothing, though British airmen were hidden there. But my uncle was taken away and brought to the prison of Bochum in Germany. This was in November 1941. My uncle died there after suffering very great hardships, in December 1942. No news ever came about what had happened to him after his arrest, till after the war. In May 1945 a Belgian priest who had been imprisoned with him in Bochum and had assisted him in his last moments came to break the news of my uncle's death to the family.

G.O'C.: *Let us come back to your Jesuit training and to your wish to go to India as a missionary.*

J.D.: During this eventful period I developed the wish to go to India as a missionary. No one was ever sent to the "foreign missions" who had not clearly expressed to the superiors his wish to go and work there. In my case, even though I had been for a long time attracted to India because of its rich cultural and religious patrimony, I had not from the beginning been thinking in terms of a missionary vocation. Here again the call came by way of osmosis, if I may say so. A large group of my companions was already destined to go to India, in view of which they did special courses in preparation for their work there. This was called the "Indian Juniorate," made up of courses on Indian history and philosophy, Indian religion, English, and Sanskrit. The course was directed by Fr. Pierre Johanns, who had lived many years in Calcutta where he had done pioneering work in the field of interreligious dialogue with Hinduism at the highest academic level. He had had to return to Belgium because of failing health and soon assumed the direction of the special courses for those destined for India. My attraction to India grew out of my contact with this extraordinary master and with those companions of mine who aspired to live and work there; and the day came when I began to think that I too was called to the same vocation. Attraction to India grew into fascination, and eventually I informed the major superiors of my desire to enroll for the Calcutta mission. I was confident that the authenticity of my vocation would be recognized by the superiors, and I rejoiced greatly when they notified me of their approval.

The third period of my early training consisted in three years of philosophy, from 1945 to 1948, to attain a licentiate in that discipline. This was to be done in Louvain at the Jesuit Philosophical Faculty of Eegenhoven. But this time we could not even begin the curriculum in what should have been our residence. Saint Albert College, Eegenhoven, had been burned down by the Germans during the war, and the community of Jesuit students in philosophy was in exile at the College of Saint Paul, Godinne, in the province of Namur. The conditions here were, however, quite favorable, and, under the direction of a remarkable group of professors, I became deeply interested in philosophy, which would serve me well later for my specialization in theology. The Louvain Jesuits had developed under the guidance of Joseph Maréchal what was called the Louvain Jesuit school of philosophy, as a transcendental response to the agnosticism of Emmanuel Kant. One entered with intellectual pride into a heritage of such quality. Eventually the Eegenhoven College was rebuilt, and we shifted from Godinne back there during the summer holidays following my second year of philosophy. I could thus do my third and last year of philosophy where I should have started the first year, near the great Louvain University. That brought the number of my places of residence to seven in seven years. Conditions were returning to normal, on the political and economic front, and we could give ourselves fully to intellectual pursuits and studies. This then is a short account of my first Jesuit years, of which I have kept a very fond memory.

G.O'C.: *You left for India at the end of 1948, sailing from Naples to Bombay. What were your first impressions of this country, which had gained independence in the previous year, in 1947, and shortly after had witnessed the assassination of Mahatma Gandhi? Where did you live in India in those early years and what did you do? What impact did the religious traditions and cultures of India make on you in that early period?*

J.D.: It was in December 1948 that I had to say farewell to my family and leave for our Calcutta mission. The departure was of course very painful, less for those who went than for those who stayed. As far as I was concerned, I was seeing my dream fulfilled and my vocation followed, however hard it was to depart. It was much harder and painful for the family which I left behind. My father with whom I had in the preceding months shared my thoughts on the matter was wondering why I should go so far in order to answer God's call. I could be a good priest and Jesuit at home, where there was so much work to be done. However, he did not attempt in any way to change my decision any more than he had done earlier, when it was a question of my joining the Society of Jesus. He agreed that I had to follow my vocation, provided I was sure that God was calling me there—which, of course, was no more easy to prove rationally than it had been in the first instance. To appreciate the cost to the family members we must recall that in those days a vocation for the "foreign missions" in India meant that one was leaving family and country once for all; there would be no return. The bridges were being cut. That later things turned out differently was not foreseen or envisaged. And so when the time came I said farewell to my father, expressing my trust that we would meet again in heaven, when and if both of us got there. I expressed the same hope as I took leave of my two brothers and my sister.

My journey to India has a story of its own. We went as a group of four Jesuits, two students, myself and another, and two young priests. We left Brussels by train on December 8, 1948, for Genoa, where we were supposed to board a ship of the Lloyd Triestino Company due to leave soon. When we reached Genoa we were told that the date for sailing was delayed by a full month. So we decided to leave our luggage with the company at Genoa and board the ship at Naples, where it would call on its way to Bombay. This gave us a wonderful opportunity to visit Italy, spending Christmas in Rome and getting there the blessing of our Father General on our missionary vocation. Eventually we left Naples early in January 1949. The ship turned out to be a semi-cargo-boat which had been at the bottom of the sea during the war and had been refloated. It was no luxury liner; in fact the third class, where we found ourselves, resembled the hard conditions we had known at home during some of our early years as Jesuits. The ship took almost a month to reach Bombay from Naples; because of strong wind it got stuck in Port Said, unable to go across the Suez Canal. We were allowed to cross the canal by road, to visit Cairo, and board the ship again there after three days.

There was no question at that time of my becoming a theology professor in India. I had come to know closely in Belgium, before coming to

India, Fr. Pierre Johanns, the founder of what came to be known as the "Calcutta Jesuit School of Indology." During my first years in Calcutta I came into close contact with those who had been his colleagues there, like Fr. George Dandoy, and his successors, Frs. Pierre Fallon, Julien Bayart, Robert Antoine, and Richard de Smet, all involved in inter-religious dialogue at a very high academic level in Calcutta University or elsewhere. I myself was then destined by my superiors to follow a similar vocation after completing my formation. Only when I became later a student of theology was my destination changed to becoming a professional theologian.

After two years spent on the staff of Saint Xavier's High School I gave a full year to studying the Bengali language, without which life in Calcutta as a priest had become inconceivable. I threw all my energy and intellectual capacity into that study, and soon became thrilled by it. It was hard work at the beginning, and the first steps were especially painful. But after some time it became extremely rewarding. I was gradually discovering the modern Bengali language of which the great poet and Nobel Prize winner for literature, Rabindranath Tagore, had been the creator and had become the leading figure. It was infinitely rewarding to be able gradually to read in the original language the exquisitely fine, deeply religious poems of the father of the modern Bengali language, as well as his essays and treatises. His immense literary production represents even today the unsurpassed cultural and religious heritage of the Bengali land, and indeed one of the most exquisite cultural and literary products in the rich Indian heritage. I may emphasize the fact that many of Tagore's religious poems were already, in those 1940s, being used in the Christian liturgy and sung at masses in the Catholic Church, for the unmistakable Christian resonance which they evoked. This too, and the familiarity with the religious poems of other Hindu bhakti saints, had some impact on me, as the question was becoming ever more pressing: how do all these riches and divine gifts relate to our own Christian heritage? I was getting ready to undertake my theological studies.

G.O'C.: *You proceeded to Kurseong, in North Bengal, for your theological studies. How did those years go and what do you remember of life there?*

J.D.: Yes, in January 1952, I went to our Jesuit theological faculty of Saint Mary's College in Kurseong, a little town on a slope of the Himalayas at an altitude of some 2,000 meters, 500 kilometers north of Calcutta. The site was simply gorgeous. From our house, to the south we had a view of the plain of Bengal extending for hundreds of kilometers when the visibility was clear; and to the north, a magnificent view of the eternal snows of the Himalayan peak of Kinchinjunga, one of the highest and most majestic peaks of the Himalayan range. The situation—so we thought in those days—was ideal for lifting our thoughts toward immortal values through the study of theology. Later, after the Second Vatican Council (1962-65), the situation would be different, and it would appear incongruous to continue thinking out the faith which we were to announce to people in such isolation from the world. Our theological faculty would be transferred from the heights of Kurseong to the center of Delhi, the capital city of India. The contrast could not have been greater, but was not regretted by anyone.

Meanwhile I started my theological studies in Kurseong in earnest. The student body was made up of a hundred or so Jesuit scholastics, belonging to all the Jesuit missions in India; the vast majority were still at the time of foreign nationality. The professors also were still almost all foreigners, mostly Belgians. The students and staff would later undergo a complete change. Almost all professors and students are now Indian nationals belonging to the different Jesuit provinces of India, to whom are added some from other Asian countries; both the students and staff are also open to non-Jesuit members. We were proud in those days of belonging to Saint Mary's College, Kurseong, which was the first and at that time still the only Ecclesiastical Faculty in India, besides being the scholasticate of the Society of Jesus situated at the highest altitude. The academic level of the faculty fitted its prestigious situation. The theological faculty of Kurseong in those days compared well with theological faculties in Rome, Paris, or anywhere else, for the rigorous academic studies and the excellence of the teaching provided by the professors. I remember with special gratitude Fr. Joseph Putz, the dean of the faculty, who became a *peritus* at the Second Vatican Council, who was my mentor—in Indian terms, I should say my guru—from whom I learned enormously, not merely by way of acquiring much knowledge, but even more by way of a real openness to the world, of attention to the surrounding culture and concrete situation, and of a honest desire for a true renewal of theology. Eventually, I was destined to become his successor in teaching such fundamental subjects of systematic theology as Christology, the Trinity, and the Eucharist, as well as a course on the theology of religions, which was then a very new topic. There was among us, professors and students, a lot of innovation in academic pursuits, including an "Indian Academy" through which efforts were made at relating our study of Christian theology to the Indian religious traditions. This was excellent training for what was to come later.

G.O'C.: *You were ordained a priest in Kurseong in 1954. What do you remember of your ordination day? Did your family come for your ordination? What were your feelings on that occasion?*

J.D.: I was ordained a priest in Kurseong at the end of my third year of theology on November 21, 1954, by Archbishop Ferdinand Perrier, S.J., of Calcutta. My father could not attend my ordination because of his heavy professional duties. My sister and a cousin of mine came. Their presence was of course a great joy and consolation, on this unique occasion of my priestly ordination—which for any new priest marks what is perhaps the most important landmark in his life. The presence of the family was all the more appreciated because such long journeys were still somewhat exceptional in those days. After the ordination I had the opportunity of touring India with my guests, making them discover some of the treasures of the Indian cultural patrimony. They were immensely impressed and carried home marvelous memories of a unique journey. For me too this organized visit to some of the most striking sites of ancient Indian civilization was precious, making me appreciate more deeply the enormous treasures of humanity found in an ancient civilization, much more ancient in fact than that from which we came. This too helped to further confirm my vocation to India.

G.O'C.: *After ordination you continued your theological studies in India, then went to Rome. Tell us about that.*

J.D.: I finished my fourth year of theology in Kurseong at the end of 1955. I was now in possession of a licentiate in theology and henceforth destined by my superiors to pursue postgraduate studies in theology in view of returning to Kurseong to teach. Before proceeding with the doctoral studies, however, I went to Hazaribagh in Bihar where, under the direction of Fr. Louis Schillebeeckx, elder brother of the great Dominican theologian Edward Schillebeeckx, I did my tertianship, the Jesuit third year of probation, a one-year period destined to deepen one's spiritual, Jesuit, and priestly life. That was 1956. There followed another year of study in the Calcutta University to familiarize myself more deeply with Indian philosophy and the Indian religious traditions. The plan had been that I should now proceed to Rome to do my doctorate. I applied for Indian citizenship, the laws for which had just been voted by the Indian parliament. This would have allowed me to stay out of India for two full years, the minimum required to complete my studies in Rome. The central government of India did not, however, accept my request. Since as a foreigner I would be allowed to stay out of India for only eighteen months with certitude of recovering my permanent permit of residence on my return, I first proceeded to De Nobili College, Poona, by then the second Jesuit theological faculty in India, where, under the direction of Fr. Joseph Neuner, another great theologian who also became a *peritus* at the Council, I began work on the topic of my thesis. I then proceeded to Rome in September 1957 to continue my work at the Gregorian University, where I obtained the doctorate in theology early in February 1959.

G.O'C.: *You were in Rome when Pope Pius XII died and John XXIII was elected. What do you remember of this?*

J.D.: I returned to Rome from a holiday in Belgium on October, 9, 1958, the day of the death of Pius XII, and attended the solemn funeral. I was there for the election of John XXIII on October 28. I remember very well the excitement which accompanied the event. I was living in the San Roberto Bellarmino College. We used to go up to the terrace of the house to see whether the smoke coming from the Sistine Chapel was black or white. In fact, it was impossible to make out with certainty what color it was, and we had to go down each time to the radio to get the correct information. Eventually, for once the smoke happened to be clearly white, and the radio confirmed the news that the election had taken place. I remember the rush that ensued, as the city of Rome literally ran to the Vatican; the traffic was totally interrupted to leave room for the people rushing through the streets. By the time I reached Saint Peter's Square, it was already crammed. We waited for quite some time before anything happened. The excitement of the crowd grew. Finally, Cardinal Ottaviani appeared on the balcony of the basilica and pronounced in a loud voice: "*Habemus Papam*, His Eminence Cardinal Giuseppe Roncalli, who has chosen the name John XXIII." A lot of whispering went around the piazza at that moment, as people had not understood the name clearly and the name mentioned came somewhat as a surprise to many. People inquired about the identity of the new pope and exchanged information and reactions. For the Italians who made up the majority of the crowd, one thing mattered supremely, namely, that an Italian cardinal had been elected. And so it was. The crowd became more and more excited, till the moment when Pope John XXIII appeared on the balcony of the basilica. The enthusiasm of the crowd that filled the piazza down to the Via della Conciliazione reached its peak and became a frenzy of joy. The pope appeared, smiling and waving to the crowd, and the crowd responded to him with applause and outstretched arms. His appearance was short and ended with the first papal blessing of the people. As the crowd began to disperse, newspapers were already on sale with the new pope's photo and an account of his life on the front page. Only the papal attire was missing, as the photo showed the new pope dressed as a cardinal. Everybody bought a copy of the paper on his way home.

G.O'C.: *As all this was happening you were researching and writing your thesis. What was your topic?*

J.D.: As the subject of my thesis I chose the religious anthropology of Origen, the Greek theologian of the third century, undoubtedly one of the greatest luminaries among the Fathers of the church. In those centuries the Fathers faced the enormous problem of inserting the Christian message into the context of the Greek culture; similarly, we theologians were now being faced with the problem of inserting it into the great cultures of the East. By no means a smaller task! I could learn a lot from the way such an intellectual genius as Origen had gone about it. I learned a tremendous amount, even if I had to finish the work within the eighteen months allotted to me before getting back to India. I landed in Bombay in February 1959, one day before the expiry of my return visa. As I passed through the police checkpost, the officer looked at my passport and remarked: "You are just on time." I answered: "Yes, but I am on time!"

G.O'C.: *After completing your doctoral studies in Rome, you returned to Kurseong to begin your teaching career. Meanwhile the Second Vatican Council was being prepared, and then officially started in 1962. This coincided with your early years as a professor. Were you able to follow the Council in India? What impact did it have on you and on your thinking and teaching? What did you do to implement the conciliar trends and decisions in the place where you were teaching and ministering?*

J.D.: Yes, it is then that I began my career as a theologian and a professor at Saint Mary's College, Kurseong. In 1959, Pope John XXIII announced his decision to call a new ecumenical council, Vatican II. This is not the place to describe the contrasting reactions with which the announcement was received, especially in Rome, going from enthusiasm on the one hand, to skepticism or sheer consternation on the other. But in the context of the Indian church, which was then in the process of coming into its own as a local church, the New Pentecost called for by the pope appeared as a precious gift of God to the church, and a unique God-given opportunity, in the Indian context, for thoroughly rethinking traditional ways and opening new vistas. We followed the preparation of the Council from 1959 to 1961, and thereafter its four sessions and intersession periods from 1962 to 1965 with the utmost interest, not to say with passion. The distance from Rome notwithstanding, we were fairly well informed about what was going on at the Council, especially when the Council work was in process, through daily, weekly, and monthly chronicles appearing in *La Croix,* the *Tablet, Informations Catholiques Internationales,* and other papers, which we received by air mail.

To start one's teaching career in this context, with the lively discussions going on at the Council about burning questions for the life of the church, was nothing less than thrilling and, as I thought, a very special grace. It forced me to do some thorough rethinking of some received theological views and to open myself up to new horizons and perspectives from which my teaching could only profit. I could take a critical distance from some traditional and apparently untouchable ways of doing things. Let me give a rather commonplace example. The untouchable teaching medium in theology had been Latin, a venerable tradition which looked immovable, since even Pope John XXIII seemed to confirm it with the apostolic constitution *Veterum sapientia* (1962). In Kurseong the practice had been for a professor to say one sentence in Latin, and then to translate it into English to make himself understood by the students. I thought this out, and came to the conclusion that this way of proceeding was a sheer waste of time. Besides, I had been commissioned to teach and make myself understood, rather than to talk Latin. So I was the first professor to start my teaching career straightaway in English, which raised some eyebrows on the faculty.

The Council constituted an enormous challenge in all spheres connected with theological training and teaching, starting with the liturgical reform which was being initiated, passing on to a new notion of the church, from "perfect society" to "the People of God," and a reversal of perspective on the mystery of the church, from pyramidal and hierarchical to communional and sacramental. More importantly still, in the Indian context, there was a new attitude toward the other religious traditions, recommending dialogue and collaboration. It would take time to assimilate all these new insights and to sort out the concrete applications. Yet there was a desire not to waste time in making a start but rather to forge ahead with determination and courage. Some of the first steps in implementing the Council's spirit and letter which were taken in the limited context of the Kurseong theological faculty may be mentioned here. These modest steps are symptomatic of the enthusiasm with which the Council was being received and followed.

The community chapel of Saint Mary's College was thoroughly transformed, to adapt it to the renewed conciliar liturgy, after the promulgation of the Constitution *Sacrosanctum concilium* on December 4, 1963. The idea and realization of the project came from the students, who themselves planned and executed the work of transformation with the talents at their disposal. To meet the cost of the transformation, which with the means at our disposal was not too high, I wrote some articles for an American theological periodical. The cost being met, the permission of the superiors to go ahead followed. With a team of four students especially gifted in handicrafts and painting, we worked day and night during the holidays at the end of the school year 1967. The result was a thorough transformation of the sanctuary in view of the new liturgy. The altar facing the wall was replaced by an altar table facing the people. All around the sanctuary were stalls for the concelebrants. [The space was] dominated, in the middle of the transept, by an impressive icon of Christ the Pantocrator painted in Indian style. The two side altars, on the right and left sides of the sanctuary, had disappeared and were replaced, on the right side, by the table for the preparation of the gifts in view of the Eucharistic celebration, surmounted by a very fine painting of the Virgin Mary in Indian style; and, on the left, by the organ, which had come down from the loft. The beautiful tabernacle, grafted with precious stones—the only thing that remained from the previous sanctuary—was located, on the right side, against the wall between the altar table and the table for the preparation of the gifts; on the opposite side, on the left, was found the ambo for the proclamation of the word of God, carved in wood in lotus-like shape and surmounted by the sacred *OM*, the Indian symbol for the word of God. In the loft of the chapel no less than six altars for private masses, three on the left and three on the right, had disappeared.

This venture all happened due to the interest and hard work of students working with modest means at their disposal but with great enthusiasm and putting to use the remarkable talents with which they had been gifted by God. Much more substantial adaptations to the new liturgy no doubt would follow thereafter, and on a much bigger scale, but the modest transformation of the Saint Mary's Chapel was one of the first realizations made in India, of which there was good reason to be proud. I still treasure some beautiful photos of the results.

Another achievement, of a more academic nature but also related to the liturgy, was the composition of a eucharistic prayer for India, drawing from the Indian religious tradition by way of phraseology and, more deeply, assuming into the Christian Eucharist the age-long search for God by people and of people by God which had characterized that tradition. In this case too the work was done by the students. I ran a seminar over a whole semester of teaching to bring this about. The structure and development of the eucharistic prayer had to be established on solid theological ground before its composition could be attempted. In the work of composition we looked for parallel expressions in the Christian Scriptures and in the Sacred Books of India to express the content of the Christian Eucharist: names for God, to whom the eucharistic prayer is addressed; the Paschal mystery of the death-resurrection of Jesus Christ of which the eucharistic celebration is the memorial; intercessory prayers which would be deeply inserted into the Indian context; and above all a long development in the "Preface" or Proclamation of the history of salvation, with explicit reference to the Indian salvation history, the record of which is found in the religions of the Indian tradition, and the three *margas* or ways—knowledge, devotion, and work—along which union with God has been sought over the centuries. The preparation of the eucharistic prayer has been a concrete example of the way in which students were endeavoring to relate their theological studies to the pastoral work which would be theirs later, and of their determination to make the Christian message meet at a deep level the religious tradition of the country. The work has been very successful. The "eucharistic prayer for India," as it came to be known, is the only such prayer which has been proposed to the Indian episcopal conference for approval. It did receive the approval of the Indian bishops, and, though it failed to receive official recognition by the Roman Congregation of Rites, is even today largely used in India. We of course used it in our own eucharistic celebrations in groups, in which it was often preceded by readings from, and common meditation on, strikingly parallel texts chosen from the Sacred Books of India on the one hand and, on the other, from the Bible, Old and New Testaments.

Still connected with the liturgy, I was nominated a consultor for the Liturgical Commission of the episcopal conference of India. The work produced by that commission over the years following the Council was enormous. It was all engineered and directed by Fr. D. S. Amalorpavadass, the dynamic director of the Bangalore Biblical, Liturgical and Catechetical Centre. We were a group of a dozen people who spent weeks working together on different projects at the Centre and became close friends by working for the creation of an Indian liturgy. The results over a few years included a full "Ordinary of the Mass" for India, and three volumes of alternative second readings for the Office of Readings in the Liturgy of the Hours. These readings were culled from various books among the Sacred Scriptures of India. The criterion for choosing them for inclusion in the Christian Liturgy of the Hours was the Christian response they

evoked and their openness to a Christian understanding and interpretation. This was a fine practical exercise in interreligious dialogue, done in
the knowledge of the differences and without syncretism, but also with
full awareness of the mutual resonances available between the traditions.
All this material is available in print, though it was never officially published because of lack of ecclesiastical approval.

There were too the regular All-India Liturgical Meetings held in Bangalore, in which the progress of the liturgical renewal in the country was
reviewed and suggestions made for speeding up the implementation of
the Council. One of my contributions to these—as also to other meetings
and seminars—consisted in staying up at night on the eve of the closing
of the meetings, drafting the conclusions or recommendations, or else the
statement or declaration. People seemed to think that I had a special gift
for drafting conclusions.

G.O'C.: *Eventually the Kurseong theological faculty was transferred to Delhi,
and you went there to continue your teaching career. Tell us a little about this.*

J.D.: After the Council it became somewhat preposterous to have the
theological training of future Jesuit priests located in the clouds of the
Himalayan mountains. Contact with the world at large and in particular
with the Indian reality became a must. The decision to transfer to the
capital city of Delhi was not an easy one to take, or to realize. The decision
was taken by Fr. Pedro Arrupe, general of the Society of Jesus, and executed in the winter of 1971. Incidentally, I made the trip from Kurseong
to Delhi on motorcycle. I thought that, rather than risking damage to my
motorcycle if sent to Delhi by train, I had better bring it there myself by
making the trip by road. I had become quite accustomed to ride a rather
powerful motorcycle of Yugoslavian manufacture, called Yawa. When I
went to see my rector in Kurseong to ask him for the permission to make
the trip by road on motorcycle, he thought I was crazy but gave me the
permission without hesitation And so I made the trip of exactly 2,000
kilometers from Kurseong to Delhi in three days on my Yawa, with a
young scholastic behind me who was a light passenger. We both enjoyed
the experience.

G.O'C.: *How did the change affect your work and which new activities did
it bring about for you? You became one of the prized theological advisers of the
Indian Bishops' Conference. Can you tell me how this came about? What were
the big issues on which you were consulted? What remains in your mind from
these years?*

J.D.: The theological work in Delhi continued, but it also implied from the start new obligations and responsibilities. On the one hand, there were more opportunities for pastoral work, including regular weekend ministry, retreats, and conferences; on the other hand, I was much in demand with the New Delhi archbishop, Angelo Fernandes, himself a theologian and a prominent figure of the Indian Episcopal Conference, for help in preparing papers and contributions to Conference assemblies. Eventually, I became for all practical purposes, though never with an official title, the main theological adviser of the Episcopal Conference of India. I attended regularly the yearly plenary assemblies of the Conference, and several times was requested to deliver at the Conference the keynote address on the subject under consideration for deliberation by the bishops.

One year—it was in January 1976—I gave the keynote address on the belonging of the religious to the particular church in which they happened to be working. I developed the theme of the religious belonging to the particular church and of their obligation to fall in line with the pastoral plan of the diocese, explaining that the "exemption" of the religious had to be understood correctly, against some misconceptions of the past. It did not mean that the religious were totally independent, constituting as it were a church within the church, but, their availability for transfer to some other local church for the sake of greater service notwithstanding, as long as they found themselves working in a particular church they were expected to fit loyally into it, in harmony with the residential bishop and the diocesan clergy and in collaboration with the mission of the local church. The bishops of India appreciated my talk very much and had it published in the Acts of the General Assembly for that year; it was also printed in *Vidyajyoti* 40 (1976): 97-111. On the contrary, some of my Jesuit confreres thought I had been selling out the religious to the bishops.

Another time the theme proposed for deliberation by the bishops at the General Assembly of the Conference was "The Church's Response to the Pressing Needs of India." This was in Mangalore in January 1977. Again I was requested to give the keynote address, on a theme which, I must confess, I thought was somewhat beyond my capacity. I tried to make the best of it, pointing especially to the need for the church to give a witness of solidarity with the poor and depressed classes in a context like that of India, to become, that is, not merely a church for the poor but with the poor and of the poor. I also stressed developing a sense of self-reliance and of dependence on local resources rather than continuing to depend principally on foreign funds and help—an attitude detrimental to the witness of the local church as well as to its legitimate autonomy. Again I stressed the need to go ahead with vigor and determination with the program of renewal laid out by the Second Vatican Council, especially in the fields of the liturgy, of lay participation, of collegiality at all levels of the church's life. Once again the talk was well received by the bishops, who entrusted to me the task of writing, during the night on the eve of the last day of the meeting, the conclusions to be read and approved the next morning by the bishops, while they themselves proceeded that evening to the residence of the archbishop of Mangalore for a reception and dinner, to celebrate the hard work done during their meeting. Both the talk and the Conclusions were again published in the Acts of the General Meeting of January 1977. These are but examples, but I choose them from the occasions which left a deeper impression on my mind.

Being in Delhi opened up also new opportunities to attend important theological meetings and sessions which during those years were being multiplied and played an important part in the theological renewal initiated by Vatican II. They included topics like "Ministries in the Church," or the Christian Understanding of "non-Biblical Scriptures," or again "The Indian Church in the Struggle for a New Society." These were either national meetings and seminars held at the Bangalore Centre, at the level of the Indian subcontinent; or they were all Asia meetings sponsored by the Indian Episcopal Conference among others, in the context of the Federation of Asian Bishops Conferences (FABC). These meetings were highly successful in developing in the Indian and the Asian churches a spirit of renewal and the awareness of being churches no longer merely in India and Asia, but of India and Asia. As far as I am personally concerned, they gave me the opportunity to make my little contribution to that growing awareness, as also of nourishing my theological teaching with the present reality on the Indian and Asian scene. My involvement in writing during those years consisted mostly of contributions to all those meetings, as well as of articles about current church and theological problems in our review *The Clergy Monthly*, later called *Vidyajyoti: Journal of Theological Reflection*, of which I became assistant editor in 1973, and of which I assumed the chief editorship from March 1977 till May 1984.

My involvement with the Indian bishops also took another form. One of the big issues under discussion in India during those years was the question of the relationship between the various individual churches, the Latin, the Syro-Malabar, and the Syro-Malankara, on the question of territorial jurisdiction. The Latin church was universally present in India while the other two churches' territorial jurisdiction was almost entirely limited to Kerala. The two Oriental churches claimed the right to do evangelization and to open dioceses on territories belonging to the Latin church; the Latin bishops had strong reservations against such a practice, which would multiply cases of double jurisdiction everywhere in the country, a practice which seemed to contradict the ancient tradition even of the East, as Patriarch Athenagoras himself admitted. Two bishops in the same territory had been compared by the ancient tradition to two cocks on the same dung heap! The question was historically very complex, and the accumulated ill feelings had made it even more delicate. I personally felt quite unprepared to become involved in this difficult matter, especially as a foreigner. Yet I was asked, in the name of the Latin bishops, to accompany the representatives of the Latin side and to assist them at some meetings which took place at the Bombay Regional Seminary of Goregaon, to discuss the matter and try to come to an agreement. These meetings, though courteous, were tense. They took place within a small group of bishops representing all three sides, with an even more limited number of experts on all sides. I thought discretion on my part was in order during these meetings. This notwithstanding, I was later requested to write, in the name of the Latin bishops and with the help of another theologian of the Latin church, Fr. Felix Wilfred, a long memorandum destined to be sent directly to the pope, in which the viewpoint of the Latin bishops in the difficult issue was exposed at length. The solution recommended in the report was very far sighted. It suggested that the only decisive solution to the problem would consist in the creation of one Indian rite, common to all three individual churches, and of course open to further adaptation to local cultural, linguistic and other traditions. On the one hand, the local differences had to be considered seriously and the long traditions of the individual churches fully honored; on the other hand, the three individual churches should give the priority to their common vocation of becoming and being together the church of India, through communion and cooperation. The solution proposed involved sacrifices on the part of all, which not all on any side were prepared to assume. Nor was it to be thought that the central authority in Rome would have been well disposed toward this solution. What happened is that the Oriental churches were granted their request of creating dioceses in Latin territories, with the problems, human and structural, involved. Universalism and particularism are difficult to combine.

G.O'C.: *You also became a consultor of the Federation of Asian Bishops' Conferences. How did this come about? What were the high and low points of this work? What memories do you treasure from this period?*

J.D.: The Federation of Asian Bishops' Conferences was created in 1970 and held its first plenary assembly in Taipei, Taiwan, in 1974. This assembly produced an important document on evangelization in the Asian continent which was sent to Rome in preparation for the 1974 synod of bishops. I was privileged to accompany Archbishop (later Cardinal) Lawrence Picachy of Calcutta, as his secretary to the synod, at which he acted as one of the president-delegates. The 1974 synod of bishops has been in my opinion the most interesting of all the bishops' synods in Rome after the Council. My comparison is based on my presence at successive synods, three in all, one being the 1985 Extraordinary Synod of Bishops called by Pope John Paul II to celebrate the twenty years of the closure of the Second Vatican Council in 1965. By then I had been transferred to Rome at the Gregorian University.

In the 1974 Synod on Evangelization, even though I had been invited by Archbishop Picachy to accompany him, I was not allowed to enter the synod hall in the capacity of his secretary. I was forced to have resort to the subterfuge of joining the Jesuit team set up by the Jesuit curia in Rome, at the request of the Vatican, to provide freely the simultaneous translation during the general assemblies of the synod. We were a team of as many as twelve Jesuit priests doing the job in different languages. This was hard work, but it gave me the opportunity to get the pulse of the synod from within, to witness the different attitudes among bishops from different continents, to follow the evolution of a new and broader concept of the church's evangelizing mission which was being elaborated at the synod. Evangelizing no longer merely consisted in proclaiming Jesus Christ and converting people to Christianity; it included the church's involvement in the integral liberation of human beings and in interreligious dialogue with the members of the other religious traditions. This was enormously important for the future of the church's life and mission, especially in the continents of the Third World, Asia in particular. An assessment of the 1974 synod is not easy to make. I attempted one in an article entitled "Synod of Bishops 1974," published in *Vidyajyoti* 39 (1975): 146-69.

A great difficulty arose at the synod due to the incompatibility between the two special secretaries appointed by the Vatican, one being Fr. Domenico Grasso, professor of pastoral theology at the Gregorian University, the other Fr. D. S. Amalorpavadass, the director of the Bangalore Centre in India. The two men had thoroughly different theological approaches and were unable to work together at composing a document which would be voted on by the bishop members and approved by them as the synod document. Instead, each one composed by himself the complete draft of a document, and both brought their own composition separately to the president-delegates of the synod. (I worked during the nights, together with Fr. Amalorpavadass and Fr. Arevalo of Manila, at the composition of the Amalorpavadass document, which went to forty pages.) The two texts were incompatible in their approach, one very conservative and looking to the past—the Grasso one—the other, of Amalorpavadass, very progressive and open toward the future, to the point that they hardly reflected the deliberations and represented the conclusions of the same ecclesial event. No wonder that the hybrid text, made up of bits from both the original productions and worked out during the night on the eve of the official closing of the synod by Msgr. A. Descamps, member of the synod in his capacity as secretary of the Pontifical Biblical Commission, was rejected by the assembly. The 1974 synod of bishops ended without having published a document of its own and had to be satisfied with requesting the pope to publish a document of his own in the light of the documentation of the synodal event. This was the origin of the apostolic exhortation *Evangelii nuntiandi* of Paul VI, published at the end of 1975. This shift from a synodal document to a postsynodal papal document became the pattern thereafter, and at the first general assembly of the 1977 synod that followed, the bishops were informed by the synod's general secretary that their task consisted in informing the pope in view of a document to be published by him.

This failure notwithstanding, the 1974 synod of bishops has been the most important and the most successful of the entire series after the Council. For one thing, the concept of the mission of the church was much broadened in relation to the world around in the spirit of the pastoral constitution *Gaudium et spes* of the Second Vatican Council; for another, the door was open, in the spirit of the declaration *Nostra aetate*, for a new approach to the mission in relation to the members of the other religious traditions, which would allow for dialogue and collaboration instead of perpetuating mistrust and antagonisms. To which it must be added that Paul VI's apostolic exhortation *Evangelii nuntiandi*, in spite of its great merits, did not—unhappily—do full justice to the new awareness which had gripped the synod fathers, of the church as being a universal communion of local churches, each with its "legitimate autonomy" and its own mission of being fully integrated in the human reality of the land. I commented on the apostolic exhortation *Evangelii nuntiandi* in an article entitled "Apostolic Exhortation *Evangelii nuntiandi*" in *Vidyajyoti* 40 (1976): 218-30.

My involvement in the work of the Federation of Asian Bishops' Conferences, which in the course of time became very well structured into different "Offices," each one dealing with a special concern for the evangelizing mission, consisted in attending and contributing to several meetings and seminars held in the name of the FABC, as for instance the

"Asian Colloquium on Ministries in the Church," held in Hong Kong in 1977. When later I received my appointment as a member of the Theological Advisory Commission of the FABC, I had to decline the invitation because I had by then received the news of my transfer to Rome. My departure for Rome would have made it impossible to attend the regular meetings of the Commission, though I always remained very much in touch with its thinking and have quoted abundantly from the documents it issued. As for the Indian Theological Association of which I was a member and remained one after I had left India, I attended and took an active part in its meetings over the years, even—insofar as possible—after leaving the country, on such topics as "Searching for an Indian Ecclesiology" (1983), "Towards an Indian Theology of Liberation" (1985), "Towards an Indian Christian Theology of Religions" (1989), and "Responding to Communalism" (1991).

G.O'C.: *While you were in India, you were involved in the editing of a volume on the doctrinal documents of the Catholic Church entitled* The Christian Faith. *You are still engaged in this work. Could you explain the project, how it started and what it has meant to you?*

J.D.: In 1938 Josef Neuner and Heinrich Roos published in German a collection of major doctrinal documents of the Catholic Church: *Der Glaube der Kirche in den Urkunden der Lehrverkündigung*. They were assisted by two young Jesuits: Alfred Delp (1907-45) and Karl Rahner (1904-84). Rahner edited subsequent editions of this collection of documents, until Karl-Heinz Weger took over—from the eighth edition in 1971. In India Fr. Neuner and myself realized that after Vatican II (1962-65) it was clearly desirable to prepare a fresh collection of the church's doctrinal documents, which would leave out irrelevant texts and include more documents, in particular from conciliar and postconciliar teaching. The introductions to chapters and introductions to specific documents were written in the light of Vatican II's doctrine and the best current scholarship. Existing translations needed correction and in some cases had to be redone. New chapters were introduced to cover significant fields of modern teaching and theology, making in all twenty-three chapters, from "Revelation and Faith" (ch. 1) to "Christian Fulfilment" (ch. 23), with an opening section of "Symbols and Professions of Faith." In doing this work, Neuner and I had the help of eight other professors of two faculties, Vidyajyoti (Delhi) and Jnana Deepa Vidyapeeth (Pune). The result was *The Christian Faith in the Doctrinal Documents of the Catholic Church*, published in 1973 by Theological Publications in Bangalore, India. From 1973 to 2001 the work went into seven editions, which were successively revised and brought up to date. The work has kept the same twenty-three chapters but has grown in length from 711 pages in the 1973 edition to 1,135 pages in the seventh edition of 2001, from which an Italian translation was made, published in 2002 by San Paolo, Cinisello Balsamo (Milan). In preparing the sixth edition (of 1995) and the seventh edition (2001), I enjoyed the help of ten collaborators from the Gregorian University. The book continues to prove a valuable instrument of theological learning of the two thousand years of the church's official teaching.

G.O'C.: *How did your years in India change your thinking on the whole question of Christianity and the other major world religions? You have said that you considered your exposure to the reality of God's gifts to other peoples, in your case especially to the Indian people, to be "the greatest grace" you received from God in your teaching career. Could you explain what you mean? Could you give some examples of how this exposure gave you a deeper insight into the mystery of God's plan for humanity?*

J.D.: I have said many times, and continue to think today in the light of what I have seen and lived thereafter, that my exposure to the Indian reality has been the greatest grace I received from God as far as my vocation as a theologian and a professor is concerned. One cannot live thirty-six years in India without being deeply affected by the experience. This is true at the level of sheer human reality. I was coming from a small West European country where all the prejudices regarding the superiority of the West over the rest of the world were still very much alive. Western—and Christian—civilization was the only civilization worthy of the name. We had learned in theory that the Indian civilization was much older and at least as rich as ours, but this abstract knowledge did not change our mentality deeply. We still considered ourselves humanly superior and were convinced of the mission of the Western world to spread its own civilization everywhere.

It strikes me as odd that even today the mentality of so many people in the West remains one-sidedly centered on the European continent. They continue to think and to act as though Europe and the Western world in general were the center of the world. Now, this is a myth which should long have been exploded. By sheer numbers it is no longer possible to think that the future of the world lies on this side; it belongs, whether we like it or not, to the so-called Third World, and especially to the Asian continent. The fact that the population of China and India together make up today well over 2 billion people out of the 6 billion that cover the planet Earth should revise our scale of values and re-dimension our own claims. The world tomorrow will be very different from that which we have known in the past; it has already changed enormously and is destined to change even more. The backbone will no longer be the Western hemisphere—it has already shifted from there—but those continents to which in the past Europe claimed to bring civilization by way of conquest. A long exposure to a vast reality such as that of the Indian subcontinent brought a cultural shock and forced me to open my eyes to much larger horizons and perspectives.

The same is all the more true if one thinks not only of the size of the countries and the numbers of their population but of the rich, ancient cultural heritage of such Eastern countries as India and China. One cannot but admire the exquisite beauty of ancient Hindu temples and Buddhist monasteries. The artistic patrimony of these and other Eastern countries compares well with our own Western cultural heritage. To discover it gradually on the occasion of journeys undertaken for professional purposes is each time a cultural thrill. India is certainly a land of contrasts and of large-scale differences—as are, moreover, many countries in the Third World. There is the shocking contrast between the rampant poverty of large masses and the luxury living of the privileged classes. But there are also the exquisite human values found eminently, perhaps preeminently, among the poor and the underprivileged by way of mutual solidarity, mercy, and compassion toward fellow humans. Through the most ordinary contacts with people one is made to feel and to sense their deep humanity, their sense of human dignity, the richness of their spiritual and religious life. And this is where we touch upon the main aspect of the problem.

If I consider my exposure to India as a grace from God in my professional work as a theologian, the main reason is that the exposure to its religious reality forced me to revise altogether my former evaluation of the meaning of the religious traditions which nourished the spiritual life of the people I was meeting on my way. Despite the privileged education I had received in Belgium before I left for India, including already some initiation into the Indian religious traditions, nevertheless I went there with the prejudices of our Western civilization and our Christian tradition. We thought we were the best, not to say the only ones, where civilization is concerned; we also had it engrained in us that Christianity was the only "true religion," and therefore the only one with an unquestionable right to exist. Of course, there were human values to be found in the religious life of the people we met and in the religious traditions to which they belonged—we had happily got beyond a purely negative appraisal. But these values were at best the expression in the various cultures of the universal aspiration toward the Infinite Being, innate in human nature itself. I came to realize that such a position was untenable and that we would have to revise altogether our premises. The religious traditions of the world did not represent primarily the search of people for God through their history, but the search of God for them. The theology of religions, which was still in its infancy, would have to make a complete turn from a Christian-centered perspective to one centered on the personal dealings of God with humankind throughout the history of salvation.

In this perspective the religions could be seen to be the "gifts of God to the peoples" of the world and to have a positive significance in God's overall plan for humanity and a saving significance for their members. With this discovery, the challenge for a theology of religions became how to combine the Christian faith in Jesus Christ universal savior with the positive meaning in God's plan of salvation of the other religious traditions and their saving value for their adherents. My entire theological work thereafter has wrestled with the need to overcome the apparent dilemma between these two affirmations, and to show that far from contradicting each other they are complementary, if one succeeds in going beyond the appearances.

So my literary production while teaching in India was centered on this central problem; it would become even more so after my transfer to Rome. I think I have been able to formulate a theological perspective which makes sense of both affirmations, and I have developed it gradually with greater precision and a more secure foundation in the Christian revelation and tradition. My efforts remain, however, partial and open to improvements; theology is never ended. The theology I have developed and the teaching I have imparted are very different from what they would have been without my Indian exposure. My mind and my intellectual make-up have been turned upside down by the experience. I realize almost every day, in conversation with colleagues in Rome, how much my scale of values differs from that of the majority among them and how much my theology arouses in some of them suspicion and misgivings. I attribute those differences to the grace of exposure which has been mine and to the lack of the same among many. One does not fall in love with what one does not know.

Part of my grace of exposure to the Indian reality is the personal acquaintance—in some cases the close friendship—which I have been privileged to entertain with all the men and women who in recent decades have been in India the pioneers for the establishment of a monastic life deeply rooted at once in the Christian tradition and the Indian religious

reality, or for an interreligious dialogue with the other religious traditions at a deep theological level. I had been in Belgium a disciple of an
extraordinary master, Pierre Johanns, the founder of the "Calcutta Jesuit
School of Indology." During my early years in Calcutta, I came to be
acquainted closely with his former colleagues and successors, all engaged
in the meeting of Christianity and Hinduism at a deep theological level.
Later I came to know personally the pioneers of the movement all over
India. I can only mention them by name: Jules Monchanin and Henri Le
Saux (Abhishiktananda), the co-founders of the Saccidananda ashram of
Shantivanam; Francis Mahieu Acharya, the founder of the Monastery of
Kurisumala; Bede Griffiths who, after Monchanin's death and the departure of Abhishiktananda for Uttarkashi, where he lived as a hermit at
the sources of the Ganges, took over the direction of the Saccidananda
ashram; Raimon Panikkar, the synthesis of East and West; Sisters Van-
dana and Sara Grant, the co-foundresses of the ecumenical ashram of
Pune; and others. All those men and women impressed me very much and
influenced deeply my thinking as I was developing my own view of the
relationship between Christianity and the religions of the world. While
not being always in agreement with their theological positions, I could
not but admire the earnestness with which they engaged in the problem
and the breadth of vision with which they attempted to solve it. My own
theological development would not have been what it became without my
personal knowledge of those pioneers.

G.O'C.: *In 1984 you were called to work at the Pontifical Gregorian University in Rome. How did this come about? Your first contact with the Gregorian
after your own studies there came when you were invited to teach a course in the
1981–1982 academic year, and again in 1982–1983. What prompted the invitation? How did you yourself view it?*

J.D.: My transfer to the Gregorian University in Rome took place in May
1984. I will explain later the reasons and circumstances of that painful transfer. Yes, I had been invited by Fr. René Latourelle to come and
give a course there in 1981 on the theology of religions, for the second
cycle of the faculty of theology. Father Latourelle was a far-sighted man
who found it odd that the curriculum of studies still did not contain any
explicit teaching on the theology of the religions of the world. The exclusivist mentality, traditional in Christianity, and the Roman approach to
theology still perpetuated the idea that theology was just about Christian dogma and Catholic doctrine. To indulge in discussions regarding
the relationship between Christianity and the other religious traditions

seemed adventurous. Why Fr. Latourelle invited me to come to Rome and give such a course, rather than calling on some other theologian, I do not know, as he never explained this to me. I suppose that he had come to know me through some of my writing and through the reputation which I had acquired as a reliable theologian. He thought he could trust me for my reliability in handling a difficult subject. However, it was not possible for me to be absent from Delhi for a full semester because of my many commitments there. So, I accepted the invitation provided the course could be concentrated in a period of six weeks.

I gave the course for the first time during the second semester of the 1981-1982 academic year. I was invited again by Fr. Latourelle, now dean of the faculty of theology, to give the same course during the second semester of 1982-1983. When I was in the Gregorian for the third time for the same course during the second semester of 1983-1984, I was informed by Fr. Peter-Hans Kolvenbach, General of the Society, about my permanent transfer to the Gregorian. The request for my transfer had come partly—if not exclusively—from the dean of theology at the Gregorian, with the consent of the authorities of the university. My course there seemed to be appreciated and found worthwhile by those in charge, who thought that my permanent transfer to the Gregorian was a worthwhile project. Father Latourelle had the idea of entrusting me, once I would be in Rome on a permanent basis, with teaching the course on Christology either at the first or second cycle, combining this with the special course on the theology of religions, which I had by then given three times. As far as I was concerned, the invitation to come to the Gregorian and teach for six weeks every year was most welcome. It gave me the opportunity to present to a much larger audience than I had in Delhi what was already getting organized in my mind about how an open theology of the other religions should proceed. Had I anticipated that the first invitation would eventually lead to a permanent transfer, I would have declined it politely, for I had never envisaged even the possibility of my leaving India permanently.

G.O'C.: *You started teaching as a permanent professor at the Gregorian in October 1984. It must have been a big change from India. What did you feel? What did you miss most? How did you experience your first years as a permanent teacher there? What kind of welcome did you get at the Gregorian? What was the academic atmosphere like in Rome during those early years?*

J.D.: The welcome at the Gregorian when I arrived in June 1984 as a permanent member of the Jesuit community and of the university's staff was very warm, especially on the part of the superiors. I started teaching in October 1984 at the second cycle, with optional courses and seminars on the theology of religions, on Christology, and the theology of mission. In that first year I ran my courses and seminars in French and English, my Italian still needing some brushing up. I shifted to the Italian language during the academic year of 1985-1986. The change to the Italian medium gave me a much bigger audience, and though my courses at the second cycle were optional, the audience became eventually so large that classes had to be held in the Aula Magna (the "Great Hall") of the university. If I were to compare my teaching experience in Rome with the one I had had in India, there would be, on the one hand, something to regret from the past and, on the other hand, something new that was welcome. In India I had the privilege of close contact with Indian students in theology, as they were rediscovering their cultural roots and asking radical questions on issues which they were living personally at a deep level in their own life: the relation between their Christian faith and the religious traditions of their ancestors, to which in some cases their families still belonged. Close contact with them in such situations was a deep experience; it was also a powerful incentive to forge ahead with a thorough reconsideration of the meaning of other religious traditions in God's plan for humankind.

On the other hand, the much larger audience which I found in Rome for my courses on religions and on Christology was also a powerful incentive to meet the expectations which the students were placing in me. The cosmopolitan character of the audience, which included a large number of nationalities, was also a great incentive. It gave me the feeling that what I conveyed would spread to all continents and be so multiplied. I often wondered why students flocked to me in such big numbers. They seemed to be looking to me for something they did not quite find elsewhere. Some told me confidentially that in the seminaries in South America where they had come from reading works by liberation theologians was forbidden. They chose my seminar on the Christology of liberation theologians to make up for what they had long been deprived of. Similar situations arose in the field of the theology of religions, some sharing with me the negative experiences which they had made in the past in this regard, either in their family context or even with priests and teachers.

On the other hand, the academic atmosphere in Rome was not too favorable. One could always have the suspicion of being somewhat under supervision and eventually threatened with denunciation. Students were allowed to register on a tape recorder the class given by the professor. In a crowded auditorium it would have been easy for a stranger to join among the students with a tape recorder in his pocket and to record—for whose benefit?—the teaching that was being imparted. I must confess that I never allowed myself to be deterred from saying and teaching what I thought to be true. And again I think that the students came to me because they felt in me that honesty and sincerity, that complete coherence between what I thought and what I taught, which made for the credibility of the message.

G.O'C.: *In 1985, the pope appointed you to be consultor to the Secretariat for Non-Christians (SNC), later known as the Pontifical Council for Interreligious Dialogue (PCID). Could you tell me how that came about? How did you view the appointment? What did the work consist of? What were the issues on which you were consulted?*

J.D.: How this nomination came about, I do not know. When one is nominated by the pope through the Secretariat of State as a consultor to a Roman dicastery, one is not told for which good personal qualities and through which influence the nomination has come. It all happens in a rather impersonal, formal manner, with of course all the pomp of the Vatican jargon. Nominations are for five years, liable to be confirmed for another five, but no more—according to the rules. The end of the tenure is expressed plainly by a letter of thanks from the Secretariat of State, also in the same formal manner. The thanks are as impersonal as the nomination. I was thus a consultor to the SNC, later the PCID, for ten years, from 1985 to 1995.

The regular work consisted in attending meetings of the consultant body on topics for which the authorities of the Council wanted to have their considered opinion, in view of decisions to be taken or attitudes to be fostered. As the session opened, Cardinal Francis Arinze, the president of the Council, would thank the consultors profusely for the "great sacrifices" they had made in coming to attend. An envelope would be sent round to each one to cover the basic travel expenses. The consultors might also attend some meetings organized by the Council, either in Italy or abroad, to consult more broadly on important issues having to do with the work of the Council. I was thus chosen by the Council to attend the Theological Colloquium organized by it which took place at the Papal Seminary in Poona, India, in August 1993, on Christology, ecclesiology, and the theology of religions. I delivered there a paper on "The Church, the Reign of God, and the 'Others,'" which was published with the Acts of the Colloquium in *Pro dialogo*, the periodical of the Council (85-86 [1994, no. 1]: 107-30). Organizing such meetings or seminars was for the Council a way of feeling the theological pulse at large on some burning issues connected with interreligious dialogue; holding them abroad helped to arouse less suspicion. As for meetings abroad with other groups involved in interreligious dialogue such as the Dialogue with Peoples of Living Faiths Unit of the World Council of Churches, consultors of the PCID were rarely asked to attend them; the staff of the Council kept that task to themselves.

With regard to the kind of topics for which the opinion of the consultors was sought, I may mention one which created a bit of a sensation. The Congregation for the Doctrine of the Faith (hereafter CDF) published in October 1989 a "Letter on Some Aspects of Christian Meditation" which provoked a stir even in Vatican quarters for its negative attitude toward the adoption of Eastern methods of prayer and meditation by Christians. Cardinal Arinze called a special consultation on the topic. The consultors of the PCID were unanimously negative in their reactions to the document, which they considered offensive toward the other religious traditions. Cardinal Ratzinger was known for his personal opposition to such practices which he had witnessed in Germany; he once referred to the practice of Zen as spiritual "self-abuse." Given the strong disapproval of the document by the Council, Cardinal Arinze asked Cardinal Ratzinger for an interview between the two dicasteries on the matter. This meeting took place, but on a reduced scale and only between the high officials on both sides. Questioned on the opportuneness and wisdom of such a document, Cardinal Ratzinger excused himself by saying that the document had been entirely written before he had assumed the function of prefect of the CDF; he had only put his signature on a document with which he had had nothing to do personally. Incidentally, he had become prefect of the CDF in November 1981!! This was a strange way of declining all responsibility for a document to which the signature of the cardinal prefect lent the authority of his office. It fell in line with the provision and the practice according to which, while the Vatican Councils for Christian Unity, for Interreligious Dialogue, and for Culture may not publish any document without the approval of the CDF, the Congregation is not expected to consult the Councils when publishing documents closely related to their field of operation. The matter was left where it stood.

G.O'C.: *You were assigned the delicate task of drafting the one major document which the PCID produced during the ten years while you were a consultor, "Dialogue and Proclamation" (1991), in collaboration with the Congregation for the Evangelization of Peoples, the former Congregation "de Propaganda Fide," Could you recall here your experience as the main drafter of this document? Who asked you to write the text? What were the crucial issues? Were you satisfied with the final result? Did you receive any feedback afterward?*

J.D.: The Secretariat for Non-Christians had published in 1984 a document called "The Attitude of the Church towards the Followers of Other Religions: Reflections and Orientations on Dialogue and Mission." The main drafter of that document had been Marcello Zago, the secretary of the Secretariat who later became General of the Oblates of Mary Immaculate. The aim of that document was to apply to interreligious dialogue the broadened notion of the evangelizing mission of the church which developed in the wake of the Second Vatican Council. Previously evangelizing had been practically identified with proclaiming Jesus Christ and converting others to Christianity. It had now to be made clear that other church activities belong to the evangelizing mission of the church as "integral parts," among which were involvement for integral human liberation and interreligious dialogue. Dialogue had been considered at best as a first step toward proclamation; it had to be shown that dialogue is already evangelization in its own right. The 1984 document did this very competently and opened new horizons for the practice of the evangelizing mission. At the same time it raised new questions.

If dialogue was already evangelization, how did it relate to the proclamation of the gospel and to the church's commission to announce Jesus Christ and to invite members of the other religious traditions to become his disciples in the church community? And, moreover, if dialogue was evangelizing, was there any place left or any need still to proclaim and to announce? These are the difficult questions which the new document, envisaged by what would soon be called the Council for Interreligious Dialogue, was destined to address. The document came to be published in 1991 under the title "Dialogue and Proclamation: Reflections and Orientations on Interreligious Dialogue and the Proclamation of the Gospel of Jesus Christ." But it had a long history and a difficult gestation, being several years in the making.

Why, after a long discussion between staff and consultors in which a provisional structure of the document was established, I was asked to write the first draft, I do not know. The fact is that Monsignor Michael Fitzgerald, the secretary—I suppose with the approval of President Cardinal Arinze—asked me to do the work. It was not an easy job, as one had to propose a balanced view of the relationship between the two components of the evangelizing mission. I decided to proceed in three steps: dialogue, proclamation, dialogue and proclamation. This had the advantage of showing that dialogue is already evangelization, yet that it does not supersede or replace proclamation, but is oriented toward it insofar as in proclamation the dynamism of the evangelizing mission culminates. I spent an enormous amount of time drafting and redrafting the text, all by myself, with much effort involved but also great interest and even enthusiasm, as I had long been reflecting on the issues involved. When my draft was ready, it went to the authorities and staff of what was by then the Council. The draft was first discussed among the staff together with the consultors, which brought some first amendments and suggestions. The document underwent as many as five successive drafts. It had to be sent to all episcopal conferences for comments, observations, and suggestions. As would be expected, comments came from opposite directions with different approaches in mind, and were sometimes mutually contradictory. All of these had to be taken seriously, yet a discernment had to be made as to what could and should be integrated into a new text, and what should be left out.

At one stage, the draft came up for discussion at the plenary assembly of the Council, of which Cardinal J. Tomko, prefect of the Congregation for the Evangelization of Peoples, was a member. Cardinal Tomko objected strongly to the Council for Interreligious Dialogue intending to publish a document on a topic closely related to the concerns of his Congregation without any reference to it. He demanded that henceforth the drafting committee should be so enlarged as to include representatives of his Congregation. This was fair enough and lightened my own personal burden. Lengthy discussions ensued at the broadened drafting committee in the presence of the two cardinals, in which it was not always easy to find a meeting ground, as the concerns of the two dicasteries and the mindsets were so different. I remember clearly Cardinal Tomko stating emphatically at one such session that he did not accept the 1984 document of the Secretariat where it was said that in dialogue "Christians meet the followers of other religious traditions in order to walk together toward truth" (13); to which I remarked politely that the document had received the approval of the pope and had been published in the *Acta Apostolicae Sedis*.

The enlarged drafting committee, though somewhat hybrid, worked well together, each side taking the responsibility for the part of the document of its immediate competence, while the revision of the third part was done together by both sides. This must be taken into account in evaluating the final outcome of the document: it explains why there are found in it some apparent discrepancies. These came primarily from a somewhat one-sided insistence on the side of proclamation to stress the Lord's command to preach the gospel—which of course was not denied—for which the other side had to make allowance. Many amendments by way of compromise had thus to be introduced into the text. At one stage I wondered whether of the five drafts the first was not perhaps the best, the most consistent and most robust. This, however, was a personal impression at a moment of stress and on a point on which I was too personally involved to be a good judge. It is clear, in fact, that its shortcomings notwithstanding, the document said something new and worthwhile, especially on the subject of a Christian approach to the meaning of the other religions and of their positive meaning for the religious life of their followers and the mystery of their salvation in Jesus Christ. The last draft of the document was eventually presented to the plenary assembly of the PCID at its meeting of April 1990.

There was lively discussion at that meeting, and eventually more amendments had to be introduced. I recall strong objections raised by Bishop Kloppenburg of Brazil against what is perhaps the most important number (n.29) of the document: "It is in the sincere practice of their own religious tradition that the members of other religions respond positively to God's invitation and receive salvation in Jesus Christ." A long discussion took place on this text, which eventually had to be changed to read as follows: "It will be in the sincere practice of *what is good in their own religious traditions and by following the dictates of their conscience* that. . . ." The idea of the amendment was of course to tone down the role which the other religious traditions have in the salvation of their followers. Even in this wording the text still met with misgivings. At that stage Cardinal Decourtray of Lyon intervened angrily to say: "If we are not prepared to say that much we had better go home and forget about publishing a document." This settled the matter and the text remained as it now stood. When it came to voting it obtained a unanimous vote, except for one vote *juxta modum* and in the absence of Cardinal Tomko, who had chosen to abstain from the voting session.

However, there still remained the need to get the *placet* of the CDF. In view of this, a meeting took place at the CDF headquarters between the heads and secretaries of the three dicasteries and a few consultors, on September 20, 1990—a meeting which I was not invited to attend. That meeting produced some more amendments, happily of a light nature. The text was now ready for publication and was published on May 19, 1991, signed by Cardinals Arinze and Tomko. I have written an extensive account of the genesis and the painful birth of the document, with a commentary added, in W. Burrows (ed.), *Redemption and Dialogue* (Maryknoll, NY: Orbis Books, 1993), 118-58. My experience of having been the main drafter of an official document published by the Vatican remains a mixed one. I was happy to be able to contribute to an important document, destined to have a lasting influence on the future of the mission. It struck me, however, that, after having done all the spade work, consultors are in the end left out of consideration in the last stage of the procedure. No thanks for the work done were ever forthcoming. *Servi inutiles sumus.*

G.O'C.: *In October 1986, the pope, for the first time ever, invited the leaders of the major world religions to Assisi to pray for peace. This was seen as one of the "prophetic" gestures of this pontificate. What, if any, was your involvement in that event? How did you view it? Looking back with the hindsight of more than sixteen years, and also with the experience of another similar event in 2002, what are your reflections now?*

J.D.: Though a consultor of the Pontifical Council for Interreligious Dialogue, I was not involved in any way in the preparation of the 1986 Assisi event; nor was I able to be present in Assisi myself, due to pressing work. I did follow the event with the utmost interest and have no hesitation in saying that it has been a "prophetic" event of the pontificate of Pope John Paul II. It is well known that Assisi 1986 met, even at the Vatican, with resistance before and with criticism after. It did take courage on the part of the pope to go ahead in the face of opposition. In his discourse to the Roman Curia in December 1986 the pope explained the meaning of the event and justified it as an expression of the new spirit and attitude of dialogue advocated by the Second Vatican Council. The speech delivered by the pope on that occasion is a robust theological statement of the foundation for a positive evaluation of the other religions and of interreligious dialogue.

The event did of course raise lively discussion, both before and after. Was there no danger of religious syncretism, leading to relativism, involved in such a happening? The most delicate point was the justification for praying together between Christians and the members of other religious traditions. The Vatican, in the person of the pope himself and of Cardinal Etchegaray, to whom was entrusted the organization of the event, took a prudential approach to the problem. It was stated clearly, almost as a leitmotif, that "We went to Assisi together to pray; we did not go to Assisi to pray together." The pope and the cardinal said explicitly that shared common prayer between Christians and others is not possible. The same would be repeated by Cardinal Walter Kasper on the occasion of the second Assisi event, in January 2002. And so, in 1986, different places were assigned in the morning to the different religious traditions, where they were invited to pray for peace in the world, while in the afternoon all assembled together on the piazza of the Basilica of Saint Francis, where they listened with deep attention to prayers formulated by heads of the different religious groups and traditions. In 2002 the procedure was revised so as to ensure even more clearly the absence of any kind of syncretism. The presence in Assisi of so many representatives of different religious traditions having come together there to pray for world peace was by itself a very significant event and a witness to the world of the harmony and collaboration which should reign between the religions of the world. It was truly a "prophetic" event. Yet the question could be asked, and was asked in fact, whether the procedure followed in Assisi was the only one conceivable if all danger of syncretism and relativism was to be avoided.

In a summit meeting like that of Assisi, where the entire planning was done by the Vatican authorities without the possibility of joint planning with the heads of the other traditions—these were only invited to answer positively the request made to them by the Vatican authorities—and considering, moreover, the fact that Assisi 1986 was a premiere, the procedure followed was the only one which could possibly be acceptable to all. Nevertheless, witnessing with great attention prayers formulated by members of other traditions is not the only practice possible in interreligious meetings. Is it altogether excluded that Christians and members of other religious traditions may pray together by truly sharing a common prayer? In the Guidelines for Interreligious Dialogue which they published in 1989, the Commission for Dialogue and Ecumenism of the Catholic Bishops' Conference of India stated: "A third form of dialogue goes to the deepest levels of religious life and consists in sharing in prayer and contemplation. The purpose of such common prayer is primarily the corporate worship of the God of all who has created us to be one large family. We are called to worship God not only individually but also in community, and since in a very real and fundamental manner we are one with the whole of humanity, it is not only our right but our duty to worship him together with others" (82). This shows that different perceptions and different ways of doing things are possible in different circumstances and situations. The practice of common prayer has been known in India for a long time, well before the 1986 Assisi event, and is in use, with the approbation of the episcopal conference, on such official occasions as the National Feast, Republic Day, or some Hindu festivals like the Festival of Lights (Diwali) and of Wisdom. We must beware of absolute rules being imposed on all times and places without need.

G.O'C.: *In those years you participated in a number of synods of bishops in Rome. Could you tell me something about those experiences, and share your reflections on those events? During the same years of teaching in Rome, you had many opportunities to attend meetings and sessions of different sorts and to give lectures in many places. Can you tell me about such extracurricular engagements?*

J.D.: I have already mentioned my participation at the 1974 synod of bishops in Rome on evangelization, in my view the most important and the most interesting of the series so far. My other experiences of being present inside the synod hall during all the proceedings, always in the humble quality of contributing gratuitously to the simultaneous translation with a team of Jesuit confreres, refer first to the Extraordinary Synod in 1985 on the occasion of the twentieth anniversary of the closure of the Second Vatican Council, and later to the "Synod on the Vocation and Mission of Lay People in the Church and the World" of 1987. To be right inside the synod hall during the proceedings has the enormous advantage of getting the feel of the assembly, of appreciating the different attitudes of episcopal conferences of the various continents to the issues involved, of watching the reactions in the assembly to what is being said by the synod members in their interventions, also on the face of the pope who is present at all the sessions. However, I became somehow disillusioned with the synods as these are being run. I declined the invitation extended to me again after the 1987 synod to continue contributing to the simultaneous translation.

Having but a consultative role, the synods became more and more engineered and directed by the Vatican Curia. The Curia had its own way of allowing the bishops to speak out, of maneuvering the recommendations they made, and of sorting the propositions which the assemblies passed on to the pope for his postsynodal exhortations. The same thing happened in the special continental synods called by the pope on the occasion of the third millennium: for Europe, America, Africa, Asia, and Oceania. I did not attend those, but I followed closely the one on Asia. It was disappointing to see how recommendations and requests made by the bishops, especially those of Japan and Indonesia, in view of a more effective recognition of the legitimate autonomy of the local churches, had quietly fallen by the wayside in the final set of propositions passed on to the pope, and completely disappeared in the postsynodal document. These issues involved, for instance, the possibility of granting to the episcopal conferences the right officially to approve translations of liturgical texts. This request has been made ever since Vatican II and was still refused at these continental synods. The present practice of reserving this right to the Holy See has led through the years to ludicrous stories.

The 1985 synod is an exception to the rule that set in after the 1974 experience, insofar as the pope allowed the publication by the synod, in its own name, of the Final Report, entitled "The Church, Led by the Word of God, Celebrating the Mystery of Christ for the Salvation of the World." The fact that Cardinal Godfried Danneels of Brussels-Malines was *Relator* and theologian Walter Kasper, later archbishop and cardinal, special secretary of the synod, probably has something to do with its success and outcome. The Final Report is a dense document which shows the deep continuity between the Council and the postconciliar church. It would go a long way in fostering the positive "reception" of the Council's ecclesiology, insisting as it did on the concept of communion as the fundamental insight of Vatican II on the mystery of the church; such a concept, if consistently applied, would lead naturally to the principles of collegiality to be applied at all levels of the church's life, and of subsidiarity in the exercise of authority. One can only hope that the postconciliar institution of the synods of bishops in Rome may one day be so revised as to realize better the hopes of the Council.

It is not possible here to recall all the meetings and congresses which I was privileged to attend during my years of teaching in Rome, much less all the occasional lectures and addresses which I delivered in so many places in Italy and abroad—not to mention the regular courses given also in Italy and abroad. I must be very selective and limit myself to mentioning only a few with a special significance or impact on my own career. There is no doubt that, as compared with being stationed in India, my permanent residence in Rome offered much greater opportunities for answering invitations which came to me from so many quarters. One instance was my attendance at the Symposium on "Christianity and Religions" organized by the theological faculty of North Italy, in Milan, in February 1992. While in Rome, Msgr. Giuseppe Colombo, dean of the faculty, had come personally to the Gregorian to invite me. I delivered on that occasion a communication entitled "Ways of Salvation or Expressions of the 'Religious Man'?" I had published recently my book *Jesus-Christ à la rencontre des religions* (Paris: Desclée, 1989), which had soon been translated into Italian under the title *Gesù Cristo incontro alle religioni* (Assisi: Cittadella, 1989, 1991). This book was the first of what would become later a trilogy on the theology of religions. My communication at the Symposium was extremely well received, as it contrasted strongly with the rather traditional views expressed by the members of the Milan faculty and the somewhat abstract linguistic approach of their discourse on "Religion" (in the singular). I myself was surprised—and so was Msgr. Colombo, who sat on my right as chairperson of the session—at the very enthusiastic applause I received from the hundreds of students who had filled to capacity and beyond the Aula Magna of the Milan Seminary. I did not talk about "Religion" in the abstract; I had in mind the concrete religious traditions which surround us and asked what significance they have for us Christians. The title of my talk indicates clearly what I was trying to say: namely, that we must go beyond the view of the other religions expressed by such great theologians of last century as Henri de Lubac and Hans Urs von Balthasar, for whom those religions represent at best the expression of the innate human aspiration toward the Infinite. The reception I got on that occasion encouraged me to pursue the line I had traced for myself. The Acts of the Symposium have been published under the title *Cristianesimo e religione* (Milan: Glossa, 1992).

An occasion worth remembering is the Interdisciplinary Seminar organized by the theological faculty of South Italy, San Luigi section, Naples, in 1996. The theme of the Study Week was "Universalism of Christianity." The study was centered on the theology of religions which I had by then developed in many writings and was now coming up for friendly discussion, evaluation, and criticism by the theological staff of San Luigi. I truly admired the initiative of the faculty, under the guidance of Fr. Saturnino Muratore, of inviting every year a prominent theologian for a week of solid discussion of his work. I thought this was an example which other theological faculties would do well to emulate—to begin with, that of the Gregorian University to which I belonged. Such initiatives can go a long way in promoting theological discussion and collaboration. I did find myself very much at home at San Luigi, although, as would be expected, opinions differed between the participants, and dissent by some on some critical points was expressed plainly and sincerely.

Since the session was centered on my own production, I was asked to introduce the topic with a long communication and, thereafter, to animate the debate and bring out the conclusions at the end. My communication was called "Universalism of Christianity: Jesus Christ, the Reign of God and the Church." The staff members of the Naples faculty, San Luigi section, each gave a communication on a theme related to the main topic of the conference. There is no room here to mention all the observations and suggestions made in the course of the rich and long discussions that ensued. Let it suffice to quote from the conclusions I brought at the end of the proceedings:

> It seems to me that on some of the points which have been discussed, we have reached a certain, though not complete convergence. The perspective of the theology of religions is changing rapidly: from the problematic of the possibility of salvation for the others, we have passed to that of a positive role of the traditions in the mystery of salvation; and today the question is: what could be the meaning of those traditions in the divine plan for humankind? Would the

religious traditions be a sign in human cultures of the depth of the divine mystery, and at the same time of the prodigality with which God is communicating himself to people? In any case, it seems that in the future the theology of religions is called to become a theology of religious pluralism.

This was in 1996, one year before I was to publish the solid book on the topic of religious pluralism which would be questioned by the CDF. What happened in Naples shows that I was already in possession of what I would soon expose at length. The Acts of the Naples Interdisciplinary Seminar have been published in Mario Farrugia (ed.), *Universalità del Cristianesimo: In dialogo con Jacques Dupuis* (Cinisello Balsamo: San Paolo, 1996).

In 1997, I was invited to become a member of the Italian Theological Association, which I readily accepted. Strangely I was and still am the only Jesuit professor of the Gregorian to be a regular member of the Association, which, however, was founded by two professors of the Gregorian, Frs. M. Flick and Z. Alszeghy. Since my nomination I have attended regularly the yearly Congresses of the Association, which I always found stimulating. The general theme of the 26th Congress in September 1997, held at Troina, Sicily, was "Christianity, Religion and Religions." A section of the study had to do with "The Uniqueness and the Universality of Jesus Christ and Religious Pluralism." Incidentally, my book *Toward a Christian Theology of Religious Pluralism* had just been published in the Italian edition: *Verso una teologia cristiana del pluralismo religioso* (Brescia: Queriniana, 1997). The Council of Presidency of the Association had thought of asking me to give the main paper on that topic. But, on learning that I had been rather seriously ill, they were afraid that I might not be able to attend and found it safer to approach another Christologist for the paper. That is how, without even checking with me about my eventual availability, they entrusted the talk on Christology and the Religions to Fr. Angelo Amato, professor of Christology at the Salesian Pontifical University in Rome. I did attend the Congress all right and was present all through its proceedings.

I found the talk by Prof. Amato very negative with regard to the ongoing discussion on the theology of religions; he pointed with one-sided insistence to dangerous opinions being held by recent theologians, some of those Catholic. The speaker had brought with him a copy of the Italian edition of my book just off the press and, holding it in his hands, made reference to it during his address. While admitting that he had had no time to study it seriously, he nevertheless expressed his negative opinion about it. I thought I should react about this publicly and, during the discussion that followed, asked for the right to speak. I made a long improvised intervention in which, among other things, I observed that, if Fr. Amato, instead of doing theology of religions in isolation in a Roman university, would go to spend some time in India, allowing himself to be exposed to the Indian reality, he would probably return with some of his ideas changed. I got an enormous applause from the audience.

When he took up the issue again at the end of the discussion, Fr. Amato became apologetic, stating that, personally, he could not in conscience go beyond the evaluation of the religions which he had exposed in his paper. One of course has a right to one's own opinion and a right to share it with others; but some tolerance toward other opinions would also be in order. As for myself, I had succeeded in making an enemy, as later events would show. The proceedings of the Troina meeting have been published in Maurizio Aliotta (ed.), *Cristianesimo, religione, religioni: Unità e pluralismo dell'esperienza di Dio alle soglie de terzo millennio* (Cinisello Balsamo: San Paolo, 1999). The talk of Prof. Amato is found on pp. 145-72.

Incidentally, I may mention that this was already the second time when I publicly disagreed with Prof. Amato. At the International Mariological Congress held at Loreto, March 22-25, 1995, which I attended, Prof. Amato had given a lecture entitled "L'incarnazione e l'inculturazione della fede." As I thought his concept of the inculturation of the faith was very short and based on a purely Western approach, I intervened in the discussion which ensued after the talk, pleading for a much broader view of the inculturation process, for which models should be sought not in Italy but in countries of the Third World, Asia in particular. My later intervention at Troina would only confirm the difference between my views and those of the dean of the faculty of theology of the Salesian University.

In fairness to him, however, I must mention that in a book previously edited by him, *Trinità in contesto* (Rome: LAS, 1993), dedicated to a reconsideration of the Trinitarian mystery in different contexts, cultural and religious, Prof. Amato included my contribution "La teologia nel contesto del pluralismo religioso. Metodo, problemi e prospettive"—a context which, however, he considered in his presentation of the book as "radically provocative."

G.O'C.: *You were well known for your good relations with the students at the Gregorian, and you clearly enjoyed teaching them. What was it that you saw in them that inspired you? What did they give you, and what did you think was the main thing you gave them? What are your main recollections of those years of teaching in Rome?*

J.D.: I have already partly answered this question. I have compared my years of teaching in Delhi with the ones spent in teaching at the Gregorian, and remarked on what I enjoyed and what I missed on both sides. It is true that through those years I enjoyed very good relations with the students. It is also true, however, that the teaching profession was very absorbing and demanding. As my reputation grew as a teacher, the work became more and more heavy. I found myself totally engaged each week, through the whole weekend, with reading, correcting, and annotating the written work of students, either for their licentiate dissertations, or, more importantly, for their doctorate theses in theology. Comparisons are odious, but I sometimes had the impression that some professors were sending me students from whom they were expecting a lesser performance. Yet it would be very unfair to establish scales of value and merit between the students of different continents, or of different countries or even regions. We were there for all those who had been sent to us by their superiors, either ecclesiastical or religious, to take a licentiate or a doctorate in theology, and it did not belong to us but to the academic authorities to accept them or not as students of the Gregorian University. I made it a point to be at the disposal of all, especially those coming from the Third World. This was a way of continuing to identify myself with the India to which I still felt I belonged. There was, moreover, I must say, an enormous amount of goodwill and of intellectual capacity that came to us from countries of the Third World and from India, in particular.

I have mentioned the large number of students who attended my courses and the cosmopolitan character of the audience. This always prompted me to share the best with them. To the question of what I received from the students, I would stress that personal contact with them was a very enriching experience, as they explained what were their special interests, their preoccupations, and the problems they were meeting with in their own countries. One got one's own horizons enormously broadened by such experiences. I was very edified by the ardor and enthusiasm with which the students devoted themselves to their work and studies. To deal permanently with young people—though, of course, all the students were already mature persons—also forced one to remain young and to adapt to new generations. Over the years there were among the students differences of mentality, and one could almost feel a different sensibility and different reactions about current problems between generations which succeeded each other at a quick pace. All this was very enriching and made one wonder at the enormous human—and Christian—potential we were privileged to deal with.

As for what I personally have been able to give to the students, I am not, of course, a good judge. They would be able to answer that question better than I. All I can say is that I have always tried to share with them what I had personally experienced of the faith, and especially of the person and the mystery of Jesus Christ. Throughout my teaching career, I have been teaching the course on Christology, which I considered a great privilege. I can say sincerely that over my forty years of teaching trying to deepen my understanding of the mystery of Christ has been a continuing passion. It also helped to enrich my own personal relation with the Lord. If, as I hope, I have been able to convey to the students my passion for Jesus Christ and helped them to increase their own love for the Lord, I will consider myself fully rewarded for my labor. The course on the theology of religions was of course closely related to Christology. I have always been convinced that the mystery of Jesus Christ is at the center of a Christian theology of religions. I always combined both very closely, as my literary production on Christology and on the theology of religions amply shows. Over the years I discovered that far from endangering faith in Jesus Christ, a positive approach to the other religions helps to discover new depths in the mystery. This also is something which I hope I have been able to convey to my students. I may add that, judging from the many marks of appreciation I have received from former students over the years, I seem to have succeeded to an extent in my endeavor. To sum up, let me say that my teaching career has always been for me a source of joy and inspiration; I only regret that age inexorably puts an end to it.

G.O'C.: *From 1985 to 2002 you were director of the university's prestigious review* Gregorianum. *How did this come about? What particular memories do you have of that work?*

J.D.: I had been full-time at the Gregorian only a short while when Fr. Urbano Navarrete, who was then rector of the university, asked me to take the direction of the review *Gregorianum*. I pointed out that it could be found strange by some members of the staff that such an important responsibility was entrusted to someone new to the university. The rector thought that my recent arrival did not raise any problem and should not even enter into consideration. He insisted on my accepting the job, which I did. The request may have been made because I had been since 1973 assistant editor of our theological review in Delhi, called *Vidyajyoti: Journal of Theological Reflection*, and chief editor of the same from 1977 until my transfer to Rome in 1984. Between the last issue of the review in Delhi for which I assumed the responsibility and the first issue of *Gregorianum* which came under my direction, there was a gap of hardly six months. I remained director of *Gregorianum* until 2002. In all, then, I bore the responsibility of editor of a theological review for a full thirty years, which, I would suppose, is not so common.

The job was quite heavy and demanding, though I always did it with cheerfulness and without experiencing any major problem. Material to publish was never lacking, though over the years I had to depend more on what came from outside than on contributions by professors of the Gregorian. Not all felt a vocation to be writers. This was somewhat an anomaly, as the review was primarily intended as the organ of the university. Nevertheless, material was always in abundance, which allowed for selection in the choice of what was approved for publication by the editorial board. The theological review of a pontifical university in Rome is of course closely followed at the Vatican, and prudence was in order in choosing articles to be published. I intended once to publish a number [of articles] on the topic of "Doing Theology on Five Continents." I had invited the collaboration of some prominent theologian from each of the five continents, including Jon Sobrino for South America, George Soares Prabhu for Asia, and others. When all the material was ready and had been approved by the review's editorial board, I thought it my duty to inform the rector about the project. The matter was somewhat delicate and I did not want to put before the superiors a *fait accompli*. To my great dismay, the rector—it was then Fr. Gilles Pelland—thought that the publication of such articles was impossible and vetoed it. He explained his decision by saying that the Gregorian was closely watched by the Vatican and I should not create additional problems with the publication of dangerous material. It is true that some of the material contained in the articles was somewhat explosive, as it claimed the right and the duty of developing local theologies in the local churches of the various continents, in keeping with local conditions and circumstances, while in Rome and in the Vatican in particular, the idea of one theology valid for all times and all places was still prevalent. I had the painful duty of expressing my regrets to the authors who had contributed the articles. As fate would have it, those articles were published in various reviews and some quoted and referred to many times for their exceptional quality.

For the rest I was never personally questioned by the Vatican about my work as editor of the review. Occasionally the rector would inform me that such and such an article had not been appreciated in high quarters, but it never went beyond that. It was not difficult to guess the reasons for the disapproval. In those circumstances the freedom of the editor in choosing material for publication is limited. I often said that I sometimes published things which I would have preferred not to publish, and, on the other hand, was not able to publish material which I would have liked to publish. It was out of the question to try to make *Gregorianum* into an avante-garde review; current church problems were rarely alluded to. The material published concentrated mostly on highly academic studies, often of high quality, but considered inoffensive and harmless in terms of current discussions. When I was new to the job, I once asked Fr. Zoltan Alszeghy, a senior member of the editorial board, why *Gregorianum* never commented on recent Roman documents. He smiled and said: "Since we can never express criticism where this would be called for, it is better to keep quiet altogether."

All these restrictions notwithstanding I did enjoy the job of editor, for which I thought myself somehow gifted, and made the best of the circumstances to maintain a high standard of scholarship within the parameters left open to us. I regret, however, that *Gregorianum* has not contributed more to the Second Vatican Council, first when the Council was in preparation and then in progress, and after the Council to its "reception" and interpretation.

G.O'C.: *How has your understanding of the role of the theologian developed over the years, as you taught theology first in India and then in Rome? How did you rate the academic freedom you enjoyed in those years? From your long years as a teacher and professor, what is the principal lesson you have learned? What would be your advice to someone starting out on a similar teaching career today?*

J.D.: I have mentioned earlier the differences between the circumstances of my teaching in India, in Kurseong and Delhi, and later in Rome at the Gregorian. The situations were different on both sides: the audience in India was limited mostly to Indian students, but in Rome was very cosmopolitan; the problems and preoccupations were also different. But these differences notwithstanding, I always found myself at home with the students and enjoyed teaching them. I did not allow any fear to deter me from conveying to the students what were my deep convictions, based as these were on my personal perception of the content of Christian faith. This had been my practice in India and I remained faithful to it, no matter what could be the implications, when I found myself teaching in Rome. I could never tolerate some discrepancy between what I deeply believed and what I conveyed to others in teaching. This was part of my understanding of the teaching profession. I would have been unable to allow double standards to separate my faith and my teaching. I was aware that we had to teach the doctrine of the church and always made it a point to base my teaching on a serious study, not only of Scripture and Tradition, but also of the recent documents of the Magisterium. But, at the same time, I was convinced that the task of the theologian does not consist merely in repeating what has always been said, much less in relaying to his audience the content of recent papal encyclicals or of decrees of the CDF. Those documents had to be taken seriously, but they needed also to be approached critically, with an eye on the context in which theology was being done and on the questions raised by that context.

In the course of time, I developed a concept of theology as hermeneutics, which could no longer proceed along a priori dogmatic lines in a merely deductive manner, but would be inductive in the first place, starting from the experience of lived reality and the questions which the context raised, thereafter to search for answers in the light of the revealed message and tradition. Theology was becoming interpretation in context, and this involved a reinterpretation. Such a way of theologizing was of course much more problematic than the traditional way, following a purely historical and dogmatic method, had been. It did imply some risks and dangers, against which one had to guard oneself carefully. But it seemed also the only way of doing theology which would really meet the concrete reality of the world in which we are living. Where the theology of religions was concerned, it meant that one could not claim to engage in it seriously without being exposed at length to the concrete reality of the other religious traditions and of the religious life of their followers. In the process, a difficult problem arose, of asking how far some doctrinal documents of the central authority were really in touch with living reality, and how far they deserved and required a blind assent on the part of the theologian, with no possibility of a responsible and prudential dissent. This is also where the question of the academic freedom of the theologian comes in.

The task of the theologian requires a certain amount of academic freedom, without which it becomes impracticable; such academic freedom must be combined with the submission on the part of the theologian to the authority of the Magisterium. To find the right balance between those two loyalties is of course problematic. What is desirable is that there may reign between the church's doctrinal authority and the theologians a climate of deep mutual trust and cooperation. It was such a climate between bishops and experts, between the Magisterium and the theologians, that made the Second Vatican Council possible. We know too well that such a climate was not present from the start at the Council, and had to grow progressively as the Council attained its maturity. The question with which we are faced nowadays consists in asking whether the same climate of trust and cooperation is alive today and to what extent. There is no denying the fact that the academic freedom of the theologian has been seriously curtailed in the postconcilar period, which Cardinal Ratzinger himself has referred to as a time of "restoration."

Already in the "Instruction on the Ecclesial Vocation of the Theologian," *Donum veritatis* (1990), by the CDF, the role of theologians is being undervalued and made to consist principally in relaying the content of doctrinal church documents. On the other hand, little space is left to the members of the church for any right to responsible and prudential dissent, especially on questions related to morals. Moreover, we have been witnessing an inflation of the central Magisterium, with the affirmation, in the apostolic letter *Ad tuendam fidem* (1998)—not *ad promovendam*—and the commentary of the same by the CDF, of an intermediary category of truths between those which are clearly contained in revelation and can be taught infallibly by the Magisterium and those which, though belonging to the ordinary Magisterium, are not contained in revelation and therefore cannot become the object of infallible pronouncements nor are intended as definitive statements. The intermediary category consists of truths which, though not revealed, are so closely connected with the content of faith and so required for preserving it that they can be stated definitively by the Magisterium as belonging to the doctrine of the Catholic Church. Concrete examples of those truths are given, on which theological discussion is thus closed authoritatively. Add too the fact that the doctrinal authority of the episcopal conferences as an intermediary instance between the central authority and the local bishops is being undermined, and that the individual bishops still tend to be considered as "vicars" of the pope in Rome. Again, restrictive interpretations of the doctrine of the Second Vatican Council are proposed, to which, however, an authoritative character is given which concretely seems to exclude the validity of other interpretations. All this curtails greatly the academic freedom of the theologian. The consequences of this are evident in the present situation. Theologians are afraid to speak out lest they should suffer reprisals from the doctrinal authority. This is the climate in which I have been teaching theology. In India it did not affect much my freedom of speech; being far away from Rome is a great asset, as one is less likely to be taken note of by the doctrinal congregation. In Rome, and especially if one is teaching in a pontifical university, the matter is different; spying and denouncing by agents of the CDF are always possible. One has to make up one's mind to live with the risk, for both one's writing and one's teaching.

To those who aspire to a theological teaching career in the present time my recommendation and my advice would be to remain always true and faithful to themselves, on the one hand, and to the church, on the other. The golden rule for this is to ensure that there never grows up a discrepancy between one's life and one's speech. To combine the two loyalties is not easy, but it is the secret of an honest, sincere, and fruitful career. I would further suggest that candidates from countries of the Third World studying in Rome should not too easily allow themselves to be lured by the prospect of an eventual teaching post in a Roman university. Invitations to follow one's career in Rome can be very attractive and tempting for more than one reason, including, often, the prospect of a more comfortable life. The temptation is all the greater because it is presented as allowing for a more universal good and service. But universality is never separable from particularity, and the more universal service will often consist in helping local and particular churches to come into their own through a mature and contextual reflection upon the faith rather than being forced to fit into the stereotyped mold of a "universal" theology and teaching, valid for all times and places. The last criterion will consist in asking where the greater glory of God really lies, which is to be discerned in agreement with one's superiors.

G.O'C.: *How would you then explain how you understand authority in the church? And how do you understand the role of the theologian vis-à-vis that authority?*

J.D.: Authority in the church is to be viewed as service, not as an exercise of power to which one clings. This is pure gospel teaching. Jesus was extremely careful to make those he established in authority in his future church understand correctly the meaning of authority. He himself had come to serve, not to be served; and those in authority would have to follow his example and to conform to his model. When the ten apostles became indignant at the request made by the mother of the sons of Zebedee that her two sons might be seated at his right hand and at his left hand in his kingdom, Jesus called them to him and said: "You know that the rulers of the gentiles lord it over them, and their great men exercise authority over them. It shall not be so among you; but whoever would be great among you must be your servant, and whoever would be first among you must be your slave; even as the Son of Man came not to be served but to serve, and to give his life as a ransom for many" (Matt 20:24-28). This ought to be and remain the model for any exercise of authority in the church, whether in pastoral practice or in doctrinal matters.

Where doctrinal authority is meant and the relationship between those in authority and the theologians is concerned, one should hope that authority be exercised without imposition or pressure, and that a climate of mutual understanding and collaboration may reign. And this at all levels, without the Roman instance on claiming universal and exclusive competence, thus overriding the authority of intermediary instances, be they the local bishops or the episcopal conferences. When Pope Paul VI, at the end of the Council Vatican II, changed the name of the Roman Office for doctrine from "The Most Holy Congregation of the Holy Office" (*Suprema Sacra Congregatio Sancti Officii*) to the "Congregation for the Doctrine of the Faith," he insisted that the Congregation is primarily meant for fostering and encouraging theology in the church, not first of all for uttering condemnations. It is well understood that the Congregation must ensure the purity of doctrine and its conformity with the revealed message; but it must do this in conformity with Jesus' standard of authority and in dialogue with the theologians, whose role is to seek to deepen the comprehension of the Christian message. That this has not always been the case in the past is too obvious; that even today it is not always happening is unhappily also true, as would be evidenced by some events in which I was personally involved as the victim of questionable ways of procedure—of which, more below.

G.O'C.: *How has your teaching career and theological reflection changed your faith and understanding of God, Jesus Christ, the Holy Spirit, and the church? How did it affect your prayer life?*

J.D.: The danger is often expressed that the practice of interreligious dialogue, and, even more, the new theology of religions is very detrimental to the faith and risks leading to doctrinal relativism and indifferentism. The call of the day would consist in reaffirming "Christian identity" against such imminent dangers. The objection comes from people who have never been in contact with the reality of other religions and much less have met persons who practice them sincerely and profoundly. I think that those who, on the contrary, have made the effort of a true and sincere encounter with others have had their faith strengthened in the process and deepened by the experience. I would count myself among those. And this in more than one way.

To begin with, the shock of the encounter forces us to rethink various prejudices and exclusivist positions, as though God had revealed himself and was present only in the Judeo-Christian tradition. A purification of the faith is necessary to divest it of preconceived ideas. There will also ensue a simplification and an enrichment of the faith which will reach fuller maturity. Enrichment, I say: through the experience and testimony of the others, Christians will be able to discover at greater depth certain aspects, certain dimensions, of the Divine Mystery that they had perceived less clearly and that have been communicated less clearly by Christian tradition. Purification, at the same time: the shock of the encounter will *often* raise questions, force Christians to revise gratuitous assumptions, and destroy deep-rooted prejudices or overthrow certain narrow conceptions and outlooks. I may testify that my own faith has been purified and deepened through the process of dialogue and familiarity with the religions and their members. It became more centered on what is essential and constitutes the core of the faith, being divested in the process of popular accretions and devotions which *often* risk hiding the core of the Mystery. It forced me to "de-absolutize" what is not absolute, against theological conceptions which tend to "absolutize" through an inflation of terminology. Finally, I discovered through the practice of dialogue new dimensions of the Christian faith and, in the terms of Saint Paul, new depths and a new breadth of the Mystery. My prayer life has also been affected thereby; it too became simpler, more sincere and, I hope, deeper.

—2—

The Pangs of a Process

G.O'C.: *Your book* Toward a Christian Theology of Religious Pluralism *was published in October 1997 and was immediately recognized, by supporters and critics alike, as a landmark in the development of the theology of religions and the dialogue between Christianity—and in particular Catholicism—and the other world religions. I would like to begin this central part of our discussion by inviting you to explain to me, and to the readers who may not be well acquainted with the discussion, in the simplest language possible, the central thesis of your now-famous book. Could you summarize its main argument and explain what it is you are trying to say to the church and the world?*

J.D.: The matter can be made simple enough. The question is how to conceive the relationship existing between Christianity and the other religions. People have become more aware today of the many religious traditions which claim and receive the allegiance of millions of people around the world. What does Christian faith require us to believe and to think about the other religions? For centuries in the past the Christian view, even in official documents of the Catholic Church, has been very negative in this regard. Gradually, however, a more positive evaluation of the religions themselves and a more open attitude toward their followers have been developing. But with differences. We can for convenience sake distinguish three main theological perspectives.

A first perspective consisted in asking whether salvation in Jesus Christ, the universal savior of humankind according to Christian faith, was possible for people who had not heard his message and had not belonged to the church during their earthly life. It is admitted today by practically all Catholics that salvation in Jesus Christ is possible for them. In the years that preceded the Second Vatican Council a new perspective began to spread. It consisted no longer merely in affirming the possibility of salvation for the "others," but asked whether positive values—and which ones—could be attributed to the various religions. Different answers were given to this new question. Some held that the other religions could possess human "natural" values, which however were not by themselves conducive to salvation. Others, on the contrary, spoke of "supernatural" elements of truth and grace contained in the religious traditions, which helped their members to obtain salvation in Jesus Christ. In the post–Vatican II period, a third perspective has been developing which goes further; in this new perspective the question becomes whether Christian faith can recognize in the other religious traditions genuine "ways" of salvation for their followers, intended by God in his eternal plan for the salvation of humankind.

It is in this third perspective that my book finds its place. The challenge here consists in asking whether and how Christian faith in Jesus Christ universal savior is compatible with the affirmation of a positive role of the other religions for the salvation of their members, in accordance with the one salvific plan designed by God for the whole of humankind. I—among others—give a positive answer to the question, and build my argument on some data from both the revealed word of God and the Christian tradition. Not all theologians are, however, disposed to agree with such a positive assessment of the religions of the world, which is a far cry from much of what has been said and written in the past on the subject. Nor has the church's central teaching authority accepted the thesis without making strong reservations. Hence the discussions and the controversy to which the book has given rise. Yet, I have been and remain persuaded that the thesis of my book is saying something important to the church for the exercise of its mission to the world, and to the world itself, in this age of universal dialogue between peoples, cultures, and religions. The church is bound to recognize in a spirit of gratitude to God the divine endowments enshrined in the other religious traditions, even as it is bound to proclaim to the world what God has done in a decisive manner for humankind in Jesus Christ.

G.O'C.: *That is your central thesis. Why did this thesis spark such controversy? What is it in what you are saying that makes people react so passionately, both in a positive and a negative sense, not only in the Vatican but in other circles too? What consequences does your thesis have for the way the church does its work and sees its mission?*

J.D.: Much has been said and written in connection with what I and others have affirmed on the subject, about the need to preserve and reaffirm the "Christian identity" against theological ideas based on a "dogmatic relativism," which, if pursued to their last conclusions, would end up destroying the core of Christian faith and ruin the mission of the church. In order to preserve and reaffirm the "Christian identity" against alleged destructive tendencies, some have recourse to maximalist views and theories with no solid foundation in the living tradition and offering few credentials. I for one am convinced that the Christian identity is not to be built, and is not enhanced, by opposition to the others and a negative, hostile assessment of their traditions, but, on the contrary, in an open dialogue with them and in full recognition of what God has been doing among them through the centuries of salvation history. In conclusion to my latest book, *Christianity and the Religions: From Confrontation to Dialogue* (Maryknoll, NY: Orbis Books, 2002)—in which the thesis of the previous one is repeated and strengthened while some ambiguities and misunderstandings are dispelled—I wrote: "What we must avoid are the ways of 'defending the faith' that turn out to be counterproductive, by making it appear to be restrictive and narrow. I am convinced that a broader approach and a more positive attitude, provided that they are theologically well grounded, will help us discover, to our surprise, new breadths and new depths in the Christian message" (p. 259). And, with the church authority in mind, I added: "I am deeply convinced that the teaching Church will do well, in keeping with its oft-stated desire and claim to reproduce in its own life and practice the divine approach in the dialogue of salvation, to abstain from any ways of proposing the Christian faith which may imply insensitive and exclusivist evaluations of the others. Such an approach in 'defending' the faith can only be counterproductive; it presents it with a 'face' that is restrictive and narrow. I am convinced that a more positive approach and a more open attitude than are often enough in evidence even today, provided such an approach and attitude are theologically well founded, will strengthen the credibility of the Christian faith and help Christians themselves to discover in the Christian message new dimensions and a new depth" (p. 263).

Where the way of conceiving the mission of the church is concerned, the new perspective implies a serious reconsideration. The time is gone when the church's mission was understood to consist essentially in "saving souls" who without receiving baptism and becoming members of the church could not be saved. Once it is recognized that the other religions can be for their members "ways" or "paths" of salvation in Jesus Christ, the mission of the church no longer consists in saving souls which otherwise would be lost, but in being in the world and in history a living—and a credible—sign of what God has done and continues to do everywhere in the world through his Son Jesus Christ, the universal savior. At the same time, the church and its members, if they are truly in love with their Lord and Master, should hope and desire to be able to share with others their joy of being his disciples in the church community. Far then from diminishing the mission of the church, this view makes it much more lofty, but also much more demanding.

G.O'C.: *Some of your critics say that your vision and understanding of the place of religions in God's plan for humankind, if widely accepted, would in fact lead to the elimination of the need for mission work. Given your theology of religious pluralism, do you consider mission work as still necessary? Do you think the church should continue its missionary work in the way it has been carried out down the centuries? Otherwise, how do you think it should be done?*

J.D.: The fear that a positive approach to the other religions would undermine the urgency, or even the need, of the proclamation of the gospel has been expressed many a time. When I was in India, I often heard missionaries in the field complain with deep concern that the new theology was sapping at the very root of the work to which they had devoted all their life and energy, with great apostolic zeal and bearing many hardships. The same objection has been repeated by some in Rome, when my book *Toward a Christian Theology of Religious Pluralism* came out in 1997.

I would like first of all to dispell some confusion. The question, as you have formulated it, speaks of the danger of "eliminating the need for mission work." But the notion of the "evangelizing mission" of the church—this is the term now used by theologians—has evolved in the postconciliar period. Formerly—and it is still so in the documents of Vatican II—"mission" or "evangelization" referred exclusively to the proclamation of Jesus Christ, intended to bring about the conversion of the others to Christianity. This view was a relic of a long traditional, negative, theological approach to the religions. The persuasion had been for centuries that salvation for the members of the other religious traditions was only possible through explicit faith in Jesus Christ and the reception of the sacrament of baptism. It is enough to think of Saint Francis Xavier in India and of the mass baptisms which he was administering to people with a scant understanding of the faith in order that souls might be saved. I have often said that Francis Xavier has been canonized, not for his theology but for his extraordinary missionary zeal and his heroic performance. And I further ask whether anyone has ever been canonized for his theology, anyway!

Even when the possibility of salvation outside the church became the official doctrine of the church—through a "baptism of desire," expressed in the sincere following of conscience—the understanding of "mission" still continued to refer mostly, if not exclusively, to making converts to Christianity. Only the more positive theological approach to religions has led in the postconciliar period to a broader notion of the "evangelizing mission," as including, among other church activities, interreligious dialogue. The question should therefore consist in asking not whether mission is being threatened by the new trends but whether interreligious dialogue would eventually undermine the church's mission to proclaim Jesus Christ explicitly and to invite members of other religions to become disciples of Jesus in his church. The question supposes that it does so in fact.

Let me first of all say that the broader notion of the evangelizing mission is now the official doctrine of the church. Two documents issued by Vatican offices—"Dialogue and Mission" of the Secretariat for Non-Christians (1984) and "Dialogue and Proclamation," published jointly by the Pontifical Council for Interreligious Dialogue and the Congregation for the Evangelization of Peoples (1991), not to mention the encyclical letter of Pope John Paul II *Redemptoris missio* (1990)—state this explicitly. The evangelizing mission comprises in order: the witness of Christian life, liturgical life and prayer, involvement for integral human liberation, interreligious dialogue, and "finally" proclamation. The two documents by the Vatican offices have already been mentioned above. The 1984 document speaks of interreligious dialogue in the following terms: "There is, as well, the dialogue in which Christians meet the followers of other religious traditions in order to walk together towards truth" (13). Interreligious dialogue is already evangelization. But both documents are careful to add that, though being an integral part of evangelization, dialogue remains nonetheless oriented toward proclamation in which the dynamism of the evangelizing mission culminates. The 1991 document expresses it as follows: "Dialogue . . . does not constitute the whole mission of the church; [it] cannot simply replace proclamation, but remains oriented towards proclamation insofar as the dynamic process of the Church's evangelizing mission reaches in it its climax and its fullness" (82).

I have insisted constantly on this complementarity and dynamism between dialogue and proclamation. Through many articles, as well as in the last two books of my trilogy on the theology of religions and perhaps most clearly in the last one, *Christianity and the Religions*, I have stressed, against some theories tending to reduce evangelization to dialogue, this orientation of dialogue toward proclamation. Just as the members of the other religious traditions who, without being members of the church, can already be members of the reign of God and sharers in the mystery of salvation, yet remain oriented toward the church, similarly and analogically, dialogue with them remains oriented toward announcing Jesus

Christ to them explicitly if and when, in God's own time, the opportunity eventually arises. If the fear expressed in the question proposed here were directed to me personally, I would only beg the inquirers to go and read what I have written: *Tolle et lege*.

The reason for the twofold orientation, of the "others" to the church and, consequently, of dialogue to proclamation, is of course the fact that the "fullness of the benefits and means of salvation," entrusted by Jesus Christ to his church—of which Pope John Paul II speaks—is available only in the church. To which must be added that, while the others can be and are saved by Jesus Christ without an explicit awareness of their savior, only the church's proclamation can bring them to this explicit knowledge. In the same order, let me add further that the urge of the church to proclaim the Good News of Jesus Christ springs not merely from the command it has received from the Lord, but from the love it bears for the One who sends it. This is beautifully expressed in the 1991 document referred to above. It says: "In this dialogical approach, how could they [the Christians] not hope and desire to share with others their joy in knowing and following Jesus Christ, Lord and Savior? We are here at the heart of the mystery of love. Insofar as the church and Christians have a deep love for the Lord Jesus, the desire to share him with others is motivated not merely by obedience to the Lord's command, but by this love itself" (82). May I recall that I was involved in drafting this document and add that I claim the personal authorship of this passage!

In the light of what has now been said, some remarks may be made as to the way the evangelizing mission of the church should be pursued today. It must of course be said that a universal strategy for the exercise of the mission cannot be established which would be valid for all times and all places. Much will depend on local conditions and circumstances. This being granted, some observations may be made as to the approach to be followed today in the light of the new theology of religions and of the role of interreligious dialogue in the church's mission. Dialogue may not be looked at as a "means" for proclamation, a first approach and a first step in proclaiming Jesus Christ. Such an attitude would not do justice to the intrinsic value of dialogue as being in itself a genuine expression of the evangelizing mission. In other words, dialogue may not be "instrumentalized" in favor of proclamation. Its orientation to proclamation notwithstanding, it ought to be entered into for its own sake and on its own merit. Practically this means that the practitioner must not be anxious to proclaim in season and out of season, being preoccupied primarily with making "converts" in view of the possible increase of the numbers of the Christian community. He must leave it to God to decide when the time for proclaiming Jesus Christ explicitly has come. There are circumstances in which, proclamation not being possible, dialogue and involvement in view of integral human liberation will eventually be the only ways in which the mission of the church is concretely possible. The disciple of Jesus will aspire to help people to discover the person of his Master, who is also theirs. If he is able to share his own love for Jesus and to help others to fall in love with him, he will have accomplished much. He must leave the rest to God, who knows the seasons and the times. His primary task consists in witnessing through his own life and example. Grace will do the rest.

G.O'C.: *Given your understanding of the place of religions in God's plan for humankind, why should a person change or feel the need to change his or her religion, and become a Christian by entering the church?*

J.D.: I think I have already implicitly answered this question. In the present state of awareness and theology, no one should wish to become a Christian simply for the sake of being saved, or even of being saved more easily or more securely. Salvation depends, in all circumstances and situations, on the sincerity of one's response to God's offer of grace in Jesus Christ in the concrete situation of one's life, no matter what religious tradition one may belong to. Salvation is not made easier by being a Christian, nor can being a Christian be sought as an easier way to salvation. Being a Christian is a responsibility even more than it is a privilege. It carries with it the obligation to witness through one's life, through one's deeds and words, to the mystery of universal salvation in Jesus Christ. The only true reason then for wishing to become a Christian, that is, a disciple of Jesus in the church community, is that one has received the grace of divine faith in Jesus Christ, universal savior of humankind, and is disposed with God's grace to witness to one's newly received faith. Such a faith needs to be discerned and tested seriously before the step can be taken of passing over from one's original community of faith to the ecclesial community of the disciples of Jesus.

G.O'C.: *Your book appeared almost simultaneously in English, French, and Italian in October 1997, and was presented to the public in Paris and in Rome. I recall that you had some important theologians and church people at both presentations, and your book was very well received. Could you explain briefly who was present—and what was said about—the book? After these two presentations, other public discussions took place around your book, and the book itself won a distinguished award in the United States. Could you explain a little about that too?*

J.D.: The book *Toward a Christian Theology of Religious Pluralism* was published almost simultaneously in French, English, and Italian, in October 1997. It has had to date fifteen printings in five languages: two in French (Cogitatio Fidei 200; Paris: Le Cerf, 1997, 1999); six in English (Maryknoll, NY: Orbis Books, 1997, 1998, 1999, 2000, 2001, 2002), plus another in English, published in India (Anand: Gujarat Sahitya Prakash, 2001); four in Italian (Biblioteca di Teologia Contemporanea 95; Brescia: Queriniana, 1997, 1998, 2000, 2003); one in Brazilian Portuguese (Sao Paolo: Paolinas, 1999); one in Spanish (Santander: Sal Terrae, 2000).

The book had two solemn public presentations. The first took place in Paris on October 27, 1997, organized by the Editions du Cerf which wanted to celebrate on the same occasion the publication of number 200 in the collection Cogitatio Fidei. This session was held at the Institute Catholique de Paris. The following spoke during the proceedings: Fr. Claude Geffré, O.P., and director of the collection; Msgr. Joseph Doré, recently nominated archbishop of Strasbourg; myself; and finally Fr. Nicolas-Jean Sed, O.P., director of the Editions du Cerf. The second public presentation was held in Rome on November 22, 1997. It was organized by the Italian Theological Association and the Gregorian University. The following took part in the proceedings: Rev. Fr. Giuseppe Pittau, S.J., rector of the university; the Rev. Giacomo Canobbio, president of the Association; Msgr. Michael Fitzgerald, then secretary of the Pontifical Council for Interreligious Dialogue; Fr. Gerald O'Collins, S.J., professor of Christology at the university; and myself. Both presentations were academic performances of a high level, attended by a large and well-informed public. While formulating some questions and asking for some clarifications, the participants did not spare their praises for a book which they considered a landmark in the field of the theology of religions.

Furthermore, an ecumenical symposium on the book was organized in Venice on October 8, 1998, by the Cultural Centre of Palazzo Cavagnas and the Maitreya Centre of Studies. The initiative for this symposium was taken by the authorities of the Waldensian community of Venice. The following took part in the proceedings: Msgr. Luigi Sartori of Padova; Prof. Paolo Ricca of the Waldensian theological faculty of Rome; Doctor Antonio Rigopoulos, Indologist of the University of Venice; and myself. There should also be mentioned a symposium-debate held at the Dominican Convent of Montpellier, France, June 15-18, 1999, in my presence. In Japan, the ecumenical group for the study of interreligious dialogue, composed of academics belonging to four Christian study centers (Sophia University, Nanzam University, Oriens Centre, and NCC Centre), organized a symposium dedicated to my book on May 22, 1999. A one-day study session also took place at Besançon, in my presence, on November 16, 2002, with members of ecumenical and interreligious groups (Amitié Judéo Chrétienne, et Chrétiens en relation avec l'Islam). Such manifestations of academic interest about the book have not abated. Some are planned for the near future, among which the following may be mentioned: a one-day study session with me, to be held on May 23, 2003, at the conclusion of an interdisciplinary study of the book, protracted over six months in six sessions between professors and students of the faculty of Catholic theology of the Marc Bloch University, Strasbourg; a colloquium with the Swiss Theological Society, with participants of all the theological faculties of Switzerland, to be held on October 24-25, 2003, in Lucerne. To these must be added many presentations of themes related to the book, which I made at congresses and other conventions in all continents, and innumerable talks on the book which I gave in Italy and abroad.

All this illustrates the interest shown everywhere by the publication of a book which did not fail to draw the attention of theologians, particularly of those especially interested in the theology of religions and of interreligious dialogue. It should also be mentioned that the book obtained the "Catholic Press Association Book Award" in the United States of America for the year 1998. As for the *International Bulletin of Missionary Research*, it mentioned the book on its official list of the "Fifteen Eminent Books of the year 1997 for the study of mission."

G.O'C.: *Since October 1997, your book was in the public arena, and as you taught at the Gregorian University and responded to invitations in other places, many theologians began to review your book. Many reviews were positive, but some rather significant negative ones also appeared. Could you explain what happened?*

J.D.: The book reviews, extensive studies and briefer comments, which have appeared in all the main languages in periodicals specialized in theology, in chapters of collective or individual books, as well as in more general periodicals and in the press, can hardly be counted. I have come to know well over one hundred such comments from the first three years of publication, and the flow has not abated, even after five years. In all that literature the most varied reactions are of course found. Many book reviews and studies do not spare their praises and consider the book an event serving as a landmark in the development of the theology of religions and interreligious dialogue. Other studies address to the book serious, sometimes harsh criticism, and do not hide their severe accusations with regard to revealed doctrine and the faith of the church. I will mention below some samples of both categories of comments. Meanwhile the book rapidly became and remains even today the object not only of intense discussion but of passionate controversy. In this context I have thought it necessary and useful to answer in an irenic manner the different questions asked by peer theologians in serious studies and reviews dedicated to my book. Two articles have thus been published (besides a third one which has so far remained unpublished, not having received the superiors' approval for publication in a time of controversy): one in Italian in *Rassegna di teologia* (1999, no. 5): 667-93, entitled "La teologia del pluralismo religioso rivisitata," in which I address the questions raised in Italian periodicals; the other, more extensive, in *Louvain Studies* (1999, no. 3): 211-63, under the title "The Truth Will Make You Free: The Theology of Religious Pluralism Revisited," in which answers are offered to the questions raised in studies and book reviews in French and English. These clarifications do not seem to have fully resolved the tension. Even today there appear, under different forms including chapters of books and of works in collaboration, studies either very positive or very critical.

G.O'C.: *Within less than a year of its publication the book was subjected to a major theological investigation by the Vatican's office for orthodoxy, the Congregation for the Doctrine of the Faith. The investigation lasted two years and eight months and was carried out under total secrecy. Could you give a short account of the proceedings of the process?*

J.D.: I may mention the main stages of the proceedings followed by the Congregation in its investigation of the book. After a meeting with some consultors of the Congregation based in Rome which resulted in a negative assessment, an Ordinary Assembly of the members of the Congregation held on June 10, 1998, decided to initiate a "Contestation" against the book. Cardinal Joseph Ratzinger gave notice of this decision to Rev. Fr. Peter-Hans Kolvenbach, General of the Society, in a letter dated September 26, 1998. The letter was accompanied by two documents, one being the minutes of the meeting which stated the decision taken by the Congregation, already approved by Pope John Paul II on June 17; the other, including nine pages of questions raised against opinions attributed by the Congregation to the book, to which I was required to respond within three months under top secret. All three documents were to be considered strictly confidential (*strettamente riservati*).

The first accompanying document, in which the decision taken by the Congregation is stated, affirmed that there are found in the work of Fr. Dupuis: (a) grave errors and doctrinal ambiguities on doctrines of the

Divine and Catholic faith, concerning revelation, soteriology, Christology and the Trinity; (b) grave errors and doctrinal ambiguities about truths belonging with certitude to the doctrine of the Catholic Church, such as the relation between reign of God–reign of Christ–the church, the doctrine of the church as universal sacrament of salvation, the inspiration of Sacred Scripture; (c) dangerous affirmations or opinions which cannot be taught safely (*tuto doceri non possunt*), such as establishing a parallelism between Jesus and the Buddha, the application of the expression "Mother" to the first person of the Holy Trinity, the affirmation that religious pluralism is a reality which *de iure* belongs to the universal salvific plan of God.

In a letter addressed to me at the end of September (which I received only on October 2) Fr. Kolvenbach shared with me a copy of the three documents received from Cardinal Ratzinger. It may be noted that the decision of the Congregation did not forbid me to teach. It stated, however, that it would be consonant with the decision that "the above-said religious should abstain in his teaching and in public conversations from sustaining and defending the contested theses, till the time of the desired clarifications and rectifications."

As this raised a serious problem regarding the scope and freedom left to me in the way of teaching, Fr. Kolvenbach thought it best to cancel the course which I was to start at the Gregorian University in the same month of October, and for which more than two hundred students were enrolled. At my request that the students be informed of the true reason for the cancellation of the course, Fr. Kolvenbach allowed the university authorities to notify the students publicly about it. Accordingly, on October 17, 1998, a notice was put up in the hall of the university, signed by Fr. Sergio Bastianel, dean of the faculty of theology, which stated the following: "Some theses contained in the recent book of Fr. Dupuis, *Toward a Christian Theology of Religious Pluralism*, have been "contested" (*contestate*). He must during these months answer the questions raised by the Congregation for the Doctrine of the Faith. While he is engaged in this work, the superiors, in agreement with the person concerned, have decided that he be free from teaching in this semester." This caused me much pain, since the course due to start on that same month of October was to be my last one, as I was soon to reach seventy-five years of age, which is the age limit fixed by the statutes of the university for teaching. The notice produced a sensation among the students and resulted in the case—which the Congregation had intended to keep top secret—becoming at once publicly known and divulged by journalists the world over. Father Kolvenbach has in fact been blamed by the Congregation for having allowed the news to leak out.

Meanwhile I set myself to answer the questions directed to me by the Congregation, for which I was allowed to consult one person of my choice, with the approval of Father General. This is how Fr. G. O'Collins has been involved in the case from the start, a post which he would keep all through the proceedings. Among the questions of the Congregation, some found an easy answer; others on the contrary required serious study in order to separate the interpretations given by the Congregation to the text of my book from what I actually meant and wrote. My answer to the questions of the Congregation filled 188 pages, which were signed December 25, 1998, and sent to the CDF by Fr. Kolvenbach on January 8, 1999. Seven full months went without any reaction to the answers being communicated by the Congregation.

Father Kolvenbach received a new letter from Cardinal Ratzinger dated July 27, 1999. In this letter the cardinal stated: "While recognizing the positive steps accomplished by the author, in the Answer to the Contestation by the Congregation, in view of the clarifications of some aspects concerning the methodology, the theological propositions and the terminology used, the precisions and the explanations are not considered substantially satisfactory, especially as regards the theses 3-8 and 10-14 of the Contestation, in view of preserving the doctrine of Catholic faith from error, ambiguities and dangerous interpretations." I will refer to the theses mentioned below. The letter stated that Pope John Paul II had confirmed the new decision of the Congregation in an audience granted to the cardinal on July 2, 1999. Accompanying the letter was a document of eleven pages called "doctrinal judgment" (*giudizio dottrinale*), stating "the main affirmations of the author, considered erroneous or ambiguous or insufficient," and in need of "further rectification or precision or clarification." The list of new questions was meant "as an invitation made to the author to assent to the truth of Catholic faith stated in the list of questions, regarding the points of doctrine concerned." A "punctual and precise" answer on the part of the author to the new set of questions was expected again within three months. As many of the questions of the new list had already been answered at length in the previous response, I was satisfied this time to send sixty pages more to the Congregation in which further precisions were added to dissipate eventual ambiguities and accusations of erroneous positions against faith and Catholic doctrine. After this new answer, dated November 1, 1999, on the Feast of All Saints, was sent to the Congregation through Fr. Kolvenbach on November 2, there followed a complete silence of ten months on the part of the CDF.

On August 25, 2000, Msgr. Tarcisio Bertone, S.D.B., secretary of the CDF, addressed a letter to Fr. Kolvenbach which Father General sent to me on August 28. The letter of the secretary was accompanied by the projected text of a Notification of the Congregation about my book. It announced an official meeting by way of judicial process which was to take place at the Congregation between, on the one side, Cardinal Ratzinger, his secretary Msgr. Bertone, and Fr. Angelo Amato, consultor of the Congregation (who incidentally—as mentioned above—had previously declared himself publicly against the book), and, on the other side, Fr. Kolvenbach, General of the Society of Jesus, myself the accused, and Fr. G. O'Collins, acting as my advocate. The encounter was to take place on September 4.

In the same letter the secretary also announced the publication to take place on September 5 at the press office of the Vatican of the declaration *Dominus Iesus*, of which he was sending an advance copy in view of the forthcoming encounter. As to the Notification, it was intended to be published in *L'Osservatore Romano* soon after the publication of the declaration. The scenario was thus well planned to show the connection between the two documents. (The connection was made even clearer when later the Vatican Press published a booklet containing the text of the declaration *Dominus Iesus*, both in Latin and in Italian, to which was added the Italian text of the Notification about my book and the article commenting on it in *L'Osservatore Romano*: *Dichiarazione Dominus Iesus*. Documenti e Studi 18, Vatican City: Libreria Editrice Vaticana, 2002). I was expected to sign the projected text of the Notification about my book, thus testifying my agreement with it.

The letter of the secretary was accompanied by the text of the projected Notification filling fifteen pages, already approved by the pope in an audience with Cardinal Ratzinger on June 16, 2000, and already ordered by him for publication. The text recalled at some length the previous stages of the proceedings about the book. It then declared the following: "Though recognizing the intention of the author to keep within the limits of orthodoxy while engaging in the treatment of problematics so far unexplored, the Congregation for the Doctrine of the Faith has verified the persistence (in the book) of grievous errors and ambiguities which force it to intervene by taking a position to clarify the matter, so as to avoid that readers may be led into error or doctrinal incertitude. Such an intervention intends to enunciate the doctrine of the church regarding some aspects of the doctrinal truths concerned, and at the same time to refute the erroneous and dangerous opinions which, independently of the intentions of the author, follow or may follow because of ambiguous formulations or insufficient clarifications and explanations contained in the book." The text further noted (in a footnote) that "the present Notification applies the principles indicated in the declaration *Dominus Iesus* to the evaluation of the work of Fr. Dupuis."

There followed eight long sections in which the text recalled in a first step the doctrine of the faith on a particular topic and went on in a second step to reject opinions considered as contradicting either the faith or Catholic doctrine. This way of proceeding was bound to be understood as affirming implicitly, though this was not explicitly stated in the text, that the opinions rejected were in fact found in the text of my book. This, however, would have had to be verified in each case, which was not done here, since the text of the Notification contained no reference whatever to the pages of the book, much less any quotation from it. As a matter of fact, the propositions reproved are open to different interpretations, not all necessarily opposed to the doctrine of the faith; neither did they always correspond exactly to what I intended and wrote in my book. To give some examples: that the revelation in Jesus Christ is "limited, incomplete and imperfect" and can be "complemented" by other divine revelation (section 3) is open to different interpretations, not all opposed to faith in the "fullness" of divine revelation in Jesus Christ; the affirmation of a "salvific economy of the Holy Spirit . . . not derived from the mediation of the glorified humanity of Jesus Christ" (section 5) is not found in the book, which insists on speaking of only one economy of salvation; that the church is "one way of salvation, though the most eminent, beside those constituted by the various religions of the world which would thus be substantially equivalent or complementary to the church in the order of salvation" (section 6) contradicts openly what is said in the book. These are but examples. The merits or demerits of the objections raised by the CDF in their Notification will be examined more closely hereafter.

Meanwhile a short account must be given of the September 4 official encounter between the parties concerned. This meeting—it must be stated—was the first time, after having lived in Rome sixteen years by then, that I met Cardinal Ratzinger and had the occasion to talk to him; it is, even today, after more than eighteen years in Rome, the only time that we have met. The meeting took place at the palace of the CDF. It was due to start at 9.30 A.M. In fact, Fr. Kolvenbach, myself, and Fr. O'Collins were kept waiting in a small parlor for about half an hour before the other participants showed up. The September Roman heat was oppressive in a room without ventilation or air conditioning. The session that lasted two full hours, without a coffee break—we were told explicitly that coffee was not available—was tense though polite. Cardinal Ratzinger and his secretary opened the proceedings with some general observations. The cardinal observed that the Notification which was under discussion in view of my approval and signature did not prejudge my "subjective thought"—whatever this expression might mean; it judged the book at its face value and in its objective content. The cardinal further remarked that at no time during the proceedings so far had I expressed a wish to meet personally with someone on the staff of the Congregation, which he interpreted as a sign of my approval of the proceedings followed by the Congregation and of my agreement with its findings. He congratulated himself on what he called the process of "dialogue" which has been going on between the CDF and myself— whatever concept of dialogue might be implied in the affirmation. He hoped that the session might end with an agreement on both sides and my signature of the text of the Notification, thus attesting my agreement with it. The secretary of the Congregation followed with some formal observations regarding procedure; after which the party of the defense was invited to speak.

Father General spoke first; in a courageous intervention he denounced the defect of form of the Notification. He said: "I do not understand how in a Notification of the Congregation for the Doctrine of the Faith about the book of Fr. Dupuis, in which he is accused of grievous errors against the Divine and Catholic Faith, no reference whatever is found to the pages of the book, nor is any quotation from it being made." The message was clear; it was followed by the observations made by Fr. O'Collins immediately thereafter that as a matter of fact the errors against the faith mentioned in the text of the Notification were not found in the book. There ensued a discussion regarding the interpretation to be made of the text of the Notification, the side of the Congregation claiming that the text need not be understood each time as attributing to me the opinions rejected. To which it was countered that, given the procedure in two steps (recalling the doctrine of the faith and spelling out the errors against it) being followed in a Notification directly and explicitly aimed at my book, every reader was bound to conclude that the opinions rejected are being attributed to my text. If this were not the case, why should those errors be explicitly mentioned in a Notification dedicated to my work, especially considering the fact that the same errors were being rejected in the declaration *Dominus Iesus* to be published the following day, which represented a more authoritative document? Was there any need then for a special Notification about my book? After a protracted discussion, it was admitted by the representatives of the CDF that the Notification would have to be interpreted in such a way as not to attribute in each and every case the errors to my book.

Not much time was in fact spent on discussing which errors against the faith were or were not actually contained in the book. The intervention made by Fr. O'Collins was not challenged with any explicit reference to the text, even while all the participants had in front of them a copy of its Italian edition. Consultor Fr. Amato was conspicuously silent, though his own negative evaluation and open criticism of the book were well known, expressed as they had been publicly on previous occasions. Cardinal Ratzinger looked embarrassed by this silence on the part of the accusation. Eventually he himself raised a question with regard to the alleged incomplete nature of God's revelation in Jesus Christ. I held that, the "fullness" of revelation in Christ does not and cannot "exhaust" the mystery of God. To which the cardinal objected that, since the person who speaks in Jesus is a divine person, it must be held that he reveals God completely and definitively. My response was swift. I observed that divine revelation in Jesus has its source in Jesus' human consciousness of being the Son of God in a unique manner, not in the divine self-knowledge, which is not communicated to Jesus' human intellect. To postulate a communication to Jesus' human intellect of the divine self-knowledge would smack—though this was not explicitly said—of monophysitism. The cardinal left the matter at that and passed on to practical questions.

The first had to do with my eventual willingness to help the Congregation to improve the text of the Notification so that it might correspond better to the reality of the case. My answer was that after sending 260 pages of answers to questions raised by the Congregation, I felt tired and little disposed to help the Congregation to improve on a text stating my condemnation. To this observation the cardinal surprisingly replied that 260 pages sent to the Congregation in answer to their questions were just too much, and I could not suppose that the Congregation could possibly read and study all that material. *Sic!* The next question was straightforward, the cardinal asking me whether I was disposed to sign the text of the Notification as it stood, thereby stating my agreement with it. My answer was that I could not sign a Notification about my book in which I was being accused of grievous errors against the faith which, however, were not substantiated with references and quotations. In a last resort the cardinal asked me whether I would be prepared to sign a declaration stating that my book must be interpreted in the light of the declaration *Dominus Iesus* of the Congregation to be made public the next day, September 5, 2000, at the press office of the Vatican. My answer this time was very circumspect; I stated that such a request "was asking too much from me." It was clear to me that I simply could not agree without restriction with everything contained in the declaration, without renouncing what I considered valid reservations to be made against some affirmations of the declaration. My misgivings against the declaration will be made clear in a piece entitled "Some Reflections on Two Roman Documents."

At this stage the secretary of the Congregation informed the participants that a revised text of the Notification would in any case have to be produced, as the cardinal members of the Congregation had requested that a Notification pointing out the errors contained in Fr. Dupuis's book be produced by the Congregation. The meeting thus came to an end after two hours and more of tense discussion. The *Osservatore Romano* carried no Notification on my book in September 2000. A document already approved and ordered by the pope for publication was thus silently dropped—a rare happening, I would suppose.

G.O'C.: *Thanks, Father, for this substantial summary of the Congregation's proceedings. After more than two years' investigation, and the one face-to-face meeting of September 4, 2000, the Vatican exonerated your book from the accusation of heresy and doctrinal error that it had originally levelled against you, but it said that your book contained "ambiguities" and could mislead people into error. Could you explain how this happened?*

J.D.: After the September 4, 2000, meeting, it took three months before a new version of the Notification was communicated to me by Fr. Kolvenbach on December 6, 2000. This new version made no allusion whatever to the previous one which had been dropped after the encounter of September 4. The text was considerably shorter, consisting of seven pages. It had again been approved by the pope in a new audience with Cardinal Ratzinger on November 24, 2000, and ordered by him to be published. I was urged this time to sign the text without further discussion and without restriction (*senza clausula*), but again under strict secrecy (*in via del tutto riservata*). The structure of the new text was the same as that of its predecessor, being made up of the same eight sections in two parts, though these were considerably shorter. The introduction was much briefer with regard to the story of the case, and contained an important change. It no longer spoke of grievous errors against the faith contained in the book but only of "grave ambiguities and difficulties." The key sentence ran as follows: "While recognizing the effort (of the author) to remain within the limits of orthodoxy, in tackling problematics so far unexplored, the Congregation for the Doctrine of the Faith has found that there still remained grave ambiguities and difficulties which unhappily were not substantially dissipated and overcome in the course of the dialogue with the author and oblige the Congregation to intervene with the present Notification." The text however went on to explain the intent of the Notification as consisting in "enunciating the doctrine of the church with regard to some aspects of the doctrinal truths mentioned and at the same time to refute erroneous or dangerous opinions at which, independently of the intentions of the author, the reader could arrive because of ambiguous formulations and insufficient explanations contained in several passages of the book." The insinuation not only of ambiguities but also of errors, though they were now assigned to possible readers, thus slipped back into the text. The opinions rejected in the eight sections were substantially the same as in the previous text, though sometimes worded differently. As for the way of proceeding in two steps in each section, it remained unchanged and was still bound to be interpreted by readers as attributing to the author of the book the opinions rejected.

Yet, these "erroneous opinions" do not necessarily represent my mind or my text. Some examples of this are as follows: It is said to be against the Catholic faith to affirm "a separation not only between the Word and Jesus or a separation between the salvific action of the Word and that of Jesus, but also to hold the thesis of a salvific action of the Word as such in his divinity, independent from the humanity of the incarnate Word" (section 3)—which my book never did, being extremely cautious always to speak of a distinction between the Word as such and Jesus, never of separation, and of an essential relatedness between the two salvific actions. Again, it is stated as contrary to Catholic faith to "consider the various religions of the world as complementary to the church in the order of salvation" (section 6), and without any foundation in Catholic theology to "consider those religions as ways of salvation in their globality" (section 8)—which again the book never did. These are but examples; the distance between the opinions rejected in the Notification and the actual content of the book will be dealt with more at length hereafter.

G.O'C.: *Why did they insist so much on your signing the Notification?*

J.D.: At this stage I asked myself what to think of the urgent request made by the Congregation for my signature of the Notification without any further discussion. What use did the Congregation intend to make of my signature and what interpretation would it give it? Judging from what had recently happened in the case of Prof. Reinhard Messner of Germany, I feared that my signature might be given a meaning not intended or agreed upon by me. The Notification published in *L'Osservatore Romano* on December 6, 2000, about the work of Prof. Messner had in fact stated that "with his signature on the text the author has committed himself in the future to abide by the clarifications contained in the Notification.

Such clarifications will be the binding criterion for his theological activity and for his future theological publications."

I feared that a similar interpretation might be given by the Congregation to my own signature on the Notification about my book; I was not disposed to agree to such an interpretation of my eventual signature, which would close for me all possibility of further theological discussion of some opinions expressed in the Notification which I considered had to remain open to discussion among theologians, as they did not seem to contradict the doctrine of the faith, while on the other hand allowing for a more positive theological evaluation of the other religions. I was therefore not disposed, without any further discussion, simply to abide by everything contained in the Notification.

G.O'C.: *Why then did you sign?*

J.D.: Fr. Kolvenbach reassured me, explaining that the meaning of my signature would amount to giving serious consideration to the text of the Notification, while making sure in any further discussion to abide by what was clearly the doctrine of the faith—which I was well disposed and determined to do in submission to the church's Magisterium. Since the Notification no longer spoke of errors against the faith but of ambiguities in need of clarification, Father General further insisted on my signing the document in its new version in order to recover my freedom of speech and of action and to have done with the case. My signature had however to be somewhat delayed as I went to hospital for a surgical operation. Eventually the new text of the Notification duly signed by me was forwarded to the Congregation through Father General on December 16, 2000, together with a covering letter in which I stated the meaning I gave to my signature as follows: "I understand that the meaning of my signature is that in the future, either in conferences or in writings, I will have to take into account the text of the declaration *Dominus Iesus* and of the Notification." I trust that Father General communicated my letter to the cardinal when he sent the text signed by me.

G.O'C.: *Then what happened?*

J.D.: A further development soon took place. The publication of the Notification was delayed for reasons unknown. It finally came out, signed by Cardinal Ratzinger and Msgr. Bertone on January 24, 2001; the pope had this time confirmed his approbation of the text in an audience with the cardinal on January 19, and had again ordered its publication. A confirmation of the pope's approval was needed "in the light of further developments," said the text. This incidentally was the fifth time that a document concerned with my case was submitted to the pope's approval. The new version of the Notification was published in the *Osservatore Romano* only on February 26, 2001, accompanied with a Commentary on the Notification signed * * * (presumably written by Cardinal Ratzinger himself, as the three asterisks indicate).

Why the new delay and why a third approbation by the pope of a text which seemed to reproduce word for word the previous one? The explanation is found in the fact that to the previous text signed earlier by me, a full paragraph had been added which explained the meaning of my signature as follows: "With his signature of the text the author has committed himself to agree with the theses enunciated (in the Notification) and to abide in the future in his theological activity and in his publications by the doctrinal contents indicated in the Notification, the text of which will have to appear in eventual reprints or new editions of the book in question, and in translations of the same." None of this was found in the text submitted earlier to me for my signature. The fears I anticipated before signing were verified.

G.O'C.: *Let me understand this clearly: you say a paragraph was added by the CDF to the text you actually signed, and this was added after you had signed it, without your knowledge or consent?*

J.D.: This is exactly what happened. I had been careful to keep a photocopy of the text signed by me, in which the paragraph mentioned above was not found. A comparison between that text and the official version of the Notification published in *L'Osservatore Romano* shows clearly the addition. This addition was made without any reference to me.

G.O'C.: *What came next?*

J.D.: There followed a period of calm during which I could resume my commitments for lectures on the theology of religions and of interreligious dialogue in Italy and abroad, which had been interrupted for a while after the publication of the Notification on February 26, 2001. The case seemed to be settled, though prudence and circumspection were required in talking and writing. A sense of recovered, though limited freedom set in. Eventually I gave a lecture in Brussels, at the Institut d'Etudes Théologiques, on May 17, 2001, on "Le Verbe de Dieu, Jesus Christ et les religions du monde," which was published in *Nouvelle* *revue théologique* (2001, no. 4): 529-46, and made a communication at the International Congress of Fundamental Theology organized by the Catholic University of Lublin, Poland (September 18-21, 2001), on "Unity and Pluralism: Christianity and the Religions," which was published in the Acta of the Congress (Lublin 2001). These two writings brought new accusations from the authorities of the CDF. A personal letter of Cardinal Ratzinger to Fr. Kolvenbach followed, dated January 8, 2002. The letter pointed to a contradiction between the text of the Notification about my book—which, according to the Congregation's interpretation of my signature, I had committed myself to follow strictly—and what I had affirmed in the two articles mentioned above. In this situation the cardinal stated that the Congregation found itself obliged to "request His Paternity, with the authority that belongs to him, at least to require that Fr. Dupuis abstain in the future from intervening in word or writing on the matter." He added that, "were he to fail to dissipate such contradiction, the opportuneness of his retaining the responsibility as director of the theological review 'Gregorianum' would have to be reconsidered." A document of four pages was attached to the letter of the cardinal, which pointed to "erroneous" opinions repeated from the previous book in the two articles mentioned.

G.O'C.: *Can you say what the Congregation found problematic in these two articles?*

J.D.: The theological tenor of this document was of poor quality. My christological language, it claimed, continues to be incorrect, "as when [I] speak of the Word expressing himself through his human action in Jesus," which according to the document would seem to deny that "the Word incarnate *is* Jesus of Nazareth, one divine person incarnate." It would have to be admitted instead that "the Word as such is the Incarnate Word"—a formulation which, however, is open to serious criticism. It would seem to make the incarnation of the Word necessary or to imply that the humanity of Jesus exists eternally in the mystery of God! There returned again the false accusation of postulating a separation between the action of the Word as such and of Jesus Christ, while in fact I speak of distinction, not of separation. I was also blamed for affirming that "Jesus does not substitute himself for God," as if I implied here a denial of the divinity of Jesus Christ. The context, however, makes the meaning abundantly clear: Jesus does not—the gospel says it in so many words—substitute himself for the Father who in the New Testament is referred to as God. The Note ended by stating that "the position of the author remains doctrinally ambiguous and leads objectively to conclusions which are not conformed with the doctrine of the church on the said matters, departing on essential points from the teaching recalled in the declaration *Dominus Iesus* and in the Notification . . . , with regard to the truth of the incarnation and the value of non-Christian religions in the order of salvation."

It was noteworthy, however, that the new document did not mention errors against the faith, but against Catholic doctrine or the doctrine of the church. The minutes of a subsequent meeting between Fr. Kolvenbach and Cardinal Ratzinger which took place toward the end of January were in part more restrained. Father General sent me a copy of these minutes with no date attached. They stated the following: "No one has questioned the usefulness and the legitimacy (of Fr. Dupuis) pursuing 'in the originality of his contribution to theology at the time of dialogue' (this refers to the suggestion expressed by Fr. Kolvenbach during the meeting), provided such originality and contribution be faithful to sound doctrine, and abstain from introducing in the theological debate further elements of confusion with his ambiguous and erroneous formulations indicated in the Notification." No mention was made here of my having to be reduced to silence in both talking and writing, though the insinuation of erroneous opinions came back.

However, a letter of Fr. Kolvenbach to me followed on February 13, 2002. It stated: "Allow me to tell you . . . frankly and without ambiguity that in your publications and conferences you may no longer defend doctrinal positions which the Notification has clearly disapproved of." Meanwhile the local superiors had, for prudence sake, requested me to cancel my participation at a meeting on Muslim–Christian relations organized by the Most Rev. George Carey, archbishop of Canterbury, which was due to take place at Lambeth Palace on January 17-18, 2002, to which I had been invited by the archbishop himself. I was also asked to cancel a visit to Lisbon where I was due to give a lecture on February 6 on "Interreligious Dialogue in a Pluralistic Society." The lecture, the text of which had been sent in advance, was in fact read in Portuguese in my absence; it has been published in *Didaskalia* 32, no. 1 (2002): 69-81.

The situation was cleared up in a meeting between me and Father General which took place later in February. The General informed me of the meaning to be given to his last letter dated February 13. It did not mean abstaining completely from any discussion of some theological aspects of the Notification; but, while being allowed to continue saying and writing what I believed remained open to theological discussion, I was obliged, where I did not fully agree with some theological assertions of the declaration *Dominus Iesus* and the Notification, to inform my audience clearly about my dissent and to propose my own opinions with modesty and in full submission to the church's Magisterium.

G.O'C.: *What followed with regard to your lecturing and writing?*

J.D.: The situation being cleared up, I could again resume my activities, and the following months were heavy with commitments for lectures both in Italy and abroad. Nor are the invitations wanting for the months to come at the time of writing in December 2002: I am invited to attend congresses and give individual lectures in the course of 2003 in Bangkok (Thailand), Calcutta and Delhi (India), Cleveland (United States), Mexico (Mexico), Strasbourg, Lyon, (France), Brussels, Louvain (Belgium), Lucerne (Switzerland), Fatima (Portugal), Lund, Jönköping, Stockholm (Sweden), without counting mainland Italy and Sicily.

Let me also recall the publication in Italian in September 2001 of my new book *Il cristianesimo e le religioni: Dallo scontro all'incontro* (Brescia: Queriniana, 2001). Other editions followed in 2002: a French edition *La rencontre du christianisme et des religions: de l'affrontement au dialogue* (Paris: Le Cerf, 2002), an English edition *Christianity and the Religions: From Confrontation to Dialogue* (Maryknoll, NY: Orbis Books, 2002, 2003), and a Spanish edition *El cristianesimo y las religiones. Del desencuentro al diálogo* (Santander: Sal Terrae, 2002). (Portuguese and Polish editions are in preparation). This new volume aims at dispelling some ambiguities which may have been found in its predecessor and to further substantiate the theological positions which it upholds, while keeping without compromise to what is seen as clearly belonging to the doctrine of the faith. The new book has not so far provoked any reaction on the part of the CDF. But the recent nomination (on December 20, 2002) of Fr. Angelo Amato as secretary of the Congregation does not augur well for the future.

G.O'C.: *With the clarification brought about by Fr. Kolvenbach have we reached the end of the story?*

J.D.: There remains a last episode to be mentioned. Cardinal Ratzinger had hinted at the desirability of my responsibility as director of the review *Gregorianum* being discontinued. On May 28, 2002, I received a letter from Fr. Franco Imoda, the rector of the Gregorian University, stating that on October 1 I would cease to be in charge of the review. For good measure Fr. O'Collins, my theological adviser throughout the investigation of my writings, received a letter from the rector informing him that his responsibility as consultor of the review was also discontinued.

This brings to an end the account—so far—of the proceedings initiated by the Congregation for the Doctrine of the Faith about my book on June 10, 1998. It may be useful to mention that in a *Festschrift* on the occasion of my eightieth birthday (Daniel Kendall and Gerald O'Collins [eds.], *In Many and Diverse Ways* [Maryknoll, NY: Orbis Books, 2003]) a select bibliography under the title "The Book and the Case" indicates the abundant literature to which the book has given rise.

G.O'C.: *For a long time you remained silent about the investigation of your book by the Congregation for the Doctrine of the Faith. What are the reasons for which on my invitation you now accept to speak out, the past imposition of silence notwithstanding, to talk about the procedure followed by the Congregation, and, following the example of other theologians who have undergone similar trials, to give an account of what you have been made to suffer at the hands of the church's doctrinal authority?*

J.D.: When you suggested doing an interview book centered on "the book and the case," I hesitated for a long time before accepting the offer. I was conscious of the fact that much of the material concerned had been marked strictly reserved, the Congregation insisting on keeping the secrecy which, however, became problematic as soon as the case became public. I abstained from any comment on the contents of the investigation, as well as on the procedure and the methods employed in it. I was satisfied to respond to the theologians' questioning, in the two articles mentioned above, without making any explicit reference to the questions asked by the CDF. Even my latest book, published in Italian, French, English, and Spanish in 2001-2002, continues to observe the same silence with regard to the discussion with the Congregation. In a postscript to that book I explain that it had been entirely written before the publication of the declaration *Dominus Iesus* and of the Notification, though for various reasons it was published only after the publication of the two documents. Even so, the text remained unchanged. This silence was offset by the fact that, even without any explicit reference to the Congregation, its queries were implicitly and indirectly dealt with in the new book by responding to the theologians' questioning. Why then the present change of attitude and what is intended in this new publication?

For one thing it may be asked: how long is one bound by the secrecy imposed upon him by the church's doctrinal authority? Can the truth remain hidden forever? Can one be forced forever to remain silent without the possibility of any self-defense, while the accusations made against one have been detrimental to one's reputation as a theologian and harmful to one's person? I do not intend here to enter into a long discussion of the methods employed by the CDF in the investigation of my case. I can testify to the fact that the methods employed correspond to the norms published by the Congregation concerning "Regulations for Doctrinal Examination" (*Agendi ratio in doctrinarum examine*) (*Acta Apostolicae Sedis* [1997], 830-35).

G.O'C.: *But these norms have been much criticized!*

J.D.: Those norms have in fact been submitted to much criticism. Let it suffice to refer to the elaborate examination of those norms made by Fr. Ladislas Orsy, a world authority on Canon Law, entitled "Are Church Investigation Procedures Really Just?" published in *Doctrine and Life* (1998): 453-66. The author does not hide his reservations against the norms of the CDF, which he compares with what he calls "The Legal Wisdom of Our Age." He does so by enunciating the characteristics which ought to be verified for "investigation procedures to be really just":

> Justice demands the precise definition of an offence. . . . Justice is best served when in the process the respective roles of the judge, the prosecutor, and the defendant are kept apart. . . . Equity . . . postulates that each of the opposing parties has a similar opportunity to plead their case before the judge. . . . The duty of the judge is to presume the accused innocent (and protect him) until the evidence proves beyond reasonable doubt that he is guilty. . . . All that affects a public sentence, ought to be done openly. (Justice not only ought to be done but also ought to be seen to be done.) . . . The opportunity for appeal is an integral part of any good judicial system. . . . The penalty of automatic excommunication . . . , as all extreme penalties, . . . punishes both the individual and the community. . . . It should be enough to state with authority what Catholic doctrine is and is not, and let time, fraternal correction and divine grace have their gentle impact on the author.

To which Ladislas Orsy adds the following: "In the Catholic world, the best way of promoting and safeguarding the doctrine of faith is to create a climate of trust where the process of 'faith seeking understanding' can flourish."

In my case the damage has by God's mercy remained limited: the book was never condemned, nor withdrawn from publication; no correction to the text was imposed on me, nor were reprints or editions in other languages forbidden. As a matter of fact, the measures taken against the book and its author, besides bringing me personally to the notice of theologians the world over and eliciting much sympathy, have also helped to sell the book. Someone suggested with a grain of humor that I ought to be thankful to Cardinal Ratzinger for the fame acquired and the publicity received. Yet the fact remains that the rapid description of the proceedings given above reveals in them grievous flaws, if they are compared to the "legal wisdom of our age" as understood by canonist Orsy. Many articles have been written, some of them especially severe, to point out these flaws and defects of procedure. The methods used by the CDF have been branded as unjust, impersonal, and inhuman. However this may be, my intention here is not to enlarge on the procedural flaws, but to be of help in the search for truth on the matters involved, which are of vital importance for the church's mission in the present age.

Instead of encouraging and promoting theological research and discussion, as was Pope Paul VI's intention when in an apostolic letter *Motu proprio* published on the eve of the close of the Council (December 7, 1965) he changed the name of the Congregation and revised its statutes, the CDF, as it operates today, rather impedes and prevents theological work by the negative measures and strictures it imposes on theologians. The Holy Office has a long record of repression, but one may wonder whether the number of theologians under investigation by the CDF, even without their being aware, is not perhaps greater today than it has ever been before. Free discussion on pressing problems which today's church faces is being silenced, and magisterial interpretations and decisions are imposed which do not carry conviction and meet with scant "reception."

G.O'C.: *Has anything changed after the Council in the way in which prominent theologians have been dealt with by the Congregation in the past and the way a new generation of theologians is being treated today?*

J.D.: One thinks naturally of names like Henri de Lubac, Karl Rahner, Yves Congar, Marie-Dominique Chenu, Edward Schillebeeckx, Bernhard Häring and others, not to mention some closer to us, like Hans Küng, Gustavo Gutiérrez, Jon Sobrino, Leonardo Boff, Tissa Balasuriya, and others. In many cases those of the previous generation have been rehabilitated at a later stage in their career, and their opinions have often become commonly accepted, even by the church authority. But is there not a lesson to learn from these upheavals and turn-abouts, in view of fairer and more equitable dealings? Yet, has this lesson been learned? There is no evidence that the new norms according to which the Congregation deals with theologians under investigation today are better than those employed earlier. It strikes one for instance that in the past the accused were invited for serious discussion of their work with the authorities of the Congregation and competent persons delegated by it; a case in point is that of Fr. Schillebeeckx. Today on the contrary they are invited only to sign a Notification against their work, approved in anticipation by the pope. Is this "due process"? It strikes one equally that a substantial correspondence between a theologian suspected of doctrinal error and the prefect of the Congregation could take place in the past, for the sake of seeking clarifications, as happened in the case of the extensive correspondence between Fr. Häring and Cardinal Franjo Seper, prefect of the CDF. Today no such clarifications are sought on a personal level and through personal contact.

G.O'C.: *You say that your aim in speaking now about your case is to help in the search for truth and for a solution to the many problems, theological and otherwise, which the case has raised and continues to raise. Can you explain further?*

J.D.: Yes, I have said that my aim is to help the search for truth on theological matters bearing on the spread and credibility of the Christian message today. The point is that the present procedure seems to stifle such a search. What belongs to Catholic doctrine and what is opposed to it seem to be settled authoritatively a priori, often with questionable arguments and doubtful authorities. The account given above shows this abundantly. Now it may be asked whether the content of Catholic doctrine, if not that of the faith, is in all cases clearly definable a priori; and, moreover, whether it does not in many cases remain open to evolution and development in the light of new insights. The truth is never entirely possessed in its fullness at any time, even by church authority, and continuous search for it is incumbent on the church authority in collaboration with all church members, especially those having the charism and the commission to teach and to promote Christian doctrine.

There is room then for requesting that theological search and discussion be not prematurely closed and forbidden on important issues affecting the church's life, where no apodictic decision can be made regarding the irreformable character of some opinions as belonging with all certitude to the unchangeable doctrine of the church or being excluded by it. The theologians of past generations referred to above have not hesitated prudently to maintain and defend their positions against the CDF, and history more often than not proved them right. They have not hesitated either to make their dealings with the Congregation public in writing, either by issuing a new book by themselves or by writing their memoirs, which were published after them. I am thinking for instance of E. Schillebeeckx's short interview book, entitled *I Am a Happy Theologian* (London: SCM Press, 1994), or of B. Häring's account of his dealings with the Congregation, *My Witness for the Church* (New York/Mahwah, NJ: Paulist Press, 1992). I am also thinking of the recent book edited by Paul Collins, *From Inquisition to Freedom* (London: Continuum, 2001) in which Charles Curran, Tissa Balasuriya, Hans Küng, Paul Collins himself, and others tell the story of their dealings with the CDF.

I am thinking even more of the long private diary which Yves Congar wrote during his black years 1946-1956, during which he was mercilessly harassed by church and religious authorities to the point of being sent into exile. His true rehabilitation came when Pope John XXIII summoned him to Rome for the Second Vatican Council, of which he became one of the main architects, leaving his imprint on several Council documents. The diary of Fr. Congar during those years has been published, edited, and presented by Etienne Fouilloux, under the title *Yves Congar: Journal d'un théologien 1946-1956* (Paris: Le Cerf, 2000). It is a staggering document which reveals how much a theologian can be made to suffer at the hands of a church which he loves and to the service of which he has devoted all his life, work, and energy. Writing for himself, Congar is not afraid to put down the searching and radical questions which the situation forces him to ask, including the meaning of his persevering in his ecclesial and religious vocation. While reading this testimony, I myself was bowled over and, even while the sufferings I personally have experienced are little compared to his, I often felt expressed in his text the feelings and reactions which I myself often have had; only they were described much more vividly than I could ever have done. I am grateful to God, as Congar was, to have received the grace of perseverance, if not the restoration of serenity of mind.

I have abstained so far from publishing pieces of writing in which I have explained the reasons why and the points on which I cannot agree with some affirmations made and positions defended by the declaration *Dominus Iesus* and the Notification on my 1997 book. The regret has been expressed by some that even in the latest book, *Christianity and the Religions: From Confrontation to Dialogue*, published in 2001-2002, I still do not make explicit reference to my disagreement with the two documents. Two appendices had in fact been added to the manuscript after the two documents had been published, in which I explained my disagreement with them. These two appendices had to be replaced, however, by the postscript referred to above; superiors were afraid the text would be considered offensive by the CDF.

G.O'C.: *You have mentioned above that your 1997 book met with very divergent reactions on the part of reviewers in periodicals and in the press, some not sparing the praises addressed to the book and its author; others, on the contrary, being very critical. Before coming to the point of the issues involved in the discussion, could you give us some idea of the comments which were being made by way of positive or negative appraisal?*

J.D.: There would be much to mention in this regard. I will comment on some reactions which are more specific, some of which have moreover an instructive history of their own. At the Paris presentation of the book on October 27, 1997, published in *La vie spirituelle* (September 1997): 580-86), Claude Geffré was delighted with the fact that the book marked the 200th volume of the collection Cogitatio Fidei, of which he is the director; this was not a sheer coincidence as it had been planned in advance by the director of the collection. He went on to say:

> It is impossible to summarize the vast theological synthesis which J. Dupuis proposes. . . . One must mostly recall that he seeks to initiate a new path in the theology of religions. He claims in effect to overcome the opposition between the two different paradigms of *christocentrism* and *theocentrism* which lead to two incompatible currents continually dividing theologians, namely inclusivism and pluralism. J. Dupuis knows that I am fundamentally in agreement with his will to overcome a theology of religions or of dialogue which still remains within the orbit of a renewed theology of the salvation of the "infidels," in order to adopt a true theology of religious pluralism in which one asks about the meaning of the diversity of the religious traditions in the one plan of God. I myself am searching in that direction. And I think as he does that it is possible to maintain the singularity of Christianity based on the uniqueness of Christ as Son of God while looking positively at the other religions and their salvific value.

This did not prevent Geffré from asking some questions or even from stating his disagreement on some points. He added: "I ask myself if, beyond the labels in words, J. Dupuis is not adopting a *theocentric* model, that very one which the pluralists claim for themselves, whom however he blames

for having "crossed the Rubicon," that is for having betrayed the uniqueness of the Christic mediation." In a private correspondence that followed
the publication of his speech (the last sentence mentioned had not been
pronounced orally at the presentation of the book), Geffré pleaded guilty
for making this unhappy remark and agreed to withdraw it. Unhappily
the sentence has been made use of by less well intentioned reviewers to
discredit my book.

Father Geffré made further comments in *Profession théologien. Quelle
pensée chrétienne pour le XXIe siècle? Entretien avec Gwendoline Jarczyk*
(Paris: Albin Michel, 1999), 202-12—this time when the investigation
about the book by the CDF was already advanced. Again he congratulated himself for having chosen as number 200 of the collection "a book
which is a landmark," for "it has, as it were, an exemplary value." He
added:

> Whatever reservations might be formulated in relation to such a
> work, it is undeniable that it represents a landmark in the history
> of Christian theology, a true "epochal moment"—in the sense that
> it marks a paradigm shift in the way of doing theology. Personally,
> I see in this book the equivalent of what was some fifty years ago
> *Chrétiens désunis* of Yves Congar: there was question then of a fun-
> damental reflection on the question of Christian ecumenism, while
> the work of Jacques Dupuis presents itself as an approach equally
> essential of that broadened ecumenism to which interreligious dia-
> logue leads today.

This did not prevent C. Geffré from formulating again his own reservations—some of which will be discussed later; yet, while being asked
whether he regretted the official challenge to the book, he added:

> I am deeply pained by that decision of the Congregation of the Faith
> which puts on trial a work which, to my sense, represents in fact
> the right balance (*Un point d'équilibre*) . . . between positions which
> are not in fact tenable: an archaic preconciliar ecclesiocentrism and
> those positions which tend to question what constitutes the back-
> bone of the apostolic faith, that is the affirmation of the uniqueness
> of the mediation of Christ.

Father Geffré returned once again to the issue in his last book, *Croire et
interpreter: Le tournant herméneutique de la théologie* (Paris: Le Cerf, 2001),
128-30. This time he wrote: "I recommend strongly the book of Jacques

Dupuis, *Vers une théologie chrétienne du pluralisme religieux*. It is a work that will soon become a classic in the theology of religions. It has been subjected to investigation by the CDF. This is all the more surprising as it shows an admirable knowledge of the church tradition and witnesses to a very well balanced position which in particular takes its distance from the so-called *pluralist* theologies." This being said, Geffré repeated once more his own questioning about the book—to which, however, I had by then repeatedly reacted in writing, and to which I will return below. This lengthy account of Geffré's repeated reactions to the book witnesses to the positive, though nuanced, evaluation coming from one of the most qualified theologians in the field.

Monsignor Michael Fitzgerald, then secretary of the Pontifical Council for Interreligious Dialogue, took part in the presentation of the book in Rome on November 22, 1997. In his intervention he observed: "The book should be extremely useful in theological faculties, theological institutes, seminaries and houses of formation throughout the world." This did not prevent him from formulating some questions, especially with regard to the second, synthetic part of the book. These notwithstanding, he concluded: "I have no doubt that *Toward a Christian Theology of Religious Pluralism* will remain the best synthesis, and the standard work of reference, for a very long time." This was too much to meet with approval on the part of the CDF. When the proofs of the number of the review *Pro dialogo* which contained the communication of Msgr. Fitzgerald were sent by the Council for Interreligious Dialogue to the Congregation for their approval (as they are bound to do for any publication of theirs), the text of the speech had to be withdrawn, apparently to avoid giving the impression of a difference of opinion about my book between the Congregation and the Council. This is how the communication of Msgr. Fitzgerald appeared only much later, under the title "Jacques Dupuis. Toward a Christian Theology of Religious Pluralism," in *Pro dialogo* 108 (2001, no. 3): 334-41, after the publication of the Notification about the book by the Congregation. The last sentence had become: "It may be said that *Toward a Christian Theology of Religious Pluralism* offers a very useful synthesis and that it will probably remain a standard work of reference for a very long time." The difference between the two versions of the sentence indicates the compliance imposed on the Council by the Congregation.

Monsignor Fitzgerald came back to the point on the occasion of the 450th anniversary of the foundation of the Roman College (April 4-5, 2001) (see *Atti del Solenne Atto Accademico in occasione del 450 anniversario della fondazione del Collegio Romano 1551-2001*, 143-51). He gave a talk on

"The Pontifical Gregorian University and Interreligious Dialogue." On that occasion he declared:

> I wish to put on record here a debt of gratitude to Fr. Jacques Dupuis for his pioneering work in the field. I had the honor and pleasure of being associated with the presentation at this university of his book. . . . There was certainly not agreement on everything said in that book, and reference has been made to certain "ambiguities." Yet, since theology is a developing science, it is surely normal for theories to be presented, discussed, reshaped and brought into a new synthesis.

He surprised some in his audience by his generous support of me, even if some caution in his language showed the restrictions imposed on those who hold high positions.

The first review of my book appeared in *Avvenire*, the Italian paper under the patronage of the Italian Episcopal Conference, on November 22, 1997, entitled "Il Cristo cosmico" and signed by Enzo Bianchi, the founder and prior of the ecumenical community of Bose, in North Italy. He pointed to the theological aspects of the problem which are "treated by the author not only with competence but with extreme lucidity and a rare balance." He ended up stating: "The dense work of Dupuis offers a most precious contribution, a guide, a compass as it were, which can guide the progress of Catholic theology as it enters the third millennium. And if it is true that this work 'will, perhaps, raise as many problems as it will propose solutions' (Introduction, English edition, p. 11), it is equally true that asking the right questions is already essential for the correct approach to the problem." This was a clear commendation. Strangely enough, the same paper *Avvenire* carried five months later, on April 14, 1998, p. 20, another book review filling one entire page of the paper, signed by Inos Biffi of the theological faculty of Milan under the telling title "Il monopolio della grazia." This review was commissioned from above. It had first been requested from Msgr. Giuseppe Colombo, chairman of the theological faculty of Northern Italy who declined to write it; it was then entrusted to Inos Biffi of the same faculty, a specialist on St. Anselm and responsible for the liturgy in the Milan archdiocese. This new review was as devastatingly negative in its evaluation of the book as its predecessor had been positive. It started off stating that the fundamental affirmations of the book "seem to us unacceptable not only from the theological point of view, but also in view of the Christian faith." It further noted that the content of the book "often lacks coherence and logic, especially as regards the interpretation of biblical data." The review had two principal parts: the first discussed affirmations made in the book; the other proposed Biffi's own reflections on the same. In the second part he criticized the "new hermeneutic" of the New Testament proposed in the book, which is "at the antipodes of the correct Christian theological method," the religious pluralism by right or of principle which the book advocates, and the Trinitarian Christology proposed in it. For Biffi all of these were thoroughly unacceptable. Finally, Biffi expressed his view that "a Christian theology of religious pluralism ought to follow another path" from that indicated in the book.

At the request of Rev. Fr. G. Pittau, rector of the university, I wrote ten pages of comments on Biffi's article, which I submitted to the rector on April 26, 1998. The rector approved my note, which, however, he thought was too long for *Avvenire* to publish. He himself wrote a shorter note, based on what I had provided, in which he protested at the tone and content of the article. He sent this note to the director of *Avvenire*, requesting him to publish it. This note was never published, the director claiming later not to have received it, and the rector was subsequently blamed at the Vatican for having organized the presentation of my book which had taken place at the university six months earlier. My long note was included with the text of my first response to the questions of the CDF, signed December 25, 1998, but was never published.

Meanwhile, an article signed by Giuseppe de Rosa, "Una teologia problematica del pluralismo religioso," was published in *Civiltà cattolica* (1998, no. 3): 129-43. For each number of *Civiltà cattolica* the director has to submit the proofs to the Secretariat of State for approval. According to the nature of the material the Secretariat of State distributes it to the various Roman Congregations for scrutiny. The text of the article of G. de Rosa was sent to the CDF, where it remained for more than one month. It came out considerably altered; the questions asked in the last pages about some of the positions proposed in my book had become much more incisive. In a letter addressed to me on July 17, 1998, Fr. Gian Paolo Salvini, director of the review, admitted that even the title had been altered, the original title not including the term "problematica" but speaking simply of "Una teologia del pluralismo religioso."

At the end of the article it was stated that the question to be asked before all else is "whether some positions of the author do full justice to the data of the New Testament," especially where the "unique, total and definitive" revelation in Jesus Christ is concerned and his quality as "unique, and absolute savior" as well as "definitive and absolute revealer." It is further noted that it cannot be affirmed that "the Word and the Spirit act distinctly from Jesus, the Incarnate Word, before as well as after the incarnation"; neither is it possible to speak of a "complementarity" of revelations. Moreover, the universal mediation of the church for the salvation of people who have not heard about Jesus Christ is not done justice by speaking of a mediation of a final, rather than of an efficient order. "It can finally be asked whether in a theology of religious pluralism, such as that presented by Fr. Dupuis, proclaiming the gospel continues to have a meaning and a place" in the mission of the church. "These and other questions which the reader of the work of Fr. Dupuis asks himself—and which make this work 'problematic' and 'provocative' on a theme of the greatest importance such as that of a religious pluralism *de iure*—call for precisions and clarifications which Fr. Dupuis will not fail to give in the course of the discussions to which his work will give rise."

The courtesy with which the questions were proposed did not hide their sharpness. Their wording belonged to the CDF, even while it was attributed to the original author of the article. When the news agency *Adista* challenged the director of *Civiltà cattolica* to admit the interference with the text by the CDF, he denied it in spite of the letter he had previously sent to me. But this denial had no effect on the *Adista* staff, too well aware of the procedure imposed on the review. They maintained and repeated their accusation. This was the second time that the Congregation had interfered with a piece of writing concerned with my book. The general public and some reviewers should know this, as they sometimes base their own criticism on articles to which they attribute special weight and which they consider symptomatic of a general consensus.

Father Gerald O'Collins was involved in my dealings with the CDF from the beginning. In fact he was involved with my book well before. He had been my theological adviser throughout its writing, making suggestions and correcting my English, the language in which the book was originally written. He had also done the censorship of the book in the name of my superiors. In the *Tablet*, as early as January 24, 1998, 110-11, there appeared under the rubric "Paths to God" a review of the book by Fr. O'Collins. He wrote: "A genuinely magisterial work, it brings together a lifetime of study and experience to outline a profound theological shift in the Christian understanding of other religions. Instead of merely asking *whether* salvation can occur for members of these other traditions, Dupuis struggles with the question of *how* in God's providence these traditions mediate salvation to their members." In conclusion he wrote:

Let me end up by recognizing this book as a superb contribution to interreligious dialogue and theology. The "toward" in its title reflects Dupuis's modesty: he wishes to make some proposals for fruitful Christian lines of approach to other religions. Yet the book is also courageously adventurous. . . . One cannot hope to do much more than explore the foothills of God's majestic providence for all human beings. But when sharing in that exploring I am very happy once again to hang on to Fr. Dupuis.

The last sentence alluded to the time when many years earlier I had carried Fr. O'Collins on my motorcycle along the narrow roads in the foothills of the Himalayas to let him visit a high-altitude Buddhist monastery.

In a later letter to the editor of the *Tablet,* "In Defense of Fr. Dupuis" (December 12, 1998), 1650, Fr. O'Collins noted the similarity between many concerns expressed by Pope John Paul II and those which draw my own attention in the book. He wrote: "Like John Paul II, Fr. Dupuis recognizes those treasures of religion through which millions of non-Christians will, we may confidently hope and pray, find salvation and be united with all the redeemed in the coming kingdom of the glorious Son of God. To condemn Dupuis's book would, I fear, be to condemn the pope himself."

Another friend ought to be mentioned here, Msgr. Luigi Sartori of Padua who devoted three pieces of writing to my book. The first was a book review published in *Studia Patavina* (1998, no. 1): 220-21. He remarked: "Perhaps the originality of his [Fr. Dupuis's] position will be understood better in the future, when the actual, rather radical debate will have led to some more secure conclusion. It seems to me that his gift consists in inviting not to propose alternative doctrines: the Christian solution cannot admit that one principle or one aspect be so stressed as to obscure the others: true theocentrism assumes and values authentic Christocentrism, and so on."

Monsignor Sartori returned to the point more at length in an article "Il dibattito sul pluralismo religioso. Considerazioni sul 'caso' Dupuis," published in *Rassegna di teologia* (1999, no. 2): 297-300, when the case was on at the CDF. This time the author openly defended the efforts made in my book. He noted how nice and fruitful a serene and free debate among theologians on the work of Fr. Dupuis, dedicated to the problem of religious pluralism, would be "if there were no fear that eventual critical reflections be taken as dogmatic pronouncements uttered immediately in the name of orthodoxy, rather than as positive contributions to research." The discussions and the book reviews seemed up to a point "to have been exemplary."

"Unhappily, with the well-known launching of censorship proceedings on the part of the Roman authorities the climate is deteriorating to the detriment of the dream of that brotherly debate." Monsignor Sartori insisted on the need for all to cultivate the sense of the mystery when faced with a truly new problem, rather than rush to destructive judgments. He wrote:

> I myself am inclined to trust *a priori* Fr. Dupuis, who builds his theological reflection after having lived for about thirty years [in fact thirty-six] in that religious universe, and can succeed in interpreting it from within; and I dare to insist on the readiness to put themselves in question when I refer to those who build a theology closed up in their own sacred cell. . . . The contribution of Fr. Dupuis is only an attempt, a proposal. . . . He does not intend to reduce the uniqueness and the singularity of Christ, but to lead to a still greater understanding and valuing of his unique divine originality. . . . We must believe, we theologians also . . . that Christ is always greater than our rational stammerings.

Monsignor Sartori also wrote a preface for the Italian edition of my last book, *Il cristianesimo e le religioni: Dallo scontro all'incontro* (Brescia: Queriniana, 2001), under the title "Riflessioni confidenziali di un amico." There he said: "We should rejoice at the help which students of serious competence offer for the meeting, so urgent and decisive today, of Christianity with the other religions of the world; especially if they come from persons with a long experience of 'conviviality,' that is of lived missionary witness, within those far away 'universes.'" "I myself support the efforts of those pioneering theologians who, like Fr. Dupuis, explore new ways which they consider well-balanced (and they are so) in rethinking theology, also that theology which so far was interested, though with slow steps, even with rare stumbling steps, to place Christian faith in dialogue with the other historical faiths." Coming back to the burning question of the uniqueness and the universality of the salvific mediation of Jesus Christ, he noted: "Also Fr. Dupuis has had to tackle this delicate problem, attempting to explore acceptable ways of progress toward the truth, even if in an upward direction." These are generous words which, well beyond an avowed personal friendship and sympathy, witness to a refreshing breadth of vision and openness to the unknown.

A name which cannot be omitted is that of Fr. Angelo Amato of the Pontifical Salesian University, who played an important role in the proceedings against my book by the CDF. In the Vatican review of the Congregation for Catholic Education called *Seminarium* (1998, no. 4):

771- 809, Fr. Amato published an article entitled "L'assolutezza salvifica del Cristianesimo: Prospettive sistematiche," in which much space is spent in discrediting my work by indulging in false accusations against it. Having come to know this article, Fr. G. O'Collins, my theological adviser, addressed a long letter to Fr. Amato in which he expressed his sorrow and indicated how "scandalized" he had been at the author's apparently thorough incapacity or unwillingness to interpret my thought and writing correctly; he received an evasive answer stating that truth is not always found entirely on the same side!

In a later article, called "L'unicità della mediazione salvifica di Cristo: Il dibattito contemporaneo," which drew on the earlier piece in *Seminarium* and appeared in Mariano Crociata (ed.), *Gesu Cristo e l'unicità della mediazione* (Milan: Paoline, 2000), 13-44, Fr. Amato returned to the charge. He listed me again with Panikkar, S. J. Samartha, Geffré, and others, all of whom he charged for holding the following "theological postulates" to justify their false religious pluralism: that Jesus, Krishna and the Buddha "complete each other"; that there is "a distinction between the salvific economy of the mystery of Christ and that of the Holy Spirit to which is attributed a "plus value" independent of the paschal mystery of Christ"; that "revelation in Jesus Christ is incomplete and partial, and hence in need of being complemented by other revelations"; and "the negation of the church as "universal sacrament of salvation." All this qualified Fr. Amato to play an important role in the procedure against my book. He was present at the consultors' meeting which preceded the ordinary assembly of the members of the CDF which decided to challenge my book (June 10, 1998). He was present as consultor of the Congregation at the official meeting of September 4, 2000, with the authorities of the CDF, though, as I have noted earlier, he was conspicuously silent during that meeting. He had written the text of the declaration *Dominus Iesus*, except for its chapter 4 on ecumenism, and took an active part, together with Cardinal Ratzinger, in its presentation at the press office of the Vatican on September 5. He was responsible for writing the text of the Notification about my book, which explains the striking similarity between the condemnations made in the declaration and those mentioned in the Notification. There is every reason to think that the new denunciation of January 2002 also originated from him. It is sad to place on record such unpleasant truths, but they may help people to assess the events and decisions taken by ecclesiastical authority.

Some other reviewers, whom it gives me satisfaction to mention, deserve to be recorded here. While formulating some pertinent questions, these expressed a high appreciation for my book. In *The Thomist* (1998, no. 2): 316-19, Paul J. Griffiths wrote after raising some questions: "These criticisms notwithstanding, Dupuis's book is a major achievement. It will be an essential point of reference on the topic for a long time to come." One of the most searching studies written about the book is the long study by Prof. Terrence Merrigan, dean of the faculty of theology, Katholieke Universiteit Leuven, published in *Louvain Studies* (1998, no. 3): 338-59, under the title "Exploring the Frontiers: Jacques Dupuis and the Movement 'Toward a Christian Theology of Religious Pluralism.'" At the end of his study Prof. Merrigan wrote the following well-nuanced evaluation of the work: "What Dupuis has done is to explore the frontiers of the inclusivist theology of religions. In so doing he has exposed certain "no-go areas" and apparently even ventured into something of a no-man's-land between the three 'classical' approaches. Of course, there are pitfalls confronting every explorer. However, like all true explorers, Dupuis deserves respect and admiration for his endeavors. This is a brave and conscientious book, a comprehensive map of familiar territory, and an attempt to chart new routes. Dupuis's map may not be complete but it will surely serve those who come after him."

Professor Hans Waldenfels commented on the "Dupuis case" initiated by Cardinal Ratzinger in an extensive study in *Stimmen der Zeit* (September 1999): 597-610, under the title "On the Way toward a Christian Theology of Religious Pluralism. Observations on the 'Dupuis Case.'" He characterized the theology proposed in the book as a "theology on the way," which he himself upheld and defended.

Also writing after the "Dupuis Case" had been started was Prof. Peter C. Phan of the Catholic University of America. In a book review published in *Dialogue and Alliance* (2000, no. 1): 121-23, he wrote:

Such a theology of religious pluralism, it must be admitted, is neither revolutionary nor uncommon today and remains well within the bounds of orthodoxy. But it has been made notorious by the fact that the Vatican has subjected Dupuis's work to "review" and required him to respond to a series of "questions" concerning his theological positions. This action by the Vatican not only betrays a distressing lack of gratitude for a man who has dedicated the greater part of his life in the service of the church and theology with his most thorough and scrupulous scholarship, but also a disconcerting unawareness that his theology of religious pluralism represents the *sententia communis* of Roman Catholic theologians. Whatever the outcome of the investigation of the Roman Curia, Dupuis's book is destined to be the standard textbook on the theology of religious pluralism for many years to come. I recommend it most enthusiastically for the use of graduate and advanced undergraduate classes on the theology of religions. It is hard to find another work that matches its comprehensive treatment, lucid exposition, fair-minded criticism, and balanced judgment.

G.O'C.: *What to make of this variety of opinions?*

J.D.: The opinions mentioned here represent only a sample in a literature which is much more extensive; as I mentioned above, a select though substantial bibliography has been published under the title "The Book and the Case." Reference is made there, among many other items, to a long piece by L. Elders in *Nova et vetera* (1998): 97-117, unfairly critical but commissioned by the CDF. A Dutch colleague at the Gregorian University handed over to me a copy he had received of a longer version of the same article, printed as pp. 300-334 of an unpublished volume without a title. This was presumably documentation for use by the Congregation. A series of articles was published in *L'Osservatore Romano*, commenting on the declaration *Dominus Iesus* after its publication (September-October 2000). The series includes well-known names: A. Amato, N. Bux, M. Dhavamony, R. Fisichella, L. Ladaria, D. Valentini, three of whom were colleagues at the Gregorian; the articles did not explicitly refer to my book, but their criticism of opinions they declared to be the target of the declaration as heretical hardly disguises their intention of referring to me. R. Fisichella castigated what he branded as "schizophrenic Christology." L. Ladaria feared that distinguishing between the Word of God not incarnate (*asarkos*) and the Word of God incarnate (*ensarkos*) might speak of two distinct Words of God, thus introducing four persons in the Trinity. All this, added to what has been mentioned above, goes to show how well the CDF was supported by Romans and others in its attacks.

G.O'C.: *So far you have been making reference to individual theologians who have expressed either a positive or a negative opinion about your book. Have some institutions reacted collectively about it as institutions, either positively or negatively?*

J.D.: Two cases should be mentioned in this connection. I have had a sad experience with the Dominicans of Toulouse and the *Revue thomiste* under their direction. In *Revue thomiste* (1998, no. 4): 591-630, a long study of forty pages was published under the title "'Tout récapituler dans le Christ.' A propos de l'ouvrage de J. Dupuis, Vers une théologie chrétienne du pluralisme religieux." The article is signed by the entire "comité de rédaction" of the review, comprising seven names, though obviously it was written by one or two. This unusual way of proceeding amounts to a manifesto against the book, even though a footnote mentions that the writing of the study was completed before notice was received of the investigation of the book initiated by the CDF. The note states: "The *Revue thomiste* insists on specifying that its critique is done in another perspective, that of a theological dialogue to which every theologian who shares his reflections with the public has a right." There followed a devastating evaluation of the book, which can hardly be called "dialogue," unless we make a parody of the term. This is not the place to enter into a new discussion with the authors' criticism; I gave it pride of place in the study published by *Louvain Studies* (1999, no. 3): 211-63, under the title "'The Truth Will Make You Free.' The Theology of Religious Pluralism Revisited," referred to above.

The prior of the Dominicans of Toulouse, Henry Donneaud, returned to the attack after the conference which I gave in Brussels in summer 2001 had been published in *Nouvelle revue théologique* (2001, no. 4): 529-46, under the title "Le Verbe de Dieu, Jesus-Christ et les religions du monde." Donneaud had been the second signatory of the first article in *Revue thomiste*. Now he formulated even more trenchant accusations in a new article in *Revue thomiste* (2002, no. 1): 43-62, without taking into account the answers which I had already given in my *Louvain Studies* article to some of his questions. I myself wrote a rejoinder to this new set of accusations, under the title "Le Verbe de Dieu comme tel et comme incarné."

The second case to which I refer is that of the theological faculty of Palermo. I had been invited by phone by the dean of the theological faculty of Sicily—he did not tell me his name—to come to Palermo for a lecture. I had accepted the invitation, after his assurance that my visit had been approved by the authorities of the diocese. Yet, when I was about to fly down to Palermo, I was suddenly informed by the dean, again over the phone, that my visit had been vetoed by Cardinal Salvatore de Giorgi, the archbishop of Palermo. This was the only time, even after the investigation of my case had been started by the Congregation, that I was turned down by local church authority. Except for this instance I have received a warm welcome from local church authorities wherever I went to give lectures.

More recently two books have been published under the direction of Mariano Crociata of the theological faculty of Palermo: *Gesù Cristo e l'unicità della mediazione* and *teologia delle religioni. Bilanci e prospettive* (Milan: Paoline, 2000 and 2001). (The editor had previously written a wicked article about my book in *Ho theologos* [1998, no. 1]: 87-116.) A quick look at both volumes makes it clear that the authors, many of whom belong to the faculty of Palermo and have had their theological training at the Gregorian University, lost no opportunity to discredit my book, often with gratuitous and unfounded criticism. This way of proceeding smacks of ecclesiastical opportunism, by those who watch in what direction the wind blows. I have not thought it worthwhile to respond to these accusations, as they have been dealt with on other occasions and I do not wish to enter into sterile controversies.

G.O'C.: *During all this time since the case against your book was initiated by the CDF, have you met with any public support and encouragement on the part of the church and religious authorities?*

J.D.: Certainly; and I am happy to put this on record. First to be mentioned in order is Archbishop Henry D' Souza of Calcutta, now emeritus, but who intervened in my favor well before the time of his resignation—a detail which is not irrelevant, as often only retired bishops have the courage or the possibility to speak out. As soon as he heard about my being challenged by the CDF, Archbishop Henry D'Souza wrote me a beautiful letter, dated November 13, 1998, which was soon put on the Internet and went round the world; it was printed by, among other journals, *Jivan* (January 1999). He wrote:

> Dear Father Dupuis, I am seriously concerned over the news that you are under investigation by the Congregation for the Doctrine of the Faith. I could hardly believe the news when I was informed. . . . Well, I do not think you will have much difficulty in explaining your position. However, I am worried about the fall-out. No theologian will want to write his thoughts, if this is the approach. He who steals my purse steals trash; he who steals my name steals all I have. . . . You have been known for your orthodoxy and steady pursuit of theological reflection in conformity with the Church's teaching. It is a pity that you have had to stop teaching in order to defend yourself. I am seriously reflecting on all these events. On the one hand, there is a reaffirmation of enculturation and the need to be open to God's presence in the world and in other faiths and the teaching of other

religions. And on the other hand, there is a fear that any thought which would not be stated in the same words as in the past becomes suspect. . . . Anyway I wanted to say these few words of encouragement. You remain in my prayers. Perhaps we have to pray also for those who still build walls around the faith and rob it of the rich insights which it can get from the sharing and interchange with the Spirit's presence outside. With warm regards, Henry.

I have thought it worthwhile to quote this letter at length as it testifies not only to a warm friendship, but also to a rare sincerity and willingness to risk oneself for a cause.

After the publication of the Notification about my book by the Congregation, Archbishop Henry supported strongly the publication of an Indian edition of the book. When this edition came out (Gujarat: Gujarat Sahitya Prakash, 2001) it carried a Foreword by him in which he wrote: "I am really pleased to write a few lines as a foreword to the Indian edition of the book of Fr. Jacques Dupuis. I am particularly happy to do so after the Notification of the Congregation for the Doctrine of the Faith has cleared the book from the original concern that it contained "serious errors against essential elements of Divine and Catholic Faith. . . ." It is my belief that Fr. Dupuis has contributed very abundantly for further research, reflection and understanding in the field of interreligious dialogue. His book is a pioneering effort in the new and complex issues of religious pluralism." Later still, Archbishop Henry contributed a piece to the Festschrift which is being offered to me on the occasion of my eightieth birthday (1923-2003).

Next to be mentioned is Cardinal Franz König, archbishop emeritus of Vienna, Austria. A truly surprising article signed by him under the title "In defense of Fr. Dupuis" appeared in the *Tablet* of January 16, 1999, 76-77. The article stated:

I have been fascinated by Fr. Jacques Dupuis's latest master-work, *Toward a Christian Theology of Religious Pluralism*. I studied it intently for several weeks. . . . I was therefore all the more surprised to learn . . . that, without consulting Fr. Dupuis directly, the Congregation for the Doctrine of the Faith has sent him a number of questions via the Jesuit General, Fr. Kolvenbach, asking him to clarify certain points in his book, concerning, it would seem, his doctrine of Christ. . . . I can well imagine how heavily it must weigh even upon such a distinguished professor of Christology as Dupuis. Moreover, for the general public such a move on the part of the Congregation

for the Doctrine of the Faith sounds the alarm. It implies that something about Fr. Dupuis's book is not in order, and that the Congregation may well suspect him of directly or indirectly violating the
Church's teaching.

He added:

> The case in hand . . . is surely a sign, an indication, that mistrust, sus-
> picion and disapproval are being prematurely spread about an author
> who has the highest intentions, and has earned himself great merits
> in the service of the Catholic Church. . . . The members of the Con-
> gregation, most of whom are Westerners, are, of course, very much
> afraid that interreligious dialogue will reduce all religions to equal
> rank. But that is the wrong approach for dialogue with the East-
> ern religions. It is reminiscent of colonialism, and smacks of arro-
> gance. . . . As an emeritus bishop of the Church it is not my function
> to give the doctrinal congregation advice. But I cannot keep silent,
> for my heart bleeds when I see such obvious harm being done to the
> common good of God's Church. In tackling this exceedingly dif-
> ficult terrain, Dupuis is trying to steer a course in close conjunction
> with the Church and with papal documents as his basic orienta-
> tion. He is a theologian who always first asks: "What is the Church's
> teaching and intention?"

The cardinal concluded:

> I am convinced that slow and very careful moves are called for. The
> Congregation for the Doctrine of the Faith has moved too fast too
> soon. . . . As a bishop of the Church who has studied the subject
> of interreligious dialogue for decades, I very much hope that the
> Congregation will find better ways of tackling these all-important
> issues and will proceed with the greatest composure and not be over-
> anxious. For, on the threshold of the third millennium, these are the
> very issues that are decisive for the Church's destiny.

I have again quoted at length, given the high qualification and authority of the author in a field which has concerned him during his long career,
but also because of the extreme wisdom and straightforwardness with
which he treats the matter. The reactions to his intervention have been
most instructive. Some thought that the cardinal had just come forward
to defend a personal friend. But I had never met Cardinal König person-

ally before, nor had any personal dealings with him. As a matter of fact, though I phoned him to thank him for his support, we still have not met as I write, even though a generous cousin of mine has offered me the plane fare to visit Cardinal König in Vienna. I still hope this visit may take place one day. Others suspected that Fr. O'Collins had written the piece, which was then attributed to the cardinal to be covered by his authority. There is no limit to where imagination can go to justify a bad cause.

Cardinal Ratzinger was offended by the intervention of Cardinal König. A rejoinder was published in the *Tablet* of March 13, 1999, under the rubric "Cardinal Ratzinger replies." It was an open letter sent by him to Cardinal König which he requested the *Tablet* to publish. He pleaded that the Congregation had simply "wanted to consult (Fr. Dupuis) personally, to be assisted by his own interpretation of the book." He wrote:

> Since our action consisted simply in sending some confidential questions to Fr. Dupuis and nothing more than this, I fail to understand your statement that our attempt at dialogue implies that the Congregation "may well suspect him of directly or indirectly violating the Church's teaching." He asked with irony: "Is dialogue with authors to be forbidden to us? Is the attempt to reach confidential clarification on difficult questions something evil? Is it not rather a way of striving to serve in a positive way the further development of faith and theology? You will understand from these questions that I find it unjust and damaging when you state that you cannot keep silent when you see such obvious harm being done to the common good of God's church, which is to say, by our attempt at dialogue."

And, pushing irony further, he added: "May I ask you to read once again the encyclical *Redemptoris missio* (on the question of dialogue) which forms the foundation of our letter?" The cardinal concluded: "You will not be offended if I conclude by saying that perhaps it was not the Congregation, but Your Eminence, who, with your article, has written 'too fast too soon.'"

There would be much to comment on the cardinal's concept of "dialogue," in view of the accusations of "grievous errors against the Divine and Catholic Faith" contained in the first document which he had forwarded to me about the book through Fr. Kolvenbach on September 26, 1998.

The exchange between the two cardinals created a sensation, some papers commenting "Cardinals Take Sides in Battle of the Book" or "Cardinals Duel on Religious Pluralism." This did not prevent Cardinal

König from publishing another piece in the *Tablet* (April 7, 2001): 483-84, under the title "Let the Spirit Breathe." He referred to the book as "a pioneering achievement in the new and complex issues of religious pluralism." He further retraced with remarkable accuracy the development of the procedure against it and the genesis of the Notification, published in its third version on February 26, 2001. He went on to say: "It is evident from the way the Notification came into being that the CDF is experiencing difficulties with its procedural mechanisms." He made four points of criticism: 1. "It is shocking that Dupuis was informed of the CDF investigation by his Superior General and not approached directly." 2. "It was moreover too soon for an investigation. The book had been published only nine months before and interreligious dialogue is a relatively new, complicated and most important subject." 3. "No specific passages of the book were quoted. The CDF's accusations applied to the book as a whole." 4. "The human aspect . . . is perhaps the most important shortcoming of all. The CDF deals not only with books but also with their authors who are human beings, in this case with a distinguished theologian who taught at a renowned university and had pledged himself to fidelity to the church's teaching authority. The CDF hurt Fr. Dupuis deeply and the shock he received led to ill-health and depression, albeit, one hopes, only temporarily. . . . The Congregation has neglected the human aspect, ignoring the deep hurt it has caused, all of which could have been avoided had it adopted a different approach. No one loses authority just because they are courteous." He concluded, with respect to the christological question which is at the center of the debate: "Fr. Dupuis has always clearly confessed Jesus Christ as the Son of God and universal savior. But this very confession—as is the case also with Pope John Paul II—encourages him to seek and acknowledge the active presence of Christ and of the Holy Spirit in the religions and cultures of the world." I can only express my deep-felt thanks to Cardinal König for his far-sighted views and his courageous writing. It is in order to do just this that I have dedicated to him all the editions of my last book, published so far in Italian, French, English, and Spanish (2001-2002).

Next to be mentioned is the declaration made by the South Asian Jesuit provincials "in defense of their theologians." The declaration was signed by Fr. Lisbert D'Souza, provincial of India, for the Jesuit major superiors of South Asia. It was published in, among other reviews, *Adista* (March 29, 1999): 2-4, and in *Jivan* (April 1999): 5. The declaration is restrained and dignified, but plain and outspoken. In the context of the need for enculturation and interreligious dialogue of the local church called for by Vatican II, it states: "We appreciate, support and encourage the work of our theologians and others to build up the local Church in India and we want them to go even further and deeper, in fidelity to Christ and to the mission he has entrusted to us in the Church." With explicit reference to the case of Fr. Anthony D'Mello (about whom the *Osservatore Romano* had recently published a Notification by the CDF with strong accusations against his writings, ten years after his death) and my own case (with the proceedings initiated by the contestation of my book by the CDF well on the way), the declaration regrets the "atmosphere of suspicion, not to say mistrust, created by recent decisions of the Congregation for the Doctrine of the Faith." About my own case it states: "Jacques Dupuis taught theology for over twenty years in India. His quest for a theology of religious pluralism is marked, both by his experience of the interreligious situation in South Asia, and his loyalty to the doctrinal, magisterial and theological tradition of the Church." The declaration goes on to state:

> We think that there is a lack of appreciation of difference and of proper procedures, when decisions are taken unilaterally without a dialogue with the Asian churches. We are afraid that such interventions are eventually detrimental to the life of the Church, to the cause of the Gospel and to the task of interpreting the Word to those who do not belong to the Western tradition. We are grateful for the appreciation and support our theologians in Asia have received from many Bishops and the People of God in Asia and the world. . . . We would like to assure our theologians of our own continued support and encouragement to go ahead, joyfully and in fidelity to God, to the Gospel and to the Church, with the difficult task of making the Word of God relevant to the situation in South Asia.

The professed support of the major Jesuit superiors of India and South Asia was for me a precious encouragement. I was especially sensitive to the fact that, even though I had left India fifteen years earlier, they still considered me as one among "their theologians."

Last but not least—in fact, foremost—I ought to mention here the strong support throughout the proceedings about my case at the CDF that I received from Fr. Peter-Hans Kolvenbach, our superior general. Ever since the Congregation decided to challenge my book on June 10, 1998—a decision communicated to Father General on September 26 and by him to me on October 2—I have had any number of opportunities to meet personally with Father General, to discuss matters with him and ask for his advice. I always found in him a deep interest for my case, a sincere sympathy for a fellow Jesuit, a very sound judgment, and a marked appreciation for the cause I was defending. Father Kolvenbach had his own quiet way of dealing with the authorities of the CDF, and I have no doubt that the softening down of the measures eventually taken against me are to a great extent due to his intervention. I have recalled above his short but decisive intervention at the sad meeting of September 4, 2000, with the authorities of the Congregation.

Later, on the very day the Notification on my book was published on February 26, 2001, in *L'Osservatore Romano*, Fr. Kolvenbach sent through the Internet to the whole Society of Jesus a statement to be brought to the notice of all members of the Society. Here I cannot do otherwise than quote in full the text of a statement which is as courageous as it is cautious. It runs as follows:

> With the Notification just published by the Congregation for the Doctrine of the Faith, a long and important inquiry has ended. The book of Fr. Jacques Dupuis, professor emeritus at the Pontifical Gregorian University, which has been justly recognized for the seriousness of its methodological research, the richness of the scientific documentation, and the originality of its exploration, dares to venture into a dogmatically fundamental area for the future of interreligious dialogue. The Notification itself recognizes the intent and efforts of Fr. Jacques Dupuis to remain within the teaching of the Catholic Faith as enunciated by the Magisterium. In line with the orientations of the document *Dominus Iesus,* the Notification clearly establishes the limits of this teaching to which the author has tried to adhere, even if he has not always succeeded. Thus the Notification helps the reader to interpret the book according to the doctrine of the Church. On this solidly established dogmatic basis we hope that Fr. Jacques Dupuis can continue his pioneer research in the field of interreligious dialogue which in his recent apostolic letter *Novo millennio ineunte,* John Paul II encourages as a challenge for the evangelization in the third millennium.

This statement has been for me a most precious support, and greatly encouraged me to forge ahead with my work with courage, trust, and dedication.

G.O'C.: *Thank you, Father, for this precious information about the "reception" which your book has met with, on the part of theologians, and more importantly of superiors. At this stage I would like to go back to the very beginning. Would you, please, tell us what prompted you to write the book* Toward a Christian

Theology of Religious Pluralism *which caused you so much trouble? What is the central theme of the book and the main questions it seeks to address?*

J.D.: I felt an almost physical compulsion to write this book. I had already written in French in 1989, on the request of Msgr. Joseph Doré, the director of the collection "Jésus et Jésus-Christ" in Paris, a first book concerned with the theology of religions, entitled *Jésus-Christ à la rencontre des religions* (Paris: Desclée, 1989; repr., 1994). An English edition of that book was published by Orbis Books in 1991, with a second printing in 1993, under the title *Jesus Christ at the Encounter of World Religions.* Italian and Spanish editions followed. I mention this to show that the topic of the theology of religions, and in particular the christological aspect of the issue, has been with me for a long time.

How could it be otherwise? I lived thirty-six years in India, twenty-five of which were spent teaching Christology and wrestling with the ever more searching questions which over the years the students asked concerning the significance in God's providence of the religious traditions of their ancestors. Throughout all those years I was exposed to the religious reality of India, which constitutes for us a deep challenge. When I first went to India in 1948, I carried with me, together with my own faith convictions, the prejudices of our Western civilization and culture, and the persuasion that as Christians we possess a monopoly over the truth. I thought I had all to give, and nothing to receive. My first assignment in Calcutta was at the high school department of Saint Xavier's College, where I came into contact with over one thousand schoolboys, the vast majority of whom were, as we used to say in those days, "non-Christians." I was struck as much by the intellectual capacity of those students as by their high moral standard and spiritual excellence. They seemed to have all the natural and supernatural virtues. The question inevitably came to my mind: From where do they derive such rich spiritual endowments? And the answer imposed itself: the religious traditions to which they and their families belonged and which they practiced earnestly had something to do with it. Similar questions arose, provoked by so many human contacts of which daily life was made up. They amounted to asking in very simple terms the question of the significance of the religious traditions in the order of human worth and salvation.

The study of theology which followed and, even more, the years of teaching Christology in close contact with students preparing for the priestly ministry, whose minds were engaged with similar problems, made the questioning much more acute. I can say that throughout my career as a teacher I have been concerned with the theology of religions, which then became a theological topic in its own right. Gradually I came to realize that, while as Christians we have something infinitely precious to share with the "others," we also have to receive from them; indeed, that before talking we must listen, and that it is more precious and important to receive than to give—even if it is more difficult!

The 1989 book referred to above represented a first attempt to reflect in the direction of a theology of religions. Even though that book remained limited in scope, it already proposed "theocentric christology" as a model adapted for such a Christian theology. However, it eventually dawned upon me—with the pressing invitation of publishing houses helping in the process—that a more thorough treatment of the question was called for. I recall Fr. Rosino Gibellini of the Queriniana Publishing House, Brescia, asking me over the phone for a new book which would be a more thoroughgoing treatment of the matter. He described the book he was contemplating as being made up of two parts: one historical, in which the theological understanding of the religions by the church and the attitudes of Christians toward their members over the centuries would be examined; a second part, if not systematic, at least synthetic, would have to study the main theological questions which are raised, especially today in the age of dialogue, by the meeting of Christianity with other religions. I first resisted the invitation, stating that I had already contributed a volume on the topic, in which I thought I had said what I had to say. Eventually, I was persuaded that the project was worthwhile and ventured into writing a new book on the matter. It followed the plan which had been suggested to me. *Toward a Christian Theology of Religious Pluralism* was originally written in English and, as has been recalled here earlier, published almost simultaneously in Italian, English, and French, in October 1997.

You ask me about the main questions which I addressed in this book. It came up earlier in our conversations. However, at the risk of partly repeating myself, let me state the case once more rapidly. Since the time of Vatican II the theology of religions had been on the front stage of theological research. Radical questions were asked with regard to the relationship which obtained between Christianity and the other religious traditions. Contrary, even contradictory, positions confronted each other. The problematic of the question had also evolved. It no longer consisted in merely asking whether salvation in Jesus Christ is attainable for the "non-Christians," not even in inquiring whether the other religious traditions may contain authentic human, natural or supernatural, values. It consisted in asking what positive significance Christian theology could attribute to the other religions in the overall divine plan of salvation for humankind. Did the plurality of religions with which we are familiar today have a place in God's eternal design for the world? Was it then legitimate to speak of a religious pluralism of principle, contained in God's eternal plan of salvation? The theology of religions was becoming a theology of religious pluralism, or even an interreligious theology.

In this context my book assumed the double task mentioned above: that of tracing the problematic of the question over the centuries while facing squarely the heavily contentious record of Christian official doctrine and attitudes, and that of attempting a new approach which would allow for more positive solutions to the questions involved. Was God's personal revelation confined merely to the Judeo-Christian tradition, or did it embrace the entire history of humankind? Could then a divine revelation be recorded in the Sacred Books of other religious traditions? Similarly, was God's personal saving action toward the human race to be traced exclusively to his becoming man in Jesus Christ and, specifically, to the mystery of his death and resurrection; or was it also to be assigned to a universal action of the Word of God and of the Spirit of God through the centuries? And, consequently, could God be thought to have done saving deeds also through the founders of other religious traditions, of which these traditions would contain traces? And if so, could those traditions be said to propose today authentic ways or paths of salvation to their followers? These were searching questions which allowed no easy answer. In trying to solve them, the book proposed as a "hermeneutical key" (a key of interpretation) a "trinitarian and pneumatic Christology" which would allow us, while professing without any ambiguity the personal identity of Jesus Christ as Son of God, to recognize a positive significance of the other religious traditions in God's one design of salvation for humankind. In order to be truly Christian, an interreligious theology ought to combine, in fruitful tension, the original uniqueness of the Christ-event with the universal ambit of God's personal dealings and involvement with humankind. This is the challenge which such a theology has to face and which my book hoped to meet in some, no doubt tentative and imperfect, manner.

G.O'C.: *You have referred briefly above to the decision taken by an Ordinary Assembly of the CDF, held on June 10, 1998, to challenge your book. Could you tell us more about the background of that decision? Who brought your book to their attention? How many times did they discuss it before coming to their decision? Who was present at the meeting?*

J.D.: I have no direct information on these points. I can only say what I have heard from reliable sources speaking spontaneously without my asking them. I do not know where the denunciation of my book came from, though I know of various possibilities. It has been suggested by some that it came from inside the Gregorian University, but I have refrained from speculating on this, as it would only have made the burden heavier to carry. The Ordinary Assembly of the Congregation, held on June 10, 1998, was preceded by a meeting of the consultors of the Congregation, which resulted in a negative assessment of the book which was then communicated to the members (members of the Congregation include only cardinals and bishops). The letter of Cardinal Ratzinger, dated September 26, which was communicated to me through my Father General on October 2, 1998, spoke of only one meeting of the consultors which preceded that of the members in which the decision was taken. Father General himself had been requested to attend the meeting of the consultors. I was of course totally unaware of both meetings, until I received a copy of the letter of Cardinal Ratzinger stating the decision taken by the Congregation. Meanwhile, before October 2, when I was told what was happening to me, I was blissfully unconcerned and living in my innocent simplicity.

As I was not suspecting anything, I was engaged with my regular activities, including giving lectures and conferences. Just a week before October 2, on September 25, I spent a whole day here in Rome with a group of bishops from England who had come for their *ad limina* visit, and spoke to them on "The Evangelizing Mission of the Church in a Pluralistic Context." Cardinal Basil Hume was present and I had very friendly exchanges with him. I found the English bishops very receptive and enjoyed a full day of discussion with them on a subject at the center of my own interests, but which is also central to their own concerns in the cosmopolitan context of Britain.

Present at the meeting of the consultors, which took place before the decision by the Ordinary Assembly of the Congregation on June 10, there will have been those resident in Rome (whose names can be found in the *Annuario Pontificio* for 1998), though one of them—Msgr. Marcello Bordoni of the Lateran University, if I may mention his name—told me that he had never been consulted on my case or called to any meeting at which it was discussed. Consultors to be consulted were carefully selected! In his latest book at the time, *La cristologia nell'orizzonte dello Spirito* (Brescia: Queriniana, 1995), Msgr. Bordoni had quoted from me profusely and with approval. It may be mentioned that four professors of the Gregorian University were at that time consultors of the Congregation (K. Becker, B. Kiely, R. Fisichella, L. Ladaria). Also consultors were Fr. G. Pelland, then rector of the Oriental Institute, and Fr. A. Vannoye, of the Biblical Institute. I know for sure that at least three from the

Gregorian attended the meeting. I have also been told by Fr. K. Becker that Rino Fisichella, who later became auxiliary bishop of the Diocese of Rome and rector of the Lateran University, had been the most strongly negative about my book.

The *Agendi Ratio* for the examination of doctrine foresees that one consultor is appointed by the cardinal prefect to speak at the meeting "in favor of" the accused, *pro auctore*, that is "for the defense"; this appointment is of course done without any reference to the accused. One may speculate about who in my case was assigned that job, and with what conviction he will have done it. I think I know who it was. Father Karl Becker of the Gregorian, who incidentally has by now been consultor of the Congregation for eighteen years—against the rules of the Vatican which foresee appointments for five years, with the possibility of being confirmed for another five years, but no more—came to visit me once, claiming that, contrary to a rumor according to which he was responsible for denouncing me to the Congregation, he in fact took my defense at the meeting of consultors. This only makes sense by supposing that he was appointed by the cardinal prefect to speak *pro auctore*, that is, in my defense. But that also raises questions about the way and the conviction with which Becker would have fulfilled this task, if one recalls how his theology is at the antipodes from mine, especially in the matter at issue. Becker is satisfied with the Council of Trent's doctrine on the "baptism of desire" and the theology of the "salvation of infidels," while I claim to go somewhat beyond that! All this confirms what I said earlier about the parody of justice at work in the CDF's proceedings. However, these last pieces of information remain somewhat conjectural.

Yet, I may mention that the letter of Cardinal Ratzinger speaks of only one Ordinary Assembly of the Congregation, that of June 10 at which the decision to contest was taken. Since it was an Ordinary Assembly, only the members residing in Rome will have been present; the composition of the meeting can therefore be guessed more or less, by consulting the *Annuario Pontificio* for 1998. I know of some cardinals being present who had previously declared themselves openly against the book. One apparently admitted having voted in favor of the Contestation without having read the book. It is clear that most of the cardinals present had little knowledge of the issues involved and relied somewhat blindly on the report which had been communicated to them in which the consultors' opinions were reported. More on this remains enshrined in secrecy.

G.O'C.: *When Cardinal Ratzinger sent a letter to Fr. Kolvenbach, informing him of the Congregation's decision to proceed with the Contestation, did* *the news come like a thunderbolt out of the blue to the Father General, or did he have some hint that all was not well before receiving the letter? Did Father General call you immediately to tell you the bad news, or how did you learn about the contents of the letter? Where did you receive the news? What did the person who gave you the news say?*

J.D.: I have already partly responded to these questions. I have mentioned that Father General had been invited to be present at the consultors' meeting. From the outcome of this meeting he must obviously have sensed that a problem was in the offing. He of course did not share with me his apprehension at that time, and, as far as I know, between June and September he remained in the dark regarding the decision of the Congregation. He came to know about it through the cardinal's letter of September 26. Father General did not call me immediately. As I have stated above, he sent me a copy of the letter and of the documents attached through the rector of the Gregorian. Father Franco Imoda, the newly appointed rector of the university, was at that time undergoing medical treatment in Chicago, before taking up office. Father Francisco Javier Egaña, vice rector of the university and superior of the community of the Gregorian, was acting rector. It is he who called me to his office on October 2 to give me the news and to hand over to me a copy of the documents. I must mention that Fr. Egaña showed from the start great sympathy and understanding, an attitude which he would continue to show all through the proceedings and beyond—for which I am extremely grateful. On that day he witnessed the shock which I experienced as I was suddenly and most unexpectedly made aware of what was happening to me. There followed a long friendly conversation in which we exchanged feelings and reactions. On the same day Fr. Egaña addressed to me a long letter in which he expressed again all his sympathy and fraternal support.

As for Father General, when soon after receiving the news of the Contestation I asked to meet him, he immediately received me. He also showed much solicitude and sympathy. I wanted to know what to make of the case, what was the meaning of the restrictions imposed upon me by the Congregation, how I should react to them, how I should go about answering the Congregation's questions within the three months allowed and under top secrecy. It is during that conversation that the decision was taken to have my course at the Gregorian cancelled, with the consequences to which I have referred earlier. This was the first of many meetings which I have had since with Father General, who followed the case with constant concern throughout and whose advice never failed me. Fathers Kolvenbach and Egaña are the two superiors whose support I felt throughout the process, and without whom I am not sure I would have been able to stand my ground.

G.O'C.: *You have made reference to the two documents which accompanied Cardinal Ratzinger's letter to Fr. Kolvenbach of September 26, 1998, with regard to the decision taken by the Congregation in the Ordinary Assembly of June 10 to initiate a Contestation against your book. Could you tell us what the two documents said? What were the questions being asked?*

J.D.: The first document reported the meeting, in which the decision was formulated and explained. I have already mentioned above the important part of that document which enumerated the accusations which were addressed to my book. There was no question of initiating a "dialogue" with me to look for clarifications—whatever claims to a "dialogue" Cardinal Ratzinger made later—but of straightforward accusations, under three categories, of grave errors against the faith, as well as against Catholic doctrine, and of dangerous affirmations and opinions not to be taught. The second document was a long list of questions, filling nine pages, which I was summoned to answer within three months, as I have mentioned earlier, under top secrecy. Let me give a rapid overview of those questions. They were divided into fourteen theses.

Thesis 1 was about theological method. It accused my combination of an inductive method with the traditional deductive method, of not doing justice to Scripture, Tradition, and the Magisterium as the *norma normans* of doing theology. Thesis 2 objected in the same vein to interreligious dialogue being called a "source" of theology, as if this meant to place it on a par with Scripture. Thesis 3 objected to the distinction which I made between the action of the *Logos asarkos* and that of the *Logos ensarkos,* as if I were affirming two distinct "economies" of salvation. Thesis 4 accused me further, while speaking of "distinction," of positing in fact a "separation" between the Word of God and Jesus, as if they represented two different persons. Thesis 5 objected to the affirmation that the revelation in Jesus Christ, though representing the "fullness" of revelation, is nevertheless to be considered "limited, incomplete, imperfect and complementary." Thesis 6 objected to the idea that, while Jesus Christ is the "constitutive" savior of humankind, he is not the "absolute" savior who is God himself. Similarly, thesis 7 objected to the idea that Jesus does not exhaust the saving power of God. Thesis 8 objected to the idea of a "relational uniqueness" of Jesus 'Christ as though this would imply that it needs to be complemented by other religious traditions. Thesis 9 claimed that there is no foundation in the Bible for calling the first person of the Trinity "Mother." Thesis 10 had to do with Trinitarian monotheism. I was accused, against the most formal affirmations of my book, of holding that the three monotheistic religions have the same concept of God. Thesis 11 had to do with covenant and covenants. It objected to the idea that the covenant with Noah, understood as representing God's covenant with the religious traditions of the nations, is not abolished but continues even after the advent of the New Covenant in Jesus Christ. Thesis 12 treated the "orientation of non-Christians to the Church." It claimed that in my book justice is not done to the "singular and unique relationship" which exists between the reign of God and the church. Thesis 13 had to do with the "eschatological fulfillment." It objected to the idea of an eschatological convergence in Jesus Christ of Christianity and the other religions as contradicting the biblical faith. Thesis 14 asked whether the "pluralistic paradigm" advocated in the book does not fall into a "dogmatic relativism" which in principle attributes to all the religious traditions an equivalent saving value. Strangely enough, no thesis alluded to the parallelism between Jesus and the Buddha which I make briefly in my book, even though in the first document this figured among the dangerous opinions which cannot be taught safely. This parallelism then fell by the wayside between the first and the second document.

G.O'C.: *What was your initial reaction after reading the letter and the two documents? How did you feel? What went through your mind? What did you eventually do? Did you speak to some of your fellow professors?*

J.D.: My first reaction was of deep distress, mixed with plain revolt. I had dedicated a great part of my life and spent all my energy trying to make sense of the faith on what had become the most vexing problem raised in recent years for the Christian message. I was now being engaged, not in a friendly dialogue seeking clarifications—whatever the interpretation of the procedure which the CDF gave later—but in a process which from the outset formulated against me the most serious accusations, including that of "grievous errors against the Divine and Catholic Faith." This was done in the most secretive manner, without my having been in any way contacted personally for explanations, and done with the pope's approval. The procedure employed looked like a parody of justice. For a full week I was just unable to regain my composure and think of the answers I should give to the questions of the Congregation. Eventually, I did sort out my mind and jotted down in the margins of the document bits of answers to be given.

I have mentioned earlier that I was allowed one theological adviser whose name had to be approved by Father General. I had no hesitation in choosing Fr. Gerald O'Collins, convinced as I was that on the staff of the Gregorian he was the only person from whom I could get sound advice and substantial help. However, Fr. O'Collins was then abroad, in the United States, and I had to write to ask whether he would be willing to advise me and eventually to go through my answers to the CDF. As he generously promised me his help, we exchanged drafts and comments by fax, till he returned and I could give the last shape to the pages which I sent in answer to the Congregation's questions. In the meantime, the case had become public with the note by the dean of the theological faculty posted in the hall of the university. The community of the professors had been informed by the superior about the investigation initiated by the Congregation. I did not speak to any of them about the case—I was not supposed to—neither did they raise questions with me about it. I may report, with regret, that throughout the case little support was shown at home. A small group did show sympathy and positive interest; another small group was strongly opposed to my cause and quite vocal against it; the vast majority seemed simply unconcerned and not interested. But this may have been due, in large part, to the fact that many found it difficult to approach me on the subject. By way of contrast much sympathy and concern came from outside and from abroad.

G.O'C.: *You have explained how you have been deprived of your last year of teaching at the Gregorian. Your lessons had always attracted many students. You had had a good relationship with the students and you had enjoyed teaching. Could you say what teaching meant to you and how you felt once you were deprived of it?*

J.D.: Teaching a special course on Christology and another on the theology of religions for the second cycle at the Gregorian was quite exciting. Though those courses were optional, they attracted every time two hundred and more students for the licentiate in theology, with the result that the lessons had to be held in the Aula Magna of the university. I always felt inspired by a large audience. I was happy to be able to share with the students the direction in which I thought a positive Christian evaluation of other religions could proceed, in full agreement with the church's faith in Jesus Christ, and what this would mean for the future of interreligious dialogue and the mission of the church. Teaching meant to me sharing with my audience the deepest convictions which I had developed through many years of reflection and, let me say it, of prayer. I used to look into the eyes of the students to read their reaction to what I was trying to get across with personal conviction. I always felt a great interest and a warm "reception" on their part. I have a specially clear remembrance of the long and loud standing ovation they gave me in the Aula Magna at the end of what would in fact turn out to be my last class at the university, though no one suspected it then. It was not planned to be my last course, since I was supposed to have another year of teaching—of which, as explained above, I was deprived. In retrospect it looks as though the students had a presentiment that this was in fact going to be my last performance, and had wanted to greet it with generous applause. Incidentally, I may mention that a well-intentioned colleague on the staff suggested to the academic authorities of the university that I should be granted an extra year of teaching after I reached my seventy-five years, in compensation for the year of teaching of which I had been deprived. The suggestion was not accepted, and ever since the end of my 1997-1998 course I no longer had any opportunity to speak in public at the university. Henceforth, I could only give lectures outside.

G.O'C.: *When the news of your being questioned by the Congregation became public, many journalists, including myself, made it known to the general public by writing stories in various magazines and papers. How did you feel about this and what did you think about the way the matter was being reported? What reactions did you get from outside as the news came to spread all over the world?*

J.D.: Quite frankly, I was happy about it, though I had never anticipated that so much publicity would be given to my case. In a sense I myself was responsible for the case becoming known, since I had requested Father General that the real reason for my course being cancelled be communicated to the students. I did not want to give false reasons or make sheer pretexts for the cancellation of the course, and thought the CDF had no right to force me to tell lies in explanation. Father General took it on himself to allow the true reason for the cancellation of the course to be communicated to the students; this, as mentioned above, was done through an official notice. This way of proceeding has been commented upon in the press as a rare, commendable act of sincerity and courage. I personally was happy that the case was made public, no matter which consequences would ensue, for I thought it better for truth to be said and to be known rather than being kept secret by an imposition of silence on the part of the prosecution, as a way of cover and self-protection. Enough secrecy would in any case continue to be imposed for a long time. The coverage and comments made in the press by journalists have been overwhelmingly sympathetic to my cause and almost universally positive. They of course were mostly concerned with the procedure being used by the Congregation, which they almost unanimously condemned; as for the content of the case they had no direct information to rely upon, and could give only some hints of the theological problems involved.

From outside and from abroad I received an enormous number of messages of sympathy and encouragement; indeed so many that it was impossible to answer them, engaged as I was in writing my response to the Congregation's questioning. I would like to express here my heartfelt thanks to so many individual persons and institutions from whom and from which all that support came. They included cardinals and bishops, an impressive number of bishops from India, theologians from all over the world, including some like Hans Küng and Paul Collins who had had themselves painful dealings with the CDF, many friends, old and young, from the Society of Jesus, ex-students from all over the world, and even many persons whom I did not remember having met personally. To the letters and messages of good will, let me add the many visits which I received from theologians passing through Rome; among these I am especially sensitive to those of fellow theologians who have themselves suffered at the hands of the CDF, such as Gustavo Gutiérrez, Jon Sobrino, Tissa Balasuriya, and others.

One Indian cardinal, who did not want his name to be revealed—and therefore I will not mention it—sent me confidentially a copy of a personal letter which he wrote in my defense to Cardinal Ratzinger. He informed the cardinal that from the personal knowledge he had had of me and of my writings, as well as from the way I dealt with the Indian and Asian bishops in conferences at which I delivered a keynote address and at which my opinion and advice was sought and appreciated, he could testify to my constant intention to abide by the faith and be faithful to the doctrine of the church. He could not hide his dismay at the proceedings launched against me by the Congregation and expressed his hope that all would be well.

Among so many messages of sympathy I wish to put on record in a special manner those which were sent collectively by theological faculties and other institutions, bearing the signature of the members of the institution. Among these let me mention the Weston Jesuit School of Theology, Cambridge, Massachusetts, in the United States, the Dialogue Interreligieux Monastique, Commission Francophone d'Europe, the Calcutta Jesuit Theology Forum, and the Provincial Congregation of 1999 of the Calcutta Jesuit Province to which I belonged and continue to belong even to this day. Often these messages made reference to the fidelity to the faith which they had always witnessed in me and to the deep love which even now I was showing, by my way of reacting, for a church at whose hands I was being made to suffer. I was overwhelmed by so many marks of sympathy and discovered that I had many more friends around the world than I ever thought.

G.O'C.: *When, after the initial shock, you sat down and studied the questions raised by the Congregation, how did you rate those questions? What did they reveal to you? And what did your theological adviser, Fr. Gerald O'Collins, who was bound by the same secrecy as you were, think about them?*

J.D.: I may say that both of us shared much the same opinion from the start. Not all the questions were equally intelligent, to say the least, or showed an open and deep understanding on the part of the drafter or drafters. Let me make two examples of especially surprising questions. I was requested to justify speaking of the first person of the divine Trinity as Father-Mother. The contention was that there was no foundation whatever in divine revelation to refer to the Father as Mother. Yet, it was clear that the First Testament attributes to YHWH—who later would be referred to as the Father of Jesus—motherly as well as fatherly attributes and attitudes. I could quote Pope John Paul I, who before the recitation of the Angelus on September 10, 1978, declared: "God is a father; more than that he is a mother" (see *Insegnamenti di Giovanni Paolo II* [Vatican City: Libreria Editrice Vaticana, 1979], 61-62). I went on to explain that our knowledge of God, even revealed, is analogical and that God possesses simultaneously, in an eminent and infinite manner, all the positive qualities which find themselves distinctly realized between the sexes among humans. This was pretty plain theology.

The other example is where I was pulled up for drawing at different points in my book a parallel between Jesus and the Buddha. This seemed to the Congregation to be altogether unheard of and blasphemous. Yet the Christian Tradition abounds in similar parallels, between Jesus and Socrates, for instance. Celsus had compared the self-composure of Socrates as he was faced with death and was compelled to drink poison with the apparent collapse of Jesus in the Garden of Gethsemane and his sense of being abandoned by God on the cross. This, to Celsus, proved the superiority of the first over the second in human worth and dignity. The Fathers of the church, Origen to begin with, had to rectify the situation by showing the supreme human countenance of Jesus and his abiding closeness to his God even in the mystery of his death. Closer to us, had not Romano Guardini contributed a beautiful book on *The Humanity of Christ* (New York: Pantheon Books, 1964), in which he showed Jesus to be divinely human and humanly divine in comparison with other great human figures—whose dignity and loftiness need not, however, be underestimated in the process? As for myself I did not see what should prevent me from pointing to similar traits present in both Jesus and the Buddha, the differences notwithstanding—provided the root cause for the differences which showed up in their respective attitudes was correctly traced to the unique consciousness Jesus had of his personal identity as the Son of God, contrasting with the agnostic attitude of the Buddha with regard to the existence and nature of an Infinite Being.

Other questions revealed a disturbing misrepresentation and misinterpretation of my text, as when I was accused of "separating" the Word of God from Jesus, thereby construing them as two different persons. Or else they showed a plain misreading of what I wrote, as when I was reproached for attributing the same concept of God to the three monotheistic religions, where I affirmed that all three monotheistic religions trace their faith to the God of Abraham and thus have the same God, even while they hold vastly different concepts of that same God.

G.O'C.: *You were asked to hand in your response to the questions within three months. Could you explain briefly what you wrote?*

J.D.: It is not easy to summarize the 188 pages which I sent to the Congregation, signed on December 25. I can only indicate briefly the direction of my response to the various questions, which followed in fact the order of the fourteen "theses" sent to me by the Congregation, as they have been indicated here above. For each thesis my response consisted of two parts: (1) some observations on the quotations made from my book or the references to the same; (2) answer to the questions. In the first part I showed that often quotations and references were made out of context or given a meaning not intended by me; in the second part I refuted the accusations made against me, based as they were on misquotations and misinterpretations. Let me show this rapidly for each thesis in order.

About thesis 1 on inductive method, I answered by stating that the word of God must in all circumstances be interpreted in a specific context, which does not mean reducing Scripture to some kind of mere "control station"; the revealed word of God remains the *norma normans*. Thesis 2 follows up on thesis 1: I explained that obviously one may not put interreligious dialogue on a par with Scripture as the "originating source" of theology, as I was accused of doing. But it remains true that theological reflection is never built in a contextual vacuum and that a changing context may require a new interpretation of the revealed word.

Thesis 3 charged the distinction which I made between the action of the "Word-non-incarnate" and that of the "Word incarnate" with implying the affirmation of two different persons. To dissipate all ambiguity, I suggested distinguishing the Word *as such* from the Word as incarnate; it would be grotesque to accuse me of holding two different Words in the mystery of God, and consequently four persons in the Trinity. But there remains the fact that the New Testament itself, the Prologue of the Gospel of John in particular, postulates the distinction which I am making. Thesis 4 follows on thesis 3. I was accused of introducing a "separation" between the Word as such and the Word incarnate, resulting in the Nestorian thesis of a distinction of persons between the Word of God and the man Jesus. To show this, the text of the thesis substituted for the term "distinction," which I used constantly in this context, the term "separation." This of course makes all the difference; as for the need to distinguish really between the Word as such and the man Jesus it is required by the christological dogma itself.

Thesis 5 on "Christian revelation limited, incomplete, imperfect and complementary" accused me of contradicting what Vatican Council II affirms regarding divine revelation in Jesus Christ. I answered that the "fullness" of divine revelation in Jesus Christ must be correctly understood: it does not and cannot imply that the mystery of God is exhaustively contained in it, which would contradict the New Testament itself. No transposition takes place of the divine knowledge to the human intellect and consciousness of Jesus, which is the direct source of the divine revelation which we receive through him. To think otherwise would lead to some kind of monophysitism which consists always in affirming in one way or another mixing or confusion between the two natures of Jesus. As for the "complementarity" which may exist between Christian revelation and other revelation, it also needs to be correctly understood. It is not in any way to be understood as undermining the uniqueness and transcendence of the revelation which takes place in Jesus, based as this is on his unique relationship to the Father as Son. It remains true, nevertheless, that other revelation may emphasize real aspects of the mystery of God less prominently in evidence in the Christian revelation; in virtue of which, it is legitimate to speak of "mutual complementarity," adding, however—as I have clarified in more recent writing—that such complementarity is "asymmetrical." Thesis 6 objected to my saying that Jesus, though he is "universal savior," is not an "absolute" but "constitutive savior." This is a question of terminology. I criticize, along with many theologians today, the inflated talk of "absoluteness" which has cropped up in recent years with regard to Jesus and Christianity. Only God is absolute and should be considered as such, while Jesus' humanity is contingent and creaturely. To affirm that he is "constitutive savior" does not in fact take anything away from the universal saving significance of the Christ-event; what is constitutive is essential. It means that the Christ-event has truly universal significance for humankind.

Thesis 7, entitled "Jesus does not exhaust God's saving power," reproaches me for holding that the saving power of God is not exhaustively and exclusively contained in Jesus Christ. Yet, the saving action of the Word of God as such prior to the incarnation and the universal presence of the Spirit of God operative also before the incarnation of the Word in Jesus force us to hold that the humanity of Jesus is not the only channel of divine salvation. His humanity simply did not exist before the historical mystery of the incarnation, and therefore could not be then the channel of divine salvation. I further suggest, not without foundation in Scripture and Tradition, that a saving action of the Word as such and a vivifying action of the Spirit continue after the incarnation of the Son of God, beyond God's saving action through the humanity of Jesus. Thesis 8 objects to the uniqueness of Jesus being called "relational." The meaning of the expression, as I understand it, is that the uniqueness and universality of God's saving action in Jesus Christ must be viewed in the context of the overall divine saving plan of God for humankind, which is not confined to the Judeo-Christian tradition but extends to the entire history of salvation, starting with creation itself.

Thesis 9 has to do with my calling God "Father-Mother." I have already quoted Pope John Paul I saying that "God is a father; more than that he is a mother." I may add now that this has been confirmed by Pope John Paul II who in his catechesis of September 8, 1999, said with reference to the parable of the lost son: The hands of God are "the hands of a father and of a mother at the same time." And he explained: "The merciful father of the parable contains in himself all the characteristics of fatherhood and motherhood, and transcends them" (cf. the *Tablet* [September 18, 1999]: 1272). In a note after thesis 9 I answered the charge of construing a parallel between Jesus and the Buddha. This, which was mentioned in the first document attached to the letter of Cardinal Ratzinger, had fallen by the wayside in the second document. I reintroduced it in my response for completeness sake. I have already explained here that the comparison is made from within the Christian faith and traces the uniqueness of Jesus to his identity as the Son of God.

Thesis 10, entitled "The Identity of God," fears that by distinguishing a personal impact of each of the three divine persons in the mystery of salvation, I end up "separating them entirely," thereby holding "three different economies." Here we see the continuous confusion between "distinction" and "separation" returning. It should be clear that the two concepts are very different. And while it is true that the divine action in the world is common to the three persons, it is no less true that each of them contributes to it according to each person's specific character within the divine mystery. The same thesis accuses me of holding that the three monotheistic religions have the same "concept" of God, which, as I have already explained, contradicts explicitly what I have written: it is one thing to say that the three religions share the same God; it is another to hold that they have the same concept of that God!

Thesis 11 on "Covenant and Covenants" objected to the idea of the covenant with Noah being said to continue after the New and Eternal Covenant in Jesus Christ has been instituted. Representing as it does a "provisional economy," it should be said to be transitory. Yet this contradicts the affirmation made in the First Testament which speaks explicitly of God's covenant with Noah as an "eternal covenant," which of course does not contradict its orientation toward the New Covenant in Jesus Christ.

Thesis 12 on the orientation of "non-Christians" to the church accused me of undermining what the Second Vatican Council and other doctrinal pronouncements affirm on the matter. An orientation to the church must certainly be affirmed inasmuch as the church has received from Christ the "fullness of the means of salvation," which fullness is not available outside the church. It is also necessary to say that the church is universally united with Christ in the work of salvation. But this leaves intact the difficult question, open to different interpretations, of the way in which the church effects salvation in the case of persons not belonging to it as its members. I have suggested that in their case a universal explicit mediation of salvation on the part of the church remains a fervent hope for an unknown future. Meanwhile, what the religious traditions to which they belong contribute to their salvation must not be underestimated.

Thesis 13 dealt with "eschatological fulfillment." It objected to the idea of an eschatological convergence of Christianity and the other religions in the fullness of the kingdom of God and the *omega-Christ* in the eschaton. This idea would allegedly undermine the universal role of the church extending to the eschaton itself. But this position seems to forget that the church in history is entirely oriented to the reign of God, an orientation in virtue of which it is destined to merge into the fullness of the kingdom at the eschaton.

Thesis 14 tackled the question of "a pluralistic paradigm" for the theology of religions. It feared that such a paradigm leads necessarily to "dogmatic relativism." To affirm a religious pluralism of principle, by which is meant that the religions of the world have in themselves a positive significance in God's plan for humankind, would amount to denying (a) the uniqueness of Jesus Christ in whom alone all human beings can be saved and (b) the universal significance of Christianity in which they are destined to find salvation. However, a clear distinction ought to be made between two vastly different ways of conceiving a "religious pluralism of principle." One would hold that all the religions of the world have in principle the same potential for human salvation and that Christianity ought to abandon its pretense to a unique significance of Jesus Christ and the Christ-event. This is obviously contrary to the faith and cannot be sustained by any theologian calling himself a Christian. But the question still remains of the possibility of holding together, in a constructive tension, the church's faith in the uniqueness of Jesus Christ and a positive significance in God's plan for humankind of the other religious traditions and their saving potential for their followers—in close relationship, no doubt, to the Christ-event, in which the personal dealings of God with humankind culminate. Admittedly, holding fast to both these ends constitutes the challenge with which a Christian theology of religious pluralism is faced today; but the challenge cannot be dismissed either for fear of the consequences or out of sheer pusillanimity.

In the process of responding to the Congregation's questioning, in both the first and the second rounds, I have been led to clarify two points of terminology in order to avoid possible "ambiguities" of which I had been accused: one terminological clarification is where I substituted the term "Word of God as such" to that of "the Word of God non-incarnate" (*asarkos*) distinct from the Word of God incarnate (*ensarkos*) or, better, "as incarnate"; the other is where I have added the term "asymmetrical" to my affirmation of a "reciprocal complementarity" between Christianity and the other religions. For the rest I have held my ground everywhere and stated what I continued to believe, as I thought it my duty to do.

G.O'C.: *After you had submitted your response to the questions of the Congregation on December 25, 1998, did you receive an acknowledgment from Cardinal Ratzinger? What did he say? What followed after that? Could you tell me what it felt like as you waited for a reply from the CDF?*

J.D.: I have already mentioned that I had never met Cardinal Ratzinger before I was informed through a copy of his letter to Father General, dated September 26, 1998, of the proceedings started against my book. My only meeting with him would be that of September 4, 2000. I have never received, even to this day, a personal message from Cardinal Ratzinger. I have received only copies of his letters to Father General. I was thus left altogether in the dark about what was happening with my first long response to the questions of the CDF. The seven months that followed my response, till the next letter of Cardinal Ratzinger to Father General, dated July 27, 1999, were indeed very painful. For one thing my physical health suffered in the process. I did have several ailments, even a pulmonary thrombosis, and had to be taken to the hospital several times during the period. When he once met Cardinal Ratzinger while I was in hospital, Father General mentioned to him my state of health and my being in hospital at the time. The cardinal observed somewhat sarcastically: "So these problems have psychosomatic consequences." He neither manifested any sympathy nor asked Father General to convey to me his good wishes. To do this would have supposed a "Church with a Human Face" (see the editorial in *Vidyajyoti* [December 1998]: 887-89)—a thing which is not foreseen in the *Agendi Ratio* of the Congregation.

My state of health forced me to cancel some commitments for lectures abroad and to decline some invitations, including a long tour for lectures in Japan, India, and the Philippines, arranged for me by Fr. Adolfo Nicolas, the Jesuit provincial of Japan. Though I soon resumed lecturing both in Italy and abroad, I had, given the uncertainty caused by the complete silence on the part of the Congregation, to be very cautious in my lectures. Add the fact that I felt more and more a stranger in my own religious community, not to say alienated from it. I wondered how to interpret the silence that surrounded me, except for the handful of sympathizers whom I mentioned earlier. Was it that, not knowing how to tackle the subject, they chose to keep silent? Or did it show that the affair was simply no concern of theirs? I knew that I could not rely on much intellectual support at home, given the general tendency in theological and academic matters of the majority of my confreres and colleagues. The overall tone was a prudential conformism with official positions, allied with a determination not to become exposed to questioning.

In this context the burning questions of the day were best left untackled. I appeared out of tune with the current stand at the university, or even, in the mind of some, an embarrassment to the institution and a danger to its good reputation with the central doctrinal authority. Father Franco Imoda, the rector of the university, was primarily concerned with the reputation at the Vatican of the Gregorian University—a legitimate concern, no doubt; but in the process he seemed to give less weight than one would have wished to personal concern and interest for a confrere. I do not wish to draw too dark a picture of the situation. But this is certainly the way I felt during the seven months which followed my response to the Congregation. I must add that Fr. Egaña, my religious superior to whom I have referred earlier as being a great moral support, thought that my analysis of the situation was too severe. I wished he were right.

G.O'C.: *You heard nothing from Cardinal Ratzinger until Fr. Kolvenbach received a new letter from him on July 27, 1999. How did you receive the letter, and what did the letter say? What did you feel on receiving it?*

J.D.: The new letter of the cardinal to Fr. Kolvenbach was, like the previous one, sent to me by Father General himself. I have already mentioned that to this new letter of the cardinal one document was appended, containing a "doctrinal judgment" (*giudizio dottrinale*) of my book, filling eleven pages with new questions. Father General had met the cardinal on July 28, a meeting during which the cardinal handed him his letter of the previous day. On the very day of this meeting, Father General, while communicating to me the cardinal's letter and the attached *giudizio dottrinale,* addressed to me a long personal letter, written with his own hand, in which he gave me an account of his meeting with the cardinal. He insisted that "the cardinal has first stressed his esteem for your person and your theological work. For him there is no doubt that your work seeks nothing but the service of the church in the delicate field of interreligious dialogue. According to him the study of your book in no way seeks to destroy dialogue but to place it on the right track. . . . Next the cardinal expressed his thanks for the clarifications made in your response (to the Congregation's questions). These represent a true progress which marks an advance of theological reflection. This progress makes it possible to reduce the points still to be clarified to a precise number: they are contained in a summary of 11 pages." This referred to the eleven pages of the *giudizio dottrinale* which accompanied the letter of the cardinal. It was made clear that I was once more to answer the new questions within three months.

The cardinal suggested that I could do this by way of a short article published in some theological review, subject to the approval of the Congregation. Father General added in his letter: "After your short reaction (to the new questions), you have a right to a colloquy with the Congregation. As I asked whether the cardinal would take part himself in this colloquy, his answer was plainly negative: he does not feel technically capable of discussing the problem at that level." And again: "At the end the cardinal regretted that a theological discussion very important for the Church had taken the appearance of a process for condemnation. He is convinced of your concern to be faithful to the Magisterium of the Church while being creative on the subject."

There would be much in this letter to comment on. First, I note once more the personal interest and concern shown by Father General on my behalf. Next, I cannot help questioning the cardinal's intentions and contentions. If he was so sorry that the affair had taken the appearance of a condemnation, why, in the first place, was the accusation of "grievous errors against the faith Divine and Catholic" made from the start of the procedure in the document of June 10, 1998, under his authority? That the cardinal stated that he thinks himself unequipped to take part personally in a serious discussion on the matters involved raises the strong suspicion, which would be verified later, that he had not looked personally into the matter but simply went by the opinion of some of his consultors. I did not care for a personal interview with someone of the staff of the Congregation—and Father General himself thought it would be useless to ask for one. The reason is that I knew of at least one case when the accused had asked for such an interview and was simply directed to a consultor of the Congregation—Karl Becker, to mention his name—from whom he had received a sermon on submission to the Magisterium. Finally, a quick glance at the eleven pages of new questions making up the *giudizio dottrinale* made it clear that a short article published in a review would not dissipate all the misunderstandings. The Congregation would have expected such an article to show my acquiescence to the accusations implied in the text of the new questions, thus stating my submission to, and agreement with, the opinions expressed by the drafter or drafters of the *giudizio*.

As this was not possible, I set about answering the new questions in secret form, to be communicated within three months to the Congregation. The letter of Cardinal Ratzinger to Father General—which sounded a different tune than what had been said orally in the interview—confirmed my opinion. I have already mentioned the main passage of this letter, which said: "The precisions and the explanations (made in the response to the Contestation) are not considered substantially satisfactory, especially as regards the theses 3-8 and 10-14 [mentioned here above] of the Contestation, in view of preserving the doctrine of Catholic faith from error, ambiguities and dangerous interpretation." The theses referred to, as can be verified from the account of my response to the Contestation also given above, raised important questions to which it was not possible to give a short response to the satisfaction of the Congregation. The *giudizio dottrinale* which accompanied the cardinal's letter gave a list of "the main affirmations of the author, considered erroneous or ambiguous or insufficient." The list of the new questions was meant "as an invitation made to the author to assent to the truth of Catholic faith stated in the list of questions, regarding the points of doctrine concerned." All this goes to show that the accusation of "grievous errors against the faith Divine and Catholic" persisted—a situation which a short article published in a theological review would not dissipate, unless by way of sheer submission to some opinions which in my view remained open to theological discussion. In my new response I frequently made reference to the answers which I had already given to the same questions in my first response, as well as to the two articles written in *Rassegna di teologia* (1999, no. 5) and *Louvain Studies* (1999, no. 3) in response to the questions made by theologians in reviews of my book. Characteristically, the Congregation chose to ignore entirely those articles, while it was now asking me to write an article to meet their own demands. Willy nilly I was in for another painful exercise of having to defend myself against accusations of contradicting the faith.

G.O'C.: *Again you set out replying to the CDF's questions. By November 1, 1999, you handed your reply to Father General. Tell me about the new questions and about your response to them.*

J.D.: The new questions often repeated those asked at the previous round, to which I had already provided an answer. This raised the suspicion that the 188 pages of my response to the Contestation had not been seriously considered and studied—a suspicion which would be confirmed when, as I mentioned above, during the September 4, 2000, official meeting Cardinal Ratzinger told me plainly that 188 pages of response were much too much and I could not expect that the Congregation would go through and study all that material. In this situation I felt dispensed from making long new developments and often referred the Congregation back to what I had written in my response to the Contestation. My response this time was thus limited to sixty pages.

Let me try to state briefly the content of the *giudizio dottrinale* and of my response to it. In the introduction to my response I wrote:

> I am sincerely convinced that the positions propounded in my book are not in contradiction with the Christian faith and the doctrine of the church. I am therefore surprised to see that the *giudizio dottrinale* of the CDF affirms repeatedly that the positions of the book, which the author maintains in his response to the Contestation, contradict such or such doctrine of the faith or doctrine of the church, with-

out ever discussing or refuting the arguments with which I thought I could establish my positions and show that they contradict neither the doctrine of faith nor of the church. This is why in this new response I will often have to refer rapidly to what has been explained in the first response.

The "Judgment on the Doctrinal Questions" was made up of three sections: (1) Doctrine on God and the Trinity; (2) Christological and Soteriological Questions; (3) Ecclesiological Questions. Under the first rubric I was accused of placing the divine mystery "beyond the (three divine) persons." This accusation had already been made in the Contestation, and had been answered in my first response; it was enough in substance to refer back to what I had written then and to show the accusation to be based on a clear misreading of my text. I had insisted on affirming that the Christian mystery of the Trinity represents the Ultimate Reality as such (*an sich*).

By far the longest section on doctrine was that on "Christological and Soteriological Questions." It was made up of five subheadings: (a) the unique and universal mediation of Jesus Christ in general; (b) Christ unique and universal revealer; (c) Christ unique and universal savior; (d) the universal action of the Spirit of Jesus; (e) the complementarity of religious traditions, and religious pluralism "of principle." This enumeration is enough to "show that the new accusations bear on the same topics as those made in the main "theses" of the Contestation. The different subsections refer to the "theses" of the Contestation in the following order: subsection (a) to theses 6-8; (b) to theses 5 and 14; (c) to theses 3 and 4; (d) to theses 5, 7, and 14; (e) to theses 5, 8, and 14. In each case it was asserted, without the claim being substantiated, that those opinions, as first expressed in the book and repeated in the response, are contrary to the faith and to Catholic doctrine.

Thus, it is supposed to be contrary to faith to affirm that "Jesus does not exhaust, nor can exhaust the saving power of God" (a). But in fact it must be affirmed that God acted salvifically, as the First Testament testifies, before the humanity of Jesus ever existed, his humanity being created in time through the mystery of the incarnation. Similarly, it would be contrary to Christian faith to hold that the revelation in Jesus Christ "remains limited, incomplete and imperfect"; and more so, to speak of a "complementary uniqueness" of Christian revelation in relation to other possible revelation (b). Yet, in fact the church's christological dogma itself necessarily implies the incomplete nature of revelation in Jesus Christ, and the New Testament affirms that God's revelation will be complete only at the eschaton. Again, it is claimed that to speak of a salvific action of the Word of God as such introduces not only a distinction but a true separation—the phantasm of "separation" comes in here again—between the Word as such and the Word as incarnate in Jesus Christ, resulting in two persons (c). Yet, it is at least clear that the salvific action of the Word as such existed before the incarnation, and the New Testament, John's Prologue in particular, seems to infer that such action continues after the incarnation and the resurrection of Jesus. In the same vein, it is considered contrary to Christian faith to speak of a salvific action of the Spirit of God not derived from the communication of the Spirit by the risen Christ, an idea which would introduce an "autonomous economy" of the Spirit and deny in fact the "universal salvific meaning of the humanity of Christ, concretely of the humanity of the risen one" (d). Yet, the New Testament itself speaks more often of the "Spirit of God" at work salvifically than of "the Spirit of Christ," and the very expression "Spirit of Christ" is open to different meanings in Scripture itself. Finally, objection is raised to the idea of a "complementarity of religious traditions and of a religious pluralism of principle," which would imply "a place of the religious traditions in the plan of divine providence," "separated from and extrinsic to their orientation to the Christological economy" (e). This objection, however, falls flat in view of the repeated affirmation, both in the book and the response, of an essential orientation of the saving power of the religions to the event of Jesus Christ in which the one plan of God for humankind culminates.

The third subsection treats more explicitly the orientation of the members of other religious traditions to the church. Both the book and the response are accused of undermining the objective "universal mediation" of the church, inseparable from that of Christ himself. Yet, it is clear that the mediation of Christ and of the church cannot be placed on one and the same level, postulating for both the same universal extension. The accusation goes on to state that in the process "the salvific influence of the church toward the members of other religious traditions and that of the traditions to which they belong are practically placed on the same plane," an affirmation which contradicts explicitly what both the book and the response affirmed.

Given this summary of the accusations contained in the *giudizio dottrinale* and of the answers given to them in my response, what still needs to be added regarding the response itself which, as stated above, I submitted on November 1, 1999? One thing is that I was aware, in my way of responding to the questions and accusations, of taking heavy risks, since, apart from some minor adjustments, I kept defending the positions of my book and of my first response, while the CDF had expected a complete submission to their views, expressed publicly in a short article. Yet, I thought that I could not, in sincerity with myself and in conformity with what I believed, do otherwise than face further contradiction. Father General was informed of my attitude and encouraged me to abide by my conscience and convictions.

Another thing is that, as I have already noted with regard to the Contestation, here too the accusations made against opinions expressed in the book and in the first response as contradicting the faith or the doctrine of the church were often due to misreadings or misinterpretations of what I had intended and written. Terms were used to describe my alleged position which I never used, which indeed I formally excluded and purposely avoided throughout, as being false or at least misleading. Examples are where I was accused of holding a "separation" between the action of the Word as such and that of the Word as incarnate, and consequently a "separation" between the Word of God and Jesus Christ as representing two persons; or again, where I was accused of holding distinct "economies" of salvation, while I insisted everywhere that there is but one economy. I have often been told that one quality of my writing is its clarity of expression. Now, however, I was faced with accusations based on serious misrepresentations and misunderstanding. This confirmed my decision to stand by what I had written while endeavoring to clear out all misunderstandings and possible ambiguities.

In concluding my response to the *giudizio dottrinale* I wrote:

> On each of (the) important and difficult questions, the *Giudizio* affirms that my answer (to the Contestation) maintains the positions of the book, which in its opinion seem to be incompatible with such revealed truth or such doctrine of the Church. But the reasons and the arguments developed at length in the response for upholding the positions of the book are never refuted, or even discussed and examined. They are simply passed over in silence, dismissed, ignored, and rejected dogmatically, even where they are based on solid biblical ground, or else on truths implicitly, if not explicitly, implied in official texts of the Church's Magisterium. This situation raises the question with what attention and in what listening spirit has my response of almost two hundred pages been considered? There has been repeatedly talk about "dialogue" between the Congregation and the author (see Cardinal Ratzinger in the *Tablet* [March 13, 1999]: 385), but, in view of the procedure and the content of the documents, one asks oneself if there is no question here of a dialogue between deaf people, or rather of a double monologue.

And I added:

This my second response has been written in a spirit of authenticity, of honesty and sincerity. In any event, I remain convinced—subject to a better counsel on the part of the authentic Magisterium of the church—that the positions of the book and of the first response are compatible with and not opposed to divine revelation, expressed in Sacred Scripture and in the authentic Tradition under the guidance of the Magisterium of the Church (cf. DV 10). I have maintained them in the hope of contributing to the promotion of theological reflection and discussion on a topic so vital today for the life of the church and the credibility of its message. I maintain that in interpreting the data transmitted from revelation either in Scripture or in Tradition an inflated usage of some texts in defense of opinions received as traditional, which yet sometimes remain open to diverse interpretations and to further discussion, is to be avoided. Neither the revealed datum nor the doctrine of the church is to be considered as a self-explanatory monolithic whole, standing beyond all possibility of interpretative discussion.

My own stand was thus made clear. It remained for me to wait and see what came next.

G.O'C.: *After you submitted your response to the* giudizio dottrinale *you were made to wait till the end of August 2000 for a reaction from the Congregation. Could you tell me what happened during that period?*

J.D.: The period of seven months during which I had had to wait for an answer to my response to the Contestation had been painful enough and difficult to bear. This time I was made to wait for ten full months for some reaction from the CDF, from November 1, 1999, the date on which I had signed and submitted my second response, to August 28, 2000, when I received a new letter from Father General announcing the official meeting which was due to take place at the CDF on September 4, the day before the publication at the press office of the Vatican of the declaration *Dominus Iesus*. To say what happened during these long months of waiting is not easy, especially considering my own awareness of the risk I had taken on myself by responding to the Congregation's *giudizio dottrinale* in the straightforward manner I have just described, which was not meant to nor likely to accommodate authorities in my favor.

What happened during that period? I did not interrupt my commitments for outside lectures and communications at congresses. However, given the uncertainty about the future and for prudence sake, I had to be cautious in the choice of topics and in my way of treating them. During those months I gave talks in many places in Italy, including Assisi, Padua, Turin, Bari, Parma, Milan, and outside Italy in Brussels and Paris. As far as writing is concerned, there came the request from Fr. Rosino Gibellini, director of the Queriniana publishing house of Brescia, for a new book on the same theological theme as that of the controversial book of 1997, but destined for a broader public. At the beginning I hesitated to accept the invitation, given the situation in which I found myself. It will be recalled that the invitation to write the previous book had also come from Fr. Gibellini, who in a sense, but with the best of intentions, shared in the responsibility for my predicament. The same person was now asking from me another book on the same subject, propounding the same theological views but in a form more accessible for the nonspecialist and with a more pastoral bent. The challenge was not small. I would have to propose again my own views on the subject of the theology of religions, taking into account seriously the questioning on the part of the CDF which had been going on for two years, and answering it implicitly, without making any explicit reference to the documents—which of course remained secret. I was moreover expected to do this under a form appealing to nonspecialists and with a pastoral approach. The risks were not to be underestimated; but "who risks nothing achieves nothing," says the proverb, and I decided that the cause to be defended was well worth the risk. Interestingly, it was Fr. Gibellini who once more guided me in the composition of this new book.

And so, after about one month of hesitation I decided that I could not wait forever for some reaction from the CDF to my second response, and began to jot down some thoughts that should enter into the new book. The Congregation is known to procrastinate, hoping that time will be on its side. Surprisingly, once I put myself to work in earnest, the composition went pretty fast. I started writing in December 1999 and ended the work on March 31, 2000. A compelling reason spurred me on, namely, the rumor that the CDF was preparing a document on the subject, to be published in the course of the year 2000. I was determined to have the new book published before the document of the Congregation came out, so as to avoid added difficulties about its publication. This was the reason why I wrote the manuscript in Italian; this, I thought, would hasten the date of publication, since I was not sure, to begin with, of the possibility of having editions of this new work in French or English. However, I had to submit my manuscript to an Italian colleague, who corrected my mistakes in Italian; the colleague did this with great devotion and competence, but took a long time. I had my entire manuscript read and studied by Fr. O'Collins, who approved it while making some suggestions for improvement. I also sent it to Msgr. Luigi Sartori of Padua, who sent a positive evaluation and also sent some suggestions, all of which were inserted in the text. With other friends approving the manuscript, I could rely on five positive evaluations. I needed, however, to submit the manuscript to my Jesuit superiors to obtain their *imprimi potest*. This, given the delicate situation in which I found myself, waiting for a response from the CDF to my second response to their questioning of my previous book, became a protracted process and lasted many months. Eventually, the final *imprimi potest* signed by Fr. Francisco J. Egaña, vice rector of the Gregorian University, would be dated June 3, 2001.

Meanwhile, Cardinal Ratzinger came out with the publication of the declaration *Dominus Iesus* on September 5, 2000, well before I obtained the permission to publish. Faced with this situation, I decided to add to my manuscript an appendix in which with reference to *Dominus Iesus* I would answer directly the CDF's difficulties. Eventually, since the process of Jesuit censorship lasted even longer, I wrote a second appendix, in which I responded to the Notification on my previous book, dated January 24, 2001, which had been published in *L'Osservatore Romano* on February 26, 2001. These circumstances did not make the procedure for the *imprimi potest* of my new book easier. Eventually I was told that the main body of the book could be published, but not the two appendices, since they could be considered offensive to the Congregation, whatever their objective merit. As it was impossible to publish the book without making any reference to the two documents of the Congregation—this would have been seen as even more offensive—I wrote a postscript, to be added to the book in place of the two appendices, in which I explained that, though no explicit reference was made to the two documents now published by the CDF, yet the questions from the Congregation were everywhere implicitly present in my text. With the postscript replacing the two appendices, the last objections to the publication of the new book were overcome, and the *imprimi potest* was finally granted.

As regards this new book, it was important to draw the attention to the circumstances of its composition in the period which followed my second response to the Congregation. A clear sign that my superiors were getting nervous at the prospect of this publication is the fact that, when correcting the proofs of the 2001, no. 4 issue of *Gregorianum*, of which I was still the director, I was asked to withdraw a short, rather innocent presentation of the new book, which I had included under the rubric "Libri Nostri."

The superior requested me to drop it, because, he said, "the Gregorian is involved." I may add, with a grain of irony, that this book, entitled in the English edition *Christianity and the Religions: From Confrontation to Dialogue,* after its painful birth exists now in four languages: Italian (Brescia: Queriniana, 2001); French (Paris: Le Cerf, 2002); English (Maryknoll, NY: Orbis Books, 2002, 2003); Spanish (Santander: Sal Terrae, 2002). Two other editions are in preparation: Portuguese-Brazilian (Sao Paolo: Loyola); and Polish (Krakow: Wydawnictwo Wam).

Another writing project occupied me during the same long period of waiting for the Congregation's reaction to my second response. I have referred to the two articles which I wrote in Italian and English in *Rassegna di teologia* (1999, no. 5) and *Louvain Studies* (1999, no. 3) respectively, in which I answered questions raised about my book by theologians in different reviews in Italian, English, and French. I wanted to complete this work, taking into account more recent reviews and studies in different languages. The idea was to give a more comprehensive view of the interest and the discussion which the book had aroused, thus explaining the *status quaestionis* in the present discussion on a topic of vital importance for the church and her mission. In this new piece, which filled thirty pages under the title "Il pluralismo religioso: un bilancio provvisorio," I proceeded more synthetically than had been the case in the two previous articles, grouped the objections and answers to them under different rubrics, and covered pretty well the entire field, without making explicit reference to the authors, either foe or friend.

Here, however, the nervousness of my superiors came to a peak. I had intended to publish the piece in Italian. If no Italian review was disposed to publish it, I could eventually take advantage of my position as director of *Gregorianum* to include it in that journal. The norms have it that the director of the review acts as the normal arbiter for the selection of articles for publication. Yet, the matter being delicate, I did not want to take advantage of my position as director of the review by publishing the piece without explicitly passing it through the superiors' censorship, thus facing them with a fait accompli. I therefore referred the matter to them, asking for the permission to publish. Let me note that Fr. O'Collins had given his full approval to this publication. Even shortly after the meeting with Cardinal Ratzinger of September 4, 2000, he still wrote—on September 9, 2000: "The article is clear, coherent and brilliant, and—by a nice stroke of divine providence—meets head on a number of points that emerge in the negative part of the Notification." (He was referring to the first draft of the Notification which had been communicated to us in view of the meeting.) If a publication in Italian were to fall through, the director of

Theological Studies in the United States was disposed to publish the piece in English in his review. The superiors, however, saw things differently.

After long deliberations that went on between the vice rector and the rector of the university on the one hand, and the delegate of Father General to the Roman houses on the other, Fr. Egaña wrote to me on November 7: "Given the present delicate situation, I did consult Father Delegate, and he too agrees that the publication of the article is not opportune, not even with a note added to state that its redaction preceded the document *Dominus Iesus*. Even if the director of one of our reviews has the delegation necessary to allow the publication of articles in the review under his direction, in cases which can involve the Institution or the Province of the author of the article, the Institution or the Province must also give their approbation. This is required by a healthy analogy with the norms of publication of books in another Province." Father Egaña went on to express his regret and his continued sympathy for my cause.

The delegate of the general, Fr. Guillermo Rodríguez-Izquierdo, had written to Fr. Egaña on September 12 as follows, after consulting Father General on the matter:

1. If the article is published in *Gregorianum*, the Gregorian is committing itself in the defense of Fr. Dupuis. Father O'Collins has always defended him and his judgment may be very valid, but not all the professors of the Gregorian think as he does. That is why it is not becoming to go ahead with this publication, unless it meets with the unanimous approval of the members of the editorial board of the review and of other professors. 2. In the present case Fr. Dupuis is "under trial" and an article of this type must not be published, for his own good, before the publication of the Notification. 3. Even after the publication of the Notification it will be prudent not to publish a defense of this type in the *Gregorianum*, in order not to compromise the Faculty of Theology.

These two letters revealed a legalistic and cautious attitude, as well as a determination not to take any risk in solidarity with and in favor of a confrere and a colleague. Both pained me very much and made me think sadly of the words of Caiphas: "It is better for one man to die rather than the whole nation perish." Do not, please, create problems for the Institution. The Institution matters more than the persons; even more than the search for truth. This, then, is how a second piece composed during the long period that followed my second response to the CDF was aborted, in spite of the rather innocent nature of its content—which was not even discussed in the process—and of the utter prudence with which it had been written, without any reference being made to the Congregation's secret or public documents. The piece has been reworked and is included in the second part of the present volume under the title "The Theology of Religious Pluralism Revisited: A Provisional Balance Sheet."

G.O'C.: *On September 4, 2000, you were summoned for the official meeting at the CDF, with Father General and Fr. O'Collins who would act as your advocate. When did you receive the invitation? What was the result of the meeting and what impact did it make?*

J.D.: The letter of Msgr. Tarcisio Bertone, dated August 25, 2000, with its invitation to the September 4 meeting, was sent to me by Father General with a covering letter of his, dated August 28. I returned from a short holiday in Belgium on September 1 and received the letters that evening. Included with the invitation to the meeting were an advance copy of the text of the declaration *Dominus Iesus,* which was to be published on September 5, and a copy of the text of the Notification on my own book which the CDF intended to publish in *L'Osservatore Romano* soon after. The idea was, as I have already mentioned, to show the connection intended by the Congregation between the two documents. I had exactly two days at my disposal to study the two documents. In his covering letter Father General suggested that during the meeting I could raise the question of the alleged presence in my writing of the grievous errors against faith mentioned in the text of the Notification. Father O'Collins had received the same documents and had the same measure of time to study them in view of the meeting. At the request of Father General, the three of us met at the Gregorian on the eve of the meeting, to prepare together our own *modus procedendi* for the discussion. Father General would of course speak first, followed by Fr. O'Collins taking my defense; I myself would speak as little as possible, and only when requested to do so. And so it went. I have already described the main lines of the tense meeting when I gave a general overview of the proceedings. But it is worth reflecting on the meaning that the CDF attributed to the meeting and what it intended to achieve through it, as well as on the procedure followed. One might think that the meeting was to initiate the discussion with the Congregation to which at an earlier stage the cardinal had said I would be entitled, once I had published a short piece professing my agreement with the findings of the CDF and their critique of my book. This interpretation would be quite mistaken, as the tenure of the text of the Notification made abundantly clear. The text spoke explicitly of grievous errors against the faith which, it was alleged, were found in my book, though this was in no way substantiated through quotations and references. Quite clearly, what the CDF expected from the meeting was not a discussion of opinions, nor some clarifications regarding the interpretation to be given to my text, and not even ways of dispelling some ambiguities, but the simple admission on my part of the presence in my book of the grievous errors against the faith which were being rejected in the text of the Notification. They were requesting me to sign the text of the Notification, the intended meaning of my signature being my own confession of grievous errors against the faith and my total submission to the content of the Notification as it stood. In that context, I had no hesitation in refusing my signature, which of course produced a stir, and led to the questions which Cardinal Ratzinger addressed to me—which I mentioned above.

It may also be worthwhile to reflect on the procedure used by the Congregation and especially on the involvement of the pope's authority in the proceedings even before any hearing had taken place between the prosecution and the defense. In his article "Are Church Investigation Procedures Really Just?," published in *Doctrine and Life* (1998, 453-66) Fr. Ladislas Orsy comments on the involvement of the pope's authority at the very first stage of an investigation. I have mentioned earlier that the decision of the Contestation taken by the Congregation on June 10, 1998, and the *giudizio dottrinale* that followed on July 27, 1999, were already approved and confirmed by the pope in private audiences with Cardinal Ratzinger. Now, the decision for the Notification and its text had similarly already been approved by the pope and even ordered by him to be published, after an audience to the cardinal on June 16, 2000.

Fr. Orsy notes that, according to the norms of the Congregation, "throughout the process the pope himself is involved; hence, there cannot be any room for appeal." He comments: "We are touching a substantial structural weakness in the Regulations: it directs a trial immediately to the highest level, involving the pope himself. Sound jurisprudence would postulate a court or tribunal of first instance at a lower level from which there would be an appeal to a higher court. . . . As it is now, the pope must be involved in every single "doctrinal examination." Should ever a miscarriage of justice occur, it would immediately reflect on the papal office itself. Not a good prospect for the faithful to contemplate." And he adds: "To leave room for appeal is to acknowledge our human condition: we are fallible human beings—judges not excepted. A process with no possibility of appeal is a scary system for any lawyer to contemplate: it leaves no room for the correction of mistakes."

As a matter of course the involvement of the pope's authority at the very first stage of the proceedings is meant to exclude a priori the possibility of any appeal to higher authority. In the process, supreme authority is concretely conferred on the Congregation, whose decisions the pope is satisfied to ratify without having personally looked into the matter. The norms thus attribute practically to the Congregation an authority which does not by right belong to it. But it is one thing to impose one's authority by law; another thing is to make it credible and to ensure its "reception" by the church. As for the pope's involvement, it is indeed disturbing that a document approved by him for publication be dismissed after a first encounter between the prosecution and the defense, and its publication cancelled. The same fate would later meet a second redaction of the Notification, also approved by the pope. I have mentioned earlier that the text of the Notification which was finally published in *L'Osservatore Romano* of February 26, 2001, was its third version. That documents approved by the pope and ordered by him to be published are so easily cancelled and replaced by others is not likely to enhance the prestige of the pope's authority.

G.O'C.: *You had received before the meeting the text of the Notification about your book which the Congregation intended to publish soon after, as well as an advance copy of the declaration* Dominus Iesus. *You had little time to study the documents before the meeting. Could you explain how you reacted to them at first?*

J.D.: What struck me at first glance on reading the two documents on September 2 was the close similarity between the two documents, and the determined intention on the part of the CDF to show the connection between the two. *Dominus Iesus* had been approved by the pope on June, 16, 2000; it is dated August 6, 2000, and signed by Cardinal Ratzinger and Msgr. Bertone. It would be published on September 5. The final Notification about my book was approved by the pope and ordered by him to be published on January 19, 2001. It is dated January 24 and signed by Cardinal Ratzinger and Msgr. Bertone. Its first version was intended to be published in September 2000, soon after the publication of *Dominus Iesus.* The similarity between the two documents was made perfectly clear by the "Note" which was inserted at the beginning of the Notification, which stated: "The Congregation for the Doctrine of the Faith, because of tendencies showing up in different quarters, as also in the thinking of the faithful, has published the declaration *Dominus Iesus* on the theme of the unicity and the salvific universality of Jesus Christ and the church (August 6, 2000), in order to safeguard the essential elements of the Catholic faith. The present Notification applies the principles indicated in the declaration to the evaluation of the work of Fr. J. Dupuis." Equally striking was the similarity between the content of the Notification and that of the previous *giudizio dottrinale* to my book.

Let me briefly describe the content of the Notification in its first version presented at the September 4 meeting. It is worth noting that this text, which had been approved by the pope as early as June 16, 2000, was communicated to Father General only on August 25 and to me on August 28 and received by me on September 2. Obviously there was no wish on the part of the Congregation to provide ample time for study, and one may ask why. Be that as it may, its introduction gave a long account of the development of the proceedings so far, insisting on the persistence of grievous errors and ambiguities even in my second response to the questions of the Congregation.

There followed five main sections, each with several propositions to be accepted as doctrine of faith or as doctrine of the church. Characteristically—as would be noted by Father General in his intervention during the meeting reported above—no reference whatever to my book, or quotation from it, was found in the text, unlike the practice which had been followed in the *giudizio dottrinale*. But the note mentioned above and the manner of composition made it clear that the doctrines rejected in the Notification were errors contained in the book. The five main sections were the following: (1) About the unique and universal salvific mediation of Jesus Christ; (2) About the unicity and the fullness of revelation in Christ; (3) About the universal salvific action of the Spirit of Jesus Christ; (4) About the ordination of all humans to the church; (5) About the value and the meaning of the salvific function of the religious traditions.

This enumeration shows that the subject matter was very similar to that of the *giudizio dottrinale* which I examined above. Eight propositions were distributed between the five headings of sections. The same eight propositions would recur later, with modifications, in the second edition of the Notification. But in the present first edition they were accompanied with long developments by way of justification, borrowed from official documents of the church. The eight propositions containing the doctrine to be held: a second, negative part, containing the doctrines to be rejected. With propositions 1 and 7, and the first part of the other ones, I could find myself in substantial agreement, insofar as they stated the doctrine of the faith; not, however, with the second part where in the context the doctrines rejected were understood to refer to my book. Thus I was again implicitly accused of holding a "separation" between the Word of God and Jesus, and between the salvific action of the Word and that of Jesus—the alleged "separation" enjoyed a long life!—; a distinct "salvific economy of the Spirit," beyond the unique salvific economy of the Word incarnate;

and the views that the religious traditions are "parallel ways of salvation" or "ways equivalent" to the Christian way and that the function of the religions "can be compared to that of the Old Testament"; and so on and so forth. In sum, all the accusations made since the beginning of the procedure were coming back, notwithstanding the long explanations contained in my two responses to the Congregation.

This is enough to show how justified was the intervention of Fr. O'Collins during the meeting. Following Father General's avowal of surprise that the Notification made accusations of serious errors against the faith without substantiating them by reference to the text or quotations from the book, he showed in detail that those errors against the faith are not found in the book! I myself kept quiet at that point, watching the reaction of surprise and unease which showed up on the face of Cardinal Ratzinger and the annoyed and discomfited silence of trusted consultor Amato on the other side of the table, who, it must be remembered, had drafted the Notification as well as the declaration *Dominus Iesus,* except for its chapter 4 on Christian ecumenism. A point had obviously been made, and the questions that followed thereafter were concerned with the practical side of the meeting. The text of the Notification as it stood was already buried. The questions now were: How to avoid a misinterpretation of the Notification, attributing to me all the opinions rejected? Was I disposed to help to improve the text? Was I prepared to sign it as it stood? Was I at least prepared to declare that my book needs to be interpreted in the light of *Dominus Iesus?* I have already indicated that my answer to those questions was consistently negative. But these questions, added to the cardinal admitting that I could not have expected the Congregation to study my long responses to their questioning, confirmed my impression that the cardinal had never really studied the matter personally but had relied all along on the opinion of some trusted consultor or consultors, the leading one among whom had now badly let him down by his discomfited silence at the meeting. So much then for the content of the Notification of September 4.

There was no time to study the declaration *Dominus Iesus* in detail in just two days. My attention had to be given first to the Notification. However, as mentioned above, the relation between the two documents was evident; and a quick reading of the declaration was enough for me to make up my mind that I would have to express my disagreement with much of its content. In any case it was clear that I could not agree with the text as it stood. Hence, when Cardinal Ratzinger, looking for a last practical solution, asked me during the meeting whether I was prepared to declare that my book ought to be interpreted in the light of *Dominus Iesus,* I had no hesitation to answer "No" politely, stating that this was asking too much from me. Later I did study the declaration more closely, and wrote a first appendix to my last book in response to it. As this appendix did not meet the approval of my superiors for publication, I reworked the text again; it is now included, together with my comments on the final text of the Notification—about which later—under the title "Some Reflections on Two Vatican Documents," in *Jacques Dupuis Faces the Inquisition* (2012). This dispenses me from providing here more explanations on this subject.

G.O'C.: *How did the meeting end? What were you thinking and feeling as you left the meeting? What did Father General and Fr. O'Collins say as you walked away from the CDF office?*

J.D.: There was of course a sense of achievement, as an important point had been made. A document approved by the pope and ordered by him for publication had been dismissed in two hours—a rare performance, I would suppose! But there was no indulging in triumphalism. Monsignor Bertone had made it clear at the end of the meeting, before Cardinal Ratzinger called it off with some annoyance, that in any case another text would have to be produced, since members of the Congregation had earnestly requested that a document stating the errors contained in Fr. Dupuis's book should be written and published by the Congregation; the CDF was bound to comply with their request. We left the stuffy room where the meeting had just ended by exchanging polite but cool greetings with the prosecution, the three of us coming down the stairs of the palace of the Holy Office without exchanging a word. Finding ourselves in the piazza brought a sense of relief, notwithstanding the scorching noonday heat. As we walked together around the colonnade of the basilica, Father General was first to express his impressions. He did not hide his satisfaction with our performance and thought we had been successful in making our points discreetly but efficaciously. We thanked each other as we separated at the end of the colonnade, Father General walking alone on foot to the Jesuit curia, and the two of us taking a taxi to return quickly to the Gregorian. Father Superior was waiting for our return and immediately inquired how the meeting had gone. I gave him what I thought to be an objective account, positive about what we had achieved, but without illusion as to what the future would have in store.

G.O'C.: *What happened in the following days? What thoughts went through your mind, and how did you feel, as you waited for Cardinal Ratzinger to make the next move? What did you expect?*

J.D.: It took again four months before a second version of the Notification, approved by the pope and ordered by him for publication on November 24, 2000, was brought to my knowledge through a letter of Father General dated December 6. It carried the names of Cardinal Ratzinger and of Archbishop Bertone, but no date was attached to it, leaving the date of publication to be determined later, depending on my eventual reactions and disposition to attach my signature to the text. I shall refer to the text of the second version of the Notification later.

What happened during these other four months of waiting? I continued to give some lectures as requests came in. But my main activity during those months was in writing: I put the last touches to the seventh revised and enlarged edition of *The Christian Faith in the Doctrinal Documents of the Catholic Church*, to be published in India and in the United States early in 2001. It did appear an irony of fate that, after I had put in so much time and energy over the last thirty years in preparing seven editions of a large collection of doctrinal documents of the church, I was, for all practical purposes, accused of heresy by the church's doctrinal authority—even though the term was not explicitly used. The oddness of this situation did not escape the attention of the news media. In any case, this work kept me busy, and there was no time to indulge in mourning and depression. I was determined to fight it out at the next round, whatever the second version of the Notification would entail.

G.O'C.: *Four months later, on December 6, 2000, you received a letter of Father General, together with a new text of the Notification. What did both communications say? What happened next?*

J.D.: The letter of Father General expressed his satisfaction at the changes contained in the "final draft"—as he called it mistakenly—of the Notification. He wrote: "You see that your intervention and that of Fr. O'Collins (at the September 4 meeting) have changed considerably the dogmatic part. . . . While giving me the final text, the cardinal told me again that "there is no intention to express a judgement on the subjective thought of the author, whose intentions have never been put in discussion." The Notification is, however, required because of "the need to offer to the faithful readers a sure criterion of evaluation in agreement with the doctrine of the church." The cardinal is asking you to agree to sign the Notification . . . , and thus put an end to the entire procedure with your 'signature without reservation' (*firma senza clausula*)."

Father General asked me to let him have the text signed by me before December 15. He added: "The publication (of the Notification) should take place in January 2001," stating that as usual the document was being sent to me "as totally reserved" (*in via del tutto riservata*), though I could talk about it confidentially with the rector of the university, Fr. Imoda, and the vice rector, Fr. Egaña. As soon as he had read the second draft of the Notification, Fr. Egaña wrote me an encouraging letter. He found the new version "substantially changed," especially insofar as I was no longer accused of errors against the faith, but of ambiguous assertions which could induce the readers into erroneous opinions. He added, however: "Even if the affirmations of the Notification have a very different theological tenure, the problem remains to evaluate what consequences would follow from a signature and what consequences would follow from not signing. I see grave consequences in not signing, both for yourself and for the Gregorian and the Society. Father General seems to me also in favor of your signature, though always respecting your freedom."

These letters placed before me the alternative to sign or not to sign the new version of the Notification. This raised the question of the use the Congregation intended to make of my signature, and the meaning it would give to it. Why did they need my signature at all to their text about my book, and why their determination to obtain it by all means? I needed to know more about these matters from Father General and wrote him a long letter on December 9, explaining my misgivings about signing the text and my reservations about its content. I added:

> I certainly have no intention of going in any way against the wish of the superiors in such an important matter, and I have the impression, reading your letter to me (of December 6th), that you take it for granted that I must sign, even if the way of proceeding of the Congregation looks like imposition: "firma senza clausula," without any "quoad modum," without any further discussion, without any correction, addition or subtraction to the text. My own impression is that I am really being compelled by the CDF to sign their text as it stands. Even so, my "obedience of execution" to the will of the superiors is not in question, whatever be the possible consequences; but inner assent to the content of the Notification is a different matter. I concluded: "In short . . . if I am compelled to sign the text just as it is and without any clause attached, it will have to be with a "restrictio mentalis," though with the obedience of execution, and being prepared to assume the consequences.

Father General answered my letter on December 13. He assured me saying:

The signature means that you are taking note of the fact that the Magisterium of the church—it is the Holy Father who approves the text—judges indispensable to put readers of your book on their guard against drawing from it some conclusions—as has happened—which are not in harmony with our faith. Such conclusions drawn from your book are your responsibility only insofar as not everything in your book—if we believe the Magisterium—is clear. . . . The signature means also that you continue your theological research, taking into account mainly *Dominus Iesus* which the Magisterium of the church proposes to every Christian. . . . While taking into account this given direction, there remains a whole free space for theological research compatible with the data of the faith, even if that space happens to be narrower than you had thought. If one believes echoes coming from the cardinals of the Congregation, your work is appreciated as exceptional, but in a time when irenicism, relativism and syncretism reign, the church must proceed with such clarity as would avoid even all possibility of non-orthodox interpretation. It is not the first time in history that a theologian opens a way on which the Magisterium . . . is not yet able to follow, needing clarifications, adjustments and maturing. . . . No doubt, it is painful for all of us to see that for reasons without doubt grave, the Magisterium of the church cannot be in full agreement with your publication, given the false conclusions which some readers could derive from it. However, the signature confirms your desire to be faithful to the Magisterium of the church and allows you to continue your work in full knowledge of the situation.

I have quoted at length this letter which testifies once more to the sympathy and concern of Father General on my behalf, and at the same time to a clear-sighted and nuanced judgment of the situation.

In short, the meaning of my signature would be that in the future I would have to take seriously into account the content of the two documents of the Congregation, the declaration *Dominus Iesus* and the Notification on my own book; not, however, that I would be binding myself to agree blindly with and to abide fully by their content. It is with this understanding of the meaning of my signature—which I made explicit in a covering letter—that I made up my mind to sign the text of the Notification, relying on the opinion of Father General and of Fr. Egaña regarding the possible serious and adverse consequences, not only for myself, of my refusal to sign. I allowed myself to be persuaded to sign, mostly because I was no longer accused personally of grievous errors against the faith, but of ambiguities—though these remained unspecified—which could eventually lead readers into mistaken opinions. Which author, I asked myself, is never guilty of some ambiguity when writing on difficult matters involving new and delicate questions? I remained nevertheless suspicious as to the use or abuse which the Congregation could make of my signature—a suspicion which would be verified later. The date of my signature had, moreover, to be slightly postponed as I was due to go to the hospital for a surgical operation, and did not want to submit to surgery with the burden of that signature on my mind. Eventually, I did send to Father General the signed text of the Notification, with the covering letter already mentioned in which I stated my own understanding of the meaning of my signature, on December 16, 2000.

As for the content of the second draft of the Notification, I have already explained that it was considerably shorter than its predecessor, consisting of seven pages. The main difference was the toning down of the accusations made against me from grievous errors against the faith to ambiguities capable of leading readers into error. A long introduction of four pages retraced the story of the case from the beginning, stating the grave accusations which had been made at the earlier stages. But the end of the introduction stated:

> This Notification does not intend to express a judgment on the subjective thought of the author; it intends rather to enunciate the doctrine of the church on some aspects of the doctrinal truths involved, and at the same time to refute erroneous or dangerous opinions to which, independently of the intentions of the author, the reader could arrive because of ambiguous formulations or insufficient explanations contained in different parts of the book. In this way it is intended to offer to Catholic readers a safe criterion of evaluation, in accord with the doctrine of the church, in order to avoid that the reading of the volume might cause grave ambiguities and misunderstandings.

The structure of the main text remained the same, being made up of the same eight sections in two parts, one positive with which I could agree substantially, the other negative, stating opinions to be rejected which in the context remained implicitly, but often wrongly, attributed to my book. It is this second part of each section which prevented me from being in agreement with the text of the Notification as it now stood. As for the long developments by way of justification of the doctrine drawn from official church documents, they had completely disappeared. More on the content of the second draft of the Notification will turn up when we come to its forthcoming official appearance. My signature had been attached to this second draft, testifying to my determination to be faithful to the faith and to the church, but also to my reservations about the content of the document.

G.O'C.: *On February 26, 2001, the Notification was finally published in* L'Osservatore Romano. *Were you told about this in advance? What were your feelings when you read it in the paper? What was the reaction of your colleagues at the Gregorian or in other pontifical universities and institutes?*

J.D.: I thought that the Notification would be published soon after I had sent it back with my signature on December 16, 2000. This was not so. The new delay of two and a half months needs to be explained. To the text which I had signed a long addition was made, stating the following: "The Congregation for the Doctrine of the Faith, having gone through the ordinary procedure of examination in all its phases, has decided to write a Notification in order to protect the doctrine of the Catholic faith from errors, ambiguities and dangerous interpretations. This Notification, approved by the Holy Father in the audience of November 14, 2000, has been presented to Fr. Jacques Dupuis, and accepted by him. With the signature of the text the author committed himself to agree with the theses enunciated and to abide in the future, in his theological activity and his publications, by the doctrinal contents indicated in the Notification. The text of the Notification will also have to be included in eventual reprints or new editions of the book, and in the translations in other languages." None of this was found in the text which had been submitted to me for my signature. My misgivings about the use or abuse which the Congregation could possibly make of my signature were thus perfectly verified.

I had expressed my fear of such abuse to Fr. Egaña before I signed the previous version of the Notification. As an expert canonist he thought that my fears were without foundation: To add, he said, to a text signed after the signature has been given, is simply dishonest, and one cannot suppose that the Congregation would indulge in such a dishonest practice. Nevertheless, it had happened. The fact came to be known to the press, which commented on it. Monsignor Bertone was in fact asked for explanations on this point. His answer was that the new paragraph dealt with discipline, not with doctrine, and therefore did not need my signature. A subtle distinction to justify a dishonest practice! What right did the Congregation have to include that paragraph over my signature and to declare accepted by me an interpretation of my signature contrary to my own will? Rome, it is said, makes the law for others to observe! The inclusion of the paragraph in question explains why the final text of the Notification had to be submitted to the pope once more, for "confirmation of his approval in the light of the last developments." Thus, in an audience of January 19, 2001, the pope confirmed his approval and again ordered the text to be published. The Notification was thus approved by the pope and ordered by him to be published no less than three times! Its final text is dated January 24 and signed by Cardinal Ratzinger and Archbishop Bertone. Yet, apparently due to the celebration that followed the creation of new cardinals and filled the pages of the paper, it was published in *L'Osservatore Romano* only on February 26, and in the English edition on March 14. Festivities at the Vatican could not be upset by publishing a Notification that played a different tune.

Apart from the paragraph added to the second version after my signature, no other substantial change is found in the final text, except for the fact that the long introduction retracing the whole story of the case had been much shortened. The main text remained substantially the same, with its eight propositions made up of a positive and a negative part, continuing to attribute to me the opinions condemned. The text of the Notification was accompanied with a long "Commentary on the Notification," signed *** presumably written by Cardinal Ratzinger himself, as the three asterisks indicate. The Commentary justified the literary genre in which the Notification is written, as being the genre used for professions of faith. It also defended the style of the declaration *Dominus Iesus,* against the strong criticism by the press and religious leaders of other churches, for its negative, dogmatic tone. I need not enlarge here on my disagreements with the official text of the Notification, since my piece entitled "Some Reflections on Two Roman Documents," already referred to, is my response to both the declaration *Dominus Iesus* and the Notification on my book.

I had of course no premonition whatever about the date when the Notification might be published, and did not know what to make of the new delay after my signature of the second draft. Father General himself had no information till the middle of February. On February 17 he wrote to me saying that he was expecting the text "for the beginning of the last week of February" and could then let me have a copy of it "sotto embargo" till publication As for my immediate reaction on reading it, one can well imagine that I immediately noticed the paragraph added to the text I had signed. My apprehensions had not been without foundation, and I found the procedure of the Congregation dishonest. I shared my opinion on this with Fr. Egaña, who previously had thought my fears unfounded; he himself did not know now what to make of it. The rest of the text was well known to me and brought no surprise. The reactions of my confreres and colleagues at the Gregorian were of course mixed. There were those—not too many, I would hope—who had expected and looked forward to an explicit condemnation, and who now were probably rather disappointed at the apparent mildness of the document. Others were glad to see the end of a bad story which hopefully would leave no trace in the near future. The bulk remained apparently unconcerned, as they had been all along.

G.O'C.: *At the same time as the publication of the Notification, Father General issued a statement to all Jesuits. What did you feel on reading it?*

J.D.: The statement by Father General was issued on the very day of the publication of the Notification. It was addressed to all Jesuits around the world and had to be brought to the knowledge of all by being affixed on the notice board in all the houses of the Society. It went round the world in no time through the Internet. For some reason, in the Gregorian it remained on the notice board for the community less than half a day. Father General had come to see me in advance to share with me what he intended to write. I was taken aback when he asked me for suggestions for improving his text. I really did not think it belonged to me to correct or improve on what Father General had written in my favor; I was quite confused at his asking me. I was immensely grateful for his praise of the work I had been doing and his stress on the merits of my book; I appreciated even more what he wrote at the end of his statement: "We hope that Fr. Dupuis can continue his pioneer research in the field of interreligious dialogue which in his recent apostolic letter *Novo millennio ineunte* John Paul II encourages as a challenge for the evangelization in the third millennium." I thought the statement of Father General, besides confirming once more and in an official manner his support and sympathy for my cause, was a courageous and important initiative—not destined, I would think, to please the authorities of the CDF. In view of its importance I thought it necessary to quote it above in full.

G.O'C.: *After almost two and a half years of imposed silence and secrecy, which lasted from October 1998 till the publication of the Notification on February 26, 2001, you were now free to speak publicly again. What did it feel like to be free of suspicion and from the threat of sanctions? What did it mean to you to be free from the charge of heresy?*

J.D.: The almost two years and a half of imposed silence and secrecy to which you refer apply only to the silence enforced upon me by the CDF about the proceedings of my case. It did not prevent me from giving lectures in Italy and abroad, though I had to do this with circumspection. Those talks and papers at congresses during those years included the following: two talks at the Theological Study in Udine on October 10, 1998, a lecture to the PIME missionaries in Rome on November 11, a lecture at the Studio teologico interreligioso pugliese at Bari on November 23, and a talk at the Istituto teologico pugliese at Molfetta on the same day, a communication at the Session Servizio Missionario Giovani in Assisi (December 5-8), two conferences in Monza at the Seminario teologico internazionale on March 3, 1999, a communication at the International Congress on "L'immaginario contemporaneo" in Ferrara (May 21-23), a talk to the Monastic Interreligious Dialogue Commissions at Douai Abbey, England (June 8-10), a seminar on my book at the convent of the Dominicans in Montpellier, France (June 15-17), a communication at the Chianciano Terme Congress of the Secretariato Attivita Ecumeniche on "La preghiera respiro delle religioni" (July 24-31), a communication at the Kottayam (India) meeting of Jesuit ecumenists (August 15-21), a lecture at an International Seminar of Philosophy on "Religion and Religions starting with the "Discourses of Schleiermacher" at Assisi (November 25-28), a communication at an interdisciplinary colloquy at the University of Studies at Padua (December 8) and a lecture at the interdiocesan seminary of Padua on December 9, a lecture at the Cultural Italian Association in Turin (January 14, 2000), a lecture to SPICES, Bari, on January 31, 2000, and another at the Cultural Italian Association in Bari on February 2, five lectures in an Ecumenical Session on "Plurality of Religions and Universality of Salvation in Jesus Christ" at Lausanne (Switzerland) (February 23-25), and, also in Lausanne, a public lecture on February 24, a paper at a Congress on "Il prossimo lontano" in Padua (April 28-May 1), a lecture at a Session Dialogue Interreligieux Monastique (DIM) in Parma (April 29-30), a communication at a Session of Study on "Theology of Religions and Liturgy" in Padua (May 8-10), a lecture at Saint John in Lateran in Milan (May 24), two communications at the Convegno Missionari Regionali Emilia Romagna in Bologna (June 16-18), four lectures at a Claretian Renewal Congress in Rome (October 9-10). This list shows how my activity as a lecturer continued after I was informed in October 1998 of the procedure initiated against me by the CDF.

A certain sense of new freedom set in with the publication of the Notification; yet it cannot be exaggerated. The meaning which the official version of the Notification gave to my signature called for continued circumspection. In the mind of the CDF I had committed myself explicitly and officially to abide blindly by the entire content of both their documents. What attitude then would I have to take henceforth in lectures and what might be the reaction of the Congregation if I spoke my mind freely? At the request of my superiors I abstained from any lectures during the first months which followed the publication of the Notification, from February to May 2001. The first talks I gave were a public lecture and a paper at a seminar in Brussels in May 2001, and in September a communication at the Lublin International Congress of Fundamental Theology on "Christianity of Tomorrow"; I have referred to these earlier. The publication of those two texts would start my troubles again, as will be explained later. It would therefore be exaggerated to say that I was henceforth "free of suspicion and from the threat of sanctions." Yet, it is true that the absolution from accusations of grievous errors against the faith—the term heresy, which has bad press, was never used—brought a deep sense of relief. We had won a crucial battle, even if the war was not over.

G.O'C.: *What was the reaction of people in the church after you were cleared of heresy? Did you receive many phone calls, letters, or emails? And what was the general tone of those? Journalists clamored to have interviews with you after the publication of the Notification. To try to handle this flood of queries, you decided to respond to one and all by giving a briefing at the Gregorian on February 27, the day after the publication of the Notification. Did you feel a sense of liberation as you spoke to them? Or what did you feel?*

J.D.: Yes, there were lots of letters and messages from friends all over the world, from those who had followed the proceedings with concern and sympathy for the accused and now wanted to share with him the sense of relief which the apparent closure of the process brought about. Those many marks of understanding and friendship were for me a great support. They gave me the feeling that not only did people wish me well, but also that many shared my views, even if they did not put them publicly in writing. They were grateful for a presentation of the Christian faith and message in my writing, which they considered to make sense in the present world. Especially overwhelming was the positive reaction of the press at large, though some journalists were not deceived by the limited character of the freedom I had just recovered, as titles of some editorials and articles showed: "En liberté surveillée," "Amère victoire," and so on, while others saw the Notification as complete absolution from all accusations: "Dupuis inquiry ends with honor satisfied," "A matter of justice. Was the trial of Jacques Dupuis really necessary?" and so forth.

The phone calls on February 26 from journalists based in Rome kept me busy the whole day. Each one wanted to know more about the case, and report it in the press with some direct input from me. As it was impossible to satisfy everyone by phone, I thought of the possibility, not of holding an official press conference, which would stir things up too much, but of speaking quietly at the Gregorian to interested journalists. But this quiet talk has a story of its own, which it is worth reporting.

I informed my superior, Fr. Egaña, and Fr. Imoda, the rector of the university, of my intention. They first thought the permission to proceed should depend on the rector; the rector, in turn, was thoroughly opposed to my speaking to journalists about the outcome of my case in the precincts of the Gregorian. I could only keep quiet about the whole affair, and there could be no question of involving the Gregorian in an expression of solidarity with my recovered freedom of speech. As I did not want to disappoint the request of many journalists, I decided to consult Father General at once on the matter. I explained to him the situation: the many phone calls from journalists asking for direct information, and the strong opposition of the rector to my receiving journalists at the Gregorian, even on a discrete basis. The reaction of Father General was entirely positive in my favor. He completely supported my intention to speak to the journalists, insisting that this was a good thing to do, both for me and for the Society. The truth, he said, should be known, though I had to be prudent in the way of proposing it. This is how on the next day, February 27, at 11 o'clock, I met the journalists at the gate of the university, and we proceeded together to a hall for an informal talk. Incidentally, the rector of the university and its three vice rectors were present, though very discretely.

The session was presided over by Fr. O'Collins. When I was asked by the chair what I wanted to communicate, I expressed my sense of relief at being able to speak freely after two and a half years of enforced silence. I thanked the journalists for their interest and their generous response to my invitation for an interview. I promised to tell them the whole truth, insofar as I myself knew it, while being well aware that I did not know everything about my own case—would I ever know later?—and eventually would have to answer some of their questions by admitting to not knowing the answer. On my part I was determined to be frank and had no intention of hiding anything. I did admit that the whole procedure had been for me "a great suffering" and that my present sense of relief at recovering my freedom of speech was not without misgivings about what the future might still have in store.

The journalists obviously appreciated this attitude of openness and sincerity, and after a quick but substantial review of the proceedings of the case there followed an interesting and open exchange of questions and answers. I had to admit my lack of information about where the denunciation of my book had come from, to begin with, having no definite information on the subject but only guesses and rumors which had not been verified and which, therefore, I found it improper to report; similarly, on the personal responsibility of individual persons in the trial, about which too there was no totally reliable information. When I was asked by one journalist what I thought about the procedure followed in the trial by the CDF, I declined to comment, professing not to be a canon lawyer and directing the enquirer to specialists in the matter, such as Fr. Ladislas Orsy in his article mentioned above. The procedure foreseen in the *Agendi Ratio* was submitted by Fr. Orsy to thorough criticism. The session ended at one o'clock, with the journalists apparently satisfied, judging from the covering of the meeting in the press in the next days. From the rector and the superior who had been discretely present I heard no comment whatever. I suppose that they had wanted to check on what I would say and not say. I interpreted their silence as a sign of approval.

G.O'C.: *As you now look back on those twenty-nine months of trial and agony, what are your personal reflections?*

J.D.: Your question seems somehow ambiguous. You ask me, as I now look back on those twenty-nine months—from October 1998 to February 2001—what my reflections are. But my looking back is not on twenty-nine months of trial, but on four full years, from October 1998 to November-December 2002, the time of writing. I have already mentioned—we shall have to return to it—that the publication of the official text of the Notification did not mark the end of my period of trial. I must postpone to later—when, I do not know—my reflections on the entire story. As for what I felt at the end of the twenty-nine months, I think I have already expressed it sufficiently. There was a mixture of satisfaction, on the one hand, for the fact that the worst seemed to have been avoided and, on the other, an abiding presentiment about what could still happen. Mistrust and suspicion prevailed over a sense of peace.

G.O'C.: *What happened to your lecturing and writing after the publication of the Notification? What are your reflections now about the imposition of secrecy to which you were submitted?*

J.D.: I have mentioned earlier that I abstained from lecturing outside, between the publication of the Notification on February 26, 2001, and the months of May and September of the same year; and I have already hinted that my talks in Brussels on May 15 and 17, 2001, and my communication at the Lublin Congress (September 18-21), which were soon published, would be the starting point of new trouble. Of this more later.

I did, however, continue to give talks, both in Italy and outside, in the following months. These included a course on the theology of religions at the Pontifical Atheneum of St. Anselm in Rome (September 17-28), and the lecture for the *Tablet* Open Day in London on October 12. Incidentally, this took place in the Senate Hall of the Anglican Communion at Westminster, and I thought to myself that I certainly would never be allowed to talk in the Hall of the Synod of Bishops at the Vatican; this lecture was published in the *Tablet* in three installments (October 20, October 27, and November 3, 2001). There were also a talk at the Fondazione G. Lazzati in Milan on October 27, three lectures to ecumenical groups at the LARC XVI Conference in Raleigh, North Carolina, United States (November 6-7), and a public lecture at Duke University of Durham, North Carolina (8th November), also in the United States, a talk at an International Session at the Fondazione per la ricerca sulla pace in Venice (December 3), and another at the Istituto Superiore di Scienze religiose delle Venezie at Padua (December 4). These took me till December 2001. After the publication of the Notification I did not abstain from giving talks or writing articles. As a matter of fact the flow of invitations never abated.

Each time I was conscious of remaining under suspicion on the part of the CDF and therefore had to be especially circumspect about what I said and how I said it. I felt my freedom of speech badly curtailed, even while I remained convinced that what I was proposing was in agreement with the church's faith. This sensation of being under constant supervision, not to say of being tracked by authority and subject to eventual new denunciation, was indeed very painful to bear. One felt like being continuously pursued by a new version of the Inquisition for spreading wrong doctrines. Yet this was the price to be paid.

As for the imposition of secrecy about the proceedings on my case, to which I had been subjected for so long, what do I think about it? I thought then and continue to think today that such imposition of secrecy is deeply unjust, and is devised on the part of the authority merely as a self-protection against possible criticism of their authoritative ways of proceeding. I had played the game all the while of keeping silent and would still continue to play it thereafter, not only to avoid new repression but also in deference to directives from my superiors. But I was determined to let the thing out of the bag one day, which is precisely what I am doing through the present book.

G.O'C.: *Since early October 1998, you could no longer lecture at the Gregorian University. This was deeply painful for you, but students still came to visit you. Tell me a little about this.*

J.D.: It was indeed very painful to be deprived, in the circumstances which I have described, of my optional course on "Special Questions of Christology" in the second cycle of the faculty of theology, which I was supposed to give to a very large audience during the first semester of the academic year 1998-1999, starting in the very month of October 1998. On the other hand, I did not think it feasible in preparing each lecture to ask myself whether I was allowed or not to say this or that. This was simply not compatible with my own way of teaching, consisting of sharing with my audience what I believed with the core of my being. I therefore accepted the sacrifice of seeing my course cancelled, a sacrifice all the more painful since I was going to reach the age limit for teaching (seventy-five years) according to the statutes of the university during those months, and would not be allowed to teach any more the following year. This means that the course which I renounced would in fact have been my last one. It was not, as is sometimes said, that I received from the CDF a *ne doceat* for the future; the fact is that I was reaching the age limit for teaching. The suggestion made to the authorities by a well-wishing colleague to the effect that I should be offered an extra year of teaching in compensation for the course I had lost was not accepted.

Students continued for some time to come and consult with me, but I was no longer allowed to direct doctorate theses, apart from bringing to conclusion those which were on the way. Once teaching ends, one is soon forgotten, as students no longer have easy opportunity for direct contact. I became for many among them a mere object of curiosity because of the delicate situation in which I found myself—this is the famous Fr. Dupuis! they were saying in a low voice—except for those who knew my writing and had derived some inspiration from it. I found myself becoming fast an outsider in the university, not to say a complete stranger.

G.O'C.: *Your health suffered under the strain of the CDF process. Tell me what happened to you health-wise in those twenty-nine months.*

J.D.: I do not like to speak about my physical health. I have already mentioned that I went to hospital several times for various ailments over the period of those twenty-nine months. The whole trial has deeply affected my person and mental health. I felt, and continue even today to feel, like a broken man who can never fully recover from the suspicion, which the authority of my church—a church which I love and have served during my whole life—has thrust upon me. The joy of living has gone, perhaps never to return. I do not recall even one instance when, since October 2, 1998, I had a hearty laugh. Neither have I been able since then to enjoy any real distraction. I had periods of dejection, during which I purposely avoided all company to make sure of not allowing myself to express my feelings in a way which others would not understand. I felt left alone and disowned. There remained blind faith and prayer for perseverance.

G.O'C.: *Was your faith in God ever seriously put to the test in those twenty-nine months?*

J.D.: Thanks to God's grace I did keep the faith. It never occurred to me that I could seriously put into question my faith in God and in the Lord Jesus. I was committed to both with all my being. The church at whose hands I was suffering would be another matter. I was deeply shocked and hurt by the insensitivity and inhumanity of the central authority. While my faith in God remained unhurt, I nonetheless asked myself questions: Why? What have I done to God for having to suffer so much? The abstract answer to that question is of course simple: not God but men are the cause of evil. Yet, concretely the question lingered all the same. I was reminded of reactions of many Jews after their people had gone through the agony of the Shoah: What was God doing all the time? It is said that God allows those people whom he loves to suffer. And were they not God's chosen people? But, would they not have preferred to be less the object of God's special choice, in which case they would perhaps have had to suffer less? I do not wish to dramatize my own suffering by comparing it with the atrociously inhuman sufferings of an entire people—which would be trivial on my part. But only persons who have gone through trials similar to what I endured are in a position to understand: I was searching for explanations, and the thought occurred to me that perhaps I needed to experience this trial in atonement for my sins. Or was it that God wanted to test my faith, or let me undergo a serious setback lest I should pride myself on the success of my theological career?

G.O'C.: *Were you ever close to losing your trust in the church?*

J.D.: This is a different question. Yet, here too I found comfort in my faith. I had learnt that the church is not the Roman Curia and its bureaucracy; the church is the people of God gathered in Jesus Christ and deriving its worth and meaning from its Master and Lord. It is at once divine and human. We are the church, the depository of God's blessings to the world in Jesus Christ, but we carry this treasure in earthen vessels. Nor did I hold the simple—too simple—distinction made by some official teaching: the church is all holy even though her members may be sinful. This distinction is an implausible way of escaping from reality. I had experienced that the church itself is sinful, that some of its structures, including some of its central authority, are sinful. That is why not only the members but also the church itself is *semper reformanda*. That faith made it possible for me to remain deeply committed to the church which I loved in spite of what I was suffering at its hands. We need to be convinced that we share at once in the church's holiness and sinfulness, and that we are all responsible for improving through reform and renewal the witness which it bears to the world in its structures as well as through its members. Yet the sinfulness of some church structures needs to be denounced and corrected for its message to be credible.

This abiding faith did not prevent me from having fits of anger and of temptation. I was in good company in what I experienced. I remembered having been somewhat surprised, even shocked, when earlier I read the declaration which Leonardo Boff made on leaving the order and the priesthood. He thought he had to take that decision in order to remain faithful to himself and his vocation. What I had failed to understand then became plausible later, and I began to sympathize with the decision, even if I still did not approve of it. In any case, while it did not belong to me to judge, it did belong to me to try to sympathize with a brother who suffered, while the institution seemed to remain unconcerned. I thank God for the grace to overcome those moments of doubt and uncertainty, due to no merit of mine but through God's sheer mercy and compassion. I did pray for my perseverance and for the courage to endure.

G.O'C.: *What held you together, faith-wise, through the twenty-nine months of the CDF's investigation? Where did you draw your strength from? How did you interpret this ordeal in terms of faith?*

J.D.: I have already partly answered this question. There is such a thing as blind faith and in times of doubt and trial the only remedy seems to be to abide by such faith. Moments of spiritual consolation were few during all that time. Someone did remark to me that I often alluded to human death. I did not really wish to die, and the instinct for survival and the sheer craving for life were too strong for me to hope sincerely for death. I have always been convinced that a person who professes to wish for death must not be easily believed. It is often a way of expressing one's deep sufferings and the difficulty of enduring them. In my case, however, the determination to stand the trial and to fight it out prevailed over the tendency to give in to despair and to throw in the towel. Where did I draw the strength from? For one thing, my faith in God our Father and in his Son Jesus remained unshaken, and no disillusion with proceedings of church authority could unsettle it. I could well understand why many people today say: God and Jesus Christ, yes; the church, no. But I also knew that it is through the mediation of human beings and structures, whatever their failings, that God and Jesus become present to us. Faith required a degree of forgiveness and compassion. For another thing, even if there was a lot of indifference around me, I was not alone in my struggle. I could all along rely on the moral support of my Father General and of my superior, Fr. Egaña, as well as on the academic help of my theological adviser and advocate, Fr. O'Collins, and on the genuine concern and sympathy of so many friends outside who had rallied around me in time of adversity.

G.O'C.: *In terms of justice, how did you rate the process conducted by the CDF in your regard? Do you think the process should be revised and, if so, in what way? How do you rate the CDF process in terms of academic freedom?*

J.D.: I am neither a lawyer nor a canon lawyer. As regards the justice of the *Agendi Ratio* of 1997 or the lack of the same, I have referred to Fr. Ladislas Orsy, a specialist in the matter, and to his article entitled "Are Church Investigation Procedures Really Just?" He compares the CDF's norms with what he calls "the legal wisdom of our age," only to conclude on the injustice by modern standards of the procedures followed by the CDF. One is surprised at the assurance with which Cardinal Ratzinger defends the total fairness of these norms against every criticism from authorities in the philosophy of law. The norms are established by the CDF itself for its own convenience and protection, and therefore not likely to be repudiated without the pope's approval. For myself, however, even more than the injustice of these norms I would mention their impersonal and inhuman, and therefore un-Christian, character.

I had lived in Rome for fifteen years without any suspicion in a matter of doctrine, when out of the blue it hit me that I had been under investigation for who knows how long and that a Contestation of my work had been launched by the members of the CDF after a consultation with some of their consultors chosen for the purpose, and all of this under top secrecy. I began then to wonder for how long I had had a file at the CDF. When I was informed about the case, I was not allowed to know who were my detractors, much less anything about what appeared like a parody of a defense, the consultor who would speak *pro auctore*—Karl Becker, it would seem—being chosen by the cardinal prefect of the CDF without any reference to the accused. The roles of prosecution, defense, and the court that would pronounce judgment were all combined in the same hands. The members of the CDF who decided on the Contestation of the book had already formally judged it to contain grievous errors against the faith Divine and Catholic, even before the case had been heard. And so on. All personal contact was excluded till such time as I was called for the tragic meeting of September 4, 2000, where my signature on a Notification against my book was to be extorted from me under duress. So much for impersonality and inhumanity.

As far as dishonesty is concerned, it was dishonest to add restrictions and threats to the second version of the Notification which I had signed under pressure, thus creating the myth—that would be used against me—that I had agreed to a drastic curtailing of my freedom in speech and writing. To call all the procedures a prolonged and friendly dialogue between the authorities of the CDF and the author under trial was to my sense as trivial as it was dishonest, and it was hard to believe that high officials at the Roman Curia—in particular Cardinal Ratzinger himself—could indulge in public lies to hide the meanness of the procedure they followed. Others did not allow themselves to be easily deceived by such a parody of truth, as is shown for instance by the "Cardinals duel on the Dupuis case," to which I have referred above.

There remains the question of the possibility of having a judgment revised and revoked. This possibility does not, however, exist according to the *Agendi Ratio*. Father Orsy explains that involving the authority of the pope at the very first stage of the inquiry is meant to exclude a priori all recourse to a higher authority after a judgment has been pronounced. Tissa Balasuriya, after the condemnation of excommunication had been pronounced against him, expressed his desire to appeal to the authority of the pope, only to be told that the possibility of such an appeal was excluded by the fact of the pope's authority being already involved in the previous judgment. All one can hope is that history will show one day that such and such opinions, which were once condemned as against the faith, were in fact not only in agreement with it but also eventually became common property of theologians. This has happened many times in history, and the greatest among the theologians of the last century have at some time been suspected of error, if not of heresy, by the church's doctrinal authority, only to become later the leading theological lights of the Second Vatican Council.

There is then need for patience and hope for better days, while praying that the church at the top may learn from its mistakes and begin to admit them. Meanwhile, however, the academic freedom of theologians has been badly curtailed in recent years by the apostolic letter *Ad tuendam fidem* (1998) and Cardinal Ratzinger's detailed commentary on it. The letter defines as narrowly as possible the limits of dissent in the church, forcing Catholics to accept all levels of church teaching almost as if they were equal. A "profession of faith" followed, which has been the object of much criticism, as it asserts the existence of a new category of truths which, though not presented by the Magisterium as formally revealed, are necessary for faithfully keeping and expounding the deposit of faith and can therefore in practice be considered as irreformable.

G.O'C.: *After those twenty-nine months you read Cardinal Yves Congar's* Diary of a Theologian (1946-1956), *in which he referred to his ordeal with the then Holy Office, the precursor of the CDF. As you read those pages what thoughts went through your mind?*

J.D.: The *Diary of a Theologian (1946–1956)* (*Journal d'un théologien*) of Fr. Congar was published in Paris by Editions du Cerf in 2000, before the end, therefore, of what you call the twenty-nine months of my trial. That expression is deceptive as it would seem to imply that with the publication of the Notification on my book on February 26, 2001, my problem had been resolved and was henceforth a past story. This is not correct, as subsequent events, already alluded to above, made clear. If I got hold of Congar's diary as soon as it was available and read it through with passion almost at one stretch in spite of its 462 pages, the reason is that I myself was under accusation and thought I could learn something from it about what to make of my own case. In any event, I was in a position to sympathize deeply with what Congar had endured for ten years. I have already said that my own trials were little compared to what he had been made to suffer during those long years from 1946 to 1956.

I would also insist on a great difference between his case and mine, namely the fact that I did have the support of my Father General throughout, while he was let down even by his religious superiors. Nevertheless, there were similarities where the relations with the Roman authorities were concerned. I read Congar's account with utter excitement, not out of mere curiosity but because I identified myself existentially with his evaluation of the theological situation in which he had to operate, with the questions he asked, with the feelings he expressed, with the doubts he formulated, and even with his wondering about the meaning of his life in the church and the order. I found the reading at once staggering and enticing, for the author's thorough sincerity with himself as he jotted down his thoughts on paper, for the bluntness of his description of concrete situations, and not least for his vivid style and his mixture of tragic accents with comic anecdotes. What thrilled me in reading it is that he often expressed—better than I myself would have been able to formulate them—feelings, questions, and doubts that I had myself experienced.

I hesitate to give here some samples of the way Congar thought, for fear of distorting his thoughts by taking them out of their broad context. As samples of the direct character of his writing, I may mention that Congar referred to the Holy Office as the Gestapo and had dreams about KZ (*Konzentrazionslager*): he had been a prisoner of war during the Second World War and had been liberated only recently when his troubles with church authority began. And—should I say it or not—twice in the book he mentioned that he went to urinate on the wall of the Palace of the Holy Office to show his utter contempt. These notations and many others make one wonder whether, if the publication of the *Diary* had been made before the year 1993, Yves Congar would have been created a cardinal of the Holy Roman Church.

Perhaps the most important and tragic part of the book is the chapter entitled "Affaires de Rome," dealing with relations with Roman authorities, both in his religious order and in the Vatican, from November 1954 to August 1955. It is from that chapter that I draw here a few quotations. On November 22, 1954, Congar writes:

> There is today a side of my being which is painfully shocked, trauma-tized, by the absurdity of it all, by the total absence of consideration for [a] man apostolically committed. . . . I am hurt deeply, pain-fully. . . . They have broken something in me, and I will no longer be the same man hereafter. Of course, there is also in me a man who, in health, with realism and optimism, will find the good sides of the situation and will accommodate himself to the conditions in which he is placed. There is too a third dimension, that of prayer and of the psalms, of faith which consists in obeying God without knowing where he is leading us, of invincible hope. There is finally the man who will seek not to be defeated by evil, to remain himself in spite of all, . . . to continue to build up his own life in Christ, to show interest in people and to enter into communion with them wherever he meets them; to be, to become, fully valuable for people in view of Jesus Christ.

This mixture of feelings of depression at experiencing deep hurt and of cou-rageous determination to meet the reality of concrete situations recurs again and again, with different accents or emphases on one side or the other.

On December 11, 1954, he writes: "On the eve of being questioned on my writings and my tendencies, I cannot help asking myself questions. Shall I not be led soon to take an option? Which one? . . ." After having considered different solutions which appear to him inadequate, he expands on one:

> To resolve myself to quit teaching . . . would perhaps be the best, provided that would allow me to continue to work, even to publish: but this seems chimerical. Rome (the "Holy Office") will never admit less than an absolute submission—with guarantees *ad arbitrium suum*—or an absolute silence. This, if it were to be imposed on me, would lead sooner or later to my leaving the church. Unless, giving a new direction to my life, I would find or be offered a priestly situation without doctrinal implication: pure apostolate, pure service, education of children, a purely monastic life. But my vocation is to work about doctrine, at the "doctrinal service of the people of God."

Would not such an issue be an evasion, a reason? And having reviewed all the possibilities, he adds:

> Beside those hypotheses all of which have their difficulties I can think only of some more or less dramatic solutions, which put as many questions as they solve: To disappear? But how? I cannot, nor do I wish, to kill myself, or to have myself killed. . . . To become Orthodox? Not Anglican (humanly possible, the solution would be contrary to too many doctrinal certitudes . . .), but Orthodox? But the Catholic Church is the church for the West; there truly is something apostolic in Rome, which the Orthodox do not honor; they too have their miseries, and I would be prisoner of something different, but still a prisoner. . . . Have myself reduced to the lay state and have a position (Hautes Etudes or other), allowing myself to live and to work? But what an adventure! My mother, my family; nieces and nephews. . . . I have a priestly and Dominican vocation; and one is only happy in one's vocation. It represents God's will. I do not like this type of men [those who desert]. Then what?

One cannot help being struck by the thorough sincerity of this questioning and its drastic character. To be shocked or scandalized at it would only prove one's inability to appreciate the tragedy of a situation with no apparent exit. Rather than detract from Congar's greatness, his questioning witnesses to the depth of his humanity.

Again on February 5, 1955, he wrote: "I am reduced almost to nothing: to a total impasse. I hit against a pitiless system, which cannot either correct or even recognize, its injustices, and which is served or represented by men overflowing with goodness and piety. Yet what I need is not goodness but justice." And later, on July 30, 1955, on the eve of a meeting with his provincial regarding some directives coming from the Holy Office:

> This prospect causes in me this Saturday evening a very serious fit of discouragement, of disgust, of bottomless weariness. I see that there will never be anything to do till I die—oh deliverance; that as long as I breathe they will thrust me down—till there be no more in me a breath coming from me. I visualize again all that they have progressively closed down for me. . . . I revolt against the injustice, the lie, the iniquity. I feel like sending everything flying. I hang on to Compline and Matins, to show up all the same, to pray (?) all the same. I place myself before Christ in agony, on the cross: he, the pure and the perfect holy one, has known the assault of discouragement and has accepted to pass for a blasphemer justly condemned and chastised. I hold on to that contemplation of Christ surmounting his disgust with an Amen of his will. I unite myself to him as I can. But then again I pass extremely painful hours.

These quotations give the measure of the deep suffering imposed on Congar during those years, but also of his determination to endure. My own case appeared trivial in comparison, but the reading aroused in me deep echoes of sympathy and compassion. The similarities between his reactions and the way I myself felt were not lacking.

Another book which I read or rather reread and meditated on during those years is Henri de Lubac's *Meditation sur l'Eglise,* first published by Aubier, Paris, in 1953, and translated into English under the rather pompous title *The Splendour of the Church.* This book has been wrongly presented as de Lubac's making amends after being pushed aside by authority, while in fact the bulk of the material in it had been assembled before (see H. de Lubac, *Mémoire sur l'occasion de mes écrits* [Namur: Culture et vérité, 1989], 78-80). In chapter 6, entitled "The Sacrament of Jesus Christ," de Lubac wrote:

> It may well be that many things, in the human context of the church, deceive us. It is also possible that we be, without fault on our part, deeply misunderstood. It may happen that in its very bosom we may have to undergo persecution. The case is not unheard of, though we must avoid to apply it to ourselves presumptuously. Patience and silent love will then be of more value than anything else: we will not have to fear the judgment of those who do not see the heart, and we

will think that the church never gives us Jesus Christ better than it does on those occasions that it gives us of being configured to his Passion. We will continue, through our witness, to serve the faith the church does not desist from preaching. The test will perhaps be heavier if it does not come from the malice of some men, but from a situation which may appear inextricable; for generous pardoning is not enough then to overcome it, nor is it enough to forget one's own person. Let us, however, be happy, in front of "the Father who sees in secret," to share in this way in that *Veritatis unitas* which we implore for all on the day of Good Friday. Let us be happy, if we buy then at the price of the blood of our soul the intimate experience which will lend efficacy to our words when we will have to sustain an unsettled brother. . . .

De Lubac's testimony is comparable, with differences, to that of Congar. Both recommend a blind recourse to faith in the experience of trial and of fidelity in giving witness. But I may confess that I found myself more attuned, in my own trial, to Congar's deeply human reactions than to de Lubac's lofty considerations.

G.O'C.: *A few months after the Notification was published, you again accepted invitations/or lectures. These arrived from many parts of the world. You gave a talk in Brussels, Belgium, in May 2001, and one in Lublin, Poland, in September, both of which were published before the end of the year 2001. These writings brought new troubles for you which almost nobody knows about. I know you have spoken a little on this earlier in our conversations, but could you say a little more about what actually happened?*

J.D.: I have mentioned above that after the publication of the Notification on February 26, 2001, I resumed giving lectures outside and publishing articles in May. I have given above a list of lectures I delivered. The invitations poured in from many quarters. Was it because, with the publication of the Notification, people thought that the case was all over and I could henceforth speak my whole mind? Or was it that they wanted to know what I thought, independently from, or even perhaps because of, my disagreement with the CDF? I was aware of having to be circumspect in speaking, and even more in writing, as I remained under close supervision. However, I also thought I had to continue to speak my mind, even if cautiously. I went to Brussels in mid-May where I gave two lectures: one public on May 15 on "Les enjeux de la théologie des religions et du dialogue interreligieux aujourd'hui"; the other, on May 17, in the context of a theological seminar at the Institut d'Etudes Théologiques, dedicated to my own book of 1997. I entitled that lecture "Le Verbe de Dieu, Jésus-Christ et les religions du monde." It must be taken into account that well before May 2001, in fact as early as the end of March 2000, I had finished writing the new book which would be published in Italian in September 2001. The talk at the seminar in Brussels summed up the theme of an entire chapter of the new book, which would be available in French only in September 2002. The subject was a delicate one, since I was maintaining and further substantiating, in spite of objections raised by the CDF, what I had affirmed in my previous book: regarding a saving action of the Word of God as such before the incarnation of the Word in Jesus Christ and, likewise, an abiding saving action of the Word as such, even after the incarnation and the resurrection of Jesus' humanity—not of course without an essential relatedness with the saving action of the Word in the humanity of Jesus assumed by him at the incarnation. The director of the *Nouvelle revue théologique*—who also ran the seminar—asked me for a copy of the manuscript, and after consulting his staff, asked for permission to publish it in the review. It appeared in the October-December 2001 issue. Interestingly, Bernard Pottier, the director of the review, published in the same number an article of his own, "Note sur la mission invisible du Verbe chez Saint Thomas d'Aquin," in which, after having examined closely the texts of St. Thomas, he concluded that Aquinas seems to agree with me where he distinguishes two missions of the Word of God, one visible and one invisible. That article of mine was one of those which would initiate new trouble at the beginning of 2002.

The other article which was to launch new trouble was the paper I gave at the International Congress of Fundamental Theology at the University of Lublin, September 18-21, 2001. The theme of the Congress was "Christianity Tomorrow," an ambitious title to which, however, the organization of the Congress and its proceedings did more than justice. The theme was developed in three stages: Christianity yesterday, Christianity today, and Christianity tomorrow, thus placing in evidence the steps forward and the progress in theological outlook and thinking brought about by the Second Vatican Council and after. I found myself in the third section in the company of such prominent speakers as Bruno Forte and Walbert Bühlmann. I was impressed by the open atmosphere and the warm receptions which most participants—with a few notable exceptions—gave to views and ideas which, I thought, would have had no currency in theological circles in Poland in past generations. My communication—which, a commentator wrote, had been "intensely awaited" by the audience—was entitled in Italian "L'unità e il pluralismo. Il cristianesimo e le religioni."

In this talk I asked whether, from the viewpoint of Christianity, the plurality of religions which we know today must be seen as an evil to be tolerated and an impediment to the realization of the divine plan of salvation; or, on the contrary, can be seen as having a positive significance in the plan of God for humankind, which theology has still to discover. I declared myself in favor of the second alternative, explaining that there is only one divine plan of salvation for humankind which culminates in the saving work of the one mediator, Jesus Christ, but that the other religious traditions find their place and have a positive role to play, within that one divine plan, for the salvation of their members, in relation to the Christ event. To affirm this is not to renounce what is of the essence of Christian faith, but only to denounce the Christian exclusivism of the past; it allows for a deeper understanding of the manifold revelatory and salvific action of God throughout the entire religious history of humankind. I thought this position was rather unassailable and should represent today the common thinking of theologians. But not so in high quarters; this rather innocent talk—which was published in Lublin with the entire Acta of the Congress, even before the event—quite a feat!—would in fact soon be the second piece of my recent writing to provoke new sparks.

G.O'C.: *After the publication of these two lectures, Cardinal Ratzinger wrote a letter to Father General asking him to take procedures against you. Father General informed you. Could you recount what happened?*

J.D.: The letter of Cardinal Ratzinger to Father General, dated January 8, 2002, was a personal initiative of the cardinal. Unlike the earlier documents, it contained no reference whatever to the pope or any approval from him of a new intervention on the part of the CDF. I have already referred to this letter, as well as to the attached "Evaluation of affirmations and theological theses maintained by Fr. Jacques Dupuis after the publication of the declaration *Dominus Iesus* and of the Notification about the book 'Verso una teologia Cristiana del pluralismo religioso,'" which challenged the two articles mentioned above. This new document, which filled four pages, had nothing in common, as far as the form is concerned—the content is a different matter—with the previous documents, where explicit reference had been made to the approval by the members of the CDF after a session with its consultors. Here there was nothing of the sort, and the Evaluation seemed to come from the private initiative of a zealous consultor—it would not be hard to guess his name. Unlike previous occasions Father General did not write directly to me but sent the documents in a letter, dated January 11, to Fr. Imoda, the rector of the university, who in turn sent them to me also by letter on January 15. The impersonal mode of communication on the part of the rector was indeed striking, especially considering the content of the new documents and the serious measures which they threatened to take against me. The cardinal, as would have been expected, referred to the commitment I was supposed to have made in the text added after my signature of the second version of the Notification on my book, to abide strictly by the doctrinal content of the Notification. He thus spoke of a "contradiction" between the Notification which I had promised to follow blindly and what I was now saying and writing; with this, the use or abuse of my signature which the Congregation had intended to make, was fully verified. I have already quoted the main sentence of the cardinal's letter in which, in the new situation, he requested Father General, "with the authority that belongs to him, at least to require that Fr. Dupuis abstain in the future from intervening in word and writing on the matter." This would have amounted to reducing me to total silence on the subject to which I had devoted my whole work and energy for years.

On receiving the letter and the document attached, I immediately asked for an interview with Father General, which was also immediately granted. Father General, who himself was due to go soon to hospital for surgery, told me that he would consult on the matter and reflect before making a decision and taking any measures. He was not in the habit of rushing through decisions and would abstain from communicating to the cardinal any reaction of his before mature reflection. The operation which he was to undergo would postpone even further any decision on his part. This explains how the letter of Father General in which he communicated to me his decision on the subject was dated one month later, on February 13, 2002. Of this letter more hereafter.

In the meantime I examined the Evaluation of my two recent articles attached to Cardinal Ratzinger's letter. I have already mentioned that the theology of that document was of a poor quality, which confirmed my suspicion about its probable origin. I have already referred to some of the incompetent criticisms it made of my articles, as where it proposed the christological formula—"the Word as such is the Incarnate Word"—which seems quite incorrect, insofar as it would imply that the humanity of Jesus exists really, not only intentionally, in God's eternity, or that the incarnation of the Son of God was necessary, and not totally free on the part of God. But not everything needs to be repeated a second time.

But there were other surprising things to be found in the Evaluation, and Fr. O'Collins, with whom I shared it, agreed with me about its poor theological quality. He wrote a letter to Father General, dated January 26, in which he expressed his surprise at the content of the Evaluation, and confessed to be "much perplexed" by it, especially with the way in which it seemed to "sweep aside the doctrine of the Council of Constantinople III about the divine 'energies and operations' of the Eternal Son of God not being lost or suppressed in and through the Incarnation"—a doctrine on which I based part of my argument. To his letter Fr. O'Collins joined a three-page report on the Evaluation, in which he further substantiated his impression of theological shabbiness. The author repeated *ad nauseam* the trite accusation of a "separation" not merely of a "distinction" between the action of the Word as such and that of the Word through his human nature, and consequently between the two natures of Christ, concluding to a clear Nestorian tendency of my writing; and again that the religious traditions are "considered as such"—that is, in their entirety—"ways of salvation," while I had attributed salvific value to the elements of truth and grace contained in them, and added that their salvific value comes "from their relationship to the Christ event"; and so on and so forth. In an earlier note on the topic, dated January 17, Fr. O'Collins had already written: "I believe that the points raised (à propos of Fr. Dupuis by the Evaluation) are not convincing and it would be a serious injustice to impose on him the silence suggested (by Cardinal Ratzinger's letter). . . . Quite frankly any view (as is made in the Evaluation) of the divine activity of the eternal Logos being 'eclipsed, circumscribed' etc. as a result of the incarnation seems to be hardly consonant with Catholic faith. . . ." He went on to note: "Dupuis is not accurately represented. Approximate sentences are quoted from him. But then his words are twisted or not precisely explained. Maybe on this issue something bigger than Catholic theology is at stake." Who then was heretic and who orthodox? And who was prosecutor and who the accused? The author of the Evaluation was disqualifying himself as a fair arbiter and a competent judge—thereby appending his name incognito to the document—though with the covering approval of the cardinal prefect of the CDF.

G.O'C.: *When eventually the decision of Father General came about the measures to be imposed on you, what did it really say and what were the consequences?*

J.D.: The letter of Father General to me, dated February 13, 2002, came as a shock as in a long letter to him dated January 25 I had expressed my hope of being able to discuss again the matter with him before any decision was taken about my fate. In this my letter I made reference to the two Appendices I had intended to add to my new book, in which I explained the reasons why I could not possibly accept in their entirety the two documents of the Congregation. These two Appendices (which in the book as it was actually published in Italian in September 2001 had been replaced by a Postscript) had been reworked in what I called "Some Reflections on Two Roman Documents," and I suggested to Father General that perhaps this text could be sent to Cardinal Ratzinger for his consideration and reflection, since they threw much light on the matters concerned; this, however, was not to happen, being considered improper. Meanwhile my superiors, the rector in particular, were getting even more nervous than before about my case, and the rector contacted the general, asking him for clarifications on what was to be done with all the invitations I was receiving for lectures. It was in answer to that request from the rector that I received Father General's letter of February 13. He wrote: "It would seem that your rector and your superior expect from me some precise indication about the invitations that you receive from almost everywhere to speak on the theological field of your specialization." He went on to say: "Allow me to tell you . . . frankly and without ambiguity that in your publications and conferences you may no longer defend doctrinal positions which the Notification has clearly disapproved of." And he added: "The last letter of Cardinal Ratzinger leaves no doubt whatever on this requirement which affects you particularly as professor emeritus of the Gregorian, a prestigious pontifical university. . . . Hoping that all is now clear, I inform with this letter of mine your rector and your superior; to them belongs the first responsibility to see to the execution of the requirements of the Notification and of the recent letter of the cardinal."

Anticipating this letter, the rector had already requested me to cancel, as I reported above, two important appointments in London in mid-January 2002 and in Lisbon at the beginning of February. But this was not to be the end of the story. On receipt of Father General's letter I asked for a new appointment with him. I did not hide from him the pain which his February 13 letter had made me feel. I told him that I had hoped to talk the matter over again with him before a decision was taken, and that the apparent injustice of the measures required by the cardinal would be seriously considered in making a decision. Now on the contrary it seemed that a decision had been made without regard for the merit or demerit of the case. Father General listened to me with great patience, humility, and sincerity, and I was greatly impressed by his attitude. In the course of our conversation he told me how his letter had to be interpreted: it did not mean that I was to abstain altogether from any discussion of some theological aspects of the Notification, but wherever I did not agree perfectly with some theological assertions either of the declaration *Dominus Iesus* or of the Notification, I was obliged to inform my audience clearly about my dissent, and moreover to propose my own opinions with modesty and in full submission to any eventual further judgment on the part of the church authority. This courageous interpretation on the part of Father General of his own letter cleared up the situation, and I could once again resume my activities, though with renewed prudence and decision to tackle in my talks the less controversial aspects of the whole matter. There was no lack of invitations in the following months, nor are they wanting for the future.

G.O'C.: *And what happened to your writing?*

J.D.: I have mentioned that my new book, entitled in Italian *Il cristianesimo e le religioni: dallo scontro all'incontro,* was completed at the end of March 2000, well before the publication of the declaration *Dominus Iesus* on September 5, 2000, and of the Notification on my previous book on February 26, 2001. I have also mentioned that after the publication of the two documents of the CDF I wrote two Appendices, to be added to the book in answer to the two documents. Those two Appendices did not obtain from my superiors the *imprimi potest,* as they would be considered offensive to the CDF. They were replaced by a Postscript, in which I explained that, though making no explicit reference to the two documents of the CDF, implicitly I was everywhere in the book taking into account the difficulties which the CDF had formulated against my previous book and answering them. I maintained the theological posture of the previous book, and strengthened it further with new arguments and considerations. In this revised version the book obtained the *imprimi potest of* my superiors and the permission to publish was duly entered on the inside cover of the book. It is signed by Fr. Francisco J. Egaña as vice rector of the university, and dated June 3, 2001. The Italian edition by Queriniana, Brescia, came out in September 2001. A French and an English editions followed in September and October 2002; and a Spanish edition in December. Two more editions are in preparation in Portuguese-Brazilian and Polish. Trouble with the CDF is good advertisement!

It is interesting to note that there has been so far no reaction whatever to that new book on the part of the CDF; strangely, in fact, since the incriminated article in *Nouvelle revue théologique* (October-December 2001), of which we spoke above, is a shortened version of a chapter of the book. Is the presence on the inside cover of the *imprimi potest* granted by the authority of the university responsible for the abstention on the part of the CDF from any reaction to the book, while the article met with vehement reaction? Or has the publication of the book escaped the notice of my detractors? The second explanation is hardly believable. Perhaps the CDF thought it unwise to start openly another case, which would not enhance its prestige. The letter of Cardinal Ratzinger to Father General requesting him to take strong measures against me was confidential; the cardinal preferred such measures to be taken by my Father General, on whom, if the new case should come to be known, the blame would have to be put. In fact the new trouble which that letter initiated has remained little known; nor did I personally wish in any way to make again headlines in the mass media.

G.O'C.: *I understand that Cardinal Ratzinger's letter led to your removal as director of the* Gregorianum. *Could you explain what happened?*

J.D.: I mentioned above that the last episode to date of my trial came from inside the Gregorian University. It was the discontinuation of the direction I exercised for eighteen years (1985-2002) of the theological and philosophical review of the university, *Gregorianum*. In his letter to Father General dated January 8, 2002, after requesting Father General to take against me the measures referred to above, Cardinal Ratzinger had added: "I allow myself to further observe that, in case the contradiction [between the content of the Notification and what I was saying and writing] should not be dissipated, there would be need to reconsider the opportunity of the continuation (of Fr. Dupuis's) responsibility as director of the theological review *Gregorianum*." This was at the beginning of January. Incidentally, in our conversation about this letter Father General had told me that the cardinal's request in this regard was totally beside the point and was unjustified, as it had no connection with the accusation that the cardinal was making about my writing.

Yet, at the beginning of the month of May I heard rumors to the effect that the rector of the university, Fr. Imoda, intended to have me replaced at the direction of the journal. I went to see him and asked whether my information was correct, which he confirmed. I then represented to him my own view on the matter. I asked him whether there had been any complaint about the way in which I had fulfilled the function all along. His answer was: no, none whatsoever. I then explained that in that case I personally would like to continue for some time the responsibility as director. The reason was that with the end of all my teaching this was the only work I could still perform—and service I could still render—for the university, and I would not like to become a sort of parasite whose presence in the university and the religious community had no academic justification any longer. Nor did I want to find myself totally unemployed, with this last measure added to the restrictions imposed on my speaking and writing. I added that, if the request of the cardinal should become known, the decision to have me replaced at the direction of the review would be interpreted as the rector's desire to comply with the cardinal's request, even while Father General had considered such a request unjustified.

The rector listened to me, but his cool, indifferent way of reacting showed that his mind was already made up. And so on May 28, 2002, I received a letter from him stating that on October 1, my responsibility for the review would come to an end. This last blow added to my sense of estrangement from both the university and my religious community. I wondered whether, if he had been informed in advance of this decision, Father General would have found it advisable in the circumstances; the rector did not have to refer the matter to him, as such a decision entered into the limits of his competence. The fact remains that the decision looked like complying with a desire and a suggestion expressed by the cardinal, on which the rector seemed pleased to act. Once more the good reputation of the Institution in high quarters prevailed over consideration for persons.

G.O'C.: *As you look back on the whole affair after more than four years, what are your feelings now?*

J.D.: First of all, I do not have the feeling even today that the whole affair is over. One could perhaps have thought so—and many in fact did think so—after the publication of the Notification on my book. I had been absolved of the accusation of "grievous errors against the faith" and should beware of "ambiguities" in what I wrote. But, as has been noted above, through the CDF's doubtful dealings I was in fact constrained to abide, in speech and writing, by opinions I did not accept, about which all possibility of further discussion was closed for me by the sheer imposition of authority. What followed amply showed that such was the situation: the letter of Cardinal Ratzinger to Father General at the beginning of January 2002 threatened in fact more severe measures against me than had been considered in the previous documents. I am thankful to my Father General for having quietly abstained from abiding by the request of the cardinal to "reduce me to silence in speech and writing." I remain and will remain for a long time under suspicion and surveillance on the part of the CDF, which uses the good services of its informers. In a private friendly conversation in November 1999, Cardinal Godfried Danneels of Bruxelles-Malines had told me: "Have courage; this may last for twenty years!" But I will not be around in twenty years to still see it! To those who suggest jokingly that I may one day be on the list to become a cardinal, my answer is that Congar and de Lubac had their troubles when they were still young and could afford to wait for thirty years for their red hat. I do not have that much time at my disposal, nor have I any inclination to wear a red hat!

The directive given to me by Father General is that I may continue to say and write prudently what I believe, but where I am not in full agreement with the two documents of the CDF I must mention this explicitly to my audience for them to judge. In a sense this situation is quite comfortable, and my experience of having followed that directive for some time shows its wisdom and far-sightedness. Rarely have I, while doing so, met with disagreement on the part of any of my hearers. All, apart from isolated exceptions, seemed to agree with me, the documents of the CDF notwithstanding. People, even the nonprofessionals, have a sense of what to believe and the courage to think for themselves. The *sensus fidei* of simple believers is a criterion of the content of faith, with greater weight than documents from the doctrinal authorities wherever such documents tend to impose particular opinions about subjects which ought to remain open to discussion. One example is where the documents of the CDF want to force us to hold that revelation in Jesus Christ so completely contains the mystery of God that nothing can ever be added to it. Christian revelation would exhaust God's mystery once for all—while the New Testament witnesses to the fact that God's revelation will be complete only at the end of the world. But, however comfortable I may feel with the directive given me by Father General, the fact remains that I have to be extremely cautious about what to say, and to whom I say it. In my conferences I must avoid the more controversial aspects of the topics treated, being satisfied to deal with those raising fewer difficulties. And this is a source of great discomfort. How am I, for instance, to give an account of my recent new book without entering into questions such as the universal presence and action of the Word of God as such and of the Spirit of God; or of the positive significance in God's plan for humankind of the plurality of religions in which our world finds itself today? These points are integral parts of the synthesis I have been attempting to elaborate.

Therefore, back to the question: What are today your feelings about the whole affair? I must answer that the whole affair remains even today a great burden, which will never be cleared up. I have suffered a deep wound which can never be healed. I can never again be the same person as before, enjoy life as I did, with a sense of the freedom to which each person has a right. And it is the church that I love and to which I have bound myself unreservedly that is responsible for imposing on me this suffering. Thanks be to God, however, it is not the church as such nor the church as a whole, but those whose exercise of authority smacks more of imposition than of service. I cannot help asking myself how for almost forty years—from 1959 to 1998—I was able to teach systematic theology in India and in Rome without ever being questioned on my teaching, when suddenly, on October 2, 1998, a thunderbolt fell on me, with the news of being accused by the central doctrinal authority of the church of "grievous errors against the faith Divine and Catholic."

Father Egaña, who, as vice rector of the university, informed me and handed to me the documents of the Vatican, including the approval already given by the pope to the Contestation of my book, wrote to me a kind letter that very evening, in which he said: "This morning I was deeply moved when I saw the consternation which you experienced at receiving the reserved documentation which I handed on to you. I see the deep disturbance which a scholar who has dedicated his entire life to Christology feels when the supreme authority of the church casts doubt on his doctrine." These were not merely polite words; they corresponded very much to what I felt, and continue to feel even today.

The question has often been asked why I became a choice target for prosecution by the CDF. Several reasons may have guided their choice. I was holding a chair at the Gregorian University in Rome and thereby was especially vulnerable; my teaching was meeting with remarkable success, to the extent of arousing feelings of jealousy. But another explanation has been suggested several times: I was the target through which Asian, and Indian theology in particular, to which I had been and remained identified, would be hit indirectly. It would be easier for the CDF to hit a partisan than to attack directly those held responsible for spreading the "dogmatic relativism" of which Cardinal Ratzinger has accused the Asian theology of religions—with the risk of alienating an entire continent. The Asian and Indian theologians were not deceived by the maneuver, and soon after the Contestation of my book came to be known, they declared through the secretary of the Commission for Doctrine of the Indian episcopal conference that they would change nothing in their way of conceiving theology. Tissa Balasuriya wrote an article entitled "P. Dupuis, missionario alla rovescia?" (*Adista* [October 11, 1999]: 4-5), in which he suggested that I was evangelizing the Western world with the good news discovered and announced by the Eastern hemisphere.

More recently the same suggestion has been made by a Dutch author in a contribution to a scholarly book entitled *"Mission Is a Must." Intercultural Theology and the Mission of the Church*, edited by Frans Wijsen and Peter Nissen (Amsterdam: Editions Rodopi, 2002). In his contribution, entitled "Jacques Dupuis as a Theologian with a Reversed Mission. Some Remarks on His Controversial Theology of Religions," Pim Valkenberg asks why my work became the target of the CDF's accusations. He formulates three hypotheses, two of which he dismisses as unsatisfactory. He then writes:

> The basic question of this article was: why is Dupuis's theology of religious pluralism deemed to be so controversial as to lead to an investigation by the Congregation for the Doctrine of the Faith? This final section will provide an answer in three parts: a negative answer (Dupuis is not under investigation because he is a relativist or a pluralist), a superficial positive answer (he has been charged with undermining the mission of the church), and a more profound positive answer (he is a representative of "reversed mission").

He explains what he sees as the real reason:

> It is clear that Jacques Dupuis symbolizes an opposite idea of mission: he develops a theology of interreligious dialogue that is based on his prolonged experiences with this dialogue in the Indian context. Moreover, as a European theologian of unimpeachable loyalty to the Catholic Church, he is in a position to gain some influence right in the middle of its central administration. Finally, as editor-in-chief of one of the most respected theological periodicals and as supervisor of many Ph.D. students from India and the rest of Asia, he is able to influence a much larger audience in the world of theology. Therefore, Dupuis symbolizes a threat to a one-way idea of mission from the central authority of the church to local churches. Because he symbolizes the idea of a reversed mission from the experiences of interreligious dialogue in Asia to the local churches in Europe that are confronted more and more with a multicultural and multi-religious reality, the threat is not Dupuis himself but rather his theological roots in India.

This, perhaps, is the most lucid analysis of the situation which has been proposed up to date. It gives me a sense of purpose in the midst of suffering that has to be endured in promoting a good cause.

G.O'C.: *Now you are nearing your eightieth birthday. As you look back over all these years in the Society of Jesus and in the academic field, how do you evaluate your life's work?*

J.D.: Where my life in the Society of Jesus over the last sixty-one years is concerned—I joined in 1941—I can truly say that I never seriously doubted my vocation, even if during the last four years of trial serious, even radical questions came to my mind as to the meaning of my perseverance in it. Through God's grace I received the gift of perseverance in what I had always considered my God-given vocation. I must add—I have already mentioned it several times—that the support of Father General and of Fr. Egaña, my religious superior at the Gregorian, during the years of trial were of immense value to me.

As for my life's work in the academic field, it is not for me to evaluate it. I found the work which was entrusted to me fascinating; it corresponded fully to what were my natural inclinations, and I consecrated to it all my energy and all my talents throughout my professional career. This I say independently of the results I may have achieved, of which I am not the judge. As I review, from the viewpoint of academic performance, the long thirty-six years spent in India —twenty-five of which in teaching systematic theology—and the added fifteen years at the Gregorian, teaching Christology and the theology of religions for the second cycle in the faculty of theology, I can say that I never got weary, despondent, or disillusioned with the job. On the contrary, I always found it thrilling to try and share with others what were my deepest convictions and what was my own perception of the faith in Jesus Christ which we share but which we shall never fully comprehend. I cannot understand how some professors of theology can consider teaching a burden. This is not to say that for me teaching was easy. It swallowed up all my time and energy by way of research and of a careful preparation of classes. But it also opened the way for personal contact with the students and the direction of their written work, either at the licentiate level or that of the doctorate. I always felt much enriched by such contacts, as I myself was endeavoring to share with the students the experience of faith and knowledge that I had acquired.

Regarding writing and publications, my years spent at the Gregorian were more productive than those in India. Commitments in India were so many—including pastoral work, giving retreats, work for the episcopal conference, talks to assemblies of bishops, work for the commission of the episcopal conference for the renewal of the liturgy, many other conferences and communications at meetings and congresses, articles for *Vidyajyoti, Journal of Theological Reflection,* without forgetting the direction of that monthly review—as to leave relatively little time for other publications. In Rome I found a more congenial atmosphere and more opportunities for publishing, notwithstanding the direction of the review *Gregorianum* and the many invitations which came my way from Italy and abroad for talks and conferences. In a sense I could devote myself more exclusively to intellectual work—to the detriment of pastoral activities. I have thus been able to produce a few books, all of which have been well received, judging from the many reprints and translations into various languages which they have known. I am grateful to so many publishing houses which always seemed anxious to receive a manuscript of mine. I may mention once more that a substantial, if not altogether complete, bibliography of my writing is being published in the Festschrift for my eightieth birthday, entitled *In Many and Diverse Ways*.

Yet, with all this I am always amazed when I think of the enormous bulk of important writing done by such theologians as Henri de Lubac, Yves Congar, Karl Rahner, or Hans Urs von Balthasar, and compare it with what I myself have been able to produce—which in comparison is so little. This comparison helps to keep me humble, even while I am encouraged and consoled by the book of Qoheleth in the First Testament (12:12): "One last thing, my son: be warned that writing books involves endless hard work, and that much study wearies the body."

G.O'C.: *As you look back, do you see things that you would like to have done differently? Or things you did not do but would like to have done? And what have you learned from all this?*

J.D.: There have been two serious periods of crisis in my life. The first was my rather abrupt transfer from Vidyajyoti, Delhi, to the Gregorian University in Rome. This is a complex story. I never asked to leave India, where I had gone as a "missionary" in 1948 with the idea of living there, working there, and dying there. In those days this is the way it went with missionary vocations for far-away Asia. Never did I get tired of my life there; on the contrary, I got myself more and more involved in a work that fulfilled my aspirations and gave me total satisfaction. This is so true that looking back on the thirty-six years spent there I can hardly believe that so much time went by, almost unnoticed.

Yet, a crisis did arise in the early '80s, when India was gradually forging its way of doing theology, especially in the field of Christology, which was my specialized topic of research and teaching. Many discussions took place in those days at the local as well as at a broader level on the way in which a contextualized local theology would have to be conceived in the Asian and in the Indian context. How far could or should inculturation of the Christian message go, by way of assimilating the cultural and religious treasures of the Indian tradition? Could a return to the rich cultural and religious patrimony of India replace altogether the Christian tradition accumulated in the West through the centuries? Could even the Old, or First, Testament of the Christian Bible be replaced in the Indian context by the Sacred Scriptures of Hindu tradition and mysticism, as God's providential preparation in India for the Christian revelation contained in the New Testament? Where the mystery of Jesus Christ was concerned the call was—rightly—for a Christology from below. But could such a Christology reach an adequate enunciation of the mystery of the person of Jesus Christ without at some stage making a turn to a Christology from above, with its starting point in the existence in God of the Word who became flesh in time? Were not both approaches to be combined, as they seemed to be in the New Testament itself? Some Christologies from below could seem incomplete and unsatisfactory, not in what they affirmed but in what they did not say. In this context, both in my teaching and in discussions with my colleagues on the Delhi faculty I made myself the advocate of some cautious and prudential restraint. I became as it were the mouthpiece of a group on the staff—made up of non-Indian members, it must be said—which, without having always the courage to express themselves, thanked me for doing it in their place and name. All this happened in a relaxed friendly atmosphere, but nevertheless it was clear that opinions were divided on important issues. In the mind of some, unintentionally and unwittingly, I became a symbol of a conservative theological posture.

Furthermore, my many commitments with the episcopal conference of India were somewhat resented and considered unbecoming. I remember one clear instance when the rector had organized a full day of group dynamics among the members of the staff, which all were supposed to attend in order to dispel tensions and clear up some differences of opinions. I could not attend this session because I had to go for a few days to Cuttack-Bhubaneswar, where Bishop Henry D'Souza, at that time the local bishop and secretary of the episcopal conference, had called me to help in composing, in the name of the Latin bishops of India, a long memorandum destined for Pope John Paul II himself on the burning question of the relations between the Oriental and the Latin rites in India. This was the time when the Orientals were claiming the right to open dioceses of theirs in the territories of Latin dioceses, thus multiplying the practice of double jurisdiction which even the ancient Oriental tradition—as Patriarch Athenagoras once admitted—had considered unlawful. The question was a delicate one and my colleagues somehow resented my being involved in it; personally I thought that I had to remain loyal to the bishops, in this case to the Latin bishops, who had placed their trust in me. My absence from the group-dynamics session for the staff of our faculty—which to my sense was less important than the work I was asked to do for the bishops—was in fact disapproved of and initiated a certain distancing on my part.

Meanwhile I had been invited by Fr. René Latourelle to come as a visiting professor for a semester course on the Theology of Religions in the academic year 1981-1982. I answered that I could not be absent for a full semester from Delhi, because of my obligations there, including the editorship of *Vidyajyoti Journal,* the monthly periodical of our faculty, which required my constant attention. I did accept to come for a course concentrated over a period of six weeks. The invitation was repeated the following year by Fr. Latourelle, now dean of the faculty of theology, and I did the course again for the academic year 1982-1983. When for the third time I was at the Gregorian doing the same course in the academic year 1983-1984, I was summoned by Fr. Peter-Hans Kolvenbach who had been recently elected superior general of the Society of Jesus. Father Pedro Arrupe had previously turned down a request made by Fr. Latourelle for my permanent transfer to the Gregorian, saying that my presence in Delhi was necessary. To my great surprise and dismay, Fr. Kolvenbach announced to me that he had decided on my permanent transfer to the Gregorian University, for the Faculty of Theology. He appreciated the work I had done in Delhi and the position I had taken in the discussions among the staff, but was afraid that in the difficult circumstances my work there might become counterproductive. This was in April 1984, when I had almost finished my course in the Gregorian; Father General asked me to return to Delhi in May to prepare my transfer and be back in Rome in June—which I did, leaving the place when all, professors and students, were away for the summer holidays. They would learn about my absence when they returned in July to begin the following academic year.

This, then, was my first crisis. The sudden and unexpected transfer was felt as a deep wound; humanly speaking, I could hardly see any wisdom or meaning in the move. It appeared to me uncalled for, not to say unjustified, since I had meant to give to India my entire life and work. At the beginning it was very much a case of blind obedience to my superior general, such as the Society has taught us to practice, even if the order received may look absurd by human standards. I remained under shock all through the summer, struggling to improve my knowledge of Italian in order to cope when the academic year would start in Rome in October. Eventually, however, I thought that, rather than brooding over the matter, I had better throw myself with all my strength into the new work entrusted to me. When I started the work at the Gregorian, I soon became engrossed in it, to the extent of having no time to regret the past. Grace had been stronger than despondency. The work was indeed enticing, and it brought as many challenges as it did consolations. Much later, in a private conversation with Father General, I reminded him of his decision about my transfer and suggested that this decision had probably been among the first he had taken as superior general. He answered with a smile that it was perhaps also the first mistake he had made.

However this may be, to the question whether I should have acted differently than I did in the delicate situation described above, there is no easy answer. Had I been too rigid in my opinions and in my views; or too self-asserting in my way of acting? On the one hand, the time had come for the non-Indian members of the staff, even if they had meant to identify as fully as possible with the legitimate aspirations of their Indian colleagues, to think and to act in a low key; on the other, it was also necessary to ensure continuity in progress, unity in plurality, between the way in which the Christian message had been understood and presented in the past, and the pressing need today to root it deeply in the cultural and religious traditions of India—a work for which foreign theologians could not be the arbiters, much less the architects. Had there been any wrong done on one side, in spite of the good will that both sides meant to keep toward each other? I leave this question unanswered, as we are always bad judges in our own case. I rejoice that in spite of that unhappy episode I continue even today, in the mind of ex-colleagues and of so many friends, including Jesuit superiors and bishops in India, identified with the country and with the church there, and even more with the cause they uphold and promote, to which from far away I have continued all along to devote my strength and energy: a local church of India, not merely *in* India, deeply rooted in the country's traditions, characterized by a triple dialogue with the poor, the cultures and the religions; a "post-Western church," that is, "one with a new way of being church" fully at home in the country—to borrow from the way in which local churches in Asia and India are being described today.

The second period of crisis in my academic life is of course that initiated by the Contestation in 1998 by the CDF of my 1997 book on a Christian theology of religious pluralism. I can afford to be short here, having said so much already about this other time of crisis. But a comparison between one situation and the other may be instructive. I had sometimes been accused in Delhi of a conservative attitude in theology; I was now being looked upon in Rome as an extremist progressive theologian. I had been seen, again by some in Delhi, as a reactionary; I was now called in Rome a revolutionary, subversive of the received order. Between such contradictory assessments of my being and writing, I felt threatened with becoming a split personality and losing my own sense of identity. Who was right between my accusers on either side? Perhaps no one. The contradiction between the opposite evaluations of my work helped me to get my bearings. How could I be at the same time a reactionary theologian and a revolutionary thinker? The contradictory accusations suggested double standards of evaluation. Many people in India came to my defense in my Roman trial on the plea that they had known me as a traditional, not to say a conservative theologian, and could not therefore see what the CDF could possibly find so reprehensible in my writing; Indian bishops wrote personally to Cardinal Ratzinger telling him that they had put their confidence in me during my long years in India and were now saddened to hear that the theologian whom they had trusted for his sound theological judgment was now subject to grievous accusations. They could not believe, they said, that I would have changed so much since and become a legitimate target for the worst accusations on the part of the CDF regarding the faith Divine and Catholic. There must have been some mistake and the case should be soon reconsidered and settled amicably.

The CDF, however, did not listen to those pleas on my behalf, and following the denunciations that had been made; they applied to my case their drastic norms of procedure. The Contestation followed upon the denunciations; the doctrinal judgment upon the Contestation; and three consecutive drafts of a Notification upon the doctrinal judgment. It is in this confused and confusing situation that the question is asked whether I would like today to have acted differently in this case. Again there is no straightforward answer. On the one hand, I had to be submissive to the church's doctrinal authority and prepared to change if I were persuaded of having gone astray from the Christian faith. On the other hand, I had to remain true to myself and to the cause I was serving, as long as I was not shown clearly where I had gone wrong. It was this attitude which prompted me on September 4, 2000, to politely decline signing the first draft of the Notification which Cardinal Ratzinger submitted for my signature. Was I wrong in my refusal? I do not think so, as what followed showed abundantly. The Congregation was forced to relent, and the accusations made in the second draft of the Notification were considerably toned down, from grievous errors against the faith to some ambiguities to be avoided. But, while a slavish submission to the CDF would have cleared the situation, though only superficially and on an ambiguous basis, my determination to be true to myself and to hold my ground against an over-powerful authority was bound to prolong the ordeal to which I have been submitted and remain subject even today. Yet, I never regretted the firmness and determination I displayed on that fateful September day.

G.O'C.: *Are you convinced that you have touched the core issues in the field of religious pluralism?*

J.D.: I think so. At the time of the Second Vatican Council, Karl Rahner spoke of "elements of truth and grace" contained in the religious traditions of the world which exercised a positive influence in the mystery of salvation in Jesus Christ of their followers. This sounded rather new and daring at that time, and went beyond the "natural values" acknowledged in those traditions by such great theologians as Henri de Lubac, Hans Urs von Balthasar, and others. The Council adopted—unaware—the expression of Rahner, speaking explicitly of "elements of truth and grace," as well as of a "ray of that Truth which illumines all men," but without ever defining those terms as referring to "supernatural" endowments contributing to the salvation of the members of those religions, or ever concluding that the religious traditions are therefore "ways" or "paths" of salvation.

Subsequently Pope John Paul II affirmed unequivocally the universal active presence of the Spirit of God, a presence and activity which "affect not only individuals but also society and history, peoples, cultures and religions" (encyclical letter *Redemptoris missio*, 28), but without ever deriving from such affirmations the conclusions which seem to follow from them logically. The core question for a Christian theology of religious pluralism is precisely that of a positive role of the religions in the mystery of salvation of their members, and, consequently, of a positive significance to be attributed to those traditions in God's eternal plan of salvation for humankind. The challenge of such a theology consists in holding fast, in a constructive tension, to the Christian faith in Jesus Christ universal savior of humankind, on the one hand, and, on the other, to the positive role exercised by the other traditions, in harmony with God's eternal design, in the order of salvation for their adherents. This amounts to daring to draw the conclusions that naturally follow from the presence in those traditions of "elements of truth and grace" and from the universal action in them of the Spirit of God—if only these affirmations would be taken seriously. A question of logic, then, but one which requires courage and daring; for giving a positive answer to it amounts to going against the grain of received opinions and official church positions, inherited from centuries of Christian exclusivism, to begin with, and, later, from too narrow a stance toward the meaning of other traditions.

To take the measure of the step involved here in the context of current theological opinions among Catholic theologians, I may mention that recently I have still been accused by Frère Henry Donneaud, the prior of the Toulouse convent of the Dominicans, of unduly and gratuitously passing in my theology of religious pluralism from "a theology of the possible" to a "theology of the real." Writing in *Revue thomiste* (2002, no. 1): 43-62, under the title "Chalcédoine contre l'unicité absolue du Médiateur Jésus-

Christ?" in answer to my own article in *Nouvelle revue théologique* (2001, no. 4): 529-46, entitled "Le Verbe de Dieu, Jésus-Christ et les religions du monde," he reproached me for repeatedly and gratuitously asserting, without bringing concrete positive proofs, the reality of a divine action and divine grace operative in the religious traditions of the world. He admits the possibility that this may be the case, perhaps by way of a permanent action of the Word of God as such and of the Spirit of God, but refuses to admit that it has been shown to be so in reality: *Ab esse ad posse valet illatio,* not vice versa.

It may be noted that "proofs" in the field of revealed Scripture and Tradition do not operate as do scientific proofs in the field of positive sciences, and, moreover, that the value and bearing of testimonies on the matter do not depend on the accumulation of many affirmations. One text, the Prologue of John's Gospel, for instance, may suffice to show that the Word of God has been and continues to be "the Light which, coming into the world, illumines all men." The real point here is the difficulty which people continue to have even today about concluding logically from the universal presence of divine grace and the Spirit of God to a positive role willed by God of the other religious traditions. Such a conclusion continues to go against the grain of an accumulated tradition.

In the same vein I have been accused recently by George Cottier, theologian of the pontifical household, of a rampant "tendency towards a universal supernaturalism" (see "Sur la mystique naturelle," *Revue thomiste* 101 [2001, nos. 1-2]: 287-311), since I hold that all people are placed in the supernatural order of grace by the very reality of creation. In that concrete historical condition they are open to the gift of self which God extends through grace: *homo capax Dei.* Hence, every authentic religious experience implies an openness of the human being toward the true God, no matter how limited may be the divine manifestation and unconscious the response which is given to it. According to Cottier, I should have allowed more for a natural mysticism, which by itself does not lead to supernatural salvation, and upheld more clearly the altogether gratuitous character of divine grace. This would have toned down, if not suppressed, my position about the other religious traditions. My own answer consists in denouncing what I call a "pan-naturalism," which in order to exalt what is proper to Christianity indulges in denigrating what God has achieved and continues to achieve outside it. In answer to these two Dominican authors I have written a piece entitled "Le Verbe de Dieu comme tel et comme incarné." I have mentioned above that this study will be published in the Festschrift for Fr. Karl Neufeld of Innsbruck.

The core issue for a theology of religious pluralism in principle lies then in combining apparently contradictory, yet complementary affirmations—none of which can be sacrificed to the advantage of the other: Jesus Christ is truly the universal savior, but the saving action of the Word of God extends beyond the limits of his own humanity, and a fortiori even more beyond those of the church which is his body, to extend and to operate also outside those boundaries in the other religious traditions. In order to show the total extent of divine and Christic grace I have assembled different elements: the full compass of salvation history, starting with creation and extending to the entire history of humankind; the plurality of the covenants God has established with the human race at various stages of its history; the "many and various ways" in which God spoke to the nations through history. The Jesus Christ event must be seen in the overall framework of God's design running through this entire history. That event is unquestionably the center, apex, high point, and interpretative key of the entire historical saving process; as such it has a universal saving significance. But it must never be isolated from the entire process, as though by itself it represented and exhausted God's entire saving power. Rather, the historic (and as such particular) saving event of Jesus Christ leaves room for a saving action by God through his Word and his Spirit that goes beyond even the risen humanity of the Incarnate Word. At every step God has taken the initiative in the encounter between God and human beings. This is why it can and must be said that the world's religious traditions are "ways" or "routes" of salvation for their followers.

They are such because they represent "ways" traced by God himself for the salvation of human beings. It is not human beings who have first set out in search of God through their history; rather God has set out first to approach them and to trace for them the "ways" along which they may find him. If, as has been suggested, the world's religions are in themselves "gifts of God to the peoples of the world," the foundation for a "religious pluralism in principle" is clear. I wrote in the conclusion to my recent book, *Christianity and the Religions: From Confrontation to Dialogue,*

> If religion and the religions originate in a self-manifestation of God to human beings, the primary foundation for the principle of multiplicity is the superabundant riches and variety of God's self-manifestation to humankind. . . . It forms part of the nature of the overflowing communication of the tri-personal God to humankind to extend beyond the divine life the plural communication inherent in that very life. Religious pluralism in principle is then based on the immensity of a God who is Love and communication.

This is the logical conclusion to be drawn from the universal presence of divine grace through the Word of God and in his Spirit.

G.O'C.: *What do you think is the significance of your life's work for ordinary people? And for the church as a whole? What is the message that you hope they have picked up from your teaching, your writing, and your life?*

J.D.: The audiences I addressed in many conferences I have given in Italy and abroad were made up not only of professional theologians and specialists in the theology of religions, but also of educated Christians and scholars of other faiths—Jewish, Buddhist, Hindu, or Muslim. I have always been struck by the very positive, even enthusiastic "reception" which I met everywhere. There was obvious sympathy for the person—my "case" was known to many—but there were also clear signs of approval for my message. In some places, after I ended my talk, I received a standing ovation on the part of the audience. The local bishops present showed their approval of my ideas. To give one example: I remember how in the Regional Seminary of Molfetta, in Puglia, I found myself on the stage surrounded by all the local bishops of the region who shared in the responsibility for the seminary; they all thanked me and congratulated me profusely.

This show of sympathy and enthusiasm raises the question: why such warm "reception"—to use the theological term consecrated by today's theology for the approval of doctrine on the part of the people? The only answer I can think of is that people found in what I proposed a discourse of Christian faith which corresponded to what they were instinctively sensing, without being able to articulate it for themselves. The traditional discourse which they had heard before, sometimes *ad nauseam,* had lost its credibility, and they were looking for something which would allow them to hold firmly to their Christian commitment, while at the same time allowing for a true openness toward other religious experiences with which life put them into contact. This corresponded exactly to my own concern of combining in my life and teaching an integral faith in Jesus Christ with a genuine appreciation and a positive evaluation of the religious traditions which nourished the spiritual life of so many people around us. I think people discovered in what I said space to breathe freely in their faith and an attempt to open—or reopen—the windows of the church, so much called for by Pope John XXIII, but so much forgotten in the last decades.

As for the people of other faiths present in my audiences, they were often happily surprised to hear a Christian speaker appreciative of their own religious patrimony and encouraged to discover that Christian theology can positively evaluate their faiths. I am always much encouraged by both of these positive reactions. I am reminded of the time in India when my own students were discovering with great relief that Christian faith need not imply a negative stand toward other faiths. Through the education they had received, they had been made to wonder for a long time about the eternal fate of their ancestors who through the centuries had practiced with great devotion another religious faith. They were now thrilled to discover that their ancestors' sincere practice of their faith had been for them the way to God and a promise of eternal happiness. The communion of saints is infinitely larger than we have been prepared to admit in the past, and the covenants of God with peoples embrace the entire history of humankind: all the peoples of the earth are God's peoples living under the ark of a covenant.

The positive reactions which people spontaneously give to an open discourse on the relationship between Christianity and the other religious traditions indicate the importance to be given to the *sensus fidelium* in developing Christian doctrine. Vatican II spoke of the role which the *sensus fidelium* exercises in the church's discourse of faith. The Christian faith is the faith of the church that is of the people of God assembled in Christ. It finds its first expression in what the people believe, and the bishops, as the witnesses of the faith, are primarily the mouthpieces of the faith of the Christian people. Perhaps recent developments in theology invite the church's doctrinal authority to give more weight to the *sensus fidelium* of the church's membership than has been done in the past.

G.O'C.: *If you were to start all over again, and had the choice, would you choose to follow the same path again?*

J.D.: There have been three important options in my life: my decision to join the Society of Jesus, my request to be sent to India as a missionary, and my theological career. Each of these has entailed hardships and difficulties, the last two even moments of serious trial—of which I have already given an account. But I may say that I have never regretted or even seriously doubted any of those options. All three together constituted my God-given vocation, the only vocation in which I could possibly find happiness and fulfillment. If I were to start all over again, I am sure that, except for the mistakes I made on the way and for which I am sorry, I would follow substantially the same course. I thank God for having chosen me for the path he assigned to me with no merit on my part, and for the grace he gave me to remain faithful in the difficulties.

When I look back on my life and all the graces accumulated over almost eighty years, I cannot but admire God's providence, his fatherly care, and constant solicitude. My three options have been my response to a personal call addressed to me by God, and have brought to my life great joy and satisfaction. It would be too long to spell out here those accumulated graces, even in a summary fashion. Let it suffice to say that I have been overwhelmed by God's gratuitous love for his unworthy creature. This, perhaps, is the reason why as a theologian I have thought it my duty to show the extent of God's love for his creatures.

I have always been fascinated by Michelangelo's representation of God's creation of Adam in the Sistine Chapel at the Vatican: the meeting of the two faces of God and Adam and the movement of their two hands toward each other express in the most profound fashion the free gift of life which God makes to his creatures, and the call which he extends to them in creation itself to share in his own life. The face of God reflects the eagerness of his call and the gratuitousness of his gifts; that of Adam, the Godward direction inscribed in his creaturely being and the gratefulness of his response to God's call. I always saw depicted in the masterpiece of Michelangelo the divine vocation which God addresses to all men and women, whatever the period of history in which they lived or the religious traditions to which they belonged. All was God's gift and promise. I myself had been the recipient of such gifts, expressed concretely as they were, beyond the gift of life itself, in a threefold vocation and calling for a threefold option. To be added is the fact that all this was concretely realized in Jesus Christ, Son of God, become man to share with us his own Sonship of God his Father, and whose disciple I had been called to become in a particular way of life as a "companion of Jesus."

I wanted my Jesuit missionary vocation and my theological career to reflect what I had personally experienced of the depth of Christian faith and of the breadth of God's gifts to humankind. This, added to the concrete circumstances in which I was made to exercise my missionary vocation and my teaching career, explains probably why my theological interest became more and more concentrated over the years around the problems raised by the full extent of God's dealings with humankind in history and the meaning in this context of the religious pluralism in which our world finds itself today. It is this special concern and the theological reflections which it led me to develop which sparked off the serious crisis to which I have been subjected in the last years.

Were I to start all over again my theological career, I would still choose to give it the same bent and direction, whatever shortcomings or ambiguities my writings may have contained—which, of course, I would want to avoid. I was and remain convinced that a theology of religions and of religious pluralism must find its ground in the practice of a true and sincere encounter with the "others" and the traditions to which they belong and by which they live. Only then can we hope to build a theological discourse on the religions of the world which reflects and uncovers gratefully the gifts which God himself has dispensed to the nations through their history and the "rays of light" which his Word has been sowing among them. I consider the exposure to which I have been submitted by the circumstances of my vocation to the reality of God's gifts to other peoples as the greatest grace I received from God in my teaching career. Without it I would not have been able to develop my theological thinking, but would have remained a prisoner to the narrow horizons which I often witness in well-intentioned people—including colleagues—who have not had the same grace of being exposed to a broader reality. As I had providentially been placed in a situation in which I could appreciate God's gifts to the peoples, I thought it my duty as a theologian to contribute my part in broadening the theological horizons of the church and of its doctrinal authority, ever too inclined to put limits on God's bounty and to place itself at the center of God's plan for humankind. The center of perspective ought to be not the church itself but the reign of God which has been instituted by God in history through Jesus Christ, destined to extend to all times and places, of which the church is called to be a living sign in the world and through history. I cannot disown that perspective which I have endeavored to develop through my writings, no matter what contradiction it has met with in the past and is still meeting today. Here I am subject to the judgment of God—not of men.

G.O'C.: *As you look ahead to the fullness of divine revelation, what do you hope for?*

J.D.: I have been censored by the CDF for holding that God's revelation in Jesus Christ, no matter how unsurpassed and unsurpassable because of his personal identity as the Son of God, remains "limited, incomplete and imperfect"; that is, it remains unfinished, does not and cannot exhaust the mystery of God and remains turned toward the final revelation of God at the eschaton. As recently as October 9 of this year (2002), a senior official of the Roman Curia, Cardinal Darío Castrillón Hoyos, prefect of the Congregation for the Clergy, in a public lecture at the Vatican condemned me openly for holding that "ruinous" position. The church, he contended, must underline in its teaching "the completeness, centrality and saving universality of Christian revelation." I myself have stressed its centrality and saving universality; but the fact remains that the "fullness" of divine revelation in Jesus Christ—of which the Second Vatican Council speaks—must be understood correctly. The New Testament itself testifies to the fact that divine revelation will attain its completeness only at the end, when God's final revelation will take place. In the words of St Paul, "For now we see in a mirror dimly, but then face to face. Now, I know in part, then I shall understand fully, even as I have been fully understood" (1 Cor 13:12). So there remains something to hope for and look forward to by way of divine revelation.

What the vision of God face to face will be at the end—*in fine sine fine*, in the words of St. Augustine—we cannot tell, except to state that it will bring with it eternal happiness and fulfillment. In the context of religious pluralism, I personally like to stress the fact that the final revelation of God will also complete the reign of God established in Jesus Christ in history, in which Christians and the "others" share and which is destined to reach its plenitude in the other world. Final divine revelation and the completion of the reign of God will coincide in the eschaton. I have written to this effect in my last book, *Christianity and the Religions: From Confrontation to Dialogue:*

> The convergence between the religious traditions will reach its goal in the eschaton with the "recapitulation" (*anakephalaiosis:* Eph 1:10) of all things in Christ. This eschatological recapitulation will coincide with the final "perfection" (*teleiosis*) of the Son of God as "source of eternal salvation" (Rev 5:9), whose influence remains subject, up to this final fulfillment, to an "eschatological remainder." When the Reign of God is achieved, then will come the end when Christ "will hand over the Kingdom to his Father," and the Son himself being "subjected to the one who put all things in subjection under him," God will be "all in all" (1 Cor 15:24-28). The eschatological fullness of the Reign of God is the common final fulfillment of Christianity and the religions.

Christianity and the religions of the world are, therefore, destined to converge in the eschaton, a convergence which is already initiated in history, insofar as they share and help to spread the values of the kingdom of God. That means that at the eschaton we shall share together with the "others" the same final destiny of all human beings in God, even as in history we already belong together in God's family. This awareness of a common origin and a common destiny ought to become alive among all peoples of the world. We ought to become aware of the universal "communion of saints" willed by God for the entire humankind, which is already operative, and to put it into practice.

To give one example: Till the liturgical reform willed by the Second Vatican Council came into effect with the "introduction of new Eucharistic prayers, the only one practiced in the Latin church was the so-called "Roman Canon," in which in the prayers of intercession we read two long—too long—lists of names, not only of the apostles, but also of Roman saints and martyrs. Some of these had little appeal or significance for people in Asia and in India, and the temptation was great of substituting for some of those names others which would appeal more, including some from the Asian and Indian religious patrimony, such as founders of religions like the Buddha, or largely venerated saints and religious teachers of the Hindu or Buddhist traditions. This testifies to a certain awareness of the universality of the "communion of saints" already existing among the different religious families and destined to come to full blossom in the eschaton. We can then and must look forward to the universality of God's eschatological kingdom which will coincide with the final revelation of God.

G.O'C.: *Your investigators in the CDF clearly saw things in a different way from you. How do you know that they were in fact wrong and that you are right? What is your yardstick, or what are the indicators that help you to conclude so? The Congregation and the pope, insofar as he was involved in the case, represent the teaching authority of the church; so why should you think you have the truth on your side? What makes you confident that you have understood the faith better than they?*

J.D.: These are incisive, loaded questions which call for many explanations. I subscribe substantially to the positive part of the eight points included in the Notification about my book, insofar as they represent the authentic faith of the church. In this entire discussion a clear distinction —made by the documents of the CDF—must be kept in mind between the content of faith and the doctrine of the church. Not all that is doctrine of the church is doctrine of faith. Where the content of the faith is concerned, it must not be thought that it is at any time comprehended, even by the church's doctrinal authority, in all clarity and without any room for hesitation and discussion. The data of faith are not reached by the same method or with the same empirical scientific certitude as are mathematical formulas. The faith is never fully possessed; we rather ought to allow ourselves to be gradually possessed by it. It is not all black or white, yes or no, without nuances or distinctions. Moreover, the faith is not a static, monolithic set of propositions to be believed once for all, identical in itself at all times. Much has been written conspicuously by Cardinal John Henry Newman—to stress the development of Christian faith in its dogmatic expression through the centuries. The faith remains the same under different garbs, but it evolves through different enunciations. The question must even be asked squarely whether the faith does not, and has not, in some instances really changed.

Can the thesis be held honestly that the church has never made mistakes in the official enunciation of its faith? The Ecumenical Council of Florence, in its Decree for the Copts (1442), declared solemnly: "[The Holy Roman Church] . . . firmly believes, professes and preaches that 'no one remaining outside the Catholic Church, not only pagans,' but also Jews, heretics or schismatics, can become partakers of eternal life; but they will go to the 'eternal fire prepared for the devil and his angels' (Mt 25:41), unless before the end of their life they are joined to it" (Neuner-Dupuis, *The Christian Faith*, n. 1005). This document of faith enunciates in the most rigid form the axiom *Extra ecclesiam nulla salus;* it does so in a way which does not correspond today to the faith of the church, as the letter of the Holy Office to the archbishop of Boston (Neuner-Dupuis, *The Christian Faith*, nn. 854-57) testifies—even if the axiom continues, strangely, to be called a "dogma." Ingenious interpretations have been devised to the effect that the content of faith has remained in this instance unaltered. But objectivity and honesty seem to require that it be admitted that the church has—happily—changed its opinion on the matter. The content of faith then is liable to change, not only to evolution in enunciation, and the possibility of the church having erred sometimes in the expression of its faith must be squarely admitted.

None of this is said here as a hint that I may, in my own case, have been right against the church's doctrinal authority on some aspects of the content of the faith; I have expressed my substantial agreement with the propositions of the doctrine of the faith, as they are contained in the Notification about my book. But different perceptions of the content of faith and different emphases on its distinct aspects are possible in different contexts and circumstances, and allowance ought to be made for a certain pluralism, not only theological but dogmatic, within the boundaries of communion in the same faith. It is at that level that there exists a difference between my own account of the faith and the discourse made by the CDF. Caution is also required in specifying the agents involved on the side of the prosecution. Are we talking about the "investigators" of the case, or the entire CDF, or the pope himself? The distance between me and the other side would be bigger if one considers some documents about my writing submitted to the CDF by subordinates than it would be if one compares my views with those expressed by the Congregation itself in the official text of the Notification on my book. I have shown above that the judgments of consultors on which the case has been built have often been biased and prejudiced. I have also shown that between the accusations made against my book in the CDF's first document, that is in the Contestation of 1998, and the third, official text of the Notification in 2001, there has been a considerable toning down from grievous errors against the faith Divine and Catholic to some ambiguities to be avoided.

This goes to show that the content of faith is not after all so easily grasped and evaluated, and that there have been on the side of the prosecution also different insights and opinions. It is not so easy to decide what is and what is not in conformity with the faith, especially where different contexts and situations come into play; nor should a rash decision be made which disregards the context, by way of imposing authority and preventing theological discussion. If it were suggested that I boldly opposed authority in an attitude of self-righteousness and self-confidence of having the truth on my side, I would protest vehemently that this does not in any way represent my deep attitude. What is true, however, is that I have been and remain convinced that we were dealing with questions which remain open and that therefore I should continue to represent the case, subject to further decision on the part of church authority.

Where the involvement of Pope John Paul II in the matter is concerned, I think it is to be deeply regretted, insofar as it is impossible to believe that the pope could look personally into the matter. Why should his authority be used—and abused—by the CDF through extracting from him his signature as many as five times? The ritual of Cardinal Ratzinger meeting the pope in audience each time to obtain his signature on the spot is a fiction without credibility, designed to cover up the CDF's dealings. The personal involvement of the pope in the case amounts to little or nothing; caution then is in order when saying that his authority has been involved five times in objection to my writing. If the pope were to hear my name pronounced before him today, would he remember that I am the man with whom his authority has been engaged five times? I wonder.

So much for the content of the faith. What about the doctrine of the church? The distinction between the two is made consistently in the documents of the CDF on my case, the last version of the Notification included. And rightly. Not all that is doctrine of the church enters the content of faith. We know this better today, since in recent years the doctrinal authority of the church has emphasized truths which, though not being part of the revealed message, are nonetheless taught unanimously by church authority to be closely connected with the content of faith and as such representing irreformable doctrine. Without entering into such specifications, the Notification, in the second part to its eight propositions, reproves opinions which it considers as contradicting either the content of faith or the doctrine of the church. As regards the second category, the Notification affirms that there is no foundation in Catholic theology for holding that the religions, "considered as such," are ways of salvation (proposition 8). Now, the church's doctrine is much more than the content of faith, subject to evolution or development, and even to change. Let us give some examples of this.

The doctrine of limbo, either of infants or of adults, was for a long time commonly taught by Catholic theologians and the doctrine of the church; yet there remains no trace of such teaching in the new *Catechism of the Catholic Church*. The descent of Christ *ad inferos* after his death on the cross has been through the centuries a favorite theme for dramatic orchestrations, in both the Western and the Eastern traditions, down to the dramatic scenario of Hans Urs von Balthasar's "theology of the three days." Theology today is more sober on this topic, being better aware that the biblical meaning of the "descent into the underworld" is that Jesus has known a true, authentically human death—which leaves room for a much more restrained and simple, but no less deeply significant, view of the unfolding of the Paschal mystery of Jesus' passover to the Father through his human death and resurrection. These are but examples, among others, to show that the doctrine of the church can change and is open to different interpretations, not all equally valid or convincing.

In this context it becomes more easily thinkable that I—among others—may have had a different perception or understanding of some points in the church's doctrine than those propounded one-sidedly by the CDF. An open discussion would have been in order to evaluate the respective merits of the different positions. One example over which I thought myself entitled to dissent from the CDF's opinion is where even in the official text to the Notification they still state explicitly that "to hold that (the) religions, considered as such, are ways of salvation, has no foundation in Catholic theology, also because they contain omissions, insufficiencies, and errors regarding fundamental truths about God, man and the world" (proposition 8). I have been careful to affirm that they are ways of salvation for their followers, due to the "elements of truth and grace" and the "rays of that Light which enlightens every man" contained in them, and not through their deficiencies and shortcomings. But the same would have to be said where Christianity is concerned. No way is perfect and beyond reproach. But God can write straight with crooked lines, and use imperfect "paths" to his own end.

To state that there is no foundation in Catholic theology for holding that the religions "in themselves" can be considered ways of salvation for their followers does not correspond to reality and betrays a lack of information about the theological scene in the church today. Francis Sullivan has published an article in *America* 189 (April 9, 2001): 28-31, entitled "Ways of Salvation? On the Investigation of Jacques Dupuis," to show that the opposite is true and that Karl Rahner for one is a clear witness to the contrary position. These notes should suffice to show that my persevering in my own theological opinions did not spring from sheer stubbornness against authority. There was a case to be made in order that the truth might prevail, to which church authority and members, the *ecclesia docens* and the *ecclesia discens*, are all equally subject and should be subservient. It must be hoped that truth may one day prevail to the satisfaction of all.

G.O'C.: *How do you make sense of such opposition in the church?*

J.D.: It would be cowardly to be scandalized by it. We are dealing with mysteries, that is with truths beyond our comprehension, which we can perceive only dimly and imperfectly. This is true whether we consider the mystery of God in himself of which we can have only an analogical or symbolic knowledge, or the mystery of his dealings with humankind in history and of the share to which he calls humans in his own divine life. The mystery of salvation remains as hidden in a "cloud of unknowing" as the mystery of God himself. This is why, while affirming that God's salvation is available to people who have not heard of Jesus Christ and are not members of the church, the Second Vatican Council states that this happens "in "a way" or "in ways" known to God" (*Gaudium et spes* 22; *Ad gentes* 7)—a clear avowal on the part of the church's Magisterium of ignorance as to the concrete way in which this takes place; and this is, it must be said, an added proof that God's revelation in Jesus Christ remains incomplete. That the church confesses to not knowing does not, however, dispense theologians from reflecting on the mystery and formulating, discretely, some hypotheses as to the way in which the mystery may be understood. The history of theology is full, in the last centuries, of such "explanations," some with more credentials than others, some affirmed at one stage and later discarded by the church's doctrinal authority, some enjoying currency today but remaining open to further investigation.

I myself have suggested that the "ways known to God" may well be the historical religious traditions themselves, as "paths" traced by God himself in his search of human beings and of peoples, along which they could come in contact with him. God set out in search of people before they could set out in search of him. Christian faith and theology teach rightly that even our search for God is a gift from him. That gift, I suggest, passes through the "paths" God has traced to make the encounter possible. It is substantially that suggestion which has raised eyebrows on the part of some people in high quarters. But it is one thing is to say "No" to a certain view; another thing is to show it to be in contradiction with the core of Christian faith. That it contradicts some traditional views is readily admitted, but perhaps those traditional views must themselves be questioned anew. The plurality of theological views should not provoke scandal and anathemas but mutual acceptance. What is required is an open mind on the part of all, people in authority as well as the others, and a readiness to grow together toward the "fullness of truth" under the guidance of the Spirit of God who has been promised to the church.

G.O'C.: *As you look back on the whole investigation now, what are your deeper feelings? Do you feel bitter toward the CDF, or anybody involved, for putting you through such ordeal? At the end of the day what questions still remain in your mind?*

J.D.: These questions are not easily answered. "Bitterness" is a loaded word. What is sure is that I have been deeply shaken by the whole affair, and can never fully recover from the shock and be as I was before. There are things which, even supposing that it be possible to forgive, can never be forgotten. I believe that there is a danger, looking from the outside, of underestimating the sense of deep hurt which such a situation creates in a person. It is thought too easily that the page should be turned over, and that one should be and do things henceforth as though nothing had happened. This attitude betrays a lack of sensitivity for the suffering once endured on the part of people who have not gone through similar trials. Even friends can indulge such attitudes, to the extent sometimes of joking about the past. One remains after all alone in his wounded mind, no matter how much sympathy may have been shown to him. Life must go on, and it goes on the same, but not for the one who has once been struck and altered deeply in the core of his being.

The question of "bitterness" is a different question. Bitterness against someone would suppose that the person to be bitter against be known with certitude. This is not always the case. I have had some suspicion about who had a hand in denouncing me to the CDF, and in the procedure that followed, but no clear certitude. I have avoided investigating the matter further, beyond the knowledge—unsought for—which I have acquired through the denunciation of denunciators by other denunciators. I thought it a dirty game on the part of some whose hands are not clean to accuse others in order to excuse themselves. This, however, shows one thing, namely, that personal grudge and enmity have played a role in the whole affair; and this is not to the glory of any of the detractors.

Where the CDF is concerned, the involvement in the procedure on the part of the authorities and on the part of subordinates and consultors must be distinguished. Where consultors are concerned, I have a clear sense of a significant involvement in the case of some who had already indulged in critical comments on my work before the procedure was started and went on doing so publicly during the proceedings themselves. I thought that in such cases decency would have suggested that the persons concerned decline the request made to them by the CDF's authority to play an official role in the proceedings. This did not happen; toward such persons I feel less bitterness than pity and sorrow. Where the authorities of the CDF are concerned, and Cardinal Ratzinger in particular, it seems that he never really studied the case personally but was satisfied to abide by the opinion of some consultors whom he specially trusted—too blindly, I am afraid. My question to him then would consist in asking how he could put his signature to documents against my work without having personally investigated the matter. After all, signing documents designed to discredit persons involves a heavy responsibility on the part of the authority concerned. Perhaps the system is here more to be blamed than the persons who find themselves caught in it. But they ought to be open to criticism of the system, instead of defending it by hook and by crook as being in keeping with the demands of "due process."

As for the cardinal members of the CDF who in the first place were responsible for requesting that a Contestation of my book be initiated by the Congregation, I beg to ask: with what personal knowledge of the case—and what theological competence—did they vote in favor of the Contestation? I have often thought of the story of Susanna in the First Testament and transposed it allegorically to my case. Instead of asking each of the witnesses separately under which tree they saw the couple fornicating, I would ask each cardinal member individually about the color of the Italian edition of my book—the edition officially used in the investigation—and wonder at the variety of answers I receive, with few or none hitting on green color which is the right answer to the question. It can be seriously doubted that the cardinals had an adequate personal acquaintance with the case so as to be able to take the decision they took. Again here, perhaps, the system is more to be blamed than the persons. Curia cardinals may be members of as many as five different Congregations. Are they competent in all matters, and do they have the time at their disposal to study personally all cases? This is simply not credible. While then I question the system, I feel more pity toward the persons than resentment.

As for the questions that still remain in my mind today, I would mention in the first place the badly needed and long desired reform of the Roman Curia, and the decentralization of authority which goes together with it. But, as is being stressed by knowledgeable people, bishops—preferably retired—theologians, and laypersons, insofar as free speech in the church is permitted, the tendency to centralization and the imposition of authority have never been so strong as they are today, in the matter of doctrine as well as of discipline. A new category of truths has been discovered between what belongs clearly to the deposit of faith and is open to solemn pronouncement on the part of the Magisterium, and the church doctrine taught by the ordinary Magisterium without such decisive involvement. It consists of truths understood to be so closely connected with the revealed message and necessary for its transmission that, considered as they are by the central authority to be commonly held by the entire episcopate, they can be the object of irreformable pronouncements. This, it has been noted, is liable to lead to grave abuses on the part of the central authority. As for centralization in practical matters to the disregard of the authority of the local bishops, it is enough to point to the requirement of the approbation by the Vatican of translations of liturgical texts. This has led in the past and is still leading today to grotesque situations and ludicrous stories which we need not recall here, except to point out that even in trivial matters the authority of the episcopal conferences is being concretely denied, as well as being undermined in theory by recent documents issued by the center. There is no lack then of questions being addressed to the church today, if it wants its witness to go across in a credible way at the time of ecumenical dialogue and of the broader dialogue with cultures and religions, and with the world at large. My own case is a drop in the ocean, but the ocean is made up of drops of water.

G.O'C.: *You say you are forever wounded by the experience, but is there no healing?*

J.D.: In his recently published *Mon journal du Concile* (Paris: Les Editions du Cerf, 2002), Yves Congar repeatedly mentions that even after his official rehabilitation by Pope John XXIII, who called him as an expert at the Second Vatican Council, of which he became one of the pillars, he was still made to feel, during the proceedings of the Council and after, strong disapproval on the part of key official figures at the Vatican, who continued to look upon him as suspect and dangerous. Once suspicion has been expressed publicly by the central doctrinal authority about the validity of a theologian's position, the scars remain with him forever and the accusations are never officially withdrawn. The central authority never admits to having made a mistake; much less does it ever apologize for the harm it has done. In my own case, even though the accusations were toned down from grievous errors against the faith to ambiguities likely to lead to error, the blame still remained. I have never been told that the clarifications I made in my latest book were accepted and that the matter was settled. I have to continue to live with the possibility of new accusations and to find my support in the "reception" I receive from people, bishops, priests, and lay. Healing comes only from God, not from the church's central authority.

G.O'C.: *If you were now given the opportunity to speak freely with the pope about the way the whole investigation and process were carried out by the CDF, what would you tell him? The pope followed the whole case, and approved the different stages of the process. What would you say to him about his own role in it?*

J.D.: These are fictitious questions. No one in trouble for doctrine with the CDF has, to my knowledge, ever had the opportunity to meet the present pope and to speak to him. Where a condemnation has been pronounced, the *Agendi Ratio* excludes every appeal to the authority of the pope, on the plea that the pope's authority has been involved at every step of the investigation by the CDF. However, we can imagine the scenario of my meeting personally and privately Pope John Paul II. If this were now to happen and at some stage during the meeting I were allowed to speak my mind freely and to ask questions, I would begin by professing my loyalty to the church and to the pope's person in view of the universal ministry of unity he exercises in it. But I would not hesitate to say that, unless I be thoroughly mistaken, many of the things I have said and written confirm the line taken by him in many of his own pronouncements. He spoke with emphasis about the universal presence of the Spirit of God, stressing that every authentic prayer, even addressed to an unknown God, proceeds in all human beings from the action in them of the Spirit. I wanted to draw the theological conclusions from this, and to organize them in an explicit discourse.

It is true that in the process I found it congenial to formulate some hypotheses which to some seemed to contradict the faith or the traditional doctrine of the church; but their incompatibility with the faith has not been shown convincingly. There seems to have been a rush to denounce, even a tendency to condemn, rather than an effort to understand and a will to discuss; a total absence of a true dialogue on the plea of the urgent need to reaffirm the "Christian identity" in the face of pernicious errors. I would point out to the pope that a letter to the *Tablet* of London suggested long ago that to condemn me would amount to implicitly condemning the pope himself.

As for the pope's personal involvement in the case, I would be so bold as to ask—if I were still allowed to speak—how far he was able to look personally into the case before signing documents five times against me, and whether he was sufficiently informed, before doing so, of my past performance in the field of theological teaching and writing. Does it not seem strange that at the end of a career of forty years, spent without having ever received any blame or any warning, one finds himself suddenly faced with the strongest accusations possible about faith and doctrine? Would not the pope himself find this very odd and wish that it had been otherwise? But the years have gone by and the past cannot be undone; no provision is made in the current norms for a direct intervention of the pope beyond the decision by the CDF. Everything suggests that the supreme authority against which there is no appeal is concretely the CDF itself. At this stage I do not know what the reaction of the pope might be and how I would fare for having spoken openly. But I would at least have the satisfaction of having done so.

G.O'C.: *If the pope, or a new pope, were to ask you for your advice, suggestions, or proposals to enable him to come up with a better, more Christian and human way of dealing with such theological or doctrinal problems in the years ahead, what would you tell him?*

J.D.: This question is even more problematic than the previous ones. I do not claim to be competent to advise the pope or any successor of his about improving the procedure followed in doctrinal cases, and much less in reforming the Roman Curia in general. I can only say that my own case and my familiarity with other cases have made me sensitive to the need of such a reform. The pope himself has called, in his encyclical *Ut unum sint* (1995), for the cooperation of pastors and theologians of the Catholic and other churches, to study together with him and to devise a way in which in the changed world of today the ministry of unity of the bishop of Rome could be exercised so as to be effectively the sign of unity of all Christians. He wrote:

> I am convinced that I have a particular responsibility in this regard, above all in acknowledging the ecumenical aspirations of the majority of the Christian communities and in heeding the request made of me to find a way of exercising the primacy which, while in no way

renouncing what is essential in its mission, is nevertheless open to a new situation. . . . When addressing the Ecumenical Patriarch his Holiness Dimitrios I, I acknowledged my awareness that "for a great variety of reasons, and against the will of all concerned, what should have been a service sometimes manifested itself in a very different light." But . . . it is out of a desire to obey the will of Christ truly that I recognize that as Bishop of Rome I am called to exercise that ministry. . . . I insistently pray the Holy Spirit to shine his light upon us, enlightening all the pastors and theologians of our churches, that we may seek—together, of course—the forms in which this ministry may accomplish a service of love recognized by all concerned (n. 95).

The invitation of the pope has been gratefully received, and an impressive quantity of scholarly writing has appeared in recent years, in the Catholic Church in particular, in response to the pope's invitation. Those books are based on serious historical research into Scripture and Tradition, and especially into the history of the papacy in past centuries and its evolution toward the present state of its exercise; they suggest—often in remarkable agreement between themselves—ways in which a serious "reform of the papacy" could and should proceed. All the authors consider the reform of the Roman Curia as an important part, an indispensable one in fact, of the reform called for. Much will depend on the "reception" which is given in high circles to those books and the suggestions they make. The impression thus far is that a certain resistance not only to that literature but also to the pope's own call for dialogue and for a common search toward a better exercise of the central authority expresses itself in the Vatican. Perhaps a new ecumenical Council will be required to make with authority the decisions which are called for. But a new ecumenical Council will have to wait till such time as circumstances will allow and a sense of the urgent need for change will have grown in the church. Meanwhile, we can only hope and pray that the Spirit of God may lead the church in that direction.

G.O'C.: *Despite all the queries the CDF had about your work, the fact remains that as a professor your lectures attracted a great number of students, you were consultant for the Indian bishops and the Federation of Asian Bishops' Conferences, you were consultant here in Rome at the Pontifical Council for Interreligious Dialogue, and even today, after the Notification, your books sell well, and you are in great demand as a speaker. How do you explain such a positive response to your work? What do you think such a response is saying to the whole church? Why is it that your work is making such sense to so many ordinary believers while meeting with contradiction in high quarters?*

J.D.: I described above the work I did during my long stay in India and later here in Rome as a teacher, speaker, counselor to bishops, writer and editor in the field of theology, specially of Christology and of the theology of religions. It is not for me to sing my praises, and I do not want to dwell any longer on my achievements and my success. I leave to others the task of evaluating my work; as for myself I thank God for the full life he has granted to me and for the many opportunities he has given me; I take him as my judge as to how I have let the talents I received fructify. I did not bury them in the ground for fear of my Master, but whether I have made them fructify a hundredfold, it will be for my Master to decide. More to the point are the questions regarding the apparent contradictions between the positive "reception" I have met with—perhaps today more than before—and the serious blame and detraction I have met on the part of the CDF.

I have already mentioned in passing some of these contradictions. I recorded letters written by Indian bishops to Cardinal Ratzinger, expressing to him their shock and dismay at the news of my being reprehended by the CDF. I have mentioned the enormous support received from Archbishop Henry D'Souza, Cardinal Franz König, and other personalities of the highest rank in response to the accusations levelled against me by the church's doctrinal authority. Beside these, another contradiction can be seen in the fact that I was considered by my colleagues in India a very cautious, not to say conservative, theologian; this explained their surprise at hearing of my process by the CDF. I am happy to have had their support in my trial, and for being considered even today as one of their own, struggling for the same cause.

But there are deeper contradictions which need to be pointed out. To begin with, in the way in which the CDF itself has assessed my work. At every stage of the proceedings and in each of the documents there is a strange mixture of appreciation for the work I have been doing on an immensely important topic requiring new investigation, on the one hand, and, on the other, an accumulation of opinions to be rejected in the name of faith, which in a subtle indirect way are being attributed to my book, often wrongly. The contrast between these two aspects was considerably stronger in the first documents, in which I was explicitly accused of grievous errors on points belonging to the essence of the faith; it has been toned down later by the fact that the accusations were changed from errors to ambiguities. But a certain contrast, not to say a discrepancy, is still found, even in the official text of the Notification, between praise and accusation.

The introduction to the official text of the Notification reads as follows:

The members of the Congregation recognized the author's attempt to remain within the limits of orthodoxy in his study of questions hitherto largely unexplored. At the same time, while noting the author's willingness to provide the necessary clarifications, as evident in his *Responses,* as well as his desire to remain faithful to the doctrine of the church and the teaching of the Magisterium, they found that his book contained notable ambiguities and difficulties on important doctrinal points, which could lead a reader to erroneous or harmful opinions.

"Errors" and "ambiguities" are in fact coupled in all the documents I know published by the CDF against theologians.

But the text just quoted raises many questions: Is the CDF as certain as it claims to be about what is or is not in contradiction with the content of faith? And a fortiori, where the doctrine of the church is concerned? I have already noted that these things are not all black and white, neither where faith is concerned, nor—and much less so—in the case of the church's doctrine. Allowance must be made for the possibility of a development of doctrine, not to say a change in doctrine, especially where, as the CDF admits, we are dealing with "questions hitherto largely unexplored." There ought to be no hurry in condemning and closing the door to theological investigation. Has the CDF a convincing answer to propose to the difficult question of combining the universal and efficacious will of God for the salvation of all people and peoples and its own strictures against and resistance to hypotheses suggested by theologians in an effort to account in a credible way for the possibility of universal salvation? I did not relish, besides, the way in which the CDF expressed its implicit condemnations in smooth language. Was it a *captatio benevolentiae* devised to extract my signature? Or was it just the Roman "way of proceeding" with matters of doctrine?

Another contradiction which raises questions is the vast discrepancies between the evaluation of my book by different authors, either in reviews or in elaborate studies. Some do not hide their praise and appreciation for what they consider a pioneering work destined to stay; others call on church authority for an explicit condemnation. I have mentioned above some of those contradictory reactions from people who can make identical claims of competence as professional theologians, though perhaps not enjoying the same expert knowledge. I have referred to the two contradictory reviews carried by the same paper, *Avvenire,* sponsored by the Italian episcopal conference: Enzo Bianchi, writing on November 22, 1997, who viewed my book as "a most precious contribution, a guide, a compass as it were, which can guide the progress of Catholic theology as it enters the third millennium"; and Inos Biffi whose piece on April 14, 1998, was as devastatingly negative as its predecessor had been positive. The contrast between the two and the question, to begin with, how the same paper could in the space of five months publish two extensive reviews of the same book so broadly contradictory has never been satisfactorily answered; it is difficult not to believe that politics have had a hand in the second piece and that it was prompted from somewhere above.

It is instructive to compare the repeated comments coming from Claude Geffré, on the one hand, and from Angelo Amato, on the other, both well-known professional theologians but belonging to different worlds. One might also compare what Peter C. Phan wrote in *Dialogue and Alliance* 14 no. 1 (2000): 121-23—when the investigation by the CDF was well on the way—with what the entire "comité de rédaction" of the *Revue thomiste* (1998, no. 4): 591-663, published. Peter C. Phan wrote about the theology of religious pluralism which my book proposed:

> Such a theology of religious pluralism, it must be admitted, is neither revolutionary nor uncommon today and remains well within the bounds of orthodoxy. But it has been made notorious by the fact that the Vatican has subjected Dupuis's work to "review" and required him to respond to a series of "questions" concerning his theological positions. This action by the Vatican not only betrays a distressing lack of gratitude for a man who has dedicated the greater part of his life in the service of the church and theology with his most thorough and scrupulous scholarship, but also a disconcerting unawareness that his theology of religious pluralism represents the *sententia communis* of Roman Catholic theologians. Whatever the outcome of the investigation of the Roman Curia, Dupuis's book is destined to be the standard textbook on the theology of religious pluralism for many years to come. I recommend it most enthusiastically for the use of graduate and advanced undergraduate classes on the theology of religions. It is hard to find another work that matches its comprehensive treatment, lucid exposition, fair-minded criticism, and balanced judgement.

By contrast, the Dominicans of Toulouse wrote at the end of a devastating study:

> In a field which is vital but still in exploration, the work of Fr. Dupuis formulates clearly essential problems and opens with cour-

age worthwhile perspectives. Unhappily, he does not always succeed in founding theologically his just intuitions. The very nature of the theology advocated (a contextual theology, which uses an inadequate philosophical instrument, thereby being incapable of thinking the great categories of Christian theology along the traditional lines) is in many aspects inadequate. Even more, some developments in the theology of revelation, in Christology or in ecclesiology do not do justice to the data of Christian tradition. . . . While taking into account the positive sides of the work of Fr. Dupuis, it is to be hoped that a different theology of religions may be elaborated, which would account for the multiform solicitude of the Father for all men without thereby questioning again the character at once gratuitous and absolutely necessary of the mediation of the man Jesus Christ and of his Body which is the church, in whom and through whom the Father has willed to recapitulate all things (Eph 1:10).

The contrast, not to say the flagrant contradiction, between the two statements could not be stronger. And it is here that some questions arise: How is it possible that such contradictory evaluations of the same work be formulated by apparently equally qualified theological sources? Is there superficiality on one side or obstinacy on the other? Is it merely a question of personal sympathy and favor on the one side and of animosity and disfavor on the other? Certainly, allowance must be made, in the assessment of academic theological work, for the possibility of a priori favorable dispositions or of contrary prejudices. But these human considerations do not suffice to solve the problem. Contradictory opinions have been expressed on things pertaining to both the content of faith and the doctrine of the church, by people who cannot a priori be suspected of allowing themselves to be carried away by prejudices or questionable intentions. The only plausible explanation is that not all is equally clear where the content of faith and, a fortiori, the doctrine of the church is concerned. In both cases, the right posture consists in holding together and combining apparently contradictory, but in fact complementary, components of reality. Different authors may stress different aspects, eventually to the prejudice of complementary aspects. The one-sided stress may even be so pronounced on both sides as to result in contradictory positions, and consequently in contradictory evaluations of the same work. What is needed on the part of all is a keener awareness of the complexity of the truth and of the relativity of our own perceptions of it.

As for the discrepancy or the contradiction between the "reception" which I meet with on the part of "ordinary" people and the lack of the same on the part of the CDF, I think it would be a serious simplification to say that people are innocent regarding questions concerned with the doctrine of faith, while the CDF is the only qualified arbiter to be trusted. The opinion of the Christian people ought to be taken seriously and their enthusiasm, if any, should not simply be attributed to ignorance; or, else, to a priori prejudice, widespread today, in favor of opinions opposed to authority. Such an attitude would amount to forgetting the role which the *sensus fidelium* exercises in indicating the content of faith and Christian doctrine.

I have mentioned this point above, but it seems important to state once more that the *sensus fidelium* is the fundamental criterion upon which the Magisterium can base its affirmation of the content of faith and doctrine. If people respond positively and with enthusiasm to the suggestions I make for a Christian solution to the problems involved in a theology of religions, should this not be an indication that a Christian solution to those problems is to be sought in that direction, with which spontaneously and with their intuitive sense of the faith the Christian people find themselves attuned? Solutions to these problems proposed over the centuries by a doctrinal authority often out of touch with reality have lost credibility with the Christian people. It is high time that the authority becomes aware of this loss of credibility and open up to more humanly acceptable and more Christian solutions.

G.O'C.: *You have spent your life as a priest in teaching. Was it necessary to become a priest to do this work? Could you not have done this work also as a layperson? If you were to start all over again, would you still become a priest?*

J.D.: It was not necessary to become a priest to do the work of a theologian, at least in theory, though in my time very few laypeople had the opportunity to study theology and still less to work as theologians. However, my first priority in life has not been theology. My vocation to the religious life and to the priesthood, concretely to be a Jesuit priest, came first. This was the call God addressed to me, in which alone I would find happiness and peace. Destination to India as a missionary and to theological work came later as the concrete ways in which I was to realize my calling. Therefore, to the question whether it was necessary for me to become a priest to do the work I have done as a theologian, the answer is that in theory it may not have been absolutely necessary. But in practice mission to India and, later, theological work have been the concrete embodiment of my God-given vocation. I believe that this double destination I received through my superiors was the expression of God's will for me.

The terms of the question must therefore be reversed: it is not a question of asking whether I became a priest in the Society of Jesus in order to be able to do theology, but to see that a vocation from God passes through various stages of maturation: in my case, from Jesuit priest to missionary in India, and then to the "profession" of being a theologian, first in India and later in Rome. This is why, when looking back, I do not in any way regret the stages of development of my vocation or wish I had been given another orientation—whatever may have been the difficulties along the way or even the trials endured. I look at them all—at least from the hindsight—as God-given opportunities offered to me to prove my faithfulness and my readiness to abide by his will. This is not to say that, when times of trial came, I always and spontaneously had a positive reaction or that difficulties, trials endured, and times of crisis have left no negative mark in me. The account I have given shows the opposite. But it does mean that, while I have been and remain wounded by some events that took place in my life, I have never really contemplated the possibility of following another path than the one God had chosen for me. That determination remains stronger today than ever, by God's grace.

G.O'C.: *As a Jesuit, you were bound by a vow of obedience to your superiors. Did that make it easier or more difficult for you to get through the ordeal?*

J.D.: It is when difficulties come that one begins to realize what the vow of obedience really means. While everything goes smoothly, obedience raises no problem and is taken for granted. When, on the contrary, one is given orders from above, the rationale and the wisdom of which escape one's understanding, then obedience—and Jesuit obedience in particular—begins to make its demands felt. This happened to me a first time in 1984, when my transfer from Delhi to Rome was abruptly decided and I was required to execute orders promptly and somewhat blindly. I must admit that I found it very hard to comply with Father General's decision, all the more so as my work there was enjoying a growing success and a broad impact. I have explained above that it took me time to discover the wisdom of my transfer and to launch with gusto into the new work assigned to me. In this case obedience had been truly painful. In the case of my Roman crisis starting in 1998, on the contrary, religious obedience turned out to be a positive asset. I have recalled above the moral support which I found in my Father General and with the religious superior of the Gregorian, Fr. Egaña. But it has not been merely a question of moral support. I have benefited much from the advice received from both as to the way in which I should react in this time of trial. I always found in them general sound advice and a readiness to do things in my favor. True, I have sometimes wondered whether the superiors should not, perhaps, in the name of the Society, be more vocal in defending their men and objecting to some ways of proceeding against them; I have suspected on their part an attitude of conformity, not to say of blind subservience, that sometimes gave the interest of the institution precedence over the good of persons. Does the Society live up today to its prophetic vocation, which, as the experience of St. Ignatius shows abundantly, does not conceive obedience as blind compliance with anything coming from above, without representation being made of different legitimate views, but suggests a common discernment with the higher authority, based on dialogue and mutual openness?

This raises the question of the existence in the church of "legitimate dissent," not only on the part of theologians but eventually on the part of the religious superiors in relation to the church's central authority. Whatever the case may be, I must admit that the course I have been asked by my superiors to follow, even if it sometimes appeared to me too timid, happened to be the right course, perhaps the only possible one. Obedience to my superiors has in fact turned to my advantage. I wonder what mistakes I might have committed if I had been left to myself to devise my own way of reacting. While then it seems clear that by choosing as its preferred targets religious under obedience, the CDF expects to deal with more submissive and vulnerable persons, while laypeople can more easily escape their grasp, the reverse is also true: namely, that religious under obedience to their superiors may find in them a positive asset in the questioning of their work and the threat of repressive measures taken against them.

G.O'C.: *As you look back on your life's work, what major questions still remain unanswered in the field of religious pluralism that, in your view, would be of significance for the whole church, and for ordinary people?*

J.D.: The theology of religious pluralism raises many questions. I have entitled my controversial book of 1997 *Toward a Christian Theology of Religious Pluralism.* The *toward* was not false humility; it expressed my awareness of the difficulty of a subject still mostly unexplored and the provisional character of my reflections and proposals. In the introduction to that work I wrote: "The present introduction will, perhaps, raise as many questions as it will propose solutions. It will hopefully, at least, sort out the issues clearly in the light of recent discussions and advances and indicate avenues for solutions to new questions, consonant with the profession of Christian faith." Even that sentence, in which I am stating my awareness of the provisional character of my work, has been used against me, as betraying my own sense of its problematic and questionable nature. Let me recall that the term "problematic" was added by the CDF to the title of the article which Fr. Giuseppe de Rosa wrote on my book for *Civiltà cattolica* (1998, no. 3): 129-43: "Una teologia problematica del pluralismo religioso."

That the subject of religious pluralism is theologically problematic is readily admitted, unless we be content to repeat opinions of the past which no longer satisfy anyone. Sadly, the addition made by the CDF to the title of the article was clearly derogatory. However this may be, my book did not claim to exhaust the subject and the suggestions it made for possible solutions to the questions raised remained open to discussion. Yet, as Enzo Bianchi suggested in his review of the book in *Avvenire* (November 22, 1997): "If it is true that this work 'will, perhaps, raise as many questions as it will propose solutions,' it is equally true that to ask the right questions is already essential for the correct approach to the problem. The question, in fact, looks toward the answer (E. Jabès)." And Terrence Merrigan, in his article "Exploring the Frontiers: Jacques Dupuis and the Movement 'Toward a Christian Theology of Religious Pluralism'" in *Louvain Studies* 23, no. 3 (1998): 338-59, wrote—if I may be allowed to quote again:

> What Dupuis has done is to explore the frontiers of the inclusivist theology of religions. In so doing, he has exposed certain "no-go areas" and apparently even ventured into something of a no-man's-land between the three classical approaches. Of course, there are pitfalls confronting every explorer. However, like all true explorers, Dupuis deserves respect and admiration for his endeavors. This is a brave and conscientious book, a comprehensive map of familiar territory, and an attempt to chart new routes. Dupuis's map may not be complete but it will surely serve those who come after him.

If, then, questions have not found a definitive answer in my writing—there was no such pretense—a direction has at least been indicated along which tentative solutions may hopefully be found to the problems raised, which go beyond the outmoded problematic of the mere possibility of salvation outside the church. It seems fair to say that from where we stand now there will be no return to the obsolete views.

Questions have not, however, disappeared, and they will remain with us. It will remain problematic *how* to combine the universal efficacy of the Christ event for the salvation of humankind and the salvific value of the religious traditions in God's plan for it; and likewise, the Christian faith in Jesus Christ the one mediator between God and human beings and God's universal efficacious will of salvation extending concretely to all; or even more, the universal significance of the Christ event for human salvation and the equally universal presence and action of the Word of God as such and of the Spirit of God. But we ought to distinguish clearly in these matters between the "fact" (*an sit*) and the "how" (*quomodo sit*). While we may be entitled to affirm that apparently opposed elements must *in fact* be combined, we may never be able to show *how* they combine in fact as complementary aspects of reality. I have stressed the need to distinguish between the *an sit* we affirm and the *quomodo sit* which remains beyond our grasp in my last book, *Christianity and the Religions: From Confrontation to Dialogue*. With reference, precisely, to the universality of Jesus Christ and that of the Word of God as such, I wrote:

> Theology must always maintain a strong sense of the mystery of transcendence not only of God, but also of his plan of salvation. In this case, it must not claim to describe or define the "how" and "in which way" (*quomodo sit*) of the essential relationship between the universal action of the Word—and the Spirit—and the historical event of Jesus Christ. Theological apophatism suggests silence where, though being able to underline the fact (*an sit*), we cannot and need not explain the "how." It behooves theology to be reserved and humble.

This attitude does not imply giving up the function of theological reflection; it only witnesses to an awareness of its limitations. Dealing as it does with mysteries, theology must be satisfied to state *what* the mysteries consist of, not *how* they are to be proved or explained. If we should claim to prove the mysteries of faith or to explain how they work, we should be going beyond what is given to us to do. We would in fact claim for ourselves the knowledge which God has of himself and of his plan for us. This would amount to self-divinization. The correct attitude then consists in allowing God to be God and in being content to live by faith: a faith that seeks understanding (*fides quaerens intellectum*)—not of the "how" but of the "what." Mysteries will remain mysteries, but we shall have progressed immensely if we have acquired a deeper perception of their content. A deep abiding sense of mystery must accompany at every step our desire to probe its meaning.

G.O'C.: *If, at the end of time, Christ were to ask you to give an account of the work you have done, what would you say to him?*

J.D.: I cannot imagine myself giving to the Lord, on the other side of this life, an account of the work I have done. Nor do I think that such an account on my part would be necessary. The Lord will know my work, even better than I know it myself. I can only hope that his evaluation of it will be more positive than has been that of some censors and, alas, of the church's central doctrinal authority. On my part, I would only wish to thank God for the gift of human life and for the call to share in his own divine life in his Son Jesus; I would also thank him for the full life which, for no merit of mine, he granted to me, his unworthy servant, and for the many opportunities he offered me to learn to serve and love him. I trust that the Lord who reads the secrets of the hearts will know that my intention in writing what I have written and saying what I have said has only been to express to the best of my ability my deep faith in him and my total dedication to him. Rather than being inclined to do the talking when we meet, I hope then to hear from the Lord, in spite of my failings and shortcomings, a word of comfort and encouragement. I pray that he may invite me to enter into his glory, forever to sing his praise. May I hear him say to me: "Well done, good and faithful servant; you have been faithful over a little, I will set you over much; enter into the joy of your Master" (Matt 25:21). Amen.

Gregorian University, Rome, June 29, 2003,
in the Solemnity of Sts. Peter and Paul

— 3 —

The Aftermath of a Trial

G.O'C.: *The end of Chapter 2 on "The Pangs of a Process" has been dated on the Solemnity of Sts. Peter and Paul, June 29, 2003. A year and a half have passed since, and things have happened in the meantime, which justify adding a new chapter with the title "The Aftermath of a Trial." Earlier you told me that after the publication of the Notification on the 1997 book (February 26, 2001), you received many invitations to write articles and give lectures in different places and different continents. But you added that, whenever you did so, you were always "conscious of remaining under suspicion on the part of the CDF, and therefore had to be especially circumspect about what [you] said and how [you] said it." You remarked: "I felt my freedom of speech badly curtailed, even while I remained convinced that what I was proposing was in agreement with the church's faith. This sensation of being under constant supervision, not to say of being tracked by authority and subject to eventual new denunciation, was indeed very painful to bear. One felt like being continuously pursued by a new version of the Inquisition for spreading wrong doctrines."*

Later in the chapter, in answering one of my questions, you noted: "I do not have the feeling even today that the whole affair is over. One could perhaps have thought so—and many in fact did think so—after the publication of the Notification on my book. I had been absolved of the accusation of 'grievous errors against the faith' and should beware of 'ambiguities' in what I wrote. But, . . . through the CDF's doubtful dealings I was in fact constrained to abide, in speech and writing, by opinions I did not accept, about which all possibility of further discussion was closed for me by the sheer imposition of authority." This apprehension, as you explained then, had already been verified in events which followed, before Chapter 2 was concluded on June, 29, 2003. Similar events have recurred again since, and it is on those that we now wish to concentrate our attention in this Chapter 3, one and a half years later, at the end of November 2004. Please, give me a short account of the academic activities you have been engaged in since we ended Chapter 2, including those which triggered new accusations and new threats.

J.D.: The list is long of the academic activities I have been engaged in since June 2003. In the following list I mention the more important items in chronological order: Mexico, Universidad Iberoamericana, VII Simposio: "La teologia en los umbrales del Siglo XXI" (September 10-12, 2003), lecture on "The Religions of the World in the Second Vatican Council and the Post-Conciliar Magisterium"; Turin, Teatro aperto 2003, "Domande a Dio": Lecture on "What Theology of Interreligious Dialogue?" (September 17); Fatima, International Congress, "The Present of Man, the Future of God" (October 10-12), lecture on "Interreligious Dialogue, a Challenge to Christian Identity"; Lucerne University, colloquy "Apprendre ensemble" (October 24-25), lecture on "Interreligious Dialogue, a Challenge to the Christian Conscience"; Louvain University, Congress on Religious Experience and Contemporary Theological Epistemology (November 5-8), lecture on "Inclusive Pluralism as a Paradigm for the Theology of Religions"; Turin, Centro di Studi Comparativi Edoardo Agnelli, Convegno internazionale "Hinduismo e Cristianesimo: Prospettive per il dialogo interreligioso" (November 20-21), lecture on "An Indian Face for Jesus Christ"; Rome, Centro internazionale Dionysia, colloquy on "Nathan the Sage," lecture on "To Speak about God: God Confessed and God Sung" (November 23); Utrecht, Catholic University, symposium on "Christianity in Dialogue," lecture on "The Renewal of Christianity through Dialogue" (December 3); Krakow, Ignazianum, symposium on "Christianity in Dialogue with Religions," lecture on "Jesus Christ—Universal Saviour and the Ways of Salvation" (December 8); open debate on "The Dignity of Difference: Meeting with Jacques Dupuis" (December 8); Warsaw, Bobolanum, symposium on "Christianity and the Religions," lecture on "Jesus Christ Universal Saviour and the Ways of Salvation" (December 9); Warsaw, House of Dominican Fathers, open discussion on "the State of Interreligious Dialogue in the World Today" (December 9); Ancona, Centro Studi Oriente Occidente, symposium on "Discordanze concordi," lecture on "The Advaita Experience and Christian Consciousness" (December 11). Syracuse, New York (United States), Le Moyne College, Loyola Lecture (February 10, 2004) on "Jesus Christ Universal Saviour and the Ways of Salvation," joined with the conferring of the degree of doctor in humane letters honoris causa; New York, Interfaith Center, talk on "Jesus Christ Universal Saviour and the Ways of Salvation" (February 12); Maryknoll, New York, colloquium "On the

Implications of the Work of Jacques Dupuis for the Theology and Practice of Mission"; Naples, University of Salerno, colloquy on "The Reasons of Dialogue: Grammar of the Encounter between the Religions," lecture on "Interreligious Dialogue: A Challenge to the Christian Conscience" (February 20); San Gimignano, Centro Internazionale di Studi sul Religioso Contemporaneo, lecture on "Christianity and Religious Pluralism Today" (March 13); Parma, parish of S. Cristina, lecture on "Il dialogo interreligioso, una sfida per la coscienza cristiana" (April 19); Camaldoli, Benedictine Monastery, colloquy on "Henri Le Saux, Crossing to the Other Shore," two lectures on "Hindu Mysticism and the Christian Mystery in Abhishiktananda (Henri Le Saux)" (May 29); Gentines (Belgium), colloquy on "The New Mission: Testimony: My Experience of Mission" (July 5-9), lecture on "Interreligious Dialogue in the Evangelizing Mission of the Church"; Camaldoli, Benedictine Monastery, annual meeting of FUCI (Federation of Italian Catholic Universities), four lectures on "The Theology of Religions and of Interreligious Dialogue" (July 26-27); Genoa, World Conference of Religions for Peace (WCRP), European colloquy, "The Communications Media and the Religions," lecture on "The Challenges and the Fruits of Interreligious Dialogue" (September 11); London, Catholic Missionary Union of England and Wales, lecture on "The Church's Evangelizing Mission in the Context of Religious Pluralism" (September 20); Washington, DC, Saint Anselm's Abbey, 31st Annual Thomas Verner Moore Lecture on "Jesus Christ Universal Saviour and the Ways of Salvation" (September 25); Washington, DC, Catholic University of America, colloquium on "Renewal of Christianity through Interreligious Dialogue" (September 27). (Note: An extensive program at Notre Dame University, Indiana, planned for the following week had to be postponed because of sickness in Washington.)

That is the list until the month of November; more appointments follow, starting with one in Turin at the beginning of December, which, as I write, has already taken place. This was the last lecture of a three-week course on Asian religious traditions for professors and teachers: "Dialogo come progetto: Tradizioni religiose dell'Asia," lecture on "Interreligious Dialogue: Perspectives and Theological Knots" (December 4). I may mention that on December 5 the Rev. Stefano Rossi, S.D.B., the promoter of the course, wrote to me saying: "The prolonged applause after your lecture full of passion and in some moments vibrating, proves the syntony of thought and intent, which you have roused in the audience. In this way, the course has been crowned, to say the least, with general satisfaction. I personally thank God and I pray that what unites us may progress. May God give you strength and health to bring forward your work, especially in this time for which it is precious. . . . Stefano Rossi, S.D.B." The long list above testifies—and this is why it is worthwhile to spell it out here—to the growing interest which universities and other institutions keep showing for the theology of religions and of interreligious dialogue. It also reveals that, notwithstanding the opposition which my contribution to those topics has met on the part of the CDF, the invitations I receive from many places to lecture on those topics, far from decreasing, have rather increased in recent times. Later on in this chapter, we shall point explicitly to those academic activities in the list which have aroused new opposition and brought about new threats from high quarters. These new threats, however, being relatively recent, allowed me a certain amount of freedom between June 2003 and the middle of 2004. Other events have claimed my attention during those months of relative freedom, to which we may now turn.

G.O'C.: *On December 5, 2003, the Gregorian University celebrated your eightieth birthday with the presentation of a Festschrift in your honor. Before we come to the celebration itself, I would like you to explain what was the background to this event and in which circumstances it came about.*

J.D.: The initiative to have a Festschrift in honor of my eightieth birthday came from Fr. Gerald O'Collins, who was expertly helped by Fr. Daniel Kendall of the University of San Francisco. The two had previously worked together on various publications and again combined their skill and their work to bring this one about. William R. Burrows, managing editor of Orbis Books, Maryknoll, NY, expressed in advance his willingness and his pleasure at publishing a Festschrift in my honor. Orbis Books had published my books in English ever since I came to Rome in 1984. With the assurance of having a distinguished publisher, the project could be launched. Invitations were sent to prospective contributors who responded generously. These included prestigious names of the theological community, especially qualified in the matters to which I had devoted much of my own theological attention. I should have been kept unaware of the preparations which were being made. This, however, was not possible because of the editors' wish to include in the volume a double bibliography: one regarding my own theological production; the other referring to the discussion and controversy which my 1997 book, *Toward a Christian Theology of Religious Pluralism*, had aroused soon after its publication. This second bibliography, as mentioned earlier, is included in an appendix to the present volume. [Editor's note: Because this bibliography was already published in *Doctrine and Life*, it has not been included here.] The bibliography of my own production was not easy to establish. It was necessary to go back to the year 1960 when I first started writing, and to trace much literature of which I had been keeping no account over the years till my transfer to the Gregorian University in 1984; that literature was dispersed in many places and had to be gathered together. The bibliography on the controversy over my own book also required putting together many references found in many periodicals and books as well as in the secular press. As it stands, it makes no pretense at being exhaustive; yet it does gather an impressive number of comments on my writing, both positive and negative, which may be of interest to students desirous of studying the merits of the case.

The Festschrift was ready well before the date of my eightieth birthday, December 2003. The problem then arose of how to plan its official presentation. In the circumstances in which I found myself in relation to the church's official doctrinal authority, could a presentation of the book take place at the Gregorian University? Would such a project meet with the approval of the authorities of the university? On the other hand, holding the presentation outside would create a strange impression to say the least. One should remember that after the publication of the Notification on my 1997 book on February 26, 2001, the authorities of the university had forbidden me to speak publicly in the precincts of the university to journalists asking for information about the case. I could only keep silent, declared Fr. Imoda, the rector of the university. That a session did take place at the Gregorian, during which I spoke freely with a group of journalists interested in the matter, was due to the personal intervention of Fr. Peter-Hans Kolvenbach, General of the Society of Jesus, who, when consulted by me on the matter, said that such a session would not only be permitted but should be welcome. "Let the truth come out," he said; "this can only do good to you and to the Society." To avoid similar difficulties and opposition on the part of the university authorities over the presentation of the Festschrift, Fr. O'Collins went straight to Father General to present the case. Father General expressed his joy at the news that a Festschrift in my honor was in the offing and gave his blessing to the idea of a presentation taking place at the Gregorian University itself. This is how the presentation of the book did take place on December 5, 2003, in the Aula Magna of the university.

This prospect did not, however, please everybody among my Jesuit colleagues in the community of the Gregorian. When the forthcoming presentation came to be known through an official announcement, one Jesuit confrere expressed vociferously in public his disapproval of the initiative. He thought it scandalous that the Gregorian should hold a public function for the presentation of a Festschrift in honor of someone who was still under investigation by the CDF, of which he was a prominent consultor; in addition, he would soon become secretary of the International Theological Commission of the Vatican. (His name—to make it plain—is Luis Ladaria, professor of dogmatic theology on the theological faculty of the Gregorian.) I was out of Rome, giving lectures somewhere, when this opposition emerged; but on my return I was informed about it by several Jesuit colleagues. In conversation with Fr. Egaña, I suggested that whoever objected to the presentation of the Festschrift taking place at the Gregorian should argue this out with Father General, since he had approved the project without hesitation or reservation. (As it happened, when the presentation of the Festschrift took place on December 5 in the Aula Magna of the university, heavily attended by people from outside, the Jesuit professors of the Gregorian University were conspicuously absent and could be counted on the fingers of two hands.)

G.O'C.: *The celebration itself was a great success; tributes flowed in from many parts of the world, and several distinguished guests attended, as did representatives of several religious orders, and priests and nuns from Asia. What are your own memories of that day?*

J.D.: Yes, the celebration was a great success. It was much better attended than I had anticipated in the circumstances, though mostly by people from outside who wanted to show their sympathy and support. I discovered on this occasion that many more people knew me and sympathized with me than I was aware of. I was especially sensitive to the presence of four members of my family: one niece, Veronique, and her husband, Christian, and another niece, Anne, and a cousin, Christine. Little allusion was made to the special situation in which this celebration was taking place, and the tone of joy and thanksgiving prevailed over what could have otherwise spread a shadow of darkness over the rejoicing. The celebration was presided over by Fr. John O'Donnell, the dean of the theological faculty. On the podium with him, there were Fr. Gerald O'Collins, Fr. Daniel Kendall, William Burrows of Orbis Books, and myself. Interludes of Indian classical music and song provided by the John Damascene College added an Indian atmosphere to the celebration. After a short introduction by the dean there followed the presentation of the Festschrift in my honor by Fr. Kendall. The title of the Festschrift, *In Many and Diverse Ways* (Maryknoll, NY: Orbis Books, 2004), is a very apt title which describes the spirit and the content of the book. It quotes the first words of the Letter to the Hebrews which recalls that God spoke in many ways to his chosen people through the prophets before, in these days that are the last, he spoke through the one who is his Son, Jesus Christ. Obviously, in the title of the book the quotation from Hebrews is intended to extend to the many ways in which God spoke to the peoples of the world throughout human history, before he spoke to the people of Israel through their prophets. There followed a long exposition by Fr. O'Collins of my work first in India for thirty-six years, and thereafter in Rome, at the Gregorian University, for the last twenty years. Alluding to the situation in which I have been placed since 1998 by the CDF, he said:

> As we all know, Father Dupuis has suffered much during those years when his book *Toward a Christian Theology of Religious Pluralism* has been challenged by the ecclesiastical authority. Being close to him, I have always been deeply edified by his fidelity to Christ and his obedience to his superiors. Before the Contestation Father Dupuis was already much recognized in Asia and in Italy. Now he is very well known and much in demand in other parts of the world. The question of the relation between Christ and the religions is a very actual one. So many people, including many bishops, wish to hear Father Dupuis on this topic. Remembering the years of the Contestation and the sufferings Father Dupuis has endured, one must say: "God writes straight with crooked lines."

There followed a short speech by William Burrows of Orbis Books, Maryknoll, who expressed his joy at having been able to publish all my books ever since I came to Rome in 1984. He thought it a pleasure for a publishing house to publish manuscripts which were so well polished by the author and which offered the highest prospects of sale in the United States and abroad. To mark the occasion, He then presented me with a plaque which reproduces the cover of the Festschrift, engraved in a wooden frame.

There followed the reading in Italian, French, and English of testimonies sent for the occasion, which expressed appreciation for my theological work as well as sympathy for the suffering I had endured at the hands of the church's central authority, and attachment to my own person. To make a complete list of those testimonies would be too long. Let me recall only some, which spoke with greater authority and with a deeper knowledge of the case, either as church leaders or as specialists in the theological matters concerned. And first of all, let me refer to two cardinals and two archbishops with whom I have been closely associated.

I have made reference earlier to the circumstances in which I went to visit Cardinal König in Vienna in July 2003, to thank him for the courage with which he had defended a person he had never met personally. Now, beside his contribution to the Festschrift, entitled "Let the Spirit Breathe," he sent me a message for the presentation in which he wrote:

> I can send you in good time my best wishes and blessings for the forthcoming birthday celebration at the Gregorian. At the same time I would like to express my appreciation for your great authority in the field of interreligious dialogue, in relation to theology, but also my recognition of the courage, thanks to the strength of your faith, with which you coped with the difficult time preparing for the "Notificatio" of 2001. . . . I should also like to combine all this in brief with my sincerest wishes and blessing from above in its plenitude!

A few months later, Cardinal Franz König died in Vienna. Cardinal Avery Dulles of Fordham University had been my companion at the Bellarmino College in Rome where we were studying at the Gregorian for the doctorate. He too contributed a piece to the Festschrift and in a brief message wrote: "Congratulations for the Festschrift and on your survival 45 years after we first met at the Bellarmino. I regret that because of a trip to England I shall not be able to come to Rome for your celebration."

The two archbishops who deserve special mention here are Henry D'Souza, now emeritus archbishop of Calcutta, and Archbishop Michael Fitzgerald, already head of the Pontifical Council for Interreligious Dialogue at the Vatican. I reported above, though rapidly, my many earlier dealings with both of them. Archbishop Henry D'Souza wrote the Foreword to the Festschrift; he had done the same for the Indian edition of my 1997 book, published in Gujarat in 2001. He also sent a message for the occasion in which he wrote to the organizers of the presentation:

> It is a pity that I shall not be there for the celebration with Fr. Dupuis. He deserves all that you can give him. He has been a great theologian and the church in India is deeply indebted to him. I think his role in promoting the understanding of the theology of religions has been very significant. History will look back and remember him with gratitude for his courage and fidelity in spite of misunderstanding. I have always admired his clear mind and attractive presentation of doctrine. However, during the last few years I have also come to appreciate his great spirit of faith and love of God and the church. Have a great celebration for him.

Archbishop Michael Fitzgerald also contributed a piece to the Festschrift, but was prevented from attending the celebration because of a trip to Japan. He wrote to the organizers:

> Father Jacques Dupuis has made a major contribution to the reflection on other religions from a Christian point of view. This is a question which for theology today is unavoidable. Father Dupuis's work "Toward a Christian Theology of Interreligious Dialogue" constitutes a precious instrument for this ongoing reflection. Of course, as is the case for all instruments, it has to be used with discernment, and I am sure that Fr. Dupuis, from his long life as a Jesuit, would be the first to acknowledge this. I am sorry not to be present in Rome for the celebration, and wish to join all in thanking Jacques Dupuis for his work.

One may reasonably suppose that both the archbishops mentioned here missed their promotion to the cardinalate to which they were destined because of the courage with which they defended me against accusations from the Vatican. To substantiate this supposition, it would be enough in the case of Archbishop Henry D'Souza to recall that he has been elected several times president of the Indian Bishops' Conference (CBCI), and after a distinction was introduced between the Conference of the Latin Bishops and the Conferences of the Bishops of the two Oriental rites, he was again elected president of the Latin Conference. He was also for many years president of the Federation of Asian Bishops' Conferences (FABC); he attended many bishops' synods in Rome, and was several times elected to the postsynodal commissions. He was eminently qualified for being the new cardinal of India at the consistory of 2001; the red hat went instead to Archbishop Ivan Dias, newly appointed archbishop of Bombay, and a partisan, if not a member, of Opus Dei. Questioned on this, Archbishop Henry commented: "I prefer the truth to a red hat." In the case of Archbishop Michael Fitzgerald, let it suffice to say that he is now one of the very few heads of a Vatican dicastery, congregation, or council not to have been created a cardinal at the consistory of 2003, at which many heads of Vatican offices who had not been promoted earlier were raised to that dignity. Let us also recall that, with the exception of Archbishop Jean Jadot, who held the office for a short period (1980-1984), all the predecessors of Archbishop Fitzgerald as head, either of the Secretariat for Non-Christians or of the Council for Interreligious Dialogue, have been made cardinals. I feel sad at having here to express my regret for what two persons of great merit and for whom I have the greatest appreciation have had to suffer because of the sympathy they showed me and the courage with which they took publicly my defense.

Next I wish to mention the message sent for the occasion by Rev. Fr. Jerome Francis, S.J., provincial of the Jesuit Province of Calcutta, to which I still belong. He addressed to the organizers the following message:

> In my own name and in the name of the Calcutta Province of the Society of Jesus, I wish to associate myself with the felicitation meeting at the Pontifical Gregorian University, and the release of the Miscellanea of studies in honor of Fr. Jacques Dupuis on his 80th birthday. Father was with us for many years, at first briefly, in Saint Xavier's High School, as much appreciated teacher and sharped-eye referee of the boys' games. Later he was an eminent member of the faculty of Saint Mary's Theological College, at first in Kurseong, then later in Delhi. We were sorry to lose him to Rome, but the exploration he has made of a meaningful dialogue with people of other faiths, in particular of those faiths prominent in India, has inspired missionary work in this country and in this Province. With heartful prayer we wish him many more years of creative theological work in the service of the church.

To the name of my Father Provincial in Calcutta, I may join that of Fr. Julian Fernandes, S.J., assistant to Father General for the South Asian Assistancy of the Society. He wrote:

> You have served God and the church with the fidelity, love, and competence of a true Jesuit. I join you and your friends in thanking the Lord for all that the Lord has accomplished in you, through you—especially through your highly specialized theological research and publications. You will understand and excuse my absence—my loss, really, in missing the occasion—but I am with you in spirit.

Among the professors of theology who contributed to the Festschrift some were also prevented from attending by various commitments. They sent messages expressing their regret at being unable to attend. Among those Fr. Claude Geffré of Paris wrote to me personally:

> Cher Père Dupuis, retenu a Tokyo, je regrette vivement de ne pas être avec vos amis pour célébrer votre 80ème anniversaire. Je vou-

drais vous assurer de ma fidèle amitié, de mon admiration et de ma gratitude. C'est l'ensemble des théologiens chrétiens qui ont une dette à votre egard. En notre âge planétaire, vous avez su ouvrir des voies nouvelles en montrant qu'il était possible de confesser l'unicité du Christ Maître de l'histoire, tout en respectant la pluralité des voies vers Dieu du sein des religions et des cultures du monde. *Ad multos annos!* With my best regards.

Father Geffré confirmed here what he had written about me previously in books and periodicals, to which I have briefly referred earlier in this book. More recently still, Fr. Geffré has come back to the topic. In an important contribution, entitled "Toward a New Theology of Religions," to a book edited by Rosino Gibellini, *Prospettive teologiche per il XXI secolo* (Brescia: Queriniana, 2003), 353-72, he wrote:

> The most promising current inside Catholicism is that which seeks to overcome a theology of fulfillment with a theology of religious pluralism. Without compromising the unicity of the mystery of Christ, that is, a constitutive Christocentrisrn, such a theology does not hesitate to speak of an *inclusive pluralism* in the sense of a recognition of the values proper to other religions. . . . It is not surprising . . . that a certain number of eminent Catholic theologians—I think mostly of Edward Schillebeeckx and Jacques Dupuis—ask themselves seriously if the pluralism de facto does not send us back to a pluralism in principle or of right, which would correspond to a mysterious will of God. (p. 359)

He goes on to write even more clearly, with reference to the accusations made by the CDF against such theological views:

> It would be easy to show that many theologians, Catholic and otherwise, who accept to distinguish between religious pluralism de facto and a pluralism of right, do not in any way succumb to the ideology of a pluralism despairing of attaining to any objective truth. They would be very surprised to hear that the distinction [they draw] makes the fatal error of considering as surpassed the truths recorded in number 4 of the declaration [*Dominus Iesus*], especially the personal unity of the eternal Word and Jesus of Nazareth, the uniqueness and the universality of the mystery of Christ, etc. It is legitimate, from the theological viewpoint to interpret [pluralism] as a pluralism which corresponds to a mysterious design of God. (p. 360)

One will recognize in the charge of denying the truths mentioned here some of the errors imputed to me by the CDF. Even more recently, Geffré has taken up the same point. In a book entitled *Who Do You Say That I Am?*, edited by John C. Cavadini and Laura Holt (Notre Dame, IN: University of Notre Dame Press, 2004), he contributed an article entitled "The Christological Paradox as a Hermeneutic Key to Interreligious Dialogue." He wrote there:

> It has been the task of studies in comparative religion, for the past decades, to reinterpret the uniqueness of Christ as the only mediator and the uniqueness of Christianity as the truly salvific religion by trying to do justice to the positive value of other religions. This is only possible by going beyond a problem which still lingers within the confines of a renewed version of the old theology of *salvation of non-believers*, and adopting a true theology of religious pluralism which is concerned with the meaning of the diversity of the various religious traditions in God's plan. This transition from accepting religious pluralism as a fact to the idea of a legitimate pluralism as part of God's mysterious plan represents an important theological step forward. Jacques Dupuis's great book entitled *Toward a Christian Theology of Religious Pluralism* is the best and most official statement of this. From the perspective of a hermeneutical theology which takes account of the irreversible facts of our historical experience, I have been trying for some considerable time to show how the religious history of humankind, despite its basic ambiguity, bears witness not only to the fumbling beginnings of a quest for the mystery of the ultimate reality but also to the plurality of the gifts of God who reaches out to humans. In other words, since its beginning human history is already history of salvation long before the coming of Christ. (pp. 160-61)

The closeness of the thought of Claude Geffré to my own justifies the long quotations introduced here, in which, with the highest competence which is his, he unreservedly approves my own theological endeavor and develops his own in a way very similar to mine.

Monsignor Luigi Sartori of Padua, as recalled above, had written a beautiful preface to the Italian edition of my latest published book, under the title "Confidential Reflections of a Friend." He too contributed a piece to the Festschrift. But, being also unable to attend due to poor health, he sent me a moving message in which he wrote:

I thank God for having known and discovered you. For me, you are a model of a zealous scholar, sharp and open; severe and coherent with regard to method; above all, exemplary in the spirituality of true love. Some reservations and contestation notwithstanding (. . . on the part of those who view truth as the privilege mostly of those who express the "tradition" [in lower case] of the past), you have been able to hide your sufferings behind a veil of peace, made up of meek and strong patience. . . . You remind us that only "The Truth" deserves to win and certainly will win; not we who propose it and consider it as our property. . . . You have placed the mysteries of the Trinity and of the Incarnation once again on a high level of reflection, after so much repetition and stagnation. You have not only put in relief again the universal action of the Holy Spirit, but also that of the Word; and, it is my conviction, you have done this without prejudice to the action of the humanity of Jesus Christ, the Word incarnate. In fact, tomorrow people will realize that in this way it will be possible to attain authentic, wonderful new developments. Those mysteries will be "understood" then a little better. Oh, if I could thank you . . . in the name of future students! But I am among those who soon will no longer have a voice on this side of life. To you, on the contrary, I truly wish, and not only by way of compliment, many more years in this "earthly" church, so that you might help her to breathe in anticipation something of heaven. Your friend and disciple, D. Luigi Sartori.

This moving message witnesses not only to a true and deep friendship, but to the great courage of one able to look beyond the present time.

Some of the contributors to the Festschrift made it a point to attend the presentation. Professor Terrence Merrigan of Louvain University, dean of the faculty of theology and director of the review *Louvain Studies*, had previously written some of the most perceptive comments on my writing and published in his periodical two articles in which I answered questions posed by theologians in book reviews of my two recent books. Besides his contribution to the Festschrift, he wished to speak during its presentation and read the following testimony:

When I began teaching the "Theology of Religions" in the early 1990s, it soon became clear to me that the agenda was being set by the so-called pluralist theologians (John Hick, Paul Knitter, et al.). I learned much from them, especially (i) the need to acknowledge the "moral and spiritual goods" of other traditions, (ii) the need to engage in dialogue with them, and (iii) above all, the need to provide a responsible theological account of their presence in history. I was, however, dissatisfied with their (i) understanding of Christianity, and (ii) their doctrine of God, in particular. But where was I to look for an alternative? It was in the midst of this search that I encountered the work of Professor Dupuis. It was, for me, a relief and a delight to discover that one can engage with the reality of religious pluralism in a creative and constructive fashion, without compromising the essence of our faith, namely, the confession of Jesus Christ as God's saving word and deed for all of humankind. *As a Christian,* I am grateful to Father Dupuis for the hope he has given me that the depth and richness of our Trinitarian faith will allow us, in time, to do justice to the "otherness" of other traditions. *As a theologian,* I am grateful to him for pointing me the way to a theological space where there is room (i) to think, and (ii) to engage with others, without fear of empty compromise or arrogant intolerance. In short, thank you, Father Dupuis, for helping me to find my way in a theological minefield that must be crossed.

This message speaks for itself, and there is no need to apologize for quoting it in full. It is written by one who is today a recognized authority in the theology of religions. His appreciation of my work and his humility put me to shame.

Hans Waldenfels, S.J., is another specialist and friend who in the midst of the controversy wrote an editorial in my defense in *Stimmen der Zeit.* He too contributed to the Festschrift but had to leave Rome before the presentation of the Festschrift took place. However, he left with me a personal letter from which I quote only one extract:

Working in a similar field as you did for decades, I know how much trouble and strain is hidden in your voluminous work on religious pluralism. . . . The Festschrift is a proof that you are not a lonesome wolf searching your way in the prairie and desert of our time. No, we are many who are happy to think with you in the direction you are walking. . . . Indeed, you prepare a theology which is to be called an interreligious theology, as Claude Geffré suggested. There is some light to be seen in the foundation of pluralism which does not destroy the Christian view of history but rather strengthens it. Pluralism is to be seen as a chance we have to develop. . . . We can be happy that in all the reservations which we find in "Dominus Iesus" and in the Notification, at the end your work and thought are not touched and censured at all. We can feel rather invited to continue our path, you can continue your path. Let us do it together with the grace of the Lord.

Father Francis Sullivan, S.J., is another contributor to the Festschrift; he taught for many years at the Gregorian and was dean of its theology faculty. He is the author of an important book, entitled *Salvation outside the Church? Tracing the History of the Catholic Response* (New York: Paulist Press, 1992), a topic closely connected with my own interests. He wrote from the United States where he is now retired:

I was honored and pleased to have been invited to contribute to the volume of essays in honor of my colleague of many years, Father Jacques Dupuis. A further token of my esteem for the work he has done, especially in the theology of religious pluralism, is the fact that during the current semester I am conducting a seminar for graduate students at Boston College on the topic: "The Church and Salvation," in which one-third of our sessions will be devoted to his recent book: "Christianity and the Religions."

I must mention two more testimonies read by their authors during the celebration. One is by Peter C. Phan of Georgetown University. He had written very positively about my books in several reviews and articles. He too contributed to the Festschrift. In his spoken testimony he insisted on the Asian roots of my theology of religions and of interreligious dialogue. The other is Rosino Gibellini, the director of the Queriniana publishing house in Brescia, who had been very instrumental in helping me to make up my mind to write my two latest books on the theology of religions. In his spoken message he expressed his joy in having succeeded to convince me to do so, and stressed the success that both publications have known in Italian and other languages.

Other messages came from bishops, colleagues, and friends, old and new, from Italy and abroad, including India, whom it is not possible to mention here all individually. They include Fr. Raymond Rossignol, once rector of the Bangalore Seminary in India, who started the series of "Theological Publications in India," in which my *Christian Faith* became one of the first big enterprises, and is probably the one that has lived the longest. He wrote from Toulouse where he was being held back unexpectedly by surgery:

I was delighted in advance at the thought of joining all those who will be round you on that day to congratulate you. I have had so often the joy of collaborating with you, in India surely (*The Christian Faith*), but also in Paris, in Cambodia. . . . I keep all this in excellent memory. You certainly have served the Mission well, dear Father Dupuis. I would have liked to say it to you by word of mouth on the occasion of your 80th birthday. Be sure of my deepest esteem, of my thankfulness and of my best wishes.

Let me also mention the friends of the Community of Pro Civitate Christiana in Assisi, with whom I have been associated in many ways. The president, Marco Marchini, sent in the name of the entire community "the most affectionate, brotherly and solidary good wishes." He added: "We greatly rejoice that a great authoritative section of the official church recognizes your wise research and your evangelically prophetic witness. With open hearts we give you a great, most tender embrace, thankful as we are for your ever faithful friendship."

Finally I cannot resist the temptation of quoting at length the personal letter I received from Fr. Edouard Boné, S.J., professor emeritus of paleontology at the University of Louvain-la-Neuve, whom I had known well during my early years in Belgium. I take the liberty of quoting it in French. He wrote:

Je veux t'assurer de ma très fraternelle union en ce jour où l'Université Grégorienne, la Compagnie, tes nombreux amis de par le monde s'associent dans cette manifestation d'hommage, de félicitations et de voeux pour l'oeuvre accompli au service de l'Eglise universelle. Car c'est bien au-delà de l'Inde, à laquelle tu as pourtant consacré l'essentiel de ta vie et de ton travail immediat, que tu as rayonne, et relativement à des aspects essentiels de la pensée théologique, de l'annonce du kerygme et de l'action pastorale. Je me réjouis de constater que l'Université Grégorienne a voulu célébrer avec faste cette exceptionnelle carrière. La palette internationale des invités, la qualité des protagonistes, la richesse des témoignages sollicités pour évoquer ce demi-siècle de réflexion théologique disent mieux que je ne le puis la reconnaissance du monde académique et du peuple de Dieu pour l'admirable vie de jésuite prestée "pour l'honneur de la théologie" (Alphonse Gesché). . . . Dieu seul sait avec quel courage, quelle fidélité, et à travers quelles embuches tu as su mener cet admirable combat. . . . De tout coeur avec toi, en ce vendredi de fête! Tu dois savoir mon admiration, ma joie, mes voeux fervents pour ce qui vient! Ma reconnaissance au Seigneur pour ce qu'il a permis par toi. Très fraternellement, Edouard Boné, S.J.

This message from a true old friend moved me deeply.

Here then is an account of the many messages of congratulations and good wishes which poured in on that occasion, which often, I thought, I did not really deserve. More than to my own person, I suggest, they were addressed to the cause I have defended with some cost to my person and my good name in some quarters. It would be instructive to know how the people present reacted to the event. Some saw in it the official rehabilitation of a theologian who had been under suspicion for years, but who was now cleared by the authority of all charges and suspicions. This interpretation is, unhappily, badly mistaken. The CDF had no part whatever in the celebration. True, a large section of the theological community—from among the most qualified—had manifested in unmistakable words their entire support; but there were the others, those especially whose absence at the function was quite notorious, be they from the Gregorian University or from outside. The homage offered to me would only sharpen their tongues and increase their opposition. From the Roman Curia, and from the Council for Interreligious Dialogue in particular—where I have been an official consultor for ten full years, being moreover the main drafter of the latest document they have produced (1991)—except for the message of Msgr. Fitzgerald, there had been no sign at all of interest, let alone the presence of any representative. When Fr. O'Collins sent a copy of the Festschrift to Cardinal Walter Kasper in the Vatican, he received a word of thanks for providing an addition to the library of the Council for Christian Unity, but had not a word of appreciation or any good wish to be conveyed to me, even when I had known him personally long before he became a bishop and cardinal. Officials at the Vatican did not appreciate the initiative of presenting a Festschrift in my honor at the Gregorian. Much less would they have appreciated what they would have heard, had they been present. But it was expecting too much to suggest that they might have been present, to listen and to learn. As for myself, I abstracted from those who were absent and rejoiced with those who were present.

G.O'C.: *At the end of the ceremony you yourself had to address the audience to thank them for their kind words and to express your own feelings on the occasion. Please give me an account of what you said.*

J.D.: Some had feared that my speech at the end of the presentation of the book would be for me an occasion to come out with a diatribe against the CDF and to expose in public the methods with which they had been dealing with my case. Of the four rectors and vice rectors of the university only Fr. Egaña was present, and I guess he anticipated such an outburst. He was all the more surprised when he realized that I was viewing the occasion in quite a different way. He congratulated and thanked me at the end of the ceremony for what I had said. I started as follows:

> I am overwhelmed by the marks of deep appreciation and of true friendship which have been expressed toward me this evening either by word of mouth or by writing. It is now my turn to express my thanks and to share with you my joy. I am aware of doing this today in a rather solemn manner. One reason is that eighty years is a serious landmark in life and that a similar opportunity as the one offered to me today is not likely to present itself hereafter. According to the psalm, the span of human life is of seventy years, or eighty for those who are strong. Following this estimate, I seem to belong henceforth to the second category; but there is no saying for how long this may be. Another reason is that I cannot easily abstract from the episode which has marked my life in recent years. The rejoicing together and the mutual exchange of thanks for which this celebration is meant cannot but be situated within the context of some recent events in my life to which reference has already been made. Not that we would want to brood over the past, but these events necessarily imprint their stamp on the shape and modality of our rejoicing and of our thanksgiving today. I am sure that there is much for me to be grateful for today, be it only for the enormous publicity which my writing has received through those events; more importantly, because of the intense interest and sympathy I received from the world theological community. I have gained hundreds, even thousands of friends everywhere. The warm "reception" I receive everywhere I go to give talks and lectures is also heartening. God writes straight with crooked lines, it is said. I like to think that this has happened in my case. We can therefore look at the past and at the present situation with warm feelings of joy and peace. Let me then express my thanks to all in that spirit, and in the order in which thanks seem to be due.

I first gave thanks to almighty God for the gift of life and of a long life full of opportunities to discover with wonder his boundless magnanimity toward an unworthy creature. I added:

> His personal call to me has taken the shape of a Christian vocation, and further of a vocation to the Society of Jesus and to the

priestly ministry in the church. There is no way to tell all the graces involved in a long life spent in this manner, to which I hope to have responded, with God's help, in a way not too unworthy of the donor. I consider it a central grace in my life to have been able, through the education I received and my own continued endeavor, to deepen my knowledge and to increase my love for our Lord Jesus Christ. I may say in all sincerity that Jesus Christ has been the one passion of my life. Providentially, when I started teaching theology in India in 1959, the first course entrusted to me was that of Christology, which I have continued teaching till 1998, that is for forty years, including those in the second cycle of theology at the Gregorian. The mystery of Jesus Christ will always remain beyond our full grasp; yet, year after year I have tried to deepen my comprehension of it and to share my deep conviction with the thousands of students, both in India and in Rome, who followed my courses. If I have been able to share with them some of my own conviction and love for the Lord Jesus, I will consider myself fully rewarded.

The sentence "I may say in all sincerity that Jesus Christ has been the one passion of my life" did not escape the attention of listeners. Some wished—and they said it—they could say the same thing with the same sincerity. Comments in the press the next days also pointed to that sentence and commented on its special significance in the circumstances in which I found myself, having been accused of grievous errors against the faith in the person of Jesus Christ.

Coming down to earth, I began by remembering with emotion and admiration my parents, their deep humanity and the example of their life. I had no doubt that, without being aware of it, they were to a great extent responsible for shaping my own vocation. Next I greeted my family which, in spite of the distances which have separated us almost throughout life, have always remained very close to me. I was especially happy to see my family represented at the celebration by a niece and her husband, and by another niece and a cousin. When I was ordained to the priestly ministry in Kurseong in 1954, my family was represented by my sister and a cousin of mine, both of whom are now dead; for my last vows in Rome in 1959, my elder brother was present with my sister-in-law; now, at this celebration the presence of the family was ensured by the following generation. "Generations change," I said, "but life continues, and the family spirit endures through time."

Next, I recalled with gratitude, at least in general and without entering into specific instances, the sixty-two years spent happily in the Society of

Jesus, under the guidance of many great superiors and in the company of co-students and later of colleagues and younger students. I said: "Life has not been made up only of fun, during those long years together; yet, when looking back, one cannot but wonder at the amount of graces received through life in common in the Society." I had in mind the early years before my departure for India—during and after the war—the thirty-six years spent in India, first as a student and afterward as a professor. I added:

> I have often said that I consider my long exposure to the Indian cultural and religious reality as the greatest grace I received from God in my professional vocation as a theologian and a professor. I have learned enormously from those generations of Indian students in theology, from the close relationship I enjoyed with them, as well as from their searching, sometimes radical questioning when, after the Second Vatican Council, they were rediscovering their cultural and religious roots and endeavoring to make sense of the Christian faith and message in the pluralist context of India. I am not ashamed to say that this experience altered deeply my previous way of looking at things and that it shaped anew and altered deeply the theology I had previously entertained. It is that renewed outlook on the Christian faith, characterized by much vaster horizons and deeper insights that I have tried to convey to my students in Kurseong and Delhi and, after my transfer from Delhi to Rome in 1984, to the thousands of students in theology from all parts of the world who at the Gregorian attended my courses.

I could have added—I did not, out of discretion, and not to hurt anyone—that I wished many others had had the same opportunity of a long exposure to a broader reality, from which their thinking and teaching could have profited greatly.

Coming then to my recent years of crisis, not with an intention to brood over the past but to see in it the hidden finger of God, I first expressed my deep thanks to our Father General from whom throughout the proceedings about my case at the CDF I have received the strongest support. I had no doubt that the softening down of the measures envisaged against my 1997 book have to no small extent been due to his intervention. Father Kolvenbach was not only pleading the cause of a fellow Jesuit out of solidarity for a member of the Order; he meant through his intervention on my behalf to show his support and sympathy for the cause I was defending. I have quoted in Chapter 2 of this book the full text of the statement Father General sent to the whole Society of Jesus through the Internet on the very day of the publication in the Vatican of the Notification about my book. Let it suffice here to recall the last sentence. He wrote: "We hope that Fr. Jacques Dupuis can continue his pioneer research in the field of interreligious dialogue which in his recent apostolic letter *Novo millennio ineunte* John Paul II encouraged the challenge for the evangelization of the third millennium."

Next I expressed my thanks to the church authorities already mentioned here above who took my defense in a conspicuous manner, especially Archbishop Henry D'Souza, Cardinal Franz König and Archbishop Michael Fitzgerald, without forgetting the South Asian Jesuit provincials who through a message signed by Fr. Lisbert D'Souza, then provincial of India, sent their warm support; as well as my own Calcutta Jesuit provincial who did likewise in the name of the entire Calcutta Province. At another level, I greeted Fr. Francisco Egaña, the vice rector of the university and religious superior of the community of the Gregorian, who also gave me his moral support.

Coming to the theological community, I had to give pride of place to Fr. Gerald O'Collins, who has been on my side at each stage of the proceedings against me. Even today he remains the only member of the staff of the Gregorian University who has officially and at his own risk taken my defense publicly, in word and writing. Recently still, Fr. O'Collins published articles in my defense in *Gregorianum* 2003 and, more importantly, in *Theological Studies* 2003, under the title "Jacques Dupuis' Contributions to Interreligious Dialogue," where he justifies all the positions I have taken in my writing. Next, I thanked all the persons already mentioned above, namely the contributors to the Festschrift, the publishers of my books in the different languages, the well-wishers who, absent or present, sent or read messages of congratulations and good wishes. The list was long. I ended by saying: "I hope that I have not forgotten anyone of whom I ought to have made explicit mention. To all of you, then, my relatives, superiors, and colleagues, professors and students, friends and well-wishers, collaborators and co-workers, my sincere thanks for having come here this evening to share in my joy and thanksgiving, manifesting thereby your appreciation and friendship. May God bless you in return."

The tone of the whole speech was very positive and cheerful; one might be tempted to think that it was somewhat forced on my part, given the circumstances in which I was speaking. The truth is that I had made up my mind to look at things positively and, from hindsight, to try and discover the finger of God in the past events. I ended saying: "I do not want this my address to sound as an *apologia pro vita sua*, nor as a *nunc dimittis*. I do pray and hope that God may give me some more time to complete what I have attempted to say and write, very imperfectly. Yet, I cannot but keep in mind what the psalm reminds me of, namely, that I have reached a threshold in the span of human life." In this situation I mentioned the answer I had made one day to a somewhat inquisitive questioner who asked: "If, at the end of time, Christ were to ask you an account of the work you have done, what would you say to him?" I need not repeat here in full my answer to him, since it has been mentioned at the end of Chapter 2 of this book. Let me only repeat this sentence: "I trust that the Lord who reads the secrets of the hearts will know that my intention in writing what I have written and saying what I have said, has only been to express to the best of my ability my deep faith in him and my total dedication to him." Was it these words or the tone of my whole address that prompted intense applause on the part of those present, I do not know. What is sure is that the celebration of the Festschrift ended in an atmosphere of joy and enthusiasm on the part of all—an enthusiasm which a reception and a drink in the main hall of the university helped to heighten.

G.O'C.: *I was particularly struck by what Archbishop Henry D'Souza said in his tribute. He stated that for many years you were "THE THEOLOGIAN" of the Indian bishops, and added: "He has been a great theologian and the church in India is greatly indebted to him." What did you feel when you heard those words? What memories did they trigger?*

J.D.: I have already partly answered this question in Chapter 1 of this book. There I mentioned that for all practical purposes I was for many years the one theologian to attend the full yearly assemblies of the Indian Bishops' Conference, though an official appointment to such an office was never published. I recalled earlier some cases when I was requested to deliver the keynote address introducing the main theme for discussion at the meeting, sometimes on topics on which I felt less prepared to give an authoritative opinion. The fact is that the bishops had placed their trust in me and that my advice and opinion were always being sought for. I referred also earlier to some happenings which accompanied the work, like the case of the general assembly at Mangalore (1977), when the bishops entrusted to me on the last night of the meeting the writing of the conclusions arrived at on "The Church's Response to the Pressing Needs of India," while from the seminary where the meeting was held, they proceeded to the archbishop's house for a good time and celebration after the hard work well done. In fact, I spent the whole night writing what I thought should be said, and the conclusions were duly read out and approved the next morning, to be soon published by the Conference. Being trusted by the bishops individually and collectively involved responsibility, but also a sense of dedication and a readiness to work hard behind the scenes. Of this many other examples could have been quoted. Let it suffice to mention here one more. The Catholic Bishops' Conference of India sent a Message to All the Faithful, Clergy and Religious of India on the occasion of the forthcoming Holy Year 1975. The document is signed by Cardinal Joseph Parecattil, archbishop of Cochin, president of the Catholic Bishops' Conference of India. In fact the text—whatever its merit or demerit—came entirely from my pen. It was published in *The Clergy Monthly* 37 (1973): 281-86, at a time when I was still only assistant editor of the review. So the answer to the question about which kind of memories the recognition on the part of Archbishop Henry D'Souza triggered in me when he referred to me as "the theologian" of the Indian bishops is a happy memory, as I felt recognized for what I was worth—at least in the estimation of the bishops. That recognition gave me a sense of purpose and a determination to be fully at the service of the church in the person of its pastors.

G.O'C.: *After the celebration of the Festschrift, if I am not mistaken, you went to Krakow and Warsaw, Poland, for the presentation of the Polish edition of your latest published work,* Christianity and the Religions: From Confrontation to Dialogue. *Could you tell me what happened there? How was your new book received and how did its presentation proceed? Did that eventually become a new cause for controversy with the CDF?*

J.D.: To be at the Gregorian for the presentation of the Festschrift, I had had to fly back in a hurry from Utrecht, where on December 3 I had given a lecture at a symposium at the Catholic University on "The Renewal of Christianity through Dialogue." Now, after the presentation of the Festschrift on December 5, I had to fly to Krakow on the morning of the 6th, entrusting my family members to a generous colleague at the Gregorian, who helped them to see as much as possible of Rome in the two days at their disposal. Let me say, to begin with, that the Krakow Jesuits had already thought of making a Polish edition of the previous book, *Toward a Christian Theology of Religious Pluralism.* They gave up the idea, not because of what happened to that book with the CDF, but because of the size of the book which would have involved too much work and expense. When *Christianity and the Religions: From Confrontation to Dialogue,* which is more modest in size, came out, they no longer had any hesitation. The initiative for the Polish edition was taken by Fr. Stanislaw Obirek, S.J., who himself ensured the translation of the book into Polish. The program for the presentation of the Polish edition of the book at the Ignazianum,

Krakow, was a heavy one. I had sent in advance a summary presentation of the book in English, under the title "Jesus Christ Universal Saviour and the Ways of Salvation." This had been translated into Polish by Fr. Obirek, who read it in my presence to a large audience. That was on December 8. There followed on the same day an open debate on "The Dignity of Difference: Meeting with Jacques Dupuis," which prompted a vivid discussion and showed much sympathy and agreement. On the same evening, I took the train for Warsaw with Fr. Obirek. There, at the Bobolanum, there took place on December 9 a symposium on "Christianity and the Religions," starting with the same lecture on "Jesus Christ Universal Saviour and the Ways of Salvation," again presented by Fr. Obirek and followed by a lively debate which aroused much interest and sympathy. I also visited on the same day the House of the Dominican Fathers in Warsaw and had with them an open discussion on "The State of Interreligious Dialogue in the World Today." Someone noted that my visit to Warsaw was responsible for establishing some contact between the Jesuits and the Dominicans there. However that may be, the entire program was very interesting and roused much interest. I was struck by the receptive and open mind of the audiences to which I spoke; it witnessed to the evolution taking place in Poland today in the field of theology and of church life. What was being said, discussed, and suggested in my presence would hardly have been heard or tolerated in Polish circles, even in recent decades. I wondered later whether the organizers had taken the initiative of sending a copy of the Polish edition of my book to the pope. He had signed five times in succession documents against me, submitted for his approval by the CDF, and ordered three of those in succession to be published, without of course having ever read anything of what I wrote. Had he received a copy of the Polish edition of my latest published book, he could have realized that what I say in it is not so distant from what he himself has often—though not always—been saying and writing in recent years. I had organized his teaching in a precise and synthetic form, drawing from it conclusions that seemed to impose themselves. As things turned out, there was no comment or expressed disapproval on the part of the central doctrinal authority about the Polish edition of my book or the entire Polish program. From Warsaw I had to rush back by plane to Italy on December 10, being due in Ancona on December 11 for a lecture on "The Advaita Experience and Christian Consciousness," in the context of a symposium on "Discordanze concordi" at the Centro Studi Oriente e Occidente.

G.O'C.: *At the end of 2003 you were busy writing a new book, and you submitted it for the approval of your Jesuit superiors in March 2004. At the begin-*

ning of June 2004 you received a negative answer from them, in which the
permission to publish the book was refused to you. Could you explain what hap-
pened and what were the reasons for denying you the imprimi potest?

J.D.: Here is where another sad story begins, or rather, since the previous
sad story could never be considered to be ended, a new and even sad-
der part of the story began. The joy at the presentation of the Festschrift
could be seen only as an illusory interlude, with the danger implied in it
of allowing one to live under illusions and to relax somewhat innocently.
I was not tempted to do this; yet the new episode or episodes which followed left me even more dismayed than the previous ones. Of these I must
give a full account, dividing the matter into several parts for clarity sake.

I received from Dr. Fabrice Blée, doctor in theology, Montreal, Canada,
a letter dated August 14, 2003, in which he invited me to contribute a volume to a new theological series which he was launching in French under the
heading "Spiritualités en dialogue: une collection sur les expériences intra-
religieuses," to be published by the Médiaspaul Publishers, Montreal. The
presentation of the collection seemed most attractive. It said: "Les Editions
Médiaspaul mettent sur pied une collection unique en son genre, portant
sur un aspect avancé et prometteur du dialogue interreligieux, l'expérience
intrareligieuse. . . . Cette collection repose sur la conviction que la spiri-
tualité chrétienne à venir est appelée à émerger d'un double movement: la
recherche mystique de Dieu et l'hospitalité envers la différence religieuse."
It was a question of putting together the lived experience and reflections
of specialists who had made the demanding effort of going personally to
the core of another religious tradition in their own religious life, and, on
this basis, of entering personally into interreligious dialogue with deeply
committed persons of that tradition. One volume would be devoted to
the meeting of Christianity with each of the main religious traditions of
the East: Hinduism, Buddhism, Sivaism, etc. Questions such as that of
"Living from Several Spiritualities" or "Monastic Interreligious Dialogue"
would be the object of distinct volumes. The list of prospective contributors was very engaging. I was invited to contribute a volume which would
serve as a general introduction to the subject, by stating, from a Christian
theological viewpoint, the foundation for a theology of religious pluralism
and interreligious dialogue. I responded enthusiastically to the invitation,
and explained succinctly which direction I thought my contribution could
take. When I received a very positive response to my proposal, I began to
consider more closely how I should proceed. This took some time, as is
always the case before starting to write a book. I began drafting the text
toward the end of the year 2003. I conceived the book as a kind of succinct

presentation of what I had written over the years on those two basic topics, especially in the last years, not only in my books, but also, for special items such as the possibility of "plural belonging" or of interreligious prayer, in reviews and volumes in collaboration recently published. I gave the manuscript the title "Pluralisme religieux et dialogue." By the end of March 2004 the manuscript was completed and prepared to be submitted to the superiors for approval in view of publication.

I submitted the manuscript at the end of March to Fr. Francisco Egaña, the vice rector of the university, who was responsible, in the name of the rector, for approving manuscripts for publication. When I brought my manuscript to him, I insisted that it contained nothing which had not been previously published elsewhere with his own *imprimi potest*. I thought it worthwhile to mention this, so that he could pass this on to the censors of his choice, who, I supposed, could and would take it into account while reading the text and giving their opinion. On the night of June 1, I found my manuscript at my door with a letter from Fr. Egaña, written on May 31. On the morning of June 2, he left for Spain on a three-month sabbatical holiday between his double assignment as superior of the Jesuit community and the new one of vice rector of the university which he was to continue after the summer holidays. His letter disturbed me deeply. After the usual formulas of politeness, he stated: "I am very sorry to have to refuse the permission to publish the manuscript 'Pluralisme religieux et dialogue.' . . . After having received two contrasting opinions, I consulted two other censors, of renowned theological competence and equilibrium. Three of the censors agree in affirming that the book contains affirmations incompatible with the doctrine exposed by the church, and in particular with the declaration *Dominus Iesus*. The reason for the denial is double: one doctrinal (fundamental), and one prudential."

As a basis for the doctrinal reason, three quotations were made from the manuscript, found on its pages 109, 85, and 56. I will come back to these below. After quoting them, the letter said: "These are affirmations which do not agree with the doctrine exposed especially in the declaration [*Dominus Iesus*]." The letter went on to say: "Regarding the opportunity of the publication, you know that the Congregation has insisted that the superiors exercise a special vigilance over your writings. You know that the Congregation, though critical with regard to your second [i.e., last] book, has chosen to remain silent. I consider that to propose the question again and to reopen the debate with the Holy See does damage to you, to the Gregorian and to the Society. In a letter of February 7, 2002, Father Delegate [of the general], Guillermo Rodríguez-Izquierdo, has communicated to me that Father General has requested Fr. Dupuis not to treat directly points in discussion with the Holy See, and of explaining clearly the viewpoint of the Holy See. Father Dupuis told Father General that he would accept this way of proceeding." The letter ended saying: "Dear Father Dupuis, I am sure that you, an intelligent and always honest man, realize that such directives are not verified in this case. I therefore think that you will not find it strange that, in the name of the university, I refuse the permission for the publication of the book."

G.O'C.: *The refusal to give your new book the green light, the "imprimi potest," was deeply upsetting for you. What did you think on receiving the letter of Fr. Egaña? What did you say in the long letter you yourself wrote to him?*

J.D.: I reflected for a few days, wondering what answer I should give and wanting to make sure of not saying what I should not say, while making sure as well of saying what I should. Eventually I sent to Fr. Egaña in San Sebastian, Spain, on June 12, 2004, a six-page letter in Italian. I cannot give a full account here of this long letter; however, I must treat succinctly the two reasons which had been given for refusing the permission to publish, namely the doctrinal one and the "prudential" one.

Concerning the doctrinal reason, I wrote:

> You say that three out of four censors "agree in saying that the book contains affirmations incompatible with the doctrine expounded by the church, particularly with the declaration *Dominus Iesus*." In proof of the charge made by the censors of affirmations incompatible with the doctrine of DI, three quotations are given from my manuscript: one from p. 109, one from p. 85 (the reference to p. 60 in your letter is not correct), one from p. 56. Allow me to say that I have consulted Fr. O'Collins, professor of Christology at the Gregorian for many years. His opinion is totally opposed to that of your censors. He thinks that whoever denies what is being said in the first and the third quotations of the manuscript puts himself in implicit contradiction with the christological doctrine of the Ecumenical Council Constantinople III. . . . Where the second quotation is concerned, Fr. O'Collins is of the opinion that to deny what I am saying there is equal to denying what Pope John Paul II has written in several recent documents. On my part I would like to add that what I affirm in those quotations does not correspond to what is disapproved of in DI. As regards the first and the third quotations (both say practically the same thing), the doctrine that is condemned supposes that the action of the Word as such and that of the Word incarnate

represent two different economies of salvation, and even a separation between two activities and two persons. I on the contrary insist *ad nauseam* that there is a question of two complementary and inseparable elements in only one divine economy of salvation. On the other hand, the condemnation of the same doctrine in the *Notification* on my 1997 book supposes again that I am affirming a separation between the two activities, that of the Word as such and that of the Word through the humanity of Jesus Christ, and even a separation between two persons. This again contradicts explicitly what I have affirmed with great clarity in the 1997 and 2001 books, namely that there is question of two distinct but inseparable aspects in the one divine plan of salvation.

As far as the second quotation made by your censors, which you include in your letter is concerned, I suppose that the use of the term "other 'salvific figures'" makes them afraid. But the meaning which I give to that expression in the context of the other religions is altogether different from what is intended by Christian faith with regard to the role of Jesus Christ, universal savior of the world and unique Mediator between God and men—an object of faith which I maintain everywhere with great clarity and insistence. The meaning of the use which I make of the expression "salvific figures" in the context of the religions has been explained several times, in my published books as well as in the last manuscript, for instance on pp. 61-62. There, having reaffirmed the uniqueness of Jesus Christ, the one mediator between God and men, I speak, making use of the affirmation made by the pope, of the possibility of "participated mediations," and I explain that "d'autres figures salvifiques peuvent néanmoins être illuminées par le Verbe ou inspirées par l'Esprit, afin de devenir des 'indicateurs' de salut pour leurs adeptes, conformément au dessein général de Dieu pour le genre humain," and in essential relationship with the one Mediation of Jesus Christ. In the light of the recent papal magisterium one cannot affirm anything less.

Therefore it does not appear to me that the objections made by your censors which they justify with the three quotations, are valid and convincing, neither as regards the theological content, nor as regards the alleged contradiction with the doctrine of the church. I would like to add that the three quotations incriminated by your censors are found *ad litteram,* that is exactly the same, word for word, in my last book, published in 2001 (Italian edition), with your *imprimi potest,* namely on pp. 387, 346, and 247, respectively, of the

French edition (2002). The censors of 2001 were, it would seem, better informed than those in the last case. The judgment of these would have been more credible had they submitted a substantial evaluation of the manuscript, based on a precise study, in which the pro and the con for the publication of the manuscript would have been indicated clearly. . . . On the contrary, you hand over to me nothing resembling that, but only three quotations from the manuscript to which your censors point as being in contradiction with the doctrine of the church and of DI, while they are found *ad litteram* in the book published in 2001 with your *imprimi potest*. Such a way of proceeding lacks credibility.

This being said, I now turn to the second reason for refusing the permission to publish, namely the "prudential" one, that is, this publication being inopportune. You speak of the request made by the CDF to the superiors of exercising "a special vigilance on my writings." You tell me that I know this. As a matter of fact, I do not know it, and it was never said to me by anyone. You add: "You know that the Congregation, while being critical with regard to the second book [that of 2001], has chosen to keep quiet." I do not know that either, and it was never said to me that the CDF has been "critical with regard to the second book." This affirmation surprises me much, because we have often spoken together of the absence of any reaction on the part of the CDF about that book. You never spoke to me of a critical attitude of theirs; you were always satisfied to rejoice with me about the total absence of any reaction on the part of the CDF. Then I ask: The suspicion of a critical attitude on the part of the CDF, is it a mere impression, or a piece of information? And if it is a piece of information, is it reliable information? If this is the case, why did you never speak to me about it? Was that perhaps of no interest to me?

You add that "to propose now the question anew and to reopen the debate with the Holy See is detrimental for you, for the Gregorian and for the Society." I must say that I am not convinced that to propose anew a theology of religions which, as I have insisted with you many times when I submitted the manuscript for your censorship and again later, has been proposed three years ago in a book published with the *imprimi potest* of the superiors and without any sign of disapproval on the part of the CDF, must be detrimental "for me, for the Gregorian and the Society," unless we wish to adopt an attitude of blind conformism with an authority which unjustly intends to prevent all theological reflection and discussion.

But I ask if such blind conformism is in accordance with the spirit of Saint Ignatius.

Father Egaña had made reference to a letter of Father Delegate, in which it was said that, in answer to a request made by Cardinal Ratzinger to Father General of using his authority over me "to reduce me to silence in word and writing," and after the intimation made to me by Father General to that effect, "Father Dupuis had told Father General that he would accept that way of proceeding," that is, of "not treating directly the points in discussion." The information contained in that letter of Father Delegate (of which I had received no information) was not correct. When I met Father General to discuss the new threats hanging over my head after the letter of Cardinal Ratzinger of January 8, 2002, he spoke to me clearly as follows: "I give you clearly my directive: You may continue to say and write what you think and believe. But, where you are not in full agreement with the documents of the CDF, you must mention it to your audience, and propose your own position with prudence and discretion." That is what I have been doing faithfully ever since, only to notice each time that the audience seemed to be massively on my side. Father General had never made me promise what was implied in the letter of Father Delegate. In my letter to Fr. Egaña, I myself added: "You, Father, have heard clearly from me that directive given to me by Father General, and have expressed some surprise at hearing it—I remember it very well. Perhaps you have forgotten it; but, since you have always praised my sincerity and honesty, I hope that you will still trust me in this case."

I went on:

As things are, I am pained to read in your letter, in which you appeal to my honesty: "I am sure that you, an intelligent and always honest man, realize that such directives [those allegedly given me by Father General and accepted by me] are not verified in this case," that is, in the case of the latest manuscript. The implication is that my way of doing would be in contradiction with what I had promised to Father General, that is, implicitly, that I was being dishonest. I am struck by the parallelism between this affirmation of yours and the way of proceeding of Cardinal Ratzinger. He was referring to a promise attributed to me in a paragraph of the *Notification*, and to the contradiction between that promise and what I was continuing to write; the promise to which he was making reference I had never made since it had been introduced without any reference to me in the paragraph which had been added by the CDF to the second draft of the *Notification*, which I had signed. You, in a similar way, refer to a promise to Father General which I have not made, and which Father General did not request me to make, and you conclude to a contradiction between my promise and my way of doing in the case of the new manuscript. And you add: "You will not find it strange that in the name of the university, I refuse the permission for the publication of the book." In the light of what I have been writing in this letter, I must conclude that your conclusion does not seem obvious to me.

I have by now four important manuscripts which I have not been allowed and am not allowed to publish. One consists of thirty pages in which I was answering in a synthetic manner all the questions raised by theologians in all languages and all the reviews about my 1997 book. The permission to publish that article has been refused by you and Father Delegate; its publication was not considered opportune. The second manuscript consists of forty pages in which I explain with discretion and prudence the points on which and the reasons for which I cannot be in agreement with the two documents of the CDF. Father Rector, Imoda, refused me the permission to publish that article; he even forbade me to send it privately, through Father General, to Cardinal Ratzinger for his personal consideration; I could only keep silent. The third manuscript is the long book called *Do not Stifle the Spirit* [the very book to which I am now adding the present third chapter], in which I am reflecting on the way of proceeding of the CDF in my case. I think this is an important document. The fourth manuscript is the present one entitled "Pluralisme religieux et dialogue." I have explained here above why in this case I cannot understand the new prohibition to publish. In this situation, the only thing that remains for me to do is to decide to stop altogether writing either books or articles in the future, hoping that the manuscripts to which I am referring may be published after my death.

I ended the letter writing: "Dear Father, I know that this letter of mine will not be pleasing to you; it displeases me also to have to write it. But I could not have waited till we meet again in September to manifest to you my reactions and to let you know in which state of crisis your decision places me again. I wish you a good holiday in Spain." On June 14, I sent a copy of this long letter to Father General for his own consideration of the new situation of crisis in which I found myself due to the refusal of permission to publish my new book.

G.O'C.: *What response did you get to your long letter to Fr. Egaña?*

J.D.: I never got any answer to my letter. I had sent it, as mentioned above, on June 12, 2004. Throughout the summer holiday I kept waiting for an answer, which never came. In the situation, I even wondered whether my letter had reached its destination in Spain. Only a few days after I came back to Rome, on August 31, that is some time at the beginning of September, Fr. Egaña, who was back before me at the Gregorian, came to see me in my room. He was somewhat apologetic, but never discussed any of the points I had made in my letter, and never showed any willingness to reconsider the refusal of the permission to publish in the light of all I had explained. Though no longer religious superior of the community for the new academic year to begin soon, he remained vice rector of the university, and therefore, as far as the local authority of the university was concerned, it remained in his power to grant or to refuse permission to publish. In my long letter, as I have explained above, I had asked him from where he had got the information he had referred to: namely that, though having decided to keep quiet, the CDF had taken toward my 2001 book a negative attitude. On meeting him now, I asked *viva voce* and bluntly whether the source of such information would have been Fr. Ladaria; he did not deny. I discovered that Fr. Ladaria, a colleague at the Gregorian, has become, as I call him now, the great Spanish inquisitor. One can also surmise that Fr. Egaña was not keen to put his own name under the *imprimi potest* of another book which would also run the risk of meeting with disapproval on the part of the CDF, whether formally expressed or not. That would do him no good personally. In my long letter of June 12, 2004, I had also requested Fr. Egaña, when we would meet again in September, to return to me the copy I had lent him one year earlier of the present manuscript, *Do Not Stifle the Spirit*, in the state in which it stood till recently, before I decided to add the present Chapter 3. I explained in a covering letter that I was not submitting the manuscript for censorship in view of publication, but in order to get his own personal considered opinion. I was aware, I said, that the publication of that manuscript "would have to wait for better times," whatever this implied and whenever such better times would be forthcoming. When we met again in September, I reminded him of my request to have the manuscript returned to me; it was by now in his hands for one and a half years. On November 6, I found the manuscript lying at my door, with a short covering letter. Father Egaña admitted that in one and a half years he had not read even a hundred pages of the manuscript (out of three hundred)—which did not witness to much personal interest and concern. As for his evaluation of the manuscript he wrote: "I share with you the opinion that the manuscript must not be published. Its pages are moving in a terrain which has occasioned grave problems to you, to the

Gregorian and the Society. It is a book of personal, even secret memories, which you have painfully and scrupulously recorded." I was not requesting the *imprimi potest* for my manuscript, but his own considered opinion about it. The response to my question, however, amounted to saying that my manuscript was destined to end in the paper basket, or at best in the archives—which was not and is not, even today, my intention, as my decision to write the present Chapter 3 should sufficiently show. I am more than ever convinced that this manuscript ought to be published one day, after my death if necessary.

The reaction of Father General to my long letter to Fr. Egaña was very different. He had been absent during part of the summer. But, as soon as he came back to Rome, he wrote to me a kind letter, signed July 17, written in French in his own hand. He wrote:

> The judgment of the censors of your book shows that there is a problem to be discussed by theologians, specialists in the matter. What for you is a certitude is not one for some others. Inasmuch as the problem is presented as a *quaestio disputata* and not as an acquired position—which it is not—space is open for discussion. I understand fully your pain at seeing your book refused for reasons of prudence and in order to preserve the reputation of orthodoxy of the Gregorian. As you know it, the entire field of interreligious dialogue is a minefield [*miné*], mostly because of the publicity which is being made about any declaration, while the question is of the competence of specialists. . . . Because of the holidays, it is not possible to take concrete steps now; but in September it will be possible, with the new administration [in the Gregorian] and with the new delegate, to see what can be done for you and for your important theological research. . . .

Father General was aware of the complexity of the situation, but showed clearly his willingness to reconsider matters and to reopen the question of the possibility of having my last manuscript published.

G.O'C.: *In this situation you went to see Father General and had a long conversation with him. How did that go, and what was the outcome of your meeting?*

J.D.: Father General was extremely busy after returning to Rome, with several meetings and sessions in and outside Rome. I was on the waiting list for urgent interviews for a long time. Finally, I was called for a personal meeting on November 4. We had a long conversation together in

French which lasted more than one hour. Father General listened to me with great interest and sympathy as I commented to him on the content of my letter to Fr. Egaña, of which I had forwarded to him a copy. My question to Father General was whether the censorship of my book could not be redone, with a person of his choice entrusted with the new proceeding outside the competence of the local authorities of the Gregorian. I also asked whether the censors whose opinion would be asked could not eventually be chosen also from among non-Jesuit specialists, capable of giving a considered and reliable opinion. I was convinced that in the theological faculty of the Gregorian the only person capable of giving such a considered and well-founded opinion on the matter was Fr. O'Collins, who ever since I came to Rome in 1984 had followed my writing closely, as well as the controversy my 1997 book had aroused. His name, however, had been excluded from the group of censors appointed by the authorities of the Gregorian, because of the presumed positive assessment which he certainly would have made of my book. Together with the letter of Fr. Egaña and my response to it, I had sent in advance to Father General comments made in writing by Fr. O'Collins about the quotations from my manuscript on which the negative verdict of the censors was based. Father General showed great interest in these documents, which he thought of communicating to the authorities of the CDF for their own consideration. I myself, on returning home after our meeting, sent to Father General a copy of the articles which Fr. O'Collins had written in my defense in *Gregorianum* 2003 and in *Theological Studies* 2003. All this put together constituted a large documentation on which a fair consideration of the case could be based.

Father General listened with kindness and sympathy to my question whether a new process of censorship of my book could be considered, and showed some interest in the proposal. On the other hand he communicated to me the "verbale" [minutes] of a meeting at the CDF which had taken place in the month of July. Was it a meeting of the Roman consultors? Was it one of the members of the Congregation? Was Cardinal Ratzinger present and presiding, or was he absent because of bad health? Was the meeting then presided over by Archbishop Angelo Amato, the new secretary of the Congregation? By whom was the "verbale" written and by whom was it approved? I have no information on these points; and I guess Father General did not have either. But Father General read the text of the "verbale" out to me; I can only refer to it from memory, as I did not get a copy of the text. The "verbale" said that the two talks which I had recently given in New York and in Fatima had not pleased the CDF. I was accused once more of undermining the uniqueness of Jesus Christ.

In this situation, it was suggested again that I should be required to stop writing on these matters. I expressed to Father General my surprise at these new accusations. The New York talk must have referred to the one I gave at the New York Interfaith Center on "Jesus Christ Universal Saviour and the Ways of Salvation" on February 12, 2004. That talk was not destined to be published, and it has not been published. One wonders through which source it came to be used as ground for new accusations on the part of the CDF. In any event it did not say anything which is not found in my latest book, *Christianity and the Religions: From Confrontation to Dialogue*, which, as has been explained earlier, was published with the *imprimi potest* of the superiors and had not raised any reaction on the part of the CDF. The Fatima talk was given at an international theological congress organized by the authorities of the Fatima shrine on October 10-12, 2003. Its title was "Interreligious Dialogue, a Challenge to Christian Identity." In this case the text of the talk has been published in the Acta of the Congress under the title *O Presente do Homem—O Futuro de Deus. Congresso internacional de Fátima* (Santuário de Fátima, 2004): pp. 319-41. It was therefore easy to check whether there would be found in that text any ground for the new accusations being made against me. I sent a photocopy of the text to Father General for him to judge whether there was in it any ground for the new accusations made against me by the CDF. On November 10, 2004, Fr. O'Collins sent a letter to Father General in which he "summarized and evaluated Fr. Dupuis's contribution" to the Fatima congress. He indicated in that letter his "reasons for finding nothing objectionable in Fr. Dupuis's paper," He ended by saying: "I must confess once more that I feel amazed, saddened, and even scandalized that anyone could take exception to Fr. Dupuis's lecture, which seems to be a straightforward and enlightening theological development of what Pope John Paul II has taught about Christ and other religions." A few days later, on November 16, Fr. O'Collins wrote and sent to Father General a long memorandum in which he dismissed the presumed reasons on which the new accusations made by the CDF on the same paper could eventually be based. In this case, the whole affair looked like a parody of "due process" and betrayed an a priori determination to find fault and to condemn. This further documentation in the hands of Father General could help him ask the CDF authorities for an explanation of their misgivings. He requested Fr. O'Collins to be disposed to accompany him at the CDF for explanations. Father O'Collins manifested to Father General his willingness to oblige. On November 22, 2004, he received a letter from Father General, thanking him for his availability. Father General wrote: "Dear Father, The Superior General of the Society of Jesus thanks you for the three clear and well explained 'stumbling blocks' in Father Dupuis's theological writings. I have asked for a discussion on a high level or, at least, for a written reaction." But he added: "Probably we will have to wait till 2005. Thank you so much and sincerely yours in Our Lord." Obviously, the authorities of the CDF were not anxious to hold such a meeting, and used the usual policy at the Vatican, to procrastinate and to put time on their side, in order to avoid what is viewed as undesirable.

In this entire situation, the Father General found himself torn between two contradictory positions. On the one hand, he would be willing to reconsider the censorship in view of the publication of my manuscript, in favor of which he had in his hands ample documentation. On the other hand, the "verbale" of the CDF meeting last July was urging new drastic measures against me. What was to be done in this situation and what decision could Father General take in my favor? Such was the situation at the end of November, when more new elements came into the picture to make the situation even more complex and difficult.

G.O'C.: *Allow me to interrupt you here before you proceed to explain those new elements which came into the picture at the end of November 2004 to make the situation even more complex and difficult. I would like you to say something about your trips for lectures to the United States, which seemed to have multiplied in recent times. How did those come about and with what success?*

J.D.: It is true that in 2004 I visited the United States several times for lectures. On February 10, I was in Le Moyne College, Syracuse, New York, where I delivered the Loyola Lecture for the year 2004 on "Jesus Christ Universal Saviour and the Ways of Salvation." This was a summary presentation of my last published book, the English edition of which had been published in the United States by Orbis Books in 2002. I reached Le Moyne College on the eve of the lecture, and was told that before the lecture on the next day the title of Doctor of Humane Letters Honoris Causa would be conferred upon me. I was taken totally unaware of the honor which the college wanted to confer upon me, but was told that the university senate had voted unanimously in favor of the honor being conferred upon me. And so it went, in a ceremony in which all the rubrics and solemnity which characterize such promotions were scrupulously observed. It is from Le Moyne College that I proceeded to New York, for the talk on February 12 at the Interfaith Center, which has been mentioned earlier. I returned again to the United States in September, this time to Washington, where on September 15 I delivered at Saint Anselm's Abbey the 31st Annual Thomas Verver Moore Lecture in honor of the founder of the abbey, on the same theme as at Le Moyne College. This was followed by a colloquium at the Catholic University of America, Washington, DC, on "Renewal of Christianity through Interreligious Dialogue," on September 27. I was due to proceed from Washington to Notre Dame University, Indiana, where a heavy program of talks and meetings had been arranged for the following days. Unhappily, due to sickness, I had to give up the trip to Notre Dame University, for which I was extremely sorry. Instead, I was taken to the Jesuit residence on the campus of Georgetown University, Washington, where I was extremely well received by the rector, Fr. Brian McDermott, and the community. They had not known that I had been in Washington for a few days. Had they known, they told me, they would have arranged a program for me at Georgetown, where I would have enjoyed much larger audiences. They suggested that this could still happen at a later date. Similarly, when I wrote to Notre Dame to express my regret at having had to cancel my visit to them, they too expressed the hope that this would only be "partie remise" to a later date. In Georgetown, where I rested for a few days before flying back to Rome, I was delighted to meet Fr. Ladislas Orsy, S.J. He had followed my case all along, and was much better informed, as I found out, than he could possibly have been through information gathered from the press or even from some comments made by theologians in theological reviews. I wondered about the source of his information. As I referred to the present manuscript, *Do Not Stifle the Spirit*, he told me that as soon as this book would come out, he would write a substantial account of it in an American magazine. Meanwhile, he hoped that the best might come out of the whole affair and promised to give me whatever help I could think of asking him for. Further invitations from abroad followed; but those unwittingly brought about the more recent problems, which, as I have mentioned above, added to my precarious situation.

G.O'C.: *Closing this parenthesis, let us come, if you wish, to those more recent events which made your present situation even more problematic.*

J.D.: On November 23, I received an email from Fr. David Eley, S.J., of Regis College, Toronto, Canada, who occasionally comes to the Gregorian as a visiting professor at the Interdisciplinary Center of Social Communication. I transcribe here the substance of his letter. He wrote:

> I have been commissioned by Regis College in Toronto (president: Joseph Schner, S.J.; Dean: Ron Mercier, S.J.) to "sound you out" about a visit to Toronto, Canada. So, this is not the formal invitation;

that will come later. This is the preliminary conversation to explore what is possible for you. . . . What follows is all open to negotiation: 1) Come to Toronto for a semester, or a major part thereof. Say the fall semester 2005, that would be September to early December, 13 weeks next year. 2) You could lead a graduate course, seminar style. 3) The College would prepare a public conference for mid-October around your work, with a title something like "How Christians Engage in Dialogue with the World Religions." You would be one of the speakers. 4) Receive an Honorary Doctorate Degree at the mid-November convocation ceremony and deliver the "Chancellor's Lecture" which is the major public lecture of the year for the College. 5) You could do some side trips to other Canadian universities who would invite you, i.e. University of Sudbury (Jesuit university) and others. 6) Live in the Regis College Jesuit community, enjoy the Canadian autumn. So, that is the offer, Jacques. Appropriate compensation would be offered. Let me know if this is of interest to you. Your availability. Your preferred dates, etc. Your interests, conditions, etc. Jacques, I hope you are well. I send you my best wishes. I hope all this can happen. David Eley, S.J.

I reflected for a while about this wonderful proposal. I was only doubtful about the amount of time involved in the program. I thought thirteen weeks was a long time of absence and in my case, for several reasons, it would seem to be unpractical. I would rather think in terms of seven weeks, within which the entire program could be fitted in, with the course being concentrated into six weeks. The entire program could then be fitted in between sometime in October and middle of November. I was of course much impressed by and grateful for the intention of Regis College to confer on me another doctorate honoris causa, after the one I had received this year from Le Moyne College, Syracuse, New York. I thought this recognition of my work on the part of another important academic Jesuit institution would contribute to show that not the whole theological community agrees with the Roman negative attitude and formal disapproval of my writing. The authorities of Regis College were entitled to have their own evaluation of my work, and capable of taking their own responsibility in their desire to confer upon me an honorary doctorate. However, for a long absence, whether of thirteen weeks or of seven weeks in Canada, I needed the permission of my religious superior. I therefore went to see Fr. German Arana, the new superior of the Jesuit community of the Gregorian, whom I had previously met only once after my visit to Father General on November 4. My intention in going to see him was not at all to discuss whether I could accept the proposals made to me by Regis College, but only to ask for the permission to be out of the house for whatever period would be involved. I handed over to him a copy of the letter of Fr. Eley. I must confess that I was simply appalled and distressed at his reaction. I thought he would have been happy to hear that another doctorate honoris causa was being planned for me next year at a prestigious Jesuit institution, and that he would congratulate me about this. On the contrary, he thought with some apparent determination that this would be quite improper, given my situation with the CDF, and that I should not only decline the offer of an honorary doctorate but even forget about the entire program. However, as broader interests than my own personal one were involved in the matter, he thought it improper for him to make a decision and wished to refer the matter to Fr. Ignacio Echarte Oñate, the new delegate of Father General, whom I have personally met only once during his recent visit to the Gregorian. He sent to him a copy of the letter from Fr. Eley to me.

On November 30, Father Delegate wrote a letter to Father Superior, in response to the consultation initiated by him on my case. I personally received from Father Superior on December 11 the transcribed text of Father Delegate's letter to him. While sending the text to me, the superior insisted that "what I am communicating to you of the letter of Father Delegate is a confidential communication between him and me, and must remain such. According to our way of proceeding there remains for you the possibility of having recourse either to Father Delegate, or directly to Father General." I was therefore requested to observe total secrecy on the content of the delegate's letter. At this stage, let me say that I have been so often bound by top secrecy during the proceeding or intimidated by such intimations. I have decided to publish in this book the whole truth on the matter, including documents from different sources. I continue here the same policy. Here then is the text of the part of Father Delegate's letter to Father Superior concerning my case. He wrote:

Dear German, Yesterday you called on me to let me have a copy of the email message which Father Dupuis has received inviting him to go to Canada, at Regis College, for diverse academic activities. In the message there is question also of the possibility of honorific academic titles to be conferred during his stay. In the shortest time possible I have tried to do the necessary consultation on the case, for I know that Fr. Dupuis suffers a lot when a question concerning him remains in suspense for a time. I suppose that you know that at present Father General has presented to the Congregation for the Doctrine of the Faith (CDF) a new theological evaluation to complement and clarify the theological thought of Fr. Dupuis. I can imagine that the answer will not arrive immediately. That is why I do not believe it would be prudent for him to commit himself for new courses or conferences which could be detrimental in his relation with the CDF. From the text which you have transmitted to me, I think I can interpret that, during the projected Canadian stay, different university centers could profit by his presence to meet with him and hear from him directly his theological thought. To give a public answer to those questions could only increase the misgivings about him. Taking into account this delicate situation and the recent story, which has not yet reached a definitive solution, I believe it more prudent for Fr. Dupuis himself not to make any move in the sense that transpires from the message.

This letter contains no word whatsoever of regret for recommending a total abstention on my part for any future academic commitments and, even more so, for the acceptance of honorary academic recognitions. I myself received no message from Father Delegate on the whole issue.

After reading this text and listening earlier to the opinion expressed by Father Superior, I have the impression of being let down now by my own superiors with little knowledge on their part of the entire story. There remains for me only one possibility; that is having recourse to the authority of Father General who in the past has several times intervened in my favor in full knowledge of the situation and taken decisions in my favor which went against the request made to him by the CDF to take drastic measures against me. Meanwhile I must say sincerely that what I suffered unjustly on the part of the CDF seemed easier to bear than the impression created now of being betrayed by my own superiors.

G.O'C.: *I am sorry to hear all that. What then is going to be the next step?*

J.D.: I could not wait till I received the letter of Father Delegate on December 11 to do what you call the "next step." In his letter Father Delegate mentions that "Fr. Dupuis suffers a lot when a question concerning him remains in suspense for some time." I wonder where he got this information. But I ask whether the suffering is not justified when a case started against me by the CDF in 1998 is being prolonged after more than six years, and when a manuscript submitted for censorship last March remains pending in December. I have learned, as Congar did even during the Vatican Council II, that once suspect at the Vatican, one remains so for life. But Congar had a John XXIII to rehabilitate him by calling him to the Council where he became one of the great architects of the Council documents; yet, in spite of this he still was made to feel during the Council that he remained suspect in the mind of Vatican officials. I for one have not had a John XXIII to put an end to the proceedings against me, and I do not think that this will ever happen. However this may be, the reason why I had to take some new step without waiting is that I could not leave the proposals made to me from Canada without a response. I knew from another Canadian Father at the Gregorian that Fr. Eley was waiting for a quick answer. And so I answered his email on December 7, saying that "I was overwhelmed with joy and thanks for the proposal [he] was making to me in the name of the President and Dean of Regis College, especially by the generous offer of granting me a doctorate honoris causa." I went to explain that on my part I would only want to discuss whether the whole program could not be fitted in into a period of seven weeks, between sometime in October and the middle of November. But another element had come into the picture. I wrote:

> Both the superior (Fr. Arana) and the delegate of the general (Fr. Oñate) are new this academic year. Soon after getting your email I went to the superior to ask for the permission to be absent for the period required, in 2005. I thought he would have congratulated me and would have rejoiced with me at the prospect of a doctorate honoris causa being proposed to me by Regis College. . . . His reaction was just the opposite. He doubted very much that, given the problems I have had with the CDF, I could accept such an offer. He would have to consult the delegate about it. Since then, nothing. In case I should receive a negative answer from them, I would certainly go and discuss the matter personally with Father General who has always been very understanding and favorable to my cause. . . . I wanted to share with you my great disappointment with the attitude taken by these new superiors. I thought they would rejoice with me at the thought of the recognition that comes to me from academic institutions after so much suffering borne at the hands of the CDF. My only hope is now with Father General, and as soon as I will have been able to discuss the matter with him, I will communicate to you his decision which I hope will be positive. Let us then hope for the best.

On the same day, December 7, I received an email answer from Fr. Eley. He wrote: "Thank you for your response. I am pleased to hear from you and read the positive reaction that you have to our proposals. I will bring your response to the attention of the rector (Schner) and the dean (Mercier). I will keep the details of your response limited only to those two." He went on to say that the question of the length of time involved in the entire program remained open to discussion; and added regarding the matter of the honorary doctorate: "I am surprised and saddened at your superiors' reaction. Surely part of the message here is that Catholic colleges and universities do value your work. That might be taken on board in the light of the delicate Roman relations. I hope the delegate gives the O.K., or Father General, if it comes to that. Let me know. But in either case, whether we offer you the degree or not, you are most welcome to come for all the other involvements. . . . Warm good wishes. David Eley."

As for the Montreal manuscript, I had been requested to submit it either in June or in November. I could not leave Prof. Fabrice Blée without an answer any longer. So I wrote on December 6:

> I have finished long ago writing the manuscript you asked from me. Last March I submitted it to my superiors for the censorship. I waited till June and then received a negative answer. The reason being given was that some affirmations in it would not please the Congregation for the Doctrine of the Faith. This surprised me considerably, because the new manuscript contained nothing which had not been previously written in the 2001 book, published with the *imprimi potest* of the superiors, to which there had been no reaction on the part of the CDF. I have therefore appealed to Father General and have asked him to delegate someone entrusted with having the censorship redone with more competent people. I am waiting for a new decision which I hope will be positive. I wanted to let you know the reason for the delay in sending you the manuscript. . . . I hope to be able to send it to you without much more delay; but, alas, this does not depend on me. I hope you will understand the difficult situation in which I find myself. Thank you for your understanding, and with my best wishes.

This letter was sent by Air Mail, and no answer has reached me so far. This then is where things stand today, a situation on which it is worthwhile reflecting a little.

In my letter to Fr. Egaña of June 12, I had written: "I lost the joy of living on October 2, 1998, and have not recovered it since; now I am losing the will to survive." October 2 referred to the day when a thunderbolt fell on my head with the news that the CDF had opened a "contestation" of my 1997 book with the pope approving the decision with his signature, in which, without any previous discussion or dialogue, I was straightaway being accused of "grievous errors against the faith Divine and Catholic." The "now" referred to Fr. Egaña's letter of May 31, 2004, in which I was refused permission to publish my new manuscript. Since then the situation has only become worse. Previously Father General had supported my lecturing activity outside the Gregorian against the local superiors who wanted to prevent it and against the request made to him by Cardinal Ratzinger to reduce me to silence in speech and writing. Now the superior and the delegate were both of the opinion that I should refuse the invitation to Toronto for various academic activities, including the conferring of a doctorate honoris causa, and even apparently cancel the future appointments outside, to which I am already committed. I would have to renounce now in December 2004 the invitation to Toronto for October-November 2005, almost a year in advance, as we were waiting for clarification on the part of the CDF in response to observations sent to them which challenged their latest charges; such clarifications might be coming sometime in 2005. The fact is that it was quite unbecoming on the part of Archbishop Angelo Amato, the secretary of the CDF, to dismiss the request made by Father General for an early meeting in order to bring clarity on those latest charges of the CDF; procrastinating is a typical way of proceeding at the Vatican to dismiss unpleasant requests made by religious superiors. Such attitude on the part of the CDF is unworthy, and therefore the verbale in which the accusations were stated should be dismissed.

The refrain that the restrictions imposed on me by the superiors were due to the fear that some activities of mine would be detrimental "to me, to the Gregorian and to the Society" had become quite unbearable to me. When Rector Imoda wanted to prevent me meeting the journalists after the publication of the "Notification" on my book, Father General showed great surprise and said to me: "It is a good thing for you, for the Gregorian and the Society." When Fr. O'Collins went straight to see him about holding at the Gregorian the presentation of the Festchrift for my eighty years, Father General likewise rejoiced at the idea and declared: "It is a good thing for Fr. Dupuis, for the Gregorian and the Society." By contrast the opposite refrain has been heard too often: from the lips of Fr. Egaña, about the publication of the new book; from Rector Imoda, about lectures outside; from the new superior Arana and the new delegate Oñate about the invitation to Toronto. What a contrast between the way of doing of the superior general and that of superiors under him.

At this stage I ask: Why are the restrictions imposed on me for my good? What is there that the CDF can still do against me which they have not done yet? To excommunicate me for holding obstinately opinions against the faith? Hopefully, they will have learned from the case of Tissa Balasuriya of Sri Lanka, whose excommunication was pronounced one year and lifted the following year. Why had this happened? Because the Asian synod was in the offing and the CDF was afraid of strong reactions on the part of the Asian bishops in the aula of the synod. The CDF had made themselves quite ridiculous in the case. Fear of excommunication seemed therefore rather slight, as it would in any case raise a storm on the part of the theological community. My activities would be detrimental to the Society? What would the Society as such lose if a degree honoris causa were to be conferred on me by Regis College, Toronto? Surely, the whole Society is not responsible for all that happens in each of its institutions; hopefully too the local authorities in prestigious academic institutions are capable of assuming their responsibility and do it in a considered manner.

Detrimental then to the Gregorian? Here we touch on the main issue. That danger, and the preoccupation for the reputation of the Gregorian at the Vatican, for orthodoxy and good behavior, is being mentioned repeatedly and explicitly. To the question whether the good reputation of the institution is more important than preserving the fame of individual persons, Father Superior, questioned by me on the matter, answered "yes" without hesitation. This reminded me of the word of Caiphas, saying that it was good for one man, Jesus, to die for the nation. In this context, the nice talk about the virtues displayed by me in the whole affair, as for instance talk about my "heroic obedience" of which the superior wrote while communicating to me the letter of the delegate, sounds rather shallow. It looks as if the superiors were committed to making my obedience ever more heroic.

In sum, my hindsight on the whole story is quite different today than it had been on the day of the presentation of the Festschrift on December 5, 2003. Not that I was telling lies on that day, but I had made up my mind to be nice to everybody, which implied dissimulating much of the truth. Today I am more realistic and determined to say things as they are. The fact was that I had been abandoned by the university from the outset of the case. There had not been any message of sympathy, however discrete and unpublicized, by the theological faculty with the signature of the names of the faculty members; I had received a number of such messages from all over the world, none from the Gregorian. The men on my side were few and could be counted on the fingers of one hand. To speak openly in my favor there was only one man, and I need no longer mention his name.

The determinately opposed side was more numerous and more vocal. For the rest there was a widespread indifference and complete lack of sensitivity. This lasted through the years and is worse today. I was struck by the certitude with which the new superior, Fr. Arana, expressed his own opinion on the first time I met him and shared with him something of my story, of which he had known nothing previously. He declared with great conviction that according to him I ought to have already left the Gregorian, and that I should still leave it now. He did not know, of course, that, when I turned seventy-five years of age and the sad story started, this had been the object of a close discernment in which so many people took part: Father General himself, Delegate Rodríguez-Izquierdo, Fr. Jerome Francis, the provincial of Calcutta, the provincial of the South Belgian Province of the Society, Fr. Egaña, some old Jesuit friends from Belgium, even my own family. Father General said clearly that if, all things considered, I thought it best, I was welcome to remain for life at the Gregorian. Father Delegate was sensitive to the financial aspect of the question, and, while exhorting me to go, he informed me that the insurance does no longer pay for the health expenses of people beyond the age of eighty. I should take this into consideration. In fact I did, and I do not think it can be said that I am a heavy financial burden to the house. The truth on this point is that I am among those whose presence profits the community financially, with my royalties and stipends for talks. I had always made it a point to try and live by my work and not to be a burden to the community. I ate little, I had few expenses, I hardly ever took the monthly 150 euro allowance for personal expenses. My main expense was the car for Fiumicino when I had to take the plane for talks outside. To make the financial situation even clearer, I managed to get through the intervention of a medical doctor a health allowance granting me for life free access to public hospitals in Italy for treatment or surgical interventions, and expensive medicines free of charge. So the financial aspect should have little place in the matter.

The result of the consultation was that, since my return to Calcutta was excluded because I would no longer obtain the permanent residence permit, and, on the other hand, returning to Belgium seemed out of question because after leaving the country fifty-five years earlier, I would no longer find roots there, the best, in fact the only thing for me to do, was to remain at the Gregorian where I was and from where I would remain easily available for talks outside. Father Superior, however, without being in the know of the serious consideration which had been given to the matter, seemed quite determined to think otherwise "for my own good," though of course he did not mean to send me away. This then was the situation: I had been abandoned by the university, and I had become a stranger to the community. I was taking my meals all alone and no longer had any social contact. That is where I stand. Let us not forget either that among the members of my community there are five assiduous consultors of the CDF. Their names are well known and need not be mentioned. They reminded me constantly of a definition which has been given in Louvain in the old days of what it means to live in a religious community: it is to live with persons one has not chosen.

G.O'C.: *Do you then hope to meet Father General soon?*

J.D.: I certainly do, for he is now my only recourse, and, it is sad to say, the only person in whom I still can put all my trust. In view of having a serious discussion with him about all the elements involved, including the latest ones, I wrote to him a long letter, dated December 16, in which I give him a kind of *status quaestionis* of the whole matter, hoping that a decision may be arrived at on the important points. In this letter, after reminding Father General of the situation as it stood till recently, with the refusal of the permission to publish my latest manuscript and the "verbale" of the CDF meeting of last July, I wrote:

> Now new elements have come into the picture and I find myself in an ever more delicate and difficult situation. For this reason I would like to meet you again soon to discuss with you the present situation, and I hope you will be willing to receive me as you always did in the past. Hoping that this be possible in the near future, I thought of sending to you in advance a sort of *status quaestionis* of the situation, so that you may know all the elements before we meet. I hope that a positive decision may be possible on several points. These points are: the status of the "verbale" of the CDF of last July; the possibility of a new censorship of my manuscript submitted last March for publication, which received a negative answer at the beginning of June and remains pending even today; the invitation made to me recently from Regis College, Toronto, for several academic exercises, including the conferring on me of a doctor honoris causa degree.

Treating the three issues separately and in order, I went on to write first about the question of the minutes ["verbale"]:

> As far as the "verbale" of the CDF meeting is concerned, I think personally that it was quite unbecoming on the part of the CDF to delay the possibility of meeting you, the general of the Society, for clarifi-

cations on their misgivings which in fact seem to be unfounded. In this context, I ask whether the "verbale" should be taken as seriously as it is by the new superior and the new delegate (I will explain hereafter) for imposing on me new restrictions. Should it not rather be dismissed as not worth considering seriously?"

I went on:

Concerning the *imprimi potest* (of my last manuscript) I have explained at length in my long letter to Fr. Egaña, of which I have sent you a copy at the time, the reasons why I found the refusal unjustified. The censorship as it has been done and its rapid conclusions lacks credibility. The one person in the theology faculty at the Gregorian really capable of giving a reliable opinion on the matter, based on sure knowledge of the case, as well as of my previous writing and of the controversy it has provoked, has been excluded in the choice of the censors. It is in this situation that I raise the question whether a new procedure of censorship could not be started, entrusted to a person of your choice with the help of reliable and well-informed censors, including eventually some from outside the Society. There is no lack of specialists in the matter outside the Gregorian, capable of giving a more serious opinion and who would be willing to do so, if requested. I mention here some names: Claude Geffré, O.P., of Paris, Rev. Peter C. Phan of Georgetown University, Msgr. Luigi Sartori of Padua, Prof. Terrence Merrigan of Louvain University, Fr. Hans Waldenfels, S.J., of the University of Bonn. In the Society I would think also of Fr. Francis Sullivan of Boston College, and closer to us, of Frs. Gerald O'Collins and Herbert Alphonso; eventually too, of Frs. Lisbert D'Souza and Etienne Degrez. I am therefore asking again whether a new decision may be taken in favor of a manuscript which was to be submitted for publication in November 2004 at the latest. I have apologized to the director of the new collection for the delay in sending the manuscript, due to some technical difficulties, and expressed my hope of still being able to send it as soon as possible.

Coming to the new elements which have made the picture even darker, I wrote:

I have received an invitation from Regis College, Toronto, for several academic exercises sometime between October and November 2005, including the conferring on me of a doctorate honoris causa.

When I went to the new superior to ask for the permission to be out of the house for the period involved, I was appalled by his reaction. I had expected him to congratulate me at the prospect of a doctorate honoris causa from Regis College as a recognition of the value of the theological work I have done. Instead, he was strongly of the opinion that I should decline entirely the invitation in view of the recent "verbale" and of my past story with the CDF. However, because of the matters involved, he thought he would have to consult with Father Delegate on the matter, which he did. The opinion of Father Delegate coincided with that of Father Superior, as he expressed it in a letter he sent to him on November 30 and which Father Superior communicated with me on December 11. I just fail to understand this negative opinion, which as usual, is justified by presumed detrimental consequences "for me, for the Gregorian and for the Society." I received earlier this year, on February 10, a doctorate honoris causa at Le Moyne College, Syracuse, New York, and there have been no detrimental consequences to anybody thereafter. In the present case I am expected to decline the whole offer of academic lectures and the doctorate honoris causa now in December 2004, almost a year in advance of the dates foreseen for the event, because of a possible discussion to take place sometime in 2005 on the CDF's "verbale" of last July. Would it not at least be possible to accept the invitation and the program provisionally, leaving open the possibility of having to reconsider the case later, if this should be required in view of new difficulties arising? I must confess that the drastic measures suggested by Father Superior and Father Delegate are incomprehensible to me. I am not looking for honors to be conferred on me, but I think that the recognition of the merits of my theological work on the part of prestigious academic institutions, far from being detrimental to anyone, is "good for me, for the Gregorian and for the Society," to use the trite formula. I have been made to suffer the treatment received from the CDF; but the suffering would be even greater if I should be faced with the fact of being let down by my Jesuit superiors. Father, allow me to say that you are in the present situation my last and only recourse. This is the reason why I firmly hope to be able to discuss the whole matter with you sometime at your early convenience.

I ended the letter, expressing my regret for the trouble I was causing to Father General and thanking him in anticipation for his kind consideration of the case. This is where I stand now, hoping for an early meeting with Father General, and trusting in the open mindedness he has manifested and the positive attitude he has taken toward me in the past on several occasions, even against serious reprisals with which I was threatened.

[**G.O'C.:** *Fr. Dupuis corrected the text on Christmas Day 2004 and had it photocopied on the morning of December 26, 2004. The following evening he collapsed in the rectory of the Gregorian University and was taken to hospital. He died the next day, December 28, 2004. RIP.*]

Part II

Searching for the Truth

Editorial note: The original intent of Fr. Dupuis was to include several articles and appendixes in this book. Because all but one of those documents have already been published elsewhere, it was the decision of the editor and the publisher that those items not be included here. However, their bibliographical provenance is included below.

Congregation for the Doctrine of the Faith. "Regulations for Doctrinal Examination." Articles 23-27. *Acta Apostolicae Sedis* 89 (1997): 834.

Dupuis, Jacques. "Jesus Christ Universal Saviour and the Ways of Salvation." Published in three installments by the *Tablet* in October and November 2001. A version of it can be found at http://sedos mission.org/old/eng/dupuis_2.htm.

————. "Some Reflections on Two Roman Documents." In *Jacques Dupuis Faces the Inquisition*, ed. William Burrows (Eugene, OR: Pickwick Publications, 2012).

Kendall, Daniel, and Gerald O'Collins, eds. "The Book and the Case: A Select Bibliography." Pages 270-81 in *In Many and Diverse Ways: In Honor of Jacques Dupuis*. Maryknoll, NY: Orbis Books, 2003.

Orsy, Ladislas, S.J. "Are Church Investigation Procedures Really Just?" *Doctrine and Life* (1998): 453-66.

The only document written by Fr. Dupuis and, to the best of our knowledge, not published elsewhere is the article "The Theology of Religious Pluralism Revisited: A Provisional Balance Sheet," which is reproduced in the following pages.

— 4 —

The Theology of Religious Pluralism Revisited: A Provisional Balance Sheet

More than five years have gone by since my book *Toward a Christian Theology of Religious Pluralism* was published (Maryknoll, NY: Orbis Books, 1997) (hereafter *Toward*). Another book of mine, *Christianity and the Religions: From Confrontation to Dialogue,* came out recently (Maryknoll, NY: Orbis Books, 2002) (hereafter *Christianity*). The first book had aroused, together with a remarkable interest, a rigorous theological discussion. I have already contributed two articles in which I answered the questions asked about the first book by theologians writing in Italian periodicals, on the one hand, and, on the other hand, in English, French, and other periodicals. I am referring to my articles published in *Rassegna di teologia* 40, no. 5 (1999): 667-93 and *Louvain Studies* 24, no. 3 (1999): 211-63. In those articles I referred explicitly and distinctly to the various authors of the linguistic areas in order to answer directly their questions. While writing *Christianity,* I took seriously into consideration what reviewers said about *Toward.* I was careful to avoid some ambiguities, to provide clarifications where necessary, and to deepen the foundation of some theological positions.

I wish now to propose a *status quaestionis* by way of a provisional balance sheet of the argument. *Christianity* offers a qualified answer to this request. Here I will indicate only the principal points on which I have thought it necessary either to clarify my position or to introduce different nuances. The way of proceeding will therefore be more synthetic than in the articles mentioned above, in more than one sense: I will not refer explicitly to comments by individual authors; I will rather gather together the more important questions that have been asked on the main themes developed in both the books, which have occasioned on my part a revision or a development of my theological position. By following this way of proceeding, I hope to be able to contribute a more synthetic response to the discussion, to present, as exactly as possible, the present *status quaestionis* of the argument, and to make a further contribution to theological reflection on the subject.

The second book was entirely written (by March 2000) before the publication by the CDF of two documents: the declaration *Dominus Iesus,* published on September 5, 2000, and the Notification on my first book, published in *L'Osservatore Romano* on February 26, 2001. The two documents require serious attention. They could not be taken into account in the second book, written before their publication. They are not taken into consideration here either, because they require a distinct treatment. I have written my reactions to both documents in the previous chapter "Some Reflections on Two Roman Documents." A careful reader will, however, note the similarity that exists between the questions raised by the theologians in the book reviews of the first book and those formulated by the documents of the CDF. By answering directly the theologians, I address also implicitly the CDF.

1. Theological Method

Objections in opposite directions are made against the method used in my first book for a theology of religions. On the one hand, it is said that, though claiming to be "hermeneutical," my theology does not truly reinterpret the data of revelation nor even the traditional doctrines of the church. It merely maintains the traditional doctrines on the basis of a theology and a Christology "from above," which means that it remains methodologically "deductive." On the other hand, it has been observed that my "inductive" method is unacceptable in theology, the only true method possible in theology being the "deductive" method, which draws logical conclusions from the data of revelation and tradition.

Against such unilateral observations I note that both my books intend to combine together the inductive and the deductive methods. And not without reason. It is necessary to take seriously into account the concrete context in which the theology of religions needs to be rethought, that is, the staggering reality of the plurality of the religious traditions, as it is known and lived today. At the same time, however, such reality must be confronted and interpreted in the light of the data of revelation and tradition. In fact, while the context is considered concretely as a *locus theologicus,* the revealed message of Scripture remains nevertheless the *norma normans* for doing theology. As regards the way in which the Word of God is to be approached in view of a theological reflection in context, it must be said that, rather than isolating some verses chosen unilaterally as proof texts, it is necessary to take Scripture in its entirety. This means seeing it as a complex whole, composed of complementary elements to be held together. The interaction between context and text, between tradition and interpretation, or between inductive and deductive method, has been well explained in the document on *The Interpretation of the Bible in the Church*, published by the Pontifical Biblical Commission (1993), for instance in Section III.D.2, on the relation between exegesis and dogmatic theology. The Second Vatican Council had already noted that "At all times the church carries the responsibility of reading the signs of the time and of interpreting them in the light of the Gospel, if it is to carry out its task. In language intelligible to every generation, it should be able to answer the ever recurring questions which men ask about the meaning of this present life and of the life to come, and how one is related to the other" (*Gaudium et spes* 4, 1). This is the task of theology.

2. Scripture and Tradition

Some critics think that the book ignores the total refusal of the "pagan" religions in the Hebrew Bible, according to which they are but idolatry, superstitions, and immoral practices (cf. Deut 4:19). As for the New Testament, it states that Christian faith and baptism are in any case necessary conditions for salvation. Texts such as Acts 14:15f., 17:27-28, and Rom 2 cannot be used to show in Luke and Paul a positive attitude toward the "pagan" religions. Those texts refer only to a natural knowledge of God as creator and to the natural law, attainable by the "pagans." No text of the New Testament, in fact, states that man can obtain salvation by following the natural law practiced in his own religion.

Against such altogether negative evaluation of the data of revelation, the best answer that can be given is provided by biblicists who in recent years have studied anew the biblical material in the context of the present theology of religions. Such a study has been done by Giovanni Odasso in his book *Bibbia e religioni: Prospettive bibliche per una teologia delle religioni*.[1] Much would have to be quoted. Regarding the texts first mentioned, here

---

1. Giovanni Odasso, *Bibbia e religioni: Prospettive bibliche per la teologia delle religioni* (Rome: Urbaniana University Press, 1998).

is what the author has to say. About Deut 4:19: "The text of Dt 4:19-20, in synthesis, considers the various religious and cultural expressions of the peoples not as the fruit of reflection and of the 'discovery' of man, but as a 'gift' that man receives. At the origin of that gift, according to the faith of Israel which is expressed in the text, is found YHWH himself" (p. 174). With reference to Rom 2, the author quotes B. Stoeckle where he writes: "Creation has an original supernatural destination, inasmuch as it is 'designed for Christ'; what the pagan religions that are turned to the cosmos are offering of humanly significant values . . . is infinitely more than the influence of a 'prime mover' indifferent to salvation: here the true grace of Christ, genuine supernatural communication of salvation, is profoundly expressed" (p. 330). As for the discourse of St. Paul to the Areopagus in Acts 17, Odasso speaks of the "positive perspective with which the text of Acts 17 looks at the religious experience of humanity. . . . However, . . . the religious experience is lived within a religion, from which it can be conceptually distinguished, but not separated in reality" (p. 352).

In conclusion Odasso affirms that the evaluation that the Bible makes of the religions of the peoples is positive, notwithstanding the negative affirmations, which must not be forgotten. "If the plan of God is at work with power in all peoples and in all nations, the religions figure as the very sign of the power of God and the place where Wisdom is operative" (pp. 359-60). "The balance sheet of the biblical concept is on the positive side. The negative dimension is certainly a real fact, but it is not 'constitutive' of the religions. The religions are *a gift of God to the peoples;* they are the sign of the power of God's salvific design which works within human history to prepare humankind for the eternal banquet of the reign" (p. 360; emphasis added). And here is the final conclusion of the author: "That the religions are so many expressions of God's design is by now established, indeed because, as can be seen from the perspective disclosed by the texts of the Old and New Testaments, they are on earth *a gift of God to all peoples,* and therefore, a sign of the salvifically operative presence of Wisdom. Hence, the religions, as expression of the divine design, are necessarily related to the resurrection of Christ, precisely because the resurrection represents the ultimate fulfillment of God's saving design" (p. 372; emphasis added).

It would not have been possible to be clearer. Apropos of the questions related to Tradition, some commentators criticize my interpretation of the first Fathers of the church. "Rays of the truth," it is said, are not found in the "non-Christian" religions, but in Greek philosophy. According to Clement of Alexandria, God has given philosophy to the pagans, but philosophy does not save. As a response, the positive attitude of some Fathers must be maintained, with regard to the religious search of the nations. To say that in the religions nothing can be found beyond a natural knowledge of God amounts to retrojection on the thinking of the Fathers, in an anachronistic way, a distinction between "nature" and the "supernatural" unknown to them. In their writings philosophy and religion cannot be separated into closed compartments. When Clement says that God has made a "covenant" with Greek philosophy, he means Greek wisdom, in which he includes the religiosity of the Greeks. Such was already the undestanding of St. Paul at Athens (Acts 17). Similarly, the Logos which according to St. Justin and Irenaeus manifested himself "partly" to the nations, was not the Logos of Philo nor of the Stoics; he was that Logos who, according to the Prologue of John, was with God from the beginning (John 1:1-3). That Logos, according to Irenaeus, had "sown his seeds" among people and the peoples, thus preparing in anticipation his coming into the flesh. This ancient doctrine of the "seeds of the Word" and of the "sowing Word" must be seriously revalued. It is to be regretted that this doctrine is often reduced to some indifferent gift of human nature, being thus devalued in its deep significance of a divine manifestation to men and to the peoples through his Word. Not even the Second Vatican Council, though it uses several times in its documents the expression "seeds of the Word" (*Ad gentes* 11, 15), has explained its true significance and its importance for a theology of the religions.

As for the theology of religions implicitly present in the documents of Vatican II, it is situated by some critics, simply and without any qualification, in the perspective of the "fulfillment theory." The Council simply followed the "traditional doctrine" according to which only natural elements and values can be found in the religious traditions, never supernatural elements. However, the true situation requires some nuances. After having discussed different interpretations of the documents of the Council, I thought it necessary to maintain that there remains some ambiguity in their exact bearing. While many expressions used by the Council with regard to the religions seem to be taken over from the "fulfillment theory," as for instance to heal, to assume, to ennoble, and to bring to fulfillment, there are also found others which evoke directly the "theory of the presence of the mystery of Christ," such as, for example, the elements of "truth and grace" (*Ad gentes* 9)—an expression, it may be noted, taken over from an essay by Karl Rahner published shortly before the Council,[2] the "ray of that Truth which illumines all men" (*Nostra aetate* 2), and the "seeds

---

2. Karl Rahner, "Das Christentum und die nichtchristlichen Religionen," *Schriften zur Theologie* V (Einsiedeln: Benziger Verlag, 1962), 136-58.

of the Word" (*Ad gentes* 11, 15), to which reference has been made above. These last two themes, without doubt, evoke the Logos of the Prologue of John (John 1:4-5, 9). I could conclude that, without affirming that the religions are means of salvation for their members, yet the Council tends in the direction of attributing to them some saving value. It seems that some critics want obsessively to reduce all value found in the religions to purely natural elements—a prejudice that determines their reading of the documents.

3. History of Salvation and Covenants

It has been observed that instead of speaking about the "history of salvation" I should have spoken of "salvation in history." I agree personally with J. Sobrino and I. Ellacuría in insisting that "salvation history is salvation in history," and in recognizing the contingencies which are necessarily involved. The "history of salvation" is not linear. However, the historical contingencies do not cancel or destroy the plan of God for humankind. The divine plan is subject to the vicissitudes of human freedom; but the realization of that plan is nonetheless certain: *Dieu écrit droit avec des lignes courbes.*

Concerning the relationship between the covenant of God with Israel and the one established with humankind in Jesus Christ, some commentators deny that both can be considered as one and the same covenant. One can observe in reply that many prominent exegetes today agree in saying that the "old covenant" has not been "abolished" but "unveiled" by the "new" one. To the name of Norbert Lohfink, to whom I referred in my first book, can be added that of Erich Zenger, who wrote with regard to the "new covenant": "This is not another covenant replacing the one on Sinai. It is one and the same covenant of grace, in which the Jewish people and the peoples gathered in the church participate, in different ways of course. The covenant was established first of all with Israel, and only subsequently, 'through Jesus Christ and together with his people was the church too brought in.'"[3]

Another objection is leveled at the permanent value of the covenant with Noah as well as at the symbolic meaning attributed to it as representing a covenantal relationship of the religious traditions of the world with God. The objection has it that those religions as well as the myths

---

3. Erich Zenger, *Il Primo Testamento: La Bibbia ebraica e i cristiani* (Brescia: Queriniana, 1997), 133-35.

in which they express themselves can refer only to some natural religiosity. By way of answer let it suffice to recall the firm conclusion in the study of B. Stoeckle on the subject: according to the Bible, "Israel and the nations have thus a common base: they are in a state of covenantship with the true God and under the same salvific will of that one God."[4] That the permanent character of the Mosaic covenant serves analogically as model for a theology of religions which affirms the permanent value of the religious traditions represented by the covenant with Noah has been suggested by various authors, some of whom find there a line of thought rich with promises for a theology of religions. This, however, does not mean that Judaism is henceforth considered simply as "one religion among others"; there remains, on the contrary, the unique character and permanent value of the covenant with Moses, as promise and foundation of the Christ event. This being said, neither the covenant with Noah nor that with Moses has been revoked by the "new covenant" in Jesus Christ. The permanent character of the covenants means that also for us Christians the covenant with Noah and that with Moses perdure, inasmuch as the "new covenant" in Jesus Christ has been built on them: Jesus of Nazareth belongs to the human family with which from the beginning God has established a bond of friendship in Noah; and Israel is the people from whom he was born.

4. Word of God and Sacred Books

Both my books defend the position according to which the history of salvation, which is coextensive with the history of the world, comprises the different stages of the various covenants of God with people and the peoples. This involvement of God with humankind implies at every stage two inseparable elements: that is, some salvific action and some self-revelation. Against this continuous presence of salvation and revelation, some critics think that, while the possibility of salvation is present in every age of humankind, divine self-revelation is found present only in the Hebrew-Christian tradition, starting with the self-manifestation of God to Abraham. The gift of revelation is the exclusive privilege of the biblical authors. It seems, however, that the Bible itself witnesses to the simultaneity of revelation and salvific actions, with regard to Adam, Noah, and Moses, as a fortiori in Jesus Christ, who is at once the decisive self-manifestation

---

4. Bernhard Stoeckle, "Die ausserbiblische Menschheit und die Weltreligionen," *Mysterium Salutis* 2 (Einsiedeln: Benziger Verlag, 1967), 1053-54.

of God to humankind and the One in whom God has reconciled the world with himself. That words and deeds are always combined in the self-manifestations of God to humankind seems, moreover, clearly affirmed by the constitution *Dei Verbum* of the Second Vatican Council: "This economy of revelation is realized by deeds and words, which are intrinsically bound up with each other. As a result, the works performed by God in the history of salvation show forth and bear out the doctrine and realities signified by the words; the words, for their part, proclaim the works, and bring to light the mystery they contain" (2). At every stage in the history of salvation, God in some way reveals himself by expressing himself in actions: words and deeds are inseparable.

It is of course true that many distinctions ought to be made between the various stages of the self-manifestation of God to humankind. That is why my books defend the thesis of an *analogical* concept of the word of God, of Sacred Scripture, and of divine inspiration. A definition of those terms made a priori in such a way that they can be applied exclusively to the biblical scriptures, leading logically to the a posteriori conclusion that they are in effect verified only in their case, can be legitimately questioned. It is not possible, in fact, to exclude a priori the existence in the sacred books of the other religious traditions of traces of authentic experiences of God made by their founders and seers, through which God intends to speak a word to the nations, no matter how initial and incomplete. Such words are obviously subject to a discernment for which the obligatory criterion is the message and the mystery of Jesus Christ. It needs to be added that, while the sacred books of the other religions may have a social function willed by God in the communities of faith, and therefore are not merely "private revelation," they do not, however, have the character of "public revelation" as this is understood in the Christian tradition with regard to the biblical scriptures which constitute the mystery of the church.

Some argue, however, that I am construing a concept of "inspiration" that is vague and reductive. I have called inspiration an *analogical* concept, which means that it can have different meanings and be used in different ways in different situations. Etymologically speaking, the term is not limited to only one possible application; it refers generally to some influence of the Spirit. The word of God and divine revelation must not be interpreted in a monolithic way; they, on the contrary, represent a diversified and complex reality.

One or two critics also argue that individual gifts of grace cannot result in "public" revelation. They certainly cannot in the precise sense intended by traditional Christian theology for the Christian scriptures. If, however, one takes into account the social function of the authentic experiences of God made by the founders and the seers of the religions, traces of such experiences can be found in the sacred books and serve as channels through which God utters a word to the nations through his Word and his Spirit.

Questions are also asked concerning the fullness of God's revelation in Jesus Christ. Objections have been raised against the affirmation that the revelation of God in Jesus Christ remains "incomplete" and "finite" (since the term "relative" is ambiguous and open to misunderstandings, it has been left out in my second book). The transcendent and unsurpassable character of the fullness of the divine revelation in Jesus Christ is certainly to be preserved. The fact remains, however, that, since it comes from the human (created) consciousness of Jesus, revelation in him does not exhaust, and cannot exhaust, the divine mystery. The term "fullness" is open to some ambiguity. I have called the fullness of the revelation in Jesus Christ "qualitative," not "quantitative," which means that, while representing the deepest divine revelation possible in history, it does not exhaust the totality of the divine mystery. Since it springs from the human consciousness of him who is the only-begotten Son of God, divine revelation in Jesus is decisive and surpasses in quality all other revelation of God in history, but it remains open to a definitive fullness of the revelation of God at the eschaton.

Some have objected to the affirmation made in my first book that "in the entire history of the dealings of God with humankind, more truth and grace are found than are simply found in the Christian tradition." This affirmation would seem to undermine the "fullness" of revelation in Jesus Christ. In answer it must be said that the "complementarity" of revelations intended keeps intact the unique and transcendent character of revelation in Jesus Christ—as is explained more explicitly in the second book. Taking into account the innate limitation of the revelation in Jesus Christ, a "reciprocal but *asymmetric* complementarity" of revelations remains open. This complementarity must not be understood in the sense that Christian revelation needs some "supplement" offered to it by other divine revelations, without which it would be lacking its "fullness," but in the sense that some aspects of the divine mystery can be put into greater relief in the sacred books of other religious traditions than they are in the Christian tradition; an enrichment of Christian tradition is therefore possible. This, however, does not in any way undermine the transcendent and unsurpassable character of the revelation of Jesus Christ in history. To whoever insists that other revelations cannot be conceived as "complementary" and "parallel" to that in Jesus Christ, the answer consists therefore in saying that the complementarity which is intended does not result in "parallel" revelations, which would supply what is missing in the Christian revelation. Christian revelation does not need "supplementary revelation"—which would contradict the fullness and the "completeness" of divine revelation in Jesus Christ (cf. *Dei Verbum* 4). As the Gospel of John repeatedly illustrates, the incarnate Word is *the* Revealer and *the* Revealed.

5. The Question of Truth

Little space has been given in my books to the problem of truth. The importance of the problem of truth for a theological evaluation of the religions, and specifically of the connection between salvation and truth, has been emphasized by the International Theological Commission, which in their document on "Christianity and the World Religions" (1997) declares that salvation is "being in the truth" (13). The question of salvation cannot, so some critics observe, be detached from that of truth. This problem is situated at the frontier between theology and philosophy. As for myself, I have declared right from the Introduction of my first book the specifically theological character of my research. As regards truth in relation to salvation, it is first of all a question of asking whether in the other religious traditions there can be found elements of divine "truth and grace" (cf. *Ad gentes* 9), and what is their relationship with the self-revelation of God and salvation in Jesus Christ. As for the philosophical problem, I have alluded to it in my first book in relation to the arguments advanced by the "pluralist" theologians in defense of their new theological paradigm. I maintained against them that God remains absolute Truth, even though we never have an adequate perception of it, our knowledge of God and of his mystery being always analogical and symbolical. It has been rightly observed that even in the enunciations of faith, based on divine revelation, there remains a "distance between the affirmation . . . and the truth itself, the reality of God toward which tends the affirmation." The historical character of the enunciations marks them with the seal of provisionality: a "distance and proximity exists between the comprehension of the truth of faith itself and the truth." The content of the mystery of faith will never therefore be exhausted, not even on the part of the whole church (cf. *Dei Verbum* 8). Nevertheless, the knowledge of the divine Mystery based on revelation remains objective, that is, corresponds objectively to the divine reality, even if analogically. I have thus been able to maintain the objective value of the mystery of the divine Trinity revealed in Jesus Christ.

The insurpassable character of Christian revelation does not, however, exclude the possibility that there might be found in the other religious traditions of the world, through an authentic divine manifestation, true intuitions of the mystery of God, pointing toward the fullness of revelation in Jesus Christ: that is, "faces of the divine mystery" in relation to the self-revelation in him who is the one "human face of God." Concerning the relation obtaining between the former and the latter, one critic rightly remarks that truth in Jesus Christ is the obligatory "criterion of truth" for all evaluation of other truths. The question is asked, however, whether, instead of speaking of a "complementarity of revelations," one should not rather speak of "a complementarity *in* the comprehension of revelation." This would mean that, once the fullness of revelation has taken place in Jesus Christ, the other revelations have in a sense become henceforth "obsolete," even though the "faces of God" proposed by them can help us to deepen our comprehension of the divine mystery known through the Christian revelation. The "categorial datum," that is, the concrete form of revelation in Jesus Christ, would result in the other divine revelations throughout history being fulfilled unilaterally in Christian revelation.

Against such position I think that it must be said that, just as the various divine covenants with humankind have not become "obsolete" with the advent of the "new covenant" in Jesus Christ, so too, analogically, the revelation which God has been able to make of himself outside the Judeo-Christian tradition, through the religious experience of the seers, the memory of which is preserved in the sacred books of other religions, has not become "obsolete" either. To say it once more, some aspects of the divine mystery may be found in the sacred books of the other religions, which are less in evidence in the Christian revelation. Interreligious dialogue will not be, therefore, a one-way street. The document "Dialogue and Mission" (1984) of the Secretariat for Non-Christians has with good reason written that through dialogue Christians and the others, in a true sense, "walk together towards truth" (13). I myself wrote in my first book: "Every truth comes from God who is *the Truth* and must be honored as such, whatever be the channel through which it comes to us." And St. Thomas Aquinas endorsed the patristic axiom: *Omne verum a quocumque dicatur a Spiritu Sancto est* (*Summa Theologica* I-II, 109, 1, ad 1).

6. The Permanent Action of the Word of God as Such

Both my books refute clearly the "Logocentric paradigm" for a theology of religions, which affirms a salvific action of the Word of God separated and detached from the salvific action of the Word incarnate. According to that paradigm the members of the other religions are saved through the

Word, while Christians obtain salvation through the Word incarnate, that is through Jesus Christ. Against this paradigm I have affirmed clearly that one may not separate or detach the Word-to-be-incarnate from the Word-incarnate and that Logocentrism and Christocentrism, far from being mutually opposed, join one another reciprocally in one unique economy of salvation: they do not constitute parallel ways of salvation. This notwithstanding, I have affirmed a universal action of the Word-as-such beyond the salvific action of the Word incarnate through his humanity. Against this affirmation various objections are made, which need to be answered.

First of all, it is necessary to provide some terminological precision so as to avoid linguistic ambiguity. Clear distinctions must be made between different names and titles. The Word-to-be-incarnate refers to the Word of God considered in his eternity in the mystery of God and to his activity in history before the incarnation. The Word-incarnate refers to the Word as incarnate who acts salvifically through his human nature united to him hypostatically; in his humanity he is the man Jesus of Nazareth, who according to the Christian kerygma has become "the Christ" through his baptism (cf. Acts 10:38) and his resurrection (cf. Acts 2:36). At issue here is my affirmation that there remains a salvific action of the Word as such that is distinct from the action through the humanity of Jesus after the incarnation of the Word and after the resurrection of Christ. In my first book, I referred to this action of the Word as such with the term (somewhat ambiguous) *Logos asarkos.* I have left out that term in the second book in order to avoid the ambiguity. It is clear that there is no Logos different from the one who became incarnate in Jesus Christ and who remains incarnate in him after the resurrection; but this leaves open the possibility of a salvific action of his beyond that which passes through his humanity, even though never separated from the humanity. Is it licit to speak of a personal action of the Logos as such after his incarnation, not determined by the humanity of the risen Christ? It is necessary to distinguish here the exegetical aspect of the question from the dogmatic and theological aspects.

With regard to the universal illuminating function of the Logos I took up the exegesis of John 1:9 in the second book more deeply than had been done in the first book with reference to R. Schnackenburg. In the second book I followed primarily, but not exclusively, Xavier Léon-Dufour. According to him,[5] notwithstanding the incidental clause of vv. 6-8, from the beginning till v. 14 (that is from v. 1 to v. 13 included), the Prologue

---

5. X. Léon-Dufour, *Lecture de l'Evangile de Saint Jean,* vol. 1 (Paris: Seuil, 1988), 62-144.

of John refers to the Word-of-God-to-be-incarnate, considered before his incarnation as present in the mystery of God and operative since the beginning of human history. He explains that the Logos has been operative from the beginning of creation (vv. 2-5), as principle of light and of life, fashioning a personal relationship between God and men: as such, "coming into the world" in the manner of the Wisdom of God in Sir 24, he is source of light for all men, and to those who received him he has given "the power to become children of God" (vv. 9, 12). Léon-Dufour writes about the synergy that takes place between God and men as they welcome the Logos: "This enlightening action, insofar as it is welcomed, produces divine sonship. And this is so, even before the Logos takes a human face, that is independently from any explicit reference to Jesus Christ" (p. 109). And he adds: "The 'coming' of the Logos has already been spoken of in 1:10f.: he 'was in the world' and 'he came to his own home.' If it is true that the Logos is God communicating himself, this communication has begun not with the incarnation but since creation, and it has continued through the whole history of revelation. However, the incarnation of the Logos marks a radical change in the mode of communication" (p. 112). The change consists in the fact that "henceforth [revelation] happens through the language and the existence of a man among others: the phenomenon of concentration in a man will make it possible for the revelation of God to be formulated directly in an intelligible way, and for all people to have access to a definitive communication of God" (p. 124): Léon-Dufour goes on, however, to insist that, notwithstanding the novelty introduced by the incarnation, "this new stage does not supersede the previous one. The Logos continues to express himself through creation of which he is the author and the witness given to the light: many can receive him and become children of God. Henceforth, however, revelation is also and mostly concentrated in him who will be designated by his name: Jesus Christ (v. 17)" (p. 124). According to Léon-Dufour, we must speak not only of the universal action of the Word-to-be-incarnate before the incarnation, but also of the continuing action of the Word as such after the incarnation of the Word and after the resurrection of Jesus Christ.

Other exegetes who find a universal action of the Logos before the incarnation and of the Logos as such after the incarnation in the Prologue of John include R. Schnackenburg and J. Dupont[6] among others. One can add on this point the very firm opinion of D. Mollat, who affirms clearly that the universal action of the Logos as such remains even today. In his

6. J. Dupont, *Essais sur la Christologie de Saint Jean* (Bruges: Editions de l'Abbaye de Saint-André, 1951), 48.

introduction to the exegesis of John,[7] he writes about John 1:9: "In this verse . . . this coming of the Word into the world, implicitly referred to in vv. 4 and 5, is explicitly revealed." He continues: "It is said that the true light "enlightens all men." The present tense, "enlightens" . . . signifies that this is its proper task and its constant work. This work is to be understood in the supernatural sense of the enlightening which was declared to be the salvific illumination through which man is instructed and freed, transfigured and sanctified, and also judged. It must be stated that the illuminating virtue of this true light extends to all men. There is no one who is not reached or touched by it. A personal relationship between all men and the Word must therefore be affirmed" (pp. 23-24).

Moving on from the exegesis of the New Testament, I referred to several theologians who affirm an action of the Word as such beyond the action of the humanity of Jesus Christ. Let me recall one of them. Claude Geffré has written: "In conformity with the traditional view of the Fathers it is . . . possible to see the economy of the Son incarnate as the sacrament of a broader economy, that, namely, of the eternal Word of God which coincides with the religious history of humankind" (cited in my first book, p. 299). And again: "Without producing a ruinous dissociation between the eternal Word and the Word incarnate, it is legitimate . . . to consider the economy of the Word incarnate as the sacrament of a broader economy, that, namely, of the eternal Word of God which coincides with the history of humankind" (cited in my first book, p. 508).

One understands then how some recent authors can cite John 1:9 to affirm a salvific action even today of the Word as such. Bernard Senécal writes: "By not identifying straightaway the Logos with Jesus-the-Christ, it is easy to conceive a broad revealing action of the Logos throughout the history of salvation, not only before, but also after the incarnation."[8] The same thought is expressed by Yves Raguin, also with reference to John 1:9:

Those who will not have known the Father through the incarnate Word will be able to know him through his non-incarnate-Word. Thus, all human beings can know the Word of God, even without knowing him in his incarnation. . . . We read in the Prologue of the Gospel of John that the Word of God is the life of all things and that his life becomes the light of all human beings. Now, every human being can make in oneself this experience of life become light and

---

7. D. Mollat, *Introductio in Exegesim Scriptorum Sancti Johannis* (Rome: PUG, 1961), 21-24.

8. B. Senécal, *Jésus le Christ à la rencontre de Gautama le Bouddha* (Paris: Cerf, 1998), 213.

thus enter, through union with the Word, in the intimacy of the Father. This is how the greatest part of humankind can enter into relationship with God, source of all life and of all love, through the mediation of the Word, without having encountered Jesus and without having known him.[9]

To the question why, if the Prologue speaks so clearly in v. 9 of a universal permanent action of the Word as such, John no longer speaks of it in his Gospel after he has made reference to the event of the incarnation, we can answer that the intention of the Gospel is to show that in the becoming man of the Word and in the paschal mystery in which the Christ event culminates is found the "concentration" of the self-communication of God to humankind with its universal efficacy. If, however, it is asked whether God "remains bound" by the form of self-communication which he has freely chosen in the Christ event, perhaps it must simply be said that we cannot impose limits on the infinite freedom of God and on his overflowing generosity.

Some critics, however, object that one may not affirm that the Word acts "distinctly" from Jesus, the Incarnate Word, neither before nor after the incarnation. The claim that there can be divine self-manifestations through the Logos "beyond" the humanity of Jesus would end up, some say, in affirming a "separation" of a Nestorian type between the two natures of the incarnate Word. An initial answer to such an objection consists in emphasizing the essential "relational" character of the entire history of salvation—already repeatedly affirmed in my first book—according to which no divine self-manifestation whatsoever can be separated or dissociated from the Christ-event which enjoys universal bearing in the unique plan of salvation. The "added and autonomous" benefits that other divine manifestations may contain are in any case "relational" both to the qualitative fullness of the self-revelation of God in the Son made man, and to the decisive salvific efficacy of the paschal event of Jesus Christ, in which the salvific work of God for human beings culminates.

The argument is, however, further pursued with reference to christological dogma, and specifically to the Nestorian danger of a "separation" between the two natures of Christ. Some fear that the personal unity between Jesus Christ and the Word of God may be in danger of being forgotten. At this point appeal may be made to what John Paul II says clearly in the encyclical *Redemptoris missio:* "To introduce any sort of separation between the Word and Jesus Christ is contrary to the Christian

---

9. Y. Raguin, *Un message de salut pour tous* (Paris: Vie chrétienne, n.d.), 31.

faith. . . . Jesus is the incarnate Word—a single and individual person" (6).
This belongs without doubt to the faith. It is, however, necessary to take
into account the two complementary aspects contained in christological
dogma. While the two natures are united in Jesus Christ—according to
the formulation of Chalcedon—"without division or separation," they are
so also "without confusion or change," which means that, though being
hypostatically united, the two natures remain nevertheless "distinct" (DS
301-302). The same is said by Constantinople III with regard to the two
operations or activities of Christ (DS 635-37): they too are neither separated nor confused; they remain, however, distinct, though being in perfect harmony and communion. There can therefore be no question of an
absorption of the divine nature or action by the human through the union
of the two, nor even of a restriction or limitation. The Word loses nothing of his divine nature and action by becoming man. It is in fact the
permanent distinction of the two natures which historical monophysitism
denied, according to which the human nature was absorbed by the divine
nature, to the point that the authenticity of the human being was lost. The
danger of monophysitism remains real even today. But monophysitism can
move in two opposite directions. One form is an eventual absorption of
the human nature into the divine, often connected with a direct, impre-
cise transposition of the attributes of God to Jesus as man, based on a
mistaken interpretation of the *communicatio idiomatum*. Rather less widespread, though no less insidious, is the other form—which could be called
"reversed monophysitism"—of a possible absorption of the divine nature
into the human; in this case, by the fact of the human nature of Jesus
being united to the divine Word, the divine attributes of the person of the
Word are ignored or, at least, in some way reduced and redimensioned by
the human nature. Christological dogma tells us clearly that this is not
so, neither in one or the other sense. The four attributes of Chalcedon
concerning the union of the two natures are taken up again in Constantinople III with reference to the wills and operations. About the two wills
and operations of Christ, while it is binding to affirm their nonseparation,
it is equally binding to retain their distinction (DS 635-37). Though the
human action of Jesus is the action of the Word, the divine action remains
nevertheless distinct from the human.

If this is so, must it not also be said that the divine action, by its nature,
cannot be reduced to the mode in which it expresses itself through the
assumed humanity: namely, that it is not necessarily constrained by it?
And would it not have to be said, as a consequence, that an action of
the Word as such remains possible, though in relation with the central
event of the incarnation? There is no question here of "separation," but of

distinction: by becoming man the Word of God remains God; not even the risen humanity of Jesus exhausts the divine action of the Word. In a true sense, it is necessary to speak, *pace* one reviewer, of a "surplus of the Logos," in the sense that the divine nature transcends the human one, hypostatically united to it. Which does not mean to say that "the Word is something—or someone—other and more than Jesus Christ"; the person is that unique person of the Word, along with the permanent distinction of the two natures and actions.

One can then speak of an action of the Word of God not only before the incarnation but also after the incarnation and the resurrection of Jesus Christ, and beyond the salvific action through the humanity of Jesus, provided such continued action be not separated from the event in which there takes place the unsurpassable "concentration" of the self-revelation of God in accord with the unique divine plan for the universal salvation of humankind. The incarnate Word remains the Word of God; God remains God. Such continued illuminating and vivifying action of the Word as such is, however, related to the "concentration" of divine salvation in the incarnate Word in Jesus Christ, as also to the permanent actuality of the historical event through the risen condition of his humanity. The reason for this obligatory reference to Jesus Christ is the fact that the incarnation marks—as I have written—"the unsurpassed—and unsurpassable—depth of the self-communication of God with human beings; the supreme mode of immanence of his being-with-them," even "the interpretative key" of the whole process of the personal involvement of God with humankind throughout the whole of history.

7. The Permanent Action of the Spirit of God

To these reflections on the universal action of the Logos I added in my first book some observations concerning the permanent action of the Spirit of God, so as to be able to further explain the presence of the divine mystery of salvation realized in a unique and unsurpassable manner in Jesus Christ, yet operative also through the other religious traditions. These considerations on the Spirit of God have been further developed in my second book. On the universality of the active presence of the Spirit there generally is agreement between theologians, and it is well known that the recent Magisterium of the church has stressed it. The point under discussion is whether after the Christ-event the communication of the Spirit and his active presence in the world are either realized exclusively through the glorified humanity of Jesus Christ or can also exceed its limits. In other words, has the Spirit of God become the Spirit of Christ to such an extent as not to be able to make himself present and active beyond the communication that is made of him by the risen Christ, in such ways that his action be henceforth circumscribed, and in that sense, limited?

Before entering into this discussion, let us note that in the New Testament, and particularly in Paul, the Spirit is called either "Spirit of God" or "Spirit of Christ." The expression "Spirit of Christ" seems to refer to the communication of the Spirit made by the risen Christ, which corresponds to the promise made by Jesus to the disciples in the Gospels of Luke and John and to its realization at Pentecost. The work of the Spirit consists in establishing between the human persons and the Lord a personal relationship by which they are incorporated into Christ. The Spirit is the "point of insertion" of God through Christ into the life of human beings, and part of his work consists in making them children of the Father in the Son by means of the risen humanity. The fact remains, however, that the Spirit is also, and more frequently, called the "Spirit of God" (eg. 1 Cor 2:11; 3:16; Rom 8:9). Hence the question may be asked: After the resurrection of Jesus can there be a vivifying action of the Spirit beyond that which passes through the risen and glorified humanity?

Some object that such an idea contradicts what the Gospel of John says, namely, that "The Spirit had not been given, because Jesus was not yet glorified" (John 7:39). Against this objection, it needs to be noted that if the affirmation made in this passage were of universal application, it would follow that no grace whatever conferred before the Christ event would ever have implied the gift of the Holy Spirit—as in fact some theologians have sustained. It has, however, been shown to the contrary that the Spirit is God's necessary "point of insertion" in the life of human beings wherever God communicates with them personally, and therefore also before the Christ event. It must moreover be remembered that the Decree *Ad gentes* (4) affirms clearly that "the Holy Spirit was at work in the world before Christ was glorified." Moreover, his presence to people before the historical event of Jesus is witnessed by the First Testament itself. On the other hand, the Spirit is communicated today through the risen humanity of Jesus Christ. The contested point is whether the action of the Spirit is exclusively bound to the mediation of the glorified humanity.

Faced with the hypothesis that it be not so bound, some critics fear that some activity of the Spirit is being "detached from the Christ event." That such is not my intention should be clear from the passages in both my books in which I have repeatedly and strongly affirmed that Christocentrism and Pneumatocentrism cannot be separated from each other, the Christ event remaining always at the center in the unfolding through human history of the one plan of salvation. One cannot therefore assent to a pneumatocentric paradigm which would lead to building parallel ways of salvation: salvation in Jesus Christ for Christians, and in the Spirit for the others. As I have writtten: "The salvific economy of God is one only, of which the Christ event is at once the culminating point and the universal sacrament; but the God who saves is 'three,' where each one of the three is personally distinct and remains active in a distinct manner. God saves with 'two hands.'"

In the opposite direction, some point to the risk of an "instrumentalization" of the Spirit. But it is precisely in order to avoid all possible "instrumentalization" of the Spirit that it seems desirable to insist on the spontaneity and the freedom of the Spirit in his salvific action: the Spirit "blows where he wills" (cf. John 3:8), without being necessarily constrained by the glorified humanity of Christ and exclusively conferred through it. The metaphor used by St. Irenaeus of the "two hands" of God can be of help here. Underlying the metaphor is probably the image of God as a potter (cf. Isa 64:6-7) who with two hands produces a single work, namely, the one economy of salvation. The two hands of God, the Word and the Spirit, are paired hands. This means that, while they are united and inseparable, they are also distinct, and complementary in their distinction. The activity of each is different from that of the other; indeed, it is the concurrence or "synergy" of the two distinct activities that produces God's saving effect. Neither can be reduced to a mere "function" of the other; rather both activities converge in achieving a single economy of salvation. God acts with both divine hands. This metaphor may make it easier to understand that the communication of the Spirit through the risen Christ does not necessarily exhaust the activity of the Spirit after the Christ event.

It is well known that the Eastern Orthodox tradition has often accused the Western tradition of promoting a theological "Christomonism" in which the Holy Spirit is reduced to being a "function" of Christ. Although Yves Congar regards the accusation as exaggerated, he nevertheless recognizes that it is not entirely without foundation: indeed it offers Western theology the chance to reflect on the inadequacy of its pneumatology. While certainly no "autonomous" economy of the Spirit can be detached from that of the Word, neither can the Spirit be reduced to a "function" of the risen Christ, to the point of being, as it were, his "vicar," The fullness of the personal saving activity of the Spirit would thereby be lost.

In fact, it seems that there are different ways in which the Spirit could unduly be reduced to a "function" of Christ. One would consist in simply identifying the Spirit with the risen Christ; this opinion is based on a mistaken interpretation of the Pauline affirmation: "The Lord is the Spirit" (2 Cor 3:17).[10] More discrete and subtler, but perhaps just as unsatisfactory, would be the position that the saving and vivifying action of the Spirit consists entirely in the communication of the Spirit made by the risen Christ. That is the position being discussed here.

Vatican II affirms clearly (*Ad gentes* 4), and recent church teaching insistently reaffirms (cf. in particular the encyclical *Dominum et vivificantem* 53), that the Spirit was already present and operative before the glorification of Christ, even before the Jesus Christ event, throughout the whole of history from creation onward. Now, one does not see why, whereas before the Christ event the Spirit was at work in the world and in history, without being communicated through the risen humanity—which did not yet exist—his activity after the Christ event would have to be so tied to such communication as to be limited by it. It must certainly be kept in mind that in both cases—whether before or after the historic event—the outpouring of the Spirit is always in relation to the event in which the unfolding of the divine plan of salvation through history reaches its culminating point. In that sense it can and must be said that the gift of the Spirit before the incarnation takes place "in view" of the christological event. But that does not mean that after that event no action whatever of the Spirit as such, even in relation to that event, may be conceived. There are not two economies of salvation. But both of God's "hands" have and keep their own personal identity in the divine activity. The Word is the light "which enlightens everyone" (John 1:9); for his part, the Spirit "blows where he wills" (John 3:8).

The immanent vivifying presence of the Spirit is, in every historical situation, either before Christ or after him, the concrete reality of the gift of self and of his life which God makes to human beings in the mystery of grace: we become children of the Father through the Son in the Holy Spirit. The difference that intervenes in the gift of grace with the Christ event consists in the introduction, starting with the resurrection, of the instrumental causality of the risen humanity. However, it seems possible to say, following the Prologue of John—as explained above— that men have been able to become children of God, also before Jesus Christ, thanks to the illuminating and vivifying action of the Word of God. Yet, it must be added that it was the immanent presence of the Spirit of God which constituted them children of God, and that divine grace before the Christ event is substantially the same as after the event.

---

10. See D. L. Gelpi, *The Divine Mother: A Trinitarian Theology of the Holy Spirit* (Lanham, MD: University Press of America, 1984), 136; also E. A. Johnson, *She Who Is* (New York: Crossroad, 1992), 211.

Where God communicates Godself personally, he does so necessarily as Father through the Son in the Spirit. God gives himself to us such as he is. It seems therefore legitimate to hold that the immanent presence of the Spirit through divine grace cannot be reduced to the communication that the risen humanity of Christ makes of him, nor can it be exclusively bound to it. And, consequently, it also seems legitimate to speak of a continued action of the Spirit as such, after the historic event Jesus Christ, but always in relation to it.

According to the divine plan, the action of the Holy Spirit is always connected with and in relation to the event Jesus Christ, which represents the culminating point of the involvement of God with humankind, and, as such, the hermeneutical key of the entire unfolding of the personal divine–human dealings. But discretion is required, and even some apophatic silence, respectful of the transcendence of the mystery, in the effort to discover and to account for the "how" of that bond and that relation. The divine economy is one, but has complementary and interconnected aspects. It is of course necessary to hold that, whether before or after the Christ event, the outpouring of the Spirit is always related to the event in which the divine plan of salvation culminates. But this does not render inconceivable all action of the Spirit as such, even after the event—any more than an action of the Word as such is inconceivable.

8. Jesus Christ, Constitutive Universal Savior

I noted in my first book that the historic event Jesus Christ, while being "the universal sacrament of the will of God to save humankind," remains nonetheless by its nature a historic event, and therefore particular. This means that it is not the only possible expression of that divine will. While in Christ "the historic particularity coincides with a universal significance," "the saving power of God is not exclusively bound to the universal sign which he has chosen for his salvific action." In that sense I have been able to speak of a universal action of the Word and of the Spirit, not circumscribed to the humanity of Jesus. To say that the humanity of Jesus does not exhaust the salvific action of the Word is not, however, equivalent to saying, as is attributed to me by one critic, that even though Jesus is *totus Deus*, he is not *totum Dei*—a distinction which intentionally I have avoided because of its ambiguity. What would it mean to say that Jesus is *totum Dei*? The terminological polarity particularity–universality is intended, on the contrary, to affirm, on the one hand, the qualitative, not merely quantitative, difference concerning the event of the incarnate Son as God's involvement with men, unsurpassable because of the unique ontological Sonship of God which is communicated to Jesus in his humanity, and, on the other hand, the unique human consciousness which the man Jesus has of the mystery of God, the intensity of which is also unsurpassable because of his unique personal identity as Son of God, turned to the Father in a lived relationship of communion in the unity of nature and the distinction of persons.

Some objections have been raised against the opinion already expressed in my first book according to which Jesus is the universal, but not absolute, savior, nor is the revelation of God that takes place in him absolute, but remains limited. The two aspects must be considered separately.

As far as salvation is concerned, I have explained the reason why it seems more correct to speak of the Christ event as "constitutive" of salvation, rather than of the "absolute savior." Absoluteness is an attribute of the divine nature of God, at least if the terms are taken in their rigorous sense; otherwise, precisions would have to be given each time that one speaks of realities that are not intrinsically divine. It is God who saves absolutely. This way of speaking seems to correspond also better to that of the New Testament: "It was God in fact who in Christ was reconciling the world to himself" (2 Cor 5:19, with the emphasis in the original Greek; cf. also 1 Tim 2:4; 4:10). God is the primary, principal, and originating cause of salvation; the Jesus Christ event is the efficacious expression of it. "Constitutive savior" does not relativize the salvific work of Christ; what is constitutive belongs to the essence.

The objection insists, however, that, since Jesus is the Son of God acting and speaking in human form, his human actions and his words, even while having a historic and therefore limited character, have nevertheless a divine and absolute value. Otherwise, Jesus would be reduced to being "a salvific figure among the others." Certainly, I have never wanted to reduce Jesus Christ to one salvific figure "among the others," even the highest one. That is why I called him, in a unique sense, "constitutive" savior, inasmuch as the Christ event is truly cause, even universal cause of salvation, while the other "salvific figures" can at best be "indicators" toward a way along which their followers will meet, without being aware of it, the salvific event of Christ. It does not seem, however, either correct or opportune to attribute to the human action of Jesus (as human) actions of a divine character, absolute and infinite. The human actions of Jesus, even though being the actions of the Son of God, and, as such, salvific, remain human in their specificity. I have meant to ensure that human specificity with the term "constitutive savior."

Another objection is made against the "constitutive and relational unicity" I attribute to Jesus Christ. Such a way of speaking would involve "dissociation" between Jesus Christ and the Logos, in virtue of which the mediation of Christ would no longer be absolute. Beyond question Jesus Christ is personally the Word. It, however, remains true that neither in the intrinsic life of God nor in the order of the divine self-communication is the Word the ultimate origin, the origin without an origin, which is the Father. The Word "comes," "originates" from the Father in the divine life and is sent by the Father in history. With good reason the liturgy can call Jesus Christ "the universal sacrament of salvation" (see Roman Missal, prayer for Tuesday of the second week of Easter)—an expression never used of nor applicable to the Father. The Father is the absolute savior, as the ultimate source of the divine salvific action. The "absolute savior" is he of whom the risen Lord is the universal sacrament. Jesus Christ could perhaps be called the "absolute mediator," in the sense that he is the *analogatum princeps* for whatever participated mediations can be affirmed in relation to his. The encyclical *Redemptoris missio* (5) recognizes the existence of "participated forms of mediation of different kinds and degrees . . . (which) acquire meaning and value *only* from Christ's own mediation, and . . . cannot be understood as parallel or complementary to it." According to 1 Tim 2:4, "there is one God, and there is one mediator between God and men, the man Jesus Christ." The Father is absolute savior; Jesus Christ, the incarnate Son, is, in his humanity, *the* mediator between God and men.

This being said, I have insisted that the unicity and universality of Christ Savior are "constitutive": the Christ event has salvific value for the entire human family. All human beings are saved in Jesus Christ. The only adequate theological foundation for such an affirmation is the personal identity of Jesus, his ontological sonship as only-begotten Son of God. No other foundation can establish it theologically in an adequate manner.

Coming then to the divine revelation made in Jesus Christ, some critics insist on affirming its "definitive and absolute" character. As for myself I have affirmed clearly that in Jesus Christ is found the fullness of divine revelation which, as already mentioned above, must be understood in a qualitative sense, not quantitative sense. This revelation is unsurpassable because, as Son of God incarnate, Jesus lived in his human consciousness his interpersonal relation with the Father and the Spirit, which characterizes the intrinsic mystery of God. I did not call it "absolute" because of the limited character of the human consciousness, which by definition cannot exhaust the divine mystery. The words of Jesus recorded in the Gospels are human words; the knowledge of the mystery of God which he conveys to us, starting from his human consciousness, is the unique human knowledge possessed by him who is the Son of God. It is also in the sense of this limitation by nature that I used—less suitably, because of the ambiguity involved—the term "relative." It would have been better to be satisfied with the term "limited," in the sense indicated.

The question is also asked why I speak of the Christ event as "decisive," without calling it "definitive." In fact, while sharing a partly common meaning, the terms imply different nuances: "definitive" means "final"; "decisive," on the contrary, means rather "conclusive," or what "decides" an issue. A "decisive" battle does not yet necessarily mean the "end" of the war. Here my intention in choosing the attribute "decisive" was twofold: divine manifestations must not be excluded after the Christ event, even though it must be said that no further historic manifestation can ever equal the unsurpassable self-manifestation of the incarnation. It must be remembered that there remains till the end an "eschatological remainder": the definitive self-manifestation of God to humankind, as also the final realization of the salvific function of Christ, will coincide with the advent of the fullness of the reign of God in the *eschaton* (cf. 1 Cor 15:26-28). Obviously, such realization at the end of time can and must now be prepared and indicated already in history through prefigurations and prophetic anticipations, which however can never be identified with the full and perfect attainment of the final reality. Therefore the expression "at the end of times" of Heb 1:1 is to be understood correctly; it refers to the eschatological era in which we have entered with the Christ event (cf. the fullness of times of Gal 4:4), leaving open the distance between the "already" and the "not yet," the realization of which remains in the future of the *eschaton*. Several times in the New Testament the term "revelation" refers directly to the end of times at the *eschaton* (cf. 1 Pet 1:5-13).

The reason why I used the term "decisive," instead of "definitive," about the divine revelation in Jesus Christ was the same for my preference of "decisive" about the Christ event itself. *Dei Verbum* affirms—rightly—that Jesus Christ "completes and perfects" (*complendo perficit*) the divine revelation and that "no new divine revelation is to be expected before the glorious manifestation of our Lord Jesus Christ" (*Dei Verbum* 4). This, however, does not deny that God might still speak to the world, either in Christianity or outside it, though not "publicly" in the sense intended by the Council. In fact, where I have spoken of "differentiated revelation," I have affirmed clearly that the "initial, secret words" spoken by God to the nations through their seers, though having a social function, do not have the "official" or "public" character which must be attributed to the words of God contained in the First Testament, and a fortiori in the New Testament. Provided one takes into account these distinctions and the unsurpassable character of the revelation made in Jesus Christ, one may say that God continues even today to speak to our world. There still are prophets in the church, and St. Augustine affirmed that there also were some among the members of other religions. In the life of the church revelation in Jesus Christ continues to be "actuated" also in the proclamation of the word in the liturgy; outside of the church, it may be hinted at in the stress laid on authentic aspects of the divine mystery, or through incomplete "faces" of the mystery.

9. Ways of Salvation

With regard to the other religious traditions as possible ways of salvation for their followers, a reviewer observed that my first book misses "a critical reading of these traditions," with their limitations, their risks, the possible ideologies, the hidden logics of sin, the ambiguities contained in them. This reviewer agrees nonetheless in including historic Christianity under the same criticism. It is true that I have deliberately opposed myself to the unilaterally negative evaluations of the other religions that have been repeated through the centuries. Such seriously unjust judgments characterized the opinions, developed through the history of the church, about the uniqueness and the "absolutism" of Christianity, understood as the "only true religion." Starting from such an absolute judgment, an unduly negative evaluation of the other religions was construed, supported by a prejudicial reading of the data. Even today it is not rare to see double standards being used in the way in which historic Christianity and the other religions are compared. The danger is still real of opposing what is best in us with what is worst in the others. Examples are readily available: it is enough to think of the general accusations of superstition, of idolatry, and of the abuse of religion as ideology, in support of social injustice or of violence. There have been such abuses in the past and they still exist today in the other religions; but it is also true that these do not have a monopoly of such failings and transgressions.

It must be added that the opinions still found today, though in less negative terms, according to which the historic religions have nothing to do with the mystery of salvation of their members, seem unsustainable. According to those opinions, the salvation of each individual person outside the church represents in fact a singular exception—as though by way of substitute for the Christian faith—to a divine order of salvation which appears rigid and narrow. It must be asked whether such an attitude is not a residue of an inadequate theological reflection in the past about the divine plan of salvation. The realization of the universal will of salvation on the part of God (cf. 1 Tim 2:4) cannot be seen as consisting, in the case of the vast majority of human beings, of an ensemble of so many individual exceptions, without falling into a very restricted concept of God the savior and of his salvific will. While, therefore, it is necessary to refute clearly the "paradigm shift" advocated by the "pluralist theologians," from traditional Christocentrism to some neutral sort of Theocentrism, a "qualitative leap" seems nevertheless desirable, even necessary, in the theological comprehension of the divine plan of salvation and, consequently, in the evaluation of the other religions.

In this context, I intended to show in my first book how some elements of the religious praxis of the "others," which to our often badly informed judgment seemed altogether reprehensible, deserve on the contrary a much more positive evaluation, once they are correctly understood. One example is the "cult of sacred images," in which it is often possible theologically to discover no longer idolatry but a "searching Christology." This does not mean that one denies the presence in the other religions of ambiguities and of sin, either in the persons or in the structures. It is a question of attempting a critical evaluation, correct and just, between a sweeping condemnation and a wholesale approval.

Thus, while I affirmed that it is possible to meet in the sacred books of the other religious traditions a word of God, by way of a written memory of authentic religious experiences of the living God made by their seers, I insisted that it is a question of *a first word* of God, oriented toward the fullness of revelation in Jesus Christ. I also said clearly that not all that is found in the other sacred books can be considered by Christian theologians as word of God—some "non-truth" can be found in them—and that the mystery of Jesus Christ must be the decisive normative criterion in the difficult but necessary work of discernment of the elements of truth. A similar discernment is equally necessary with regard to the possible elements of grace and salvific values, eventually hidden in the moral code and the rites and sacramental practices of the other religious traditions. Not everything in the religions is from God, nor everything salvific.

Nevertheless, one critic disagrees with the affirmation of any positive value in the religious traditions for the salvation of their members. According to him, even today it must be held that to obtain supernatural faith which saves, the proclamation and the acceptance of the gospel is required: after the preaching of the apostles, explicit faith in Jesus Christ is necessary for salvation. It is difficult to reconcile this opinion with the official doctrine of the church, as expressed under Pius XII in the document of the Holy Office (cf. DS 3866-72). According to the critic, while it is true that the church has no monopoly over "natural" truth, the "supernatural" truths have been entrusted to it by Christ as its inheritance. The answer consists in saying that, while it is pure Pauline doctrine that supernatural faith is necessary for salvation, it does not follow that explicit faith in Jesus Christ is also necessary after the Christ event. Such a position, which was still held by St. Thomas Aquinas, has been abandoned long ago.

More insidious is the objection: Once some salvific value is recognized in the religions for the salvation of their members, Christianity is considered merely one way of salvation among others, thus forgetting the true meaning of the mediation operative in the religion of the incarnation. But Christianity, it is said, is precisely the religion in which the Absolute gives itself in a mediation: the mediation thus acquires an absolute value. The mediations chosen by God are endowed with a character of necessity: there is no other way toward God beside Jesus Christ, and there is no other "place" to be united with Christ beside the church. Let us note that the sacramentality of Jesus Christ as "sacrament of the encounter with God" and that of the church as "sacrament of Jesus Christ" seem here to be placed on the same level, both being considered equally necessary in every historic situation.

One may also note a too restrictive ecclesiological perspective, which places both mediations on the same plane and affirms of both the same necessity. On the contrary, it may be thought that the mystery of salvation in Jesus Christ can be encountered through different modalities of mediation, while maintaining that in the church is found the "complete" mediation, that is, the complete sacramental visibility of the mystery of salvation. But the affirmation of the singularity of the ecclesial mediation, as the "way" established by God in his Son, does not necessarily lead to denying or undervaluing the positive meaning of other "ways" of salvation. It is true that the mediation of the mystery of salvation, operative in the other religious traditions, remains "incomplete," and therefore "ordained" toward the complete mediation operative in the church. But this does not mean that the church is the only "place where grace is operative." For grace has no "one place" of operation. It is operative everywhere, and salvation can reach all people, in whichever historic situation or circumstances of life they may find themselves. One may recall what Cardinal Manning wrote in the nineteenth century: It is correct to say with St. Irenaeus *Ubi ecclesia ibi Spiritus*—"Where the church is, there is the Spirit"—but it would not be correct to say: "Where the church is not, there neither is the Spirit."[11] The works of the Holy Spirit have always invaded the entire family of human beings from the beginning, and they are fully active also now in the midst of those who are outside the church. This agrees with the encyclical *Domunum et vivificantem* 53, where John Paul II affirms clearly the operative presence of the Holy Spirit before the Christ event and, after the event, beyond the limits of the church.

A critic has expressed the fear that by speaking of "substitutive mediations" of salvation, the uniqueness of the mediation of the church will be forgotten. It must be well understood that the incomplete mediations operative in the other religious traditions are neither parallel nor alternative. Far from contradicting the unique mediation of Jesus Christ, they are essentially related to it; they are also, as explained above, ordained toward the complete mediation of the mystery of salvation present in the church. They remain in fact incomplete and fragmentary. The Christ event represents in the entire history of salvation the deepest personal involvement of God with humankind, to which every other manner of involvement of God with human beings is necessarily related. The church, on its part, has received the complete mediation, that is, the deepest sacramental visibility of the salvific event in Jesus Christ, toward which the other mediations remain oriented.

However, this talk of "complete" and "incomplete" is not to be understood in the sense of the "fulfillment theory," according to which the other religions represent only the expression, in the diverse cultures of the world, of a universal human desire of union with the divine mystery. The language of "fulfillment" can in fact be understood in two different ways. According to the "fulfillment theory," the gifts of nature contained in the religious traditions find in the mystery of Jesus Christ and in Christianity the only fulfillment of their natural aspirations. Here, on the contrary, we speak of elements of truth and grace contained in those religious traditions, of a certain, though incomplete, mediation in them of the mystery of salvation, which is necessarily related to the Christ event and oriented toward the ecclesial mediation. Inasmuch as the Christ event represents the supreme modality of the mediation of the divine salvific action, that event "fulfills," in a true sense, what remains incomplete in the other mediations. I have already quoted John Paul II where in *Redemptoris missio* (5), he speaks of "participated forms of mediation of different kinds and degrees," not "parallel or complemen-

---

11. Quoted by Yves Congar, *I Believe in the Holy Spirit*, vol. 2 (London: G. Chapman, 1983).

tary" to that in Jesus Christ, but which attain their meaning and value from his unique mediation. The way in which the real but incomplete mediation at work in the other religious traditions and in their founders and seers must also be remembered. I have spoken of them being "indicators of salvation for their followers," in the sense that they point toward paths in which, unconsciously, they may come in contact with the salvific mystery of Jesus Christ.

As far as the "complementarity" between the elements of truth and grace found in the religious traditions and Christianity is concerned, I have said that it must not be understood only in the sense of the "fulfillment theory," that is, as a unilateral process according to which Christianity brings to fulfillment the "stepping stones" (*pierres d'attente*) spread out elsewhere; one may on the contrary speak of a "reciprocal complementarity," which opens the possibility of a mutual enrichment. But it must not be concluded that in this manner the biblical revelation and the other sacred books are being placed "on the same plane." In fact, this "reciprocal complementarity" does not contradict the unique character of the biblical and Christian revelation; there is no question of placing all the words of God on the same plane. Much less is it intended that the other revelations fill a void left open in the Christian revelation, which without them would not attain its fullness. There remains, however, the fact that some aspects of the divine mystery can be put into greater relief in the nonbiblical scriptures than they are in the biblical ones, which, however, retain their transcendence. In order to stress correctly the complex relation of reciprocal complementarity existing between the Christian and the other revelations, I used in my second book the expression "reciprocal, *asymmetrical* complementarity." In the same way, as regards the transcendence of the Christ event in relation to other divine manifestations, it must be said that not all the manifestations of the Word have the same significance. The incarnation of the Word, compared to his "illuminating" action, has a historic density all its own.

10. The Reign of God and the Mediation of the Church

Already in my first book I spoke of the church as the sign of the presence already operative in the world of the reign of God, that is, of the mystery of salvation in Jesus Christ which, however, remains on the way toward its eschatological fulfillment. A critic expressed at this point the fear that such a perspective tends to reduce the distance between history and eschatology. The true discontinuity between history and eschatology must be emphasized, that is, the "eschatological remainder" which is in hope. In fact, the discontinuity between the reign already present and its eschatological fullness has never been denied, but it remains true that a total discontinuity cannot be accepted. I have spoken on the contrary of a continuity-in-discontinuity, or vice versa, which exists in the development through history of the divine plan of salvation, till it reaches its eschatological fullness. The two aspects of continuity and discontinuity are indivisible and inseparable. I note that also *Gaudium et spes* (39) has combined both together.

As far as the mediation of the church is concerned, one reviewer asks whether in my first book it is adequately stressed. Since the Council has spoken of the church as the Body of Christ, it is "probable"—it is said—that where the Council spoke of it as "universal sacrament of salvation" (*Lumen gentium* 48), it meant to say that the church as Body of Christ totally united with him, exercises a mediation of the efficient causal order for all men, and never only of a final order. This collaboration with Christ on the part of the church is expressed through the preaching of the gospel, the eucharistic celebration offered for the salvation of all, the prayer and the suffering of the members.

Personally I have thought it opportune to distinguish, on the one hand, a mediation of a strictly theological order expressed in the preaching of the gospel and the sacramental economy at the center of which is the eucharistic celebration and, on the other hand, prayer and intercession which do not have this character of strictly theological mediation. The first, in normal circumstances, does not reach out to members of the other religions; the other, on the contrary—and especially the intercession in the eucharistic celebration—extends to the salvation of all. I have added that, in the first case, the causality involved is of instrumental efficient order; in the other, of moral and final order.

By speaking of "probability" in the thinking of the Council, the critic shows that he is aware of the doubt that remains in this matter. Let us note in passing that already in St. Paul the metaphor of the Body for the church is understood differently in 1 Corinthians and Ephesians. However this may be, it seems clear that the modality of the causality at work in the intercession of the church remains a question open to theological discussion. That which on the contrary is of primary importance is the nonambiguous conciliar affirmation of the "necessity of the church" (*Lumen gentium* 14) for salvation. The way of conceiving this, however, will depend on the way in which we understand the relation between the reign of God and the church, the relation between the members of the other religions, the reign and the church, and, finally, the nature of the action of the church for the salvation of the persons who, though not being its members, are nonetheless ordained toward it.

Another critic asks, however, for further clarifications about the exact role of the church for the salvation of the "others," and the nature of its association with Christ the savior. Another still notes that Christ and the church cannot be mutually separated in the work of salvation, any more than the bond between Christology and ecclesiology can be broken. He refers to *Lumen gentium* 14, where the necessity of the church for salvation is affirmed without, however, a "universal mediation" being explicitly spoken of. How then must the necessity of the church for salvation, clearly affirmed by the Council, be understood and interpreted? Certainly we must affirm that between the reign of God and the church there exists a strict bond. John Paul II writes in *Redemptoris missio* 18: "While remaining distinct from Christ and the Kingdom, the church is indissolubly united to both." But we must ask in what this bond consists. The encyclical letter speaks of a "specific and necessary role" (n. 18) of the church in relation to the reign of God—an expression which by itself does not automatically involve a "universal mediation." As regards a universal instrumental efficient causality exercised by the church in the order of grace, I think—together with other theologians, among them Yves Congar whom I quoted in my first book (p. 351)—that that question remains open. It is one thing to speak of a "specific and necessary role" of the church; it is another thing to attribute to it a universal instrumental causality of grace for all men beyond its own boundaries.

A reviewer insists, however, that the "orientation" of the members of the other religions toward the church, of which *Lumen gentium* 16 speaks, means nothing if it does not refer to their being its members *in voto*, which was spoken of before the Council; and consequently it is necessary to say that the Council intends to affirm an efficient causality of the church in their regard. Alas, the censor does not take into consideration the fact that the Council—as several authors have noted—chose deliberately to leave out the terminology of being "members" *in voto* in the case of the members of other religions. The reason is that the members of the other religious traditions are simply not members of the church, according to the definition of the church given by the Council in *Lumen gentium* (8): the church is made up of two inseparable elements, divine and human, that is, the communion of grace and the human institution. On the other hand, if the members of the other religious traditions remain "ordained" toward the church, the reason is that Jesus Christ has entrusted to the church the "fullness of the benefits and means of salvation" (*Redemptoris missio* 18; cf. 55).

A recent author has rightly written, with regard to the language of the Council: "The terms of 'belonging' to the church have been put aside; the Council is content to say that 'Those who have not yet received the Gospel are ordained, in various ways, to the people of God' (*Lumen gentium* 16). This is why some are astonished by the fact that the International Theological Commission . . . has declared—twenty years after the Council—that 'belonging to the Reign cannot but constitute a belonging—at least implicitly—to the church' (10, 2). John Paul II seems to display more prudence and more flexibility, when he is content to speak of 'a mysterious relationship with the church' (*Redemptoris missio* 10)."[12]

Some reviewers do not admit that the reign of God is broader than the church; both coincide, according to traditional theological doctrine, even if there exist different degrees of their realization. The members of the other religious traditions are, as such, "potential members" of the church, that is, of the reign of God; but they must still pass from the natural state to the world of grace. This opinion does not coincide with the doctrine of the Council according to which the members of the other religious traditions, while not being members of the church, can be saved in Jesus Christ through the working of the Holy Spirit (cf. *Gaudium et spes* 22). What is new in *Redemptoris missio* (20), as compared to the doctrine of the Council, is that the reign of God present in history extends beyond the boundaries of the church, even though it is present in it in a privileged manner, and that the members of the other religious traditions can be members of the reign of God without belonging to the church as members. The reign of God represents, therefore, the universal reality of salvation present and operative in the world.

According to another critic, not only does Vatican II preserve the identification of the church with the reign of God, but the more recent ecclesial documents do likewise (*Redemptoris missio* 18, 20). The reign of God present in history is simply the church. I am criticized for "separating" the one from the other by affirming the reign to be broader than the church. Here it would have to be observed that "identification," "distinction," and "separation" are not the same thing. I reject the identification, but I reject also the separation. I hold a distinction, though with a strict bond and a necessary relation, given the fact that the church has "a specific and necessary role" in relation to the reign (cf. *Redemptoris missio* 18). The church, which is at the same time, according to Vatican II (*Lumen gentium* 8),

---

12. J. Rigal, *L'Eglise en chantier* (Paris: Cerf, 1995), 49. The document of the International Theological Commission to which the author refers is that of 1985, entitled *L'unique Eglise du Christ* (Paris: Centurion, 1985).

communion of grace and human institution, is distinct but not separated from the universal reality of the reign of God present in the world. While for the critic, the church is the very reality of salvation, and wherever there is salvation there is the church, for me as for many theologians today the reality of salvation is the reign of God universally present, of which the church, as the Council suggests, is the "universal sacrament."

I very much fear that the identification of the church with the very reality of salvation leads to forgetting that the church is a derived, relative mystery, which does not have in itself its raison d'être. The church has its raison d'être in Jesus Christ and in the reign of God instituted by God in him. Therefore, the ultimate criterion for salvation cannot consist in being related to the church, but to Christ and to the kingdom. I am therefore not persuaded that the model of an all-pervading and invading ecclesiology, in which the church is identified with the very reality of salvation, offers a more adapted and more fruitful model for an open theology of the religions than the model of the universality of the reign of God and of the sacramentality of the church in relation to it. In the regnocentric perspective, the task of the church consists in witnessing the universal operative presence of the reign in history and in the world; it also consists in serving the growth of the reign in history and in announcing it as good news for all people. Certainly the reign of God can never be separated either from the person of Jesus Christ, or from the mystery of the church (cf. *Redemptoris missio* 17-18); but, this being well understood, it remains true that a regnocentric perspective opens vaster horizons and a broader perspective for a theology of the religions and of interreligious dialogue than a directly ecclesiocentric approach can offer, which risks being too narrow and centered on the church itself.

11. Interreligious Dialogue: Complementarity and Convergence

With regard to the meaning of interreligious dialogue in the life of the church, a critic objects that according to me dialogue would henceforth be the "principal method" of mission, while announcing Jesus Christ would have become "secondary." He refers to the document "Dialogue and Proclamation" (1991) (29), which, according to him affirms only the possibility of "natural religiosity," which is open to the members of the other religious traditions and does not procure salvation. Against such a prejudicial reading of the document, I must repeat that it clearly holds the possibility for them of obtaining salvation itself "through the sincere practice of what is good in their own religious traditions." For the relationship between dialogue and proclamation, it is necessary to take into account n. 82 of the above-mentioned document, to which I have made reference in both my books, where it is said: "Dialogue . . . does not constitute the whole mission of the church; . . . it cannot simply replace proclamation, but remains oriented towards proclamation insofar as the dynamic process of the church's evangelizing mission reaches in it its climax and its fullness." Just as the members of the other religious traditions who are saved in Christ remain "oriented" toward the church according to the Constitution *Lumen gentium* 16, in the same way and logically so, interreligious dialogue remains oriented, in the evangelizing mission of the church, toward proclamation. I have refused, especially in the second book, to simply identify the evangelizing mission with dialogue, thus reducing the first to the second.

The same reviewer insists that I make dialogue into "an autonomous enterprise of evangelization." Yet, on this subject I have done nothing else than refer to the official documents of the church according to which dialogue is an "integral element" or an "authentic expression" of the evangelizing mission which, however, as recorded above, remains "oriented" toward proclamation. For this critic, dialogue can only serve as a "preparatory step" for the proclamation of Christ. Yet, the official documents intentionally abstain from such an affirmation in order to avoid the danger that dialogue be "manipulated" (cf. *Redemptoris missio* 55). The purposes of dialogue and of proclamation are different: dialogue aims at a deeper conversion toward God of both partners of the dialogue; proclamation, on the other hand, aims at inviting the others to become disciples of Jesus in the Christian community (cf. "Dialogue and Proclamation," 40-41, 83). That through the entire process the Christian hopes to be able to witness his own faith is clear: "How could they not hope and desire to share with others their joy in knowing and following Jesus Christ, Lord and Savior?" (see "Dialogue and Proclamation," 83).

Still apropos of interreligious dialogue, another critic seems to attribute to me the idea that the finality of such a dialogue is "only the eschatological conversion of the whole of humankind to God," while it would be according to him first of all a question of the "search for the truth about man." Yet, I have spoken explicitly of a mutual enrichment and a mutual collaboration through dialogue in the present time, adding that Christians and the others are called to be under God co-creators of the reign of God in history. This seems a long way from a merely eschatological conversion and convergence in the mystery of God. On the other hand, while in Jesus Christ the mystery of man is fully revealed (cf. *Gaudium et spes* 22), this does not allow us to say that the other religious traditions cannot contribute anything to our knowledge of man's mystery and meaning. It remains, however, to say that a regnocentric perspective opens new horizons for a comprehension of the evangelizing mission of the church, especially in its eschatological aspect.

But a question is also raised in the opposite direction: in a theology of the religions according to which they have, in the divine plan for humankind, a positive significance and salvific value, one asks whether announcing the gospel with the intention of making others disciples of Jesus in the Christian community still has a place and a meaning. Why should the others be "called" to become disciples of Christ in the church once the saving elements spoken of earlier are affirmed to be present in their religious traditions? The answer consists in saying that their "ordination" to the church (cf. *Lumen gentium* 16) and their eventual "vocation" to become disciples of Jesus in it are not in view of a salvation which otherwise they would not be able to attain, but in view of a possible explicit knowledge of the universal savior of humankind and because to the church has been entrusted by Christ "the fullness of the benefits and the means of salvation" (cf. *Redemptoris missio* 18). This fullness is not available outside the church. On the part of the church, it is also first of all a mystery of love, as the document "Dialogue and Proclamation" says pointedly: "Insofar as the church and Christians have a deep love for the Lord Jesus, the desire to share him with others is motivated not merely by obedience to the Lord's command, but by this love itself" (83). Only the church can communicate to them the explicit knowledge of him in whom they are saved. That is why I have thought it necessary to show, especially in my second book, that, while interreligious dialogue is by itself evangelization, it may not be said to exhaust the evangelizing mission of the church.

Coming then to the "complementarity" and "convergence" that I have affirmed between the diverse religious traditions and Christianity, one critic doubts that such language is legitimate on my part because I still hold the idea of a "fulfillment" of the other religions in Christianity. Another critic expresses the fear that my affirmation of incomplete values in the other religions which will find their complement in the Christian message does not account adequately for the significance and the intrinsic coherence of the religions in themselves, in their diversity and specificity. This is where to recall, once more, the two meanings of "complement" and "fulfillment," to which I have referred repeatedly. For the "fulfillment theory," the complementarity is in one direction only, inasmuch as Jesus Christ and Christianity—the only "supernatural" religion—fulfill the natural religiosity expressed in the other traditions. On the contrary, there is question in my books of a "reciprocal complementarity," which, without suppressing the uniqueness of Jesus Christ and the consequent irreducible singularity of Christianity, maintains nonetheless that some aspects of the divine mystery can be put into greater relief and expressed in such a way in the other religious traditions as to allow Christians to profit from contact with them. Because the complementarity is reciprocal, dialogue is not one-way traffic; it is not a monologue, but a dialogue.

Another critic asks how I can speak of the elements of truth and grace present in the other religious traditions as "added and autonomous benefits." The obvious sense is that such gifts cannot be reduced to be mere stepping stones (*pierres d'attente*) for Christian revelation and the Christian religion, if, as I have affirmed, in other salvific figures and traditions it is possible to discover truth and grace not explicitated with the same vigor and clarity in the revelation and the manifestation of God in Jesus Christ. This does not in any way contradict the transcendence of the singular manifestation of God in him—that is why I am speaking of "reciprocal *asymmetrical* complementarity"—nor the essential "relationality," in the divine plan of salvation, of such gifts of truth and grace toward the historic event in which the process of the divine self-manifestation to humankind culminates. "Autonomy" is not opposed here to "relationality." I have quoted Claude Geffré where he writes: "Without compromising the absolute commitment inherent to faith, Christianity can be considered as a *relative* reality; not, however, in the sense in which 'relative' is opposed to 'absolute,' but in the sense of 'relational.' The truth to which Christianity witnesses is neither exclusive nor inclusive of all other truth; it is related to all that is true in other religions" (quoted in *Toward*, p. 388). Because of this character of reciprocal relationality Christians can learn some divine truth from the others through interreligious dialogue.

Yet, the reviewer says he is "embarrassed" by the concept of "complementarity." That idea would contradict the fact that the church has received the fullness of the means of salvation. It would, moreover, establish "parallel ways of salvation." Besides, it would not account adequately for, nor would it show the respect due to, the other religions in their specific difference. It is clear that such is not my intention. But the fact remains that the other religious traditions may contain some divine truth from which Christians can learn, even if the same religions contain elements which are incompatible with Christianity; similarly, they can serve as "means" of salvation for their followers, even if the church alone has received from Christ the fullness of the means. As for the respect due to those religions in their difference and specificity, the "complementarity" which is being proposed does not in any way intend to absorb the other traditions, but, on the contrary, to recognize with gratitude what Christians can receive from them. Dialogue, I have insisted, must take place in full respect for the differences.

Yet, the reviewer insists that Israel and Christianity do not find themselves in a relation of reciprocal complementarity, but rather "face to face" in a "reciprocal contestation." This situation, in as far as it is true, does not in my opinion prevent a certain reciprocal complementarity between Judaism and Christianity: Christianity is not conceivable without Israel, from which it originated, while Israel, according to the plan of God, is that people from which his Son would be born. Is there not here perhaps some complementarity intended by God in his plan for humankind? However different and mutually irreducible Israel and the church may be, they remain nonetheless mutually relational. Lastly, the critic suggests that the final eschatological fulfillment in Christ of the elements of truth and grace present in the other religions may not be confused with their fulfillment "in Christianity as historic religion." I agree with that opinion. In fact I intend to distinguish clearly the partial "complementarity" which can exist between the religions and Christianity in history and the complete "convergence" in Christ of all things in the *eschaton*.

Another critic objects still more strongly to the affirmation of a "reciprocal complementarity" between Christianity and the religions. But he argues wrongly that the "relational uniqueness" which I attribute to Jesus Christ is reduced to a simple "relative uniqueness." In fact the two concepts are very different. I have affirmed about revelation in Jesus Christ and the salvific Christ event a "singular uniqueness" which I have called "constitutive" and "relational." The theological foundation for such uniqueness has been sufficiently explained and no longer needs further clarification. That which needs to be said once more is that this "constitutive uniqueness" is at the same time "relational," that is, inasmuch as the Christ event must be seen and situated in the entirety of the history of the self-manifestation of God to humankind, which culminates in Jesus Christ, without being reducible to Christ. God has neither spoken nor done salvific deeds exclusively in Jesus Christ. We must take seriously the doctrine of the "seeds of the Word" as initial words of God to the peoples, as also the salvific deeds of God in other stories beside that of Jesus Christ, while "relationalizing" those stories to that of Jesus in which the history of salvation reaches its summit.

12. Religious Pluralism in Principle

To speak of religious pluralism in principle means that the plurality of religions, such as we know it in the world today, has a positive meaning in

the divine plan for humankind. I am using the term pluralism "in principle" rather than pluralism *de iure* (that I have used in *Toward*), because
this last term can be interpreted in an equivocal manner, with juridical
connotations. In order to justify the idea of a religious pluralism in principle, one must appeal to the plan of God which foresees the religious
route of men toward the last end of their eschatological fulfillment in
Christ, along diverse paths and following diverse ways, though oriented
toward communion and unity. The fundamental reason for the affirmation
of a religious pluralism in principle is the fact that, before representing the
search for God on the part of men, the religions are "the ways" through
which God has sought men throughout the history of humankind. They
are thus part of the entire process of God's personal involvement with
humankind throughout history, which culminates, as has been said several times, in the infinite condescension with which, becoming man in the
Son, God has come to meet human beings on their own level. The Jesus
Christ event is "relational" to the entire unfolding of salvation history, and
vice versa. The involvement of God with humankind takes place through
limited historic events, mutually relational, the unfolding of which culminates in the "constitutive" event Jesus Christ.

One critic notes that religious pluralism is the sign of the "provisional
and progressive character" impressed on man's approach toward the truth.
While this is true, it does not seem enough to bring out the ultimate
foundation of the religious pluralism of principle. The reason is that, in
that case, the religions would be considered only as diverse ways in which,
in the various cultures of the world, men have sought to approach the
divine mystery, without being ever able to reach it. One would then abide
simply by the "fulfillment theory," today largely abandoned. We must, on
the contrary, say that the religions represent in the first place the "diverse
ways" (cf. Heb 1:1) in which God has sought men through their history—
a divine search to which men have been able to respond in the measure of
their limited possibilities, and not without God's grace. As I have written:
"Religious pluralism in principle is founded on the immensity of a God
who is Love and communication."

While accepting religious pluralism in principle, one critic disagrees
with regard to the theological foundation on which it must be based. He
notes that we do not know if the pluralism corresponds to a "positive will
of God"; there is a risk of extending to the whole history of humankind
a "principle of divine pedagogy" which in fact applies only to the history of Israel. Therefore, instead of founding the plurality in principle
on the diverse ways in which, through human history, God would have

manifested himself to the peoples, he prefers to found it simply on "cultural factors," that is, on the "unity-diversity of the human family," or else, on the various ways in which the peoples have sought after God in the context of their various cultures. This would suffice to justify a pluralism in the name of God, because it is God who created humankind "plural," from which the plural character of the human search for God naturally and necessarily follows.

According to me, such an explanation does not suffice, for it runs the risk of again reducing the religious traditions to being merely various expressions in the diverse cultures of the human search for God. On the contrary, the foundation of religious pluralism lies in the mystery of the pluriform communication of God to humankind in history—the "economic" Trinity, which governs the unique but plural economy of salvation. The reason is that, in every event and from the beginning, God has sought for men throughout their history, before they could think of searching for him: "Tu ne me chercherais pas *si je ne t'avais déjà trouvé*"—it can be said, in inverting the words attributed to God by Blaise Pascal. The religions cannot but contain at least traces of this divine search for humankind. If, as the empirical evidence suggests, religious pluralism will endure, must we not perhaps see in this fact the expression of a positive divine disposition, and seek to discover the positive meaning and function religions have in the divine plan of God for humankind? I have referred earlier to the weighty words of a biblicist, who wrote: "That the religions are so many expressions of God's design is by now established, indeed because as can be seen from the perspective disclosed by the texts of the Old and New Testaments, they are on earth *a gift of God to all peoples,* and, therefore, a sign of the salvifically operative presence of Wisdom" (emphasis added).[13] If the religions are "a gift of God to all peoples and . . . a sign of the salvifically operative presence of Wisdom"—that Wisdom which, "coming into the world, enlightens all men" (cf. John 1:9)—is it not legitimate to see their origin in a positive disposition of God the savior, and, consequently, to speak of a religious pluralism in principle?

13. Perspectives and Expectations

In order to help the theological discussion in progress on the topic of a Christian theology of religious pluralism I wish to insist on three deep intentions which have inspired and animated my work, and which consti-

---

13. G. Odasso, *Bibbia e religioni,* 372.

tute three criteria which should also be presupposed by whoever wishes to read it and to evaluate it with adequacy and according to truth.

1. The theme—the problem of religious pluralism—is a new and unique fact today, which invites all to a new and certainly difficult global hermeneutic of the Christian faith. There is need therefore for a strong "sense of the problem," before thinking of easy, immediate, "dogmatic" solutions. In this sense, one may say—in the true meaning of the term—that my books represent a "problematic" proposal.

2. There is also need for maintaining the "sense of mystery," of the transcendence not only of God but also of his plan of salvation, without pretending to describe precisely the "hows and "in which way," when it is only possible—and perhaps that is enough—to underline the fact. An example of this is the relationality of the action of the Word and of the Spirit with the historic event of Jesus Christ.

3. Finally, a living and prolonged experience of the praxis of meeting and of dialogue is to be considered decisive. A theological reflection from a distance cannot be very promising, that is, a discourse "about the others" without having encountered them and listened to them, without having come into contact closely with their religious life and "firm belief," which often "can make Christians ashamed" (cf. *Redemptor hominis* 6).

Among the reviewers of *Toward,* some have stressed rightly the intentional provisional character of my research. One of these concludes his review by appealing to the fact that "what can be decisive need not be definitive." Another considers the work "problematic" and "provocative," in the positive sense—I would want to suppose—that it provokes reflection and raises problems that cannot be avoided and require further clarifications. Of this I have been and remain even today well aware. It is in fact this awareness of mine which I expressed clearly in the very title: *"Toward* a Christian Theology of Religious Pluralism." The book was an introduction, which, as I have explicitly written, "will, perhaps, raise as many questions as it will propose solutions." However, as a kind reviewer has observed, "To ask the right questions is already essential for a correct position of the problem." However this may be, in the new perspective of today, theological reflection on the subject has started and must continue. There remain questions, and the answer given to those that have been considered remains tentative. One of the reviewers observed gently: "What Dupuis has done is to explore the frontiers of the inclusivist theology of religions. In so doing he has exposed certain "no-go areas" and apparently even ventured into something of a no-man's land between the three "classical" approaches. Of course, there are pitfalls confronting every explorer. However, like all true explorers, Dupuis deserves respect and admiration for his endeavors. This is a brave and conscientious book, a comprehensive map of familiar territory, and an attempt to chart new routes. Dupuis's map may not be complete but it will surely serve those who come after him."

The model of a "Trinitarian Christology" which I proposed in *Toward* to lead toward an "inclusivist pluralism" of the religions certainly requires further elaboration and a deeper study. But I remain convinced that this is the right key, if we wish to enter into a new research and a new interpretation of the biblical data and those of the Christian tradition on the religions in today's context of a lived pluralism. Scripture is not monolithic, but made up of plural aspects; neither is tradition static, but dynamic. The divine revelation which comes to us through them requires from us faithfulness and openness in our ongoing search, loyalty and courage. "Every scribe who has been trained for the Kingdom of heaven is like a householder who brings out of his treasure what is new and what is old" (Matt 13:52).

The model of a Trinitarian Christology, proposed in the two books, is designed to combine and to hold together the uniqueness and the universality of Jesus Christ in the order of salvation, on the one hand, and, on the other, a positive salvific value of the other religious traditions for their followers. I have shown that the dilemma of having to choose between Christocentrism and Theocentrism, or between "inclusivism" or "pluralism," considered as mutually opposed and exclusive paradigms, must be overcome. I have often repeated that in Christian theology, far from being mutually exclusive, Theocentrism and Christocentrism call for each other. I have thus spoken of a "Theocentric Christocentrism" or of a "Trinitarian Christology" as a model for an open theology of the religions. The model proposed can be called, as I wrote in *Christianity*, an "inclusivist pluralism," or a "pluralistic inclusivism." This means that, while retaining the inclusivistic position with a clear affirmation of Jesus Christ as universal savior, a plurality of religious "ways" with a salvific value for their followers is affirmed at the same time. Not, however, without these "ways" being essentially and organically relational to the Christ event according to the one divine plan for humankind. Such an "inclusivist pluralism"—it must be said clearly—has nothing to do with the "pluralistic paradigm" which has been developed by the "pluralist" theologians, under the premise of denying a universal saving action of Jesus Christ based on his identity as Son of God. While therefore I reject the "pluralist paradigm" based on the denial of Jesus Christ as universal savior, I hold that an inclusivist theology of religions is compatible with a pluralist model, because it is not contradictory to hold together the uniqueness of Jesus Christ savior and a positive role of the other religious paths according to the plan of God. It is in that sense that I speak of an "inclusivist pluralism."

All this being said, I reject the accusation made against me by one reviewer, according to which, while claiming to propose "a way between inclusivism and pluralism," in fact I have "crossed the Rubicon" with the pluralists. In the language of the pluralists, "to cross the Rubicon" refers to the paradigm shift from inclusivism to pluralism, a shift that implies the denial of the uniqueness of Jesus Christ, Son of God and Savior. As for myself, I affirm without ambiguity and consistently the uniqueness of Christ; the difference between the "inclusivist pluralism" which I propose and the "pluralist paradigm" of the pluralist theologians ought to be clear.

By way of conclusion let me express once more my conviction that a more open and more positive approach toward the other religious traditions in the plan of God for humankind is an urgent need for the life of the church itself. A "qualitative leap"—which has nothing to do with the "paradigm shift" toward "pluralistic theology"—is required for a theology of religions to deserve to be called Christian. What is at stake is the credibility of the Christian message today and tomorrow. We must shun every manner of "defending" the faith which turns out to be counterproductive because it makes it appear narrow and restrictive. I am convinced that a more positive and more open approach and attitude, provided it be built on solid theological ground, can help us to discover, with surprise and admiration, new depths and a new breadth in the Christian message. I hope, therefore, that we might progress together toward an ever deeper knowledge of the mystery of God and of the superabundant munificence of his plan of salvation for the whole of humankind. May we discover with admiration that God is truly "greater than our heart" (see 1 John 3:20)— and than our mind—and comprehend better "the breadth and length and height and depth" of the mystery (*mystērion*) realized in Christ Jesus!

Index of Names